# Datacasting

# Datacasting

**How to Stream Databases
over the Internet**

**Jessica Keyes**

**McGraw-Hill**

New York   San Francisco   Washington, D.C.   Auckland   Bogotá
Caracas   Lisbon   London   Madrid   Mexico City   Milan
Montreal   New Delhi   San Juan   Singapore
Sydney   Tokyo   Toronto

**Library of Congress Cataloging-in-Publication Data**

Keyes, Jessica (date).
    Datacasting : how to stream databases over the Internet / Jessica
Keyes.
        p.    cm.
    Includes index.
    ISBN 0-07-034678-X
    1. Database management.  2. Databases.  3. World Wide Web
(Information retrieval system)  I. Title.
QA76.9.D3K35898      1997
005.75'8—dc21                                                97-34674
                                                                CIP

## McGraw-Hill

*A Division of The* **McGraw·Hill** *Companies*

1 2 3 4 5 6 7 8 9 0  DOC/DOC  9 0 3 2 1 0 9 8

ISBN 0-07-034678-X

*The sponsoring editor for this book was Michael Sprague, and the production
supervisor was Clare Stanley. It was set in Century Schoolbook by the author.*

*Printed and bound by R. R. Donnelley & Sons Company.*

This book is printed on recycled, acid-free paper containing a
minimum of 50% recycled, de-inked fiber.

McGraw-Hill books are available at special quantity discounts to use as premi-
ums and sales promotions, or for use in corporate training programs. For more
information, please write to the Director of Special Sales, McGraw-Hill,  11 West
19th Street, New York, NY 10011. Or contact your local bookstore.

# Contents

## Chapter 12: IBM Web Connectors for IMS and CICS                    241

## Chapter 13: INFORMIX-Universal Web Connect                         291

# Preface

## This book is Web-enabled. Visit at www.business-america.com/datacasting

What do you get if the you combine the Internet, or an Intranet, and a relational database management system (or even Object Oriented DBMS)? Almost heaven, according to several database and Web software companies. That is why the leading database vendors, Netscape, and others are engaged in a frantic rush to release products, stake out territory, or just map strategy to make it happen.

In the past year, all the major relational DBMS companies — including Informix, Oracle, Sybase, IBM, and Microsoft — spelled out how they will let their customers combine the benefits of Web technology with databases. Ultimately, everyone wants to support heavy-duty transaction processing. The immediate goal is to tie databases more tightly to the Web through new products that can do things like accept a query from a Web browser, extract the data from a database, and format it in HTML for return to the Web. The long-range goal is nothing short of robust, secure transaction processing.

Database vendors, already secure in the art of three-tier database processing, see the Web as the ultimate in middleware — widely distributed, platform independent and easy to use.

Oracle and Sybase are reselling Netscape browsers and servers and Informix is bundling its OnLine Workgroup Sever and OnLine Workstation database products with Netscape's FastTrack Web Server.

Netscape's Enterprise Server comes with a database connection via a JavaScript API. You can take an HTML file, incorporate a JavaScript API in the server tag and embed SQL statements in the HTML file to move data between a database and a browser form or display.

IBM has a plethora of offerings for its legacy databases including Net.Data for DB/2 and a series of "IBM Connectors" for IMS and CICS.

Oracle's Web Request Broker permits real-time interactions between the Web and databases while Oracle's InterCartridge Exchange supports add-on applications on the server.

While Oracle calls its server add-ons "cartridges," Sybase uses the Sun — derived term of "servlets" to describe a Web server-side plug-in that has the capabilities of performing advanced database logic while freeing the end-user from having to add a "plug-in" to his or her browser — something any Web designer worth his e-money tries to avoid. Using its web.sql as a base, Sybase is looming large on Web-to-database middleware scene.

web.sql allows a Web server to act as a client by triggering the database based on an URL. The Web server will hand off a certain call or URL to web.sql and then pass back the data suitably encoded in HTML.

The last of the big three database vendors, Informix, has also dived into the deep end of the pool with its Universal Server. The Universal Server is designed to integrate object technology, enabling its database to handle any data type.

## Why Read This Book

Think of this book as a guide through the maze of database products and decisions. There's a lot of choices out there and you need to make the right ones. What this book offers is sort of a test drive of products that I've decided are the most interesting Web-database integration products on the market today. Not every product is here — but all the best ones are. And along with their descriptions are instructions on how to use them — plus tons of code and over 176 illustrations.

In Chapter 1, we delve into multiple ways of connecting non-dynamic data to the Web. Interestingly, the majority of Web sites today are powered by static data. In Chapter 2 we'll discuss two of the more popular database to Web products — Information Builders WebFocus and Microsoft's Visual InterDev.

In Chapter 3 we'll digress for a moment to discuss how to maximize the efficiency of your Web database. My gut feeling, given the agonizingly slow response rate of many database-driven Web sites, is that more than a few Web databases are being generated by Webmasters rather than database administrators. It's for these guys that I've included insightful tidbits of wisdom that they should write down and memorize.

I've invited several experts to share their thoughts with us. Object Design's Mark Palmer waxes eloquent on the art of deploying object databases on the Web in Chapter 4. Dr. Larry Harris, a founder of the artificial intelligence movement, tells us how we can use natural language to query a Web database in Chapter 7. If you want to know a thing or two about Java database connectivity read Dennis Minium, who is Director of Product Strategy for XDB Systems, in Chapter 8 and Kingsley Idehen, President and CEO of OpenLink, in Chapter 9. If you want the low-down on one of the better tools on the market to connect your data to the Web, then read David Isaacson's chapter on how to glue data to the Web with Sapphire/Web which can be found in Chapter 19.

There's about 65 billion lines of COBOL code out there. And much of it already accesses databases. Wouldn't it be a good idea if you had inside information on how to use COBOL to connect to the Web. Fujitsu's Ron Langer gives us the low-down, complete with code, in Chapter 20. You'll really want to read this Chapter if you're a corporate developer since Ron is going to tell you where to go to get a free COBOL development environment worth over a thousand dollars.

Chapters 22 through 25 give us an inside look at creating robust Internet applications. Here you'll find three case studies and the description of a radically different methodology and toolset to self-generate database-enabled Web applications. Margaret Hamilton of Hamilton Technologies, Inc. starts off by describing the methodology which is called Development Before the Fact (DBTF). Both Margaret and Ron Hacker then describe how they used DBTF, and its implementation toolset 001, to build an accident recording system for state governments. Then Stephen Dolha and Dave Chiste of Cadeon Strategic Technologies describe how they built a resource librarian remote query system in Canada using both the Web and databases. Finally Marc and Norman Beaulieu of NetBenefit describe how their Web site, which relies on database technology, was created.

The big three database vendors all are here too. Sybase's web.sql is described in Chapter 11, Oracle Designer/2000 is discussed in Chapter 17 and Informix's Universal Web Connect is described in Chapter 13.

IBM and Microsoft are here too. Microsoft in Chapter 18, where we discuss the Advanced Data Connector, and IBM in Chapter 12 where we discuss how to hook IMS and CICS to the Web.

There's a plethora of popular database connecting tools other than the Big three. Cold Fusion is discussed in Chapter 5, Progress Software's WebSpeed in Chapter 14, and NetObject's Fusion in Chapter 15.

Don't have a database, but would like one? Read Chapter 6 which is about the shareware product MiniSql. Have a database but no cash for the middleware? Then turn to Chapter 21 to read about WDB, a shareware interface between the Web and SQL databases.

Turn the page. There's really a solution for everyone!

# 1

# Because You Have Start Somewhere

## Introduction

*Data, data everywhere, but not a drop to drink.*

That's certainly been true of the Web — up until now that is. The Web of the past was a Web of rather flat, static data. Until the advent of porting tools and automatic HTML generators, database-derived data had to be meticulously and painstakingly hand-coded. Luckily, the Web of today is a different ballgame altogether. Essentially, that's what this book is about. How to call the plays when it comes to connecting your data to the Web.

Now, data comes in many forms. Some of it's in files. And some of it's in databases. Some of it may even be in data warehouses. In essence your goal is to broadcast some, or all, of that data on the Web. That's the reason why I've named this book *Datacasting*. Data + broadcasting = datacasting.

Datacasting requires you to make some very important decisions. The first decision is a big one. Do you need a database at all? There is a definite downside to hooking the corporate database to the Web. The primary goal of Web-database connectivity is to get as much done in one connection as possible. But the more efficient the system is in doing this, the slower the results are returned to the user. Another thing to think about is data integrity. While the concept of commits, backups and restores is what database administrators cut their teeth on in the corporate environment, it's a whole new frontier for Webmasters. Then there's the question of whether you permit access to the corporate datastores themselves or copies of these datastores. And how best to optimize those copies. Given the agonizingly slow response of more than a few database-driven Web sites I've been visiting lately, it seems these lessons have not yet been learned by more than a few Webmasters. (For these folks I've included a whole chapter pulled from the tip book of guru database administrators — see chapter 3).

So what's a Webmaster to do? The first thing to do is to recognize that there's more than one way to skin a cat. Coincidentally, there's more than one way to datacast. This chapter, also known as "Datacasting Light", will discuss some rather straightforward and simple ways of getting data on the Web.

## Data Publishing Using a Flat File

One of the easiest ways of updating data on the Web is through the use of a flat file (i.e., ASCII/TEXT). This method is most expedient if the amount of the data is small and not too many people are expected to be updating the system at the same time (folks just don't appreciate that server busy notice).

A good example of this is the now ubiquitous guest book. Everyone's got one. In fact, they probably have the same one. Matt Wright is owner and proprietor of probably one of the most popular sites on the Web. His archive contains scripts for every purpose — from search engines to the guest book discussed below (www.worldwidemart.com).

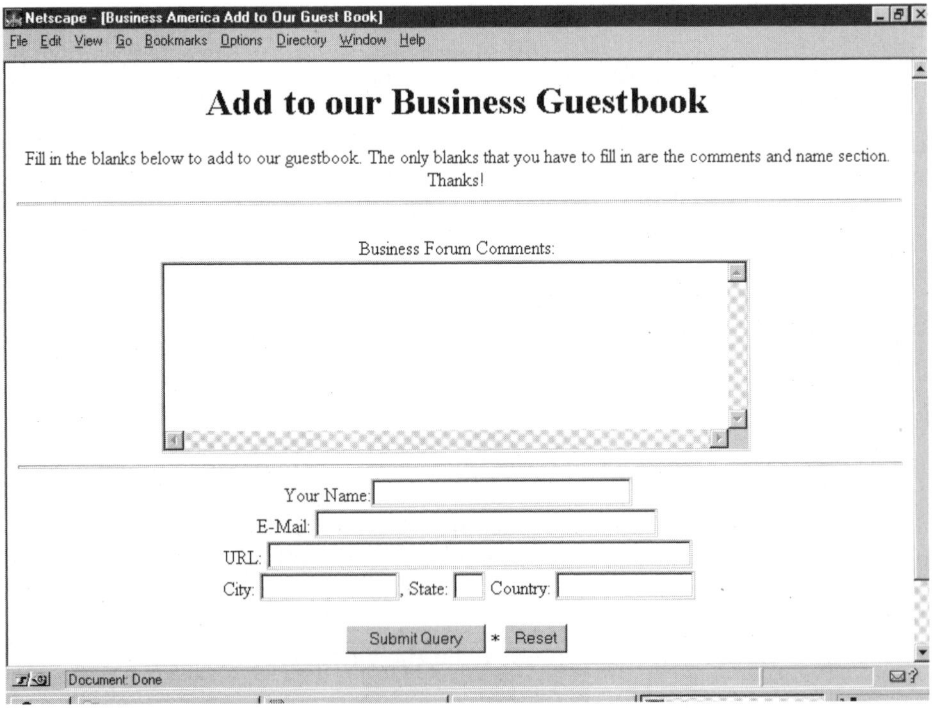

**Figure 1-1.** The Business-America forum.

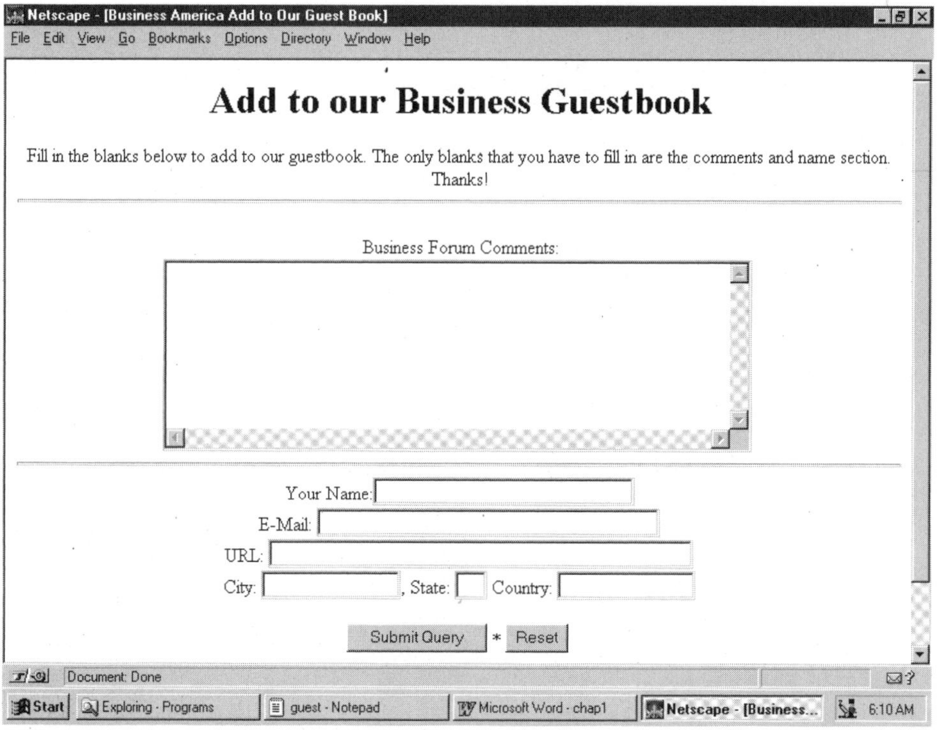

**Figure 1-2.** A typical input form.

The guest book demonstrates the principles behind using CGI and a text file to permit end-users to update and then view data on the web. I've taken Matt's script, and with just a few modifications, altered it to provide a small business forum for my www.business-america.com site. Look at the screen in figure 1-1.

Notice the comments from visitors. Essentially, it takes two HTML pages and one CGI script to perform the function of using CGI to move data between the end-user and the Web server.

The first HTML page is the "add" page which is a hyperlink to the HTML page above. Figure 1-2 shows a typical guest book add input form.

The HTML for this form follows:

```
<HTML>
<TITLE>Business America Add to Our Guest
Book</TITLE>

<body bgcolor="#ffffff" text="#000000"
link="#342567" >
<center>
<body>
<h1>Add to our Business Guestbook</h1>
```

```
                </center>

    Fill in the blanks below to add to our guestbook.
    The only blanks that you
    have to fill in are the comments and name section.
    Thanks!<hr>

    <form
    method=POST action="/cgi-bin/guest.pl">

    Business Forum Comments:<br>
    <textarea
    name=comments COLS=60 ROWS=8></textarea>
    <hr>

    Your Name:
    <input type=text name=realname size=30><br>

    E-Mail:
    <input type=text name=username size=40><br>

    URL: <input type=text name=url size=50><br>

    City: <input type=text name=city size=15>, State:
    <input type=text name=state size=2> Country: <input
    type=text name=country size=15><p>

    <p>
    <input type=submit> * <input type=reset>
    </form>
    <hr>
    <a href="guest.htm">
    Back to the Guestbook Entries</a><br>
    </body>
    </html>
```

Once the visitor clicks on the submit button, control is passed to a program in the site's cgi-bin directory. A Perl program called guest.pl then processes the input, does some light error-checking to make sure certain input fields are present, and then writes the input to the output file which is called guest.htm and displays a "thank you for adding your comments" message. This last message is dynamically generated as an HTML file directly from the Perl program.

I'm not going to get into the details of this Perl script (Matt has extensive instructions on his site). Suffice it to say, it is a simple but effective way to get quasi-dynamic data out to the Web.

## The code for the guest.pl Perl script follows:

```
#!/usr/local/bin/perl
######################################################################
Guestbook                    Version 2.3.1                        #
# Copyright 1996 Matt Wright   mattw@worldwidemart.com             #
# Created 4/21/95              Last Modified 10/29/95              #
# Scripts Archive at:          http://www.worldwidemart.com/scripts/    #
######################################################################
# COPYRIGHT NOTICE                                                 #
# Copyright 1996 Matthew M. Wright  All Rights Reserved.          #
#                                                                  #
# Guestbook may be used and modified free of charge by anyone so long as  #
# this copyright notice and the comments above remain intact.  By using this#
# code you agree to indemnify Matthew M. Wright from any liability that    #
# might arise from it's use.                                       #
#                                                                  #
# Selling the code for this program without prior written consent is   #
# expressly forbidden.  In other words, please ask first before you try   #
# and make money off of my program.                               #
#                                                                  #
# Obtain permission before redistributing this software over the Internet #
# in any other medium. In all cases copyright and header must remain intact.#
######################################################################
# Set Variables

$guestbookurl = "http://www.business-america.com/guest.htm";
$guestbookreal = "/usr/local/wwwdocs/www.business-america.com/guest.htm";
$guestlog = "/usr/local/wwwdocs/www.business-america.com/guestlog.htm";
$cgiurl = "http://www.business-america.com/cgi-bin/guest.pl";
$date_command = "/usr/bin/date";

# Set Your Options:
$mail = 0;                 # 1 = Yes; 0 = No
$uselog = 1;               # 1 = Yes; 0 = No
$linkmail = 1;             # 1 = Yes; 0 = No
$separator = 1;            # 1 = <hr>; 0 = <p>
$redirection = 0;          # 1 = Yes; 0 = No
$entry_order = 1;          # 1 = Newest entries added first;
                           # 0 = Newest Entries added last.
$remote_mail = 0;          # 1 = Yes; 0 = No
$allow_html = 1;           # 1 = Yes; 0 = No
$line_breaks = 0; # 1 = Yes; 0 = No


# If you answered 1 to $mail or $remote_mail you will need to fill out
```

```
# these variables below:
$mailprog = '/usr/lib/sendmail';
$recipient = 'you@your.com';

# Done
#############################################################################

# Get the Date for Entry
$date = `$date_command +"%A, %B %d, %Y at %T (%Z)"`; chop($date);
$shortdate = `$date_command +"%D %T %Z"`; chop($shortdate);

# Get the input
read(STDIN, $buffer, $ENV{'CONTENT_LENGTH'});

# Split the name-value pairs
@pairs = split(/&/, $buffer);

foreach $pair (@pairs) {
   ($name, $value) = split(/=/, $pair);

   # Un-Webify plus signs and %-encoding
   $value =~ tr/+/ /;
   $value =~ s/%([a-fA-F0-9][a-fA-F0-9])/pack("C", hex($1))/eg;
   $value =~ s/<!—(.|\n)*—>//g;

   if ($allow_html != 1) {
      $value =~ s/<([^>]|\n)*>//g;
   }

   $FORM{$name} = $value;
}

# Print the Blank Response Subroutines
&no_comments unless $FORM{'comments'};
&no_name unless $FORM{'realname'};

# Begin the Editing of the Guestbook File
open (FILE,"$guestbookreal") || die "Can't Open $guestbookreal: $!\n";
@LINES=<FILE>;
close(FILE);
$SIZE=@LINES;

# Open Link File to Output
open (GUEST,">$guestbookreal") || die "Can't Open $guestbookreal: $!\n";

for ($i=0;$i<=$SIZE;$i++) {
```

```perl
$_=$LINES[$i];
if (/<!—begin—>/) {

    if ($entry_order eq '1') {
        print GUEST "<!—begin—>\n";
    }

    if ($line_breaks == 1) {
        $FORM{'comments'} =~ s/\cM\n/<br>\n/g;
    }

    print GUEST "<b>$FORM{'comments'}</b><br>\n";

    if ($FORM{'url'}) {
        print GUEST "<a href=\"$FORM{'url'}\">$FORM{'realname'}</a>";
    }
    else {
        print GUEST "$FORM{'realname'}";
    }

    if ( $FORM{'username'} ){
        if ($linkmail eq '1') {
            print GUEST " \&lt;<a href=\"mailto:$FORM{'username'}\">";
            print GUEST "$FORM{'username'}</a>\&gt;";
        }
        else {
            print GUEST " &lt;$FORM{'username'}&gt;";
        }
    }

    print GUEST "<br>\n";

    if ( $FORM{'city'} ){
        print GUEST "$FORM{'city'},";
    }

    if ( $FORM{'state'} ){
        print GUEST " $FORM{'state'}";
    }

    if ( $FORM{'country'} ){
        print GUEST " $FORM{'country'}";
    }

    if ($separator eq '1') {
        print GUEST " - $date<hr>\n\n";
```

```
      }
      else {
         print GUEST " - $date<p>\n\n";
      }

      if ($entry_order eq '0') {
         print GUEST "<!—begin—>\n";
      }

   }
   else {
      print GUEST $_;
   }
}

close (GUEST);

# Log The Entry

if ($uselog eq '1') {
   &log('entry');
}


#########
# Options

# Mail Option
if ($mail eq '1') {
   open (MAIL, "|$mailprog $recipient") || die "Can't open $mailprog!\n";

   print MAIL "Reply-to: $FORM{'username'} ($FORM{'realname'})\n";
   print MAIL "From: $FORM{'username'} ($FORM{'realname'})\n";
   print MAIL "Subject: Entry to Forum\n\n";
   print MAIL "You have a new entry in the Forum:\n\n";
   print MAIL "——————————————————\n";
   print MAIL "$FORM{'comments'}\n";
   print MAIL "$FORM{'realname'}";

   if ( $FORM{'username'} ){
      print MAIL " <$FORM{'username'}>";
   }

   print MAIL "\n";

   if ( $FORM{'city'} ){
```

```
      print MAIL "$FORM{'city'},";
   }

   if ( $FORM{'state'} ){
      print MAIL " $FORM{'state'}";
   }

   if ( $FORM{'country'} ){
      print MAIL " $FORM{'country'}";
   }

   print MAIL " - $date\n";
   print MAIL "————————————————————\n";

   close (MAIL);
}

if ($remote_mail eq '1' && $FORM{'username'}) {
   open (MAIL, "|$mailprog -t") || die "Can't open $mailprog!\n";

   print MAIL "To: $FORM{'username'}\n";
   print MAIL "From: $recipient\n";
   print MAIL "Subject: Entry to the Forum\n\n";
   print MAIL "Thank you for adding to the Forum.\n\n";
   print MAIL "————————————————————\n";
   print MAIL "$FORM{'comments'}\n";
   print MAIL "$FORM{'realname'}";

   if ( $FORM{'username'} ){
      print MAIL " <$FORM{'username'}>";
   }

   print MAIL "\n";

   if ( $FORM{'city'} ){
      print MAIL "$FORM{'city'},";
   }

   if ( $FORM{'state'} ){
      print MAIL " $FORM{'state'}";
   }

   if ( $FORM{'country'} ){
     print MAIL " $FORM{'country'}";
   }
```

```perl
    print MAIL " - $date\n";
    print MAIL "————————————————————\n";

    close (MAIL);
}

# Print Out Initial Output Location Heading
if ($redirection eq '1') {
    print "Location: $guestbookurl\n\n";
}
else {
    &no_redirection;
}

#######################
# Subroutines

sub no_comments {
    print "Content-type: text/html\n\n";
    print "<html><head><title>No Comments</title></head>\n";
    print "<body><h1>Your Comments appear to be blank</h1>\n";
    print "The comment section in the forum fillout form appears\n";
    print "to be blank and therefore the Forum Addition was not\n";
    print "added.  Please enter your comments below.<p>\n";
    print "<form method=POST action=\"$cgiurl\">\n";
    print "Your Name:<input type=text name=\"realname\" size=30 ";
    print "value=\"$FORM{'realname'}\"><br>\n";
    print "E-Mail: <input type=text name=\"username\"";
    print "value=\"$FORM{'username'}\" size=40><br>\n";
    print "City: <input type=text name=\"city\" value=\"$FORM{'city'}\" ";
    print "size=15>, State: <input type=text name=\"state\" ";
    print "value=\"$FORM{'state'}\" size=15> Country: <input type=text ";
    print "name=\"country\" value=\"$FORM{'country'}\" size=15><p>\n";
    print "Comments:<br>\n";
    print "<textarea name=\"comments\" COLS=60 ROWS=4></textarea><p>\n";
    print "<input type=submit> * <input type=reset></form><hr>\n";
    print "Return to the <a href=\"$guestbookurl\">Forum</a>.";
    print "\n</body></html>\n";

    # Log The Error
    if ($uselog eq '1') {
        &log('no_comments');
    }

    exit;
```

```
}

sub no_name {
    print "Content-type: text/html\n\n";
    print "<html><head><title>No Name</title></head>\n";
    print "<body><h1>Your Name appears to be blank</h1>\n";
    print "The Name Section in the guestbook fillout form appears to\n";
    print "be blank and therefore your entry to the Forum was not\n";
    print "added.  Please add your name in the blank below.<p>\n";
    print "<form method=POST action=\"$cgiurl\">\n";
    print "Your Name:<input type=text name=\"realname\" size=30><br>\n";
    print "E-Mail: <input type=text name=\"username\"";
    print " value=\"$FORM{'username'}\" size=40><br>\n";
    print "City: <input type=text name=\"city\" value=\"$FORM{'city'}\" ";
    print "size=15>, State: <input type=text name=\"state\" ";
    print "value=\"$FORM{'state'}\" size=2> Country: <input type=text ";
    print "value=USA name=\"country\" value=\"$FORM{'country'}\" ";
    print "size=15><p>\n";
    print "Comments have been retained.<p>\n";
    print "<input type=hidden name=\"comments\" ";
    print "value=\"$FORM{'comments'}\">\n";
    print "<input type=submit> * <input type=reset><hr>\n";
    print "Return to the <a href=\"$guestbookurl\">Forum</a>.";
    print "\n</body></html>\n";

    # Log The Error
    if ($uselog eq '1') {
       &log('no_name');
    }

    exit;
}

# Log the Entry or Error
sub log {
    $log_type = $_[0];
    open (LOG, ">>$guestlog");
    if ($log_type eq 'entry') {
       print LOG "$ENV{'REMOTE_HOST'} - [$shortdate]<br>\n";
    }
    elsif ($log_type eq 'no_name') {
       print LOG "$ENV{'REMOTE_HOST'} - [$shortdate] - ERR: No Name<br>\n";
    }
    elsif ($log_type eq 'no_comments') {
       print LOG "$ENV{'REMOTE_HOST'} - [$shortdate] - ERR: No ";
       print LOG "Comments<br>\n";
```

```
      }
}

# Redirection Option
sub no_redirection {

   # Print Beginning of HTML
   print "Content-Type: text/html\n\n";
   print "<html><head><title>Thank You</title></head>\n";
   print "<body><h1>Thank You For Adding a Comment to the Forum</h1>\n";

   # Print Response
   print "Thank you for adding your comment.  Your entry has\n";
   print "been added to the Forum.<hr>\n";
   print "Here is what you submitted:<p>\n";
   print "<b>$FORM{'comments'}</b><br>\n";

   if ($FORM{'url'}) {
      print "<a href=\"$FORM{'url'}\">$FORM{'realname'}</a>";
   }
   else {
      print "$FORM{'realname'}";
   }

   if ( $FORM{'username'} ){
      if ($linkmail eq '1') {
         print " &lt;<a href=\"mailto:$FORM{'username'}\">";
         print "$FORM{'username'}</a>&gt;";
      }
      else {
         print " &lt;$FORM{'username'}&gt;";
      }
   }

   print "<br>\n";

   if ( $FORM{'city'} ){
      print "$FORM{'city'},";
   }

   if ( $FORM{'state'} ){
      print " $FORM{'state'}";
   }

   if ( $FORM{'country'} ){
      print " $FORM{'country'}";
```

```
    }
    print " - $date<p>\n";

    # Print End of HTML
    print "<hr>\n";
    print "<a href=\"$guestbookurl\">Back to the Forum</a>\n";        print
"- You may need to reload it when you get there to see your\n";
    print "entry.\n";
    print "</body></html>\n";

    exit;
}
```

## Level 2 Datacasting — Export to HTML

There are many instances when it just isn't necessary to integrate a "live" database to the Web. If your application calls for "read-only" and your volume of data is not too large, then exporting database data to HTML just might be your ticket to web-database integration.

Many reporting tools, such as Crystal Reports, include an "export to HTML" option. Some of these tools also contain a scheduler that permits you to automatically generate HTML for Web publication on a regular basis.

A good example of this is Microsoft's Access 97. With Microsoft Access, you can output two types of HTML files: static or dynamic. The static HTML files you output are a "snapshot'" of the data at the time you publish your files. In general, you use static HTML files for reports and datasheets that you update and disseminate as part of your regular business cycles, such as weekly stock-level reminders or monthly sales reports. Microsoft Access creates one Web page for each report page and one Web page for each datasheet that you output. When your data changes, you need to publish your files again, so that your users can view the new data on the Web.

Those of you with access to Access 97 (and who doesn't have it) can follow along with this mini-tutorial using the now famous sample Northwind database. The Northwind report called "Alphabetical List of Products" lists each product, the category it belongs to, the quantity per unit, and the current stock level.

The HTML pages you output will simulate the report's page orientation, margin settings, and other attributes such as color, font, and alignment. You can output most controls and features of a Microsoft Access report to HTML.

Open the Northwind sample database, Northwind.mdb (located by default in C:\Program Files\Microsoft Office\Office\Samples). In the Database window, on the Reports tab, click Alphabetical List of Products, and then on the File menu, click Save As/Export. In the Save As dialog box, click HTML Documents (*.html;*.htm); select the Autostart check box so that you can use your browser to verify the generated output; and then click Export as shown in figure 1-3.

Clicking **Export** will display the **HTML Output Options** dialog box.

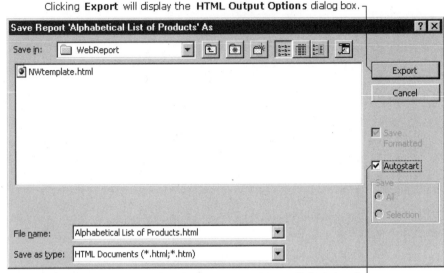

Selecting the **Autostart** check box will display and
verify your output in your default Web browser.

**Figure 1-3.** Exporting Microsoft Access data to HTML.

It's really as simple as that. Microsoft typifies the "big vendor" approach that
is building Web portability right into their database products. You'll read much
more about how to do this in a dynamic way in the later chapters of this book.

## The One Tool, Many Databases Approach

Corel, once known solely for their Drawing software, has gotten itself a good
reputation as a provider of Web-building tools. Corel Web.DATA is an excellent
approach for those with limited database or Internet knowledge, or those folks
who simply don't want to bother with more complex approaches.

Corel Web.DATA's fully graphical user interface leads you through the steps
to gather the information you want to use, organize and  determine the layout,
and include additional text and codes to enhance it. Web.DATA automatically
adds other standard HTML codes that will complete the formatting of your Web
page. Then, with a simple push of a button, your HTML page containing your
data is created and published to the Web.

All of the instructions on how to create your Web page are stored in a file
called a recipe — somewhat akin to a macro. You can use the recipe over and
over, or modify it to create different recipes or a different  look to the page. If
your data changes, all you need to do is  open the recipe and press the Process
button and your data  is immediately updated on your Web page.

Corel Web.DATA uses Open Database Connectivity (ODBC) drivers to connect to a wide variety of databases on SQL servers such as Oracle — and at less

than $300 the price is definitely right. The feature set is definitely right too. For instance, Web.DATA can join tables from the same type or different types of data sources, to create complex new views. It can join an Excel spreadsheet to a local dBASE file, and extend the view with data from an Oracle table. You can create lookups between a large number of tables from the same or different database files. Let's take a look at how Web.DATA works.

Web.DATA Example

In order to access an SQL database, we must access or create a file that has ODBC connect information. For example:

```
CONNECT = DSN = NORTHWIND; UID = Dan;
PWD = prince
SQL=SELECT * FROM CUSTOMERS
```

This connect string specifies the data source name (DSN), the user ID (UID), and the password (PWD), while the SQL string requests all information from the CUSTOMERS reference. We can also use Common Gateway Interface macros in the ODBC SQL statement to optimize SQL queries. The data source must be defined in the ODBC.INI file, in order to be accessible. The ODBC.INI file can be edited through the ODBC application in the Control Panel.

A recipe is a Corel Web.DATA file that contains the instructions for setting up the database publishing process. Once we create a recipe, we can use it repeatedly to produce a particular publication, or modify it to change the publication's style and format.

To build a recipe we must perform four mandatory steps: Select Database, Publishing Options, Field Selection, and Output Setup. With these steps we select and format our database information for publication. Corel Web.DATA has four optional steps for further customizing and formatting: Record Selection, Record Sorting, Field Attributes, and Global Attributes.

When designing a recipe, we need a place to store the recipe information. In Corel Web.DATA, we'll save all this information in an .RCP file.

To create a new recipe file:

1. Click File, New.
2. Click File, Save As.
3. Browse through the Save In list to find the default directory in which you want to save this recipe file, in this example, C:\CORELWEB\CWEBDATA\CWDATA\project\recipes.
4. In the File Name box, we type MyCDHome.
5. We now select Recipes in the Save As Type list.
6. Finally, we click Save.

The next step in creating a recipe is specifying the database (or databases) we'll use as shown in figure 1-4.

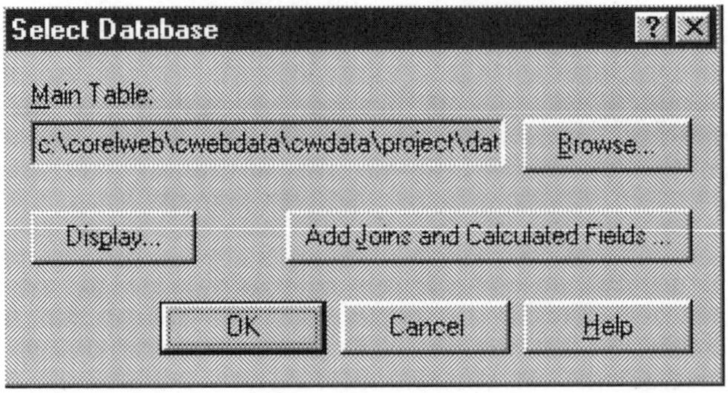

**Figure 1-4.** Selecting a Web.DATA database.

Now we need to specify how we would like this data published. Since we'll be publishing our recipe file to HTML, we need to specify the extension and the processing method. The extension list allows us to specify the browser that will open when we publish our document. Since the Internet browsers available have minor differences in their capabilities, we will customize our document to take advantage of our browser's characteristics. Here, we will be selecting HTML 3.0, as shown in figure 1-5, so we can publish our document using any browser which supports HTML 3.0. In selecting the Processing Method, we are given the option of having Corel Web.DATA publish our document in a standardized table format, or of creating a custom format ourselves. Here, we'll use Web.DATA's table formatting capabilities.

In the next step, which is shown in figure 1-6, we'll select the fields that we want to appear in our recipe. Web.DATA provides us with different areas in our document (heading blocks and the document body block) to which we can assign different fields. In this example, we will assign the fields to the document body.

As we assign attributes to the fields, notice that each field begins with the prefix t0. It indicates that these fields belong to the main database. When we

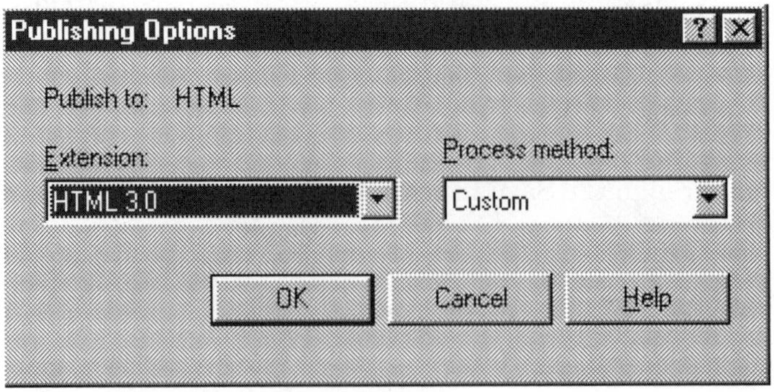

**Figure 1-5.** Selecting publishing options.

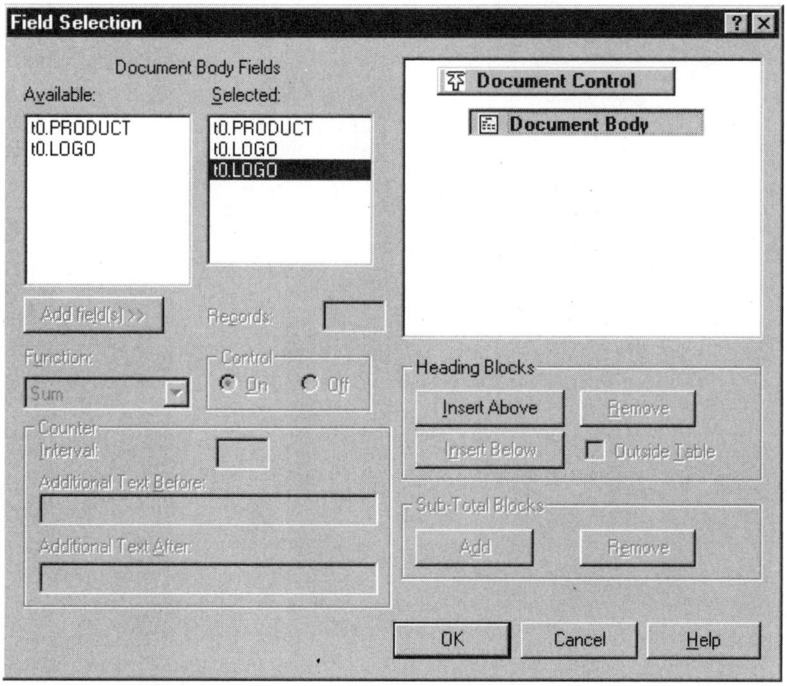

**Figure 1-6.** Field selection.

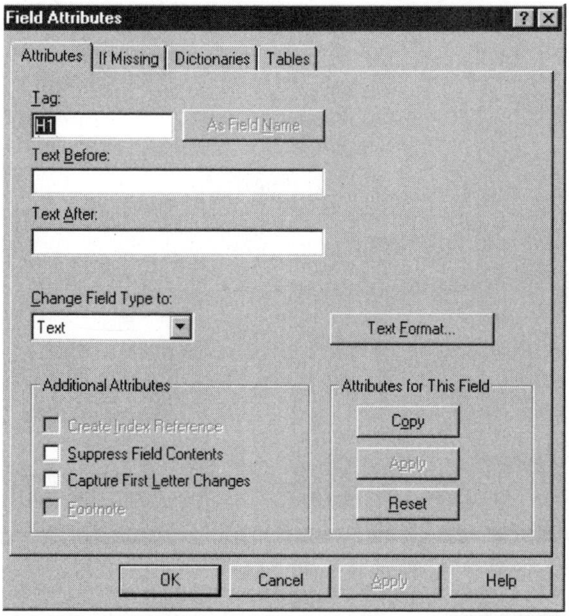

**Figure 1-7.** Selecting field attributes.

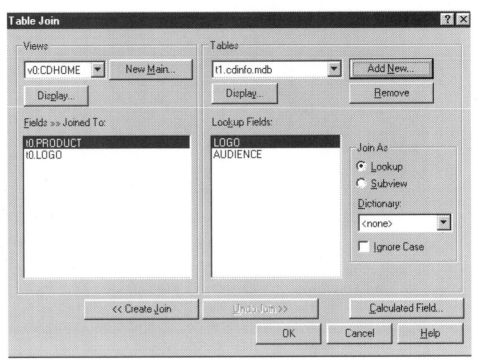

**Figure 1-8.** A Web.DATA join.

join other tables to the main table, their fields are prefixed by tn, where n is 1 for the first joined table, 2 for the second, and so on.

The t0.LOGO field is the product's filename; we will use this field twice. The first occurrence will be used to reference the product's graphic file; the second will be used to reference the product's text file.

In figure 1-7, we see the dialog to set the field attributes. Although, in our example, we will not be setting any of these attributes, the process provides Web.DATA with details on how we would like to use the fields in our table.

Now, we will add a second database (again, see figure 1-4) to the recipe file. This second database will be a Microsoft Access database. We will also create a join between the two databases to add information to our recipe.

To create a join, as shown in figure 1-8, we do the following:

1. Accept the default Look-up, in the Join As section.
2. Select t0.LOGO in the Fields Joined To list and LOGO in the Lookup Fields list.
3. Click Create Join.
4. Click Display in the Views section to see the result, which is shown in figure 1-9.

| **Table View - v0:CDHOME** | | | | |
|---|---|---|---|---|
| | **t0.PRODUCT** | | **t0.LOGO** | **t1.L** |
| 1 | The Interactive Alphabet | | Alphabet | Alphabet |
| 2 | Corel Classic Books | | Clasbook | Clasbook |
| 3 | Arcade Mania | | Arcade | Arcade |
| 4 | Blue Tortoise | | Bluetort | Bluetort |
| 5 | Wild Board Games | | Wildbord | Wildbord |
| 6 | Adventures with Edison | | Edison | Edison |
| 7 | Green Bear | | Grbear | Grbear |
| 8 | The Complete Herman Collection | | Hermlogo | Hermlogo |
| 9 | Bernard of Hollywood's Marilyn | | Marilyn | Marilyn |
| 10 | Corel All Movie Guide | | Movie | Movie |
| 11 | NN'n N Toy Makers | | Nnnnlogo | Nnnnlogo |
| 12 | Red Rhino | | Redrhino | Redrhino |

**Figure 1-9.** Web.DATA output.

## Using Web.DATA and CGI

Corel Web.DATA also offers a leg up on delivering merely static HTML. It can also be used as a CGI server application, enabling us to provide dynamic access to our databases. All we need do is install the program on the Web Server and include CGI macros in the Record Selection section of the recipe, which is somewhat akin to a macro. As a CGI server, Web.DATA receives the request from the Web Server and retrieves the information from the database. It then enhances and formats the data, and sends the results back to the Web Server, which, in turn, passes it on to the Web browser.

Two Web.DATA macros handle the CGI function:

• CGI DATA:[variable names]: Passes a list of variables from an HTML form to CorelWEBDATA running in server mode using CGI
• CGI ENV:[environment variable names]: Inserts the values of the specified system environment variables

## Conclusion

Thus far, we've discussed simple and/or static methods for getting data to the Web. While this simplistic approach will be sufficient for many data applications, it's no match for the requirement of bringing the corporate database to the Web. For this, the developer needs the help of one or more tools to assist in the creation of dynamic, database-driven Web pages. That's essentially, what the rest of this book is all about.

# Microsoft Visual InterDev and Information Builders' WebFOCUS

## Introduction

Where chapter 1 started you off nice and easy with some simple approaches to broadcasting data across the Web, this chapter will move one notch above simple and discuss two more popular approaches to connecting database data to the Web.

## Microsoft Visual InterDev

Visual InterDev is a set of development tools that Microsoft is selling as a complete Web application development toolset. While it lets you connect data to the Web, that's not all it does. It provides you with fairly robust tools to design and develop entire Web sites. This section will provide a brief mini-tutorial that will show you what it's like to use Visual InterDev as a complete Web development tool.

Microsoft Visual InterDev is based on a distributed development environment. Visual InterDev projects are located on Web servers, while the development takes place on the developer's workstations.

A Visual InterDev Web application consists of a virtual root on a Web server, and all of its folders and files. The simplest way to create a new Web application is to use the Web Project Wizard. The Web Project Wizard communicates with the specified Web server and automatically creates a new Visual InterDev Web application as shown in figure 2-1.

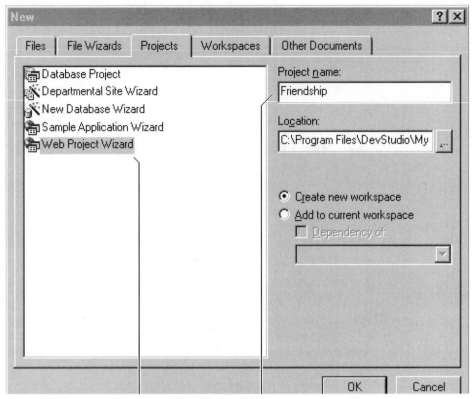

**Figure 2-1**. Creating a Web application with Visual InterDev.

## Creating a Simple Active Server Page

The basic element for any Active Server application is the Active Server Page, or .asp file. An Active Server Page (ASP) is an HTML document that contains embedded server-side scripting. Microsoft Internet Information Server 3.0 executes the server-side scripting and strips it out of the ASP before sending the page to a browser. From the client-side perspective, the ASP is a standard HTML document, viewable on any platform using any Web browser.

Visual InterDev's controls and wizards automate the process of creating Active Server Pages as shown in figure 2-2, but for purposes of this tutorial, let's construct your first simple Active Server Page by hand.

Visual InterDev creates the new ASP, adds it to your project, and then opens the new ASP in the HTML Source Editor as shown in figure 2-3.

By default, Visual InterDev generates client- and server-side script in Visual Basic Scripting Edition (VBScript), but you can easily change the script language to Microsoft's JavaScript-compatible scripting language (JScript) by choosing Options on the Tools menu.

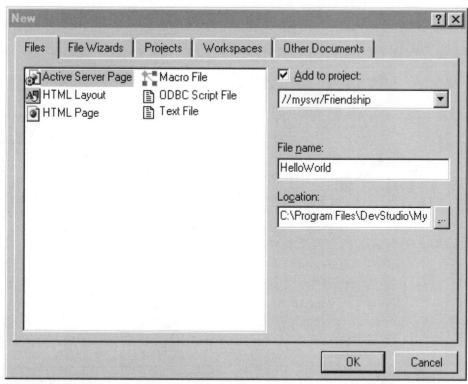

**Figure 2-2.** Creating an Active Server page.

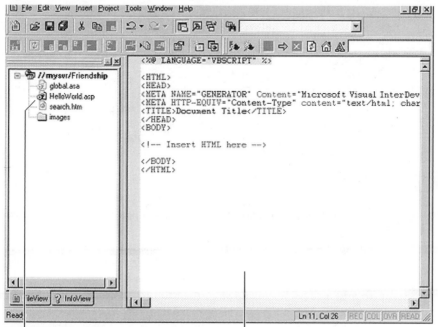

**Figure 2-3.** The ASP.

Adding External Content Files to a Web Project

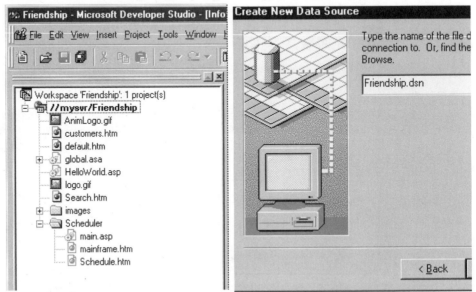

**Figure 2-4.** Adding external files.    **Figure 2-5.** Adding a new data connection.

Most developers have existing content that they'll want to add to their Web projects. Visual InterDev makes this task easy. Adding external files to a Web project involves not too much more than point and click. You click on the "Add Folder Contents" and then locate the information you wish to add. Visual InterDev copies the contents automatically, via HTTP, to your Web server as shown in figure 2-4.

You can also drag files and folders from Windows Explorer directly into a Web project, or into a folder within a project. This will publish the files, over HTTP, to the appropriate location on the Web server.

Adding a Data Connection to a Web Project

Once a template for displaying data is created, we can add a script to display dynamic information from a database — in this tutorial, the Friendship customer database.

The first step in displaying dynamic data on a Web page is to establish a connection to the customer database within the project by adding an SQL Server data connection to our Web project as shown in figure 2-5.

To add a SQL Server data connection to a Web project provide the following information: the data source (Friendship.dsn); the database(Friendship.mdb); the access driver; and the database customer (CustomerDB).

Once you establish a connection to the database, the global.asa file is copied to your local drive. In FileView, a database connection icon (for example, CustomerDB) appears below the global.asa file. This file is the "front door" to your Web application, and allows the Web server to initialize application variables such as database connections whenever a user enters your Web site for the first time. The global.asa file is executed once for each user no matter which page in your application is viewed first.

Microsoft Visual InterDev provides easy access to a range of powerful database development tools, all integrated directly within the development environment. One of these database features is Data View, which allows developers to view detailed information on each database they are using in the Web application.

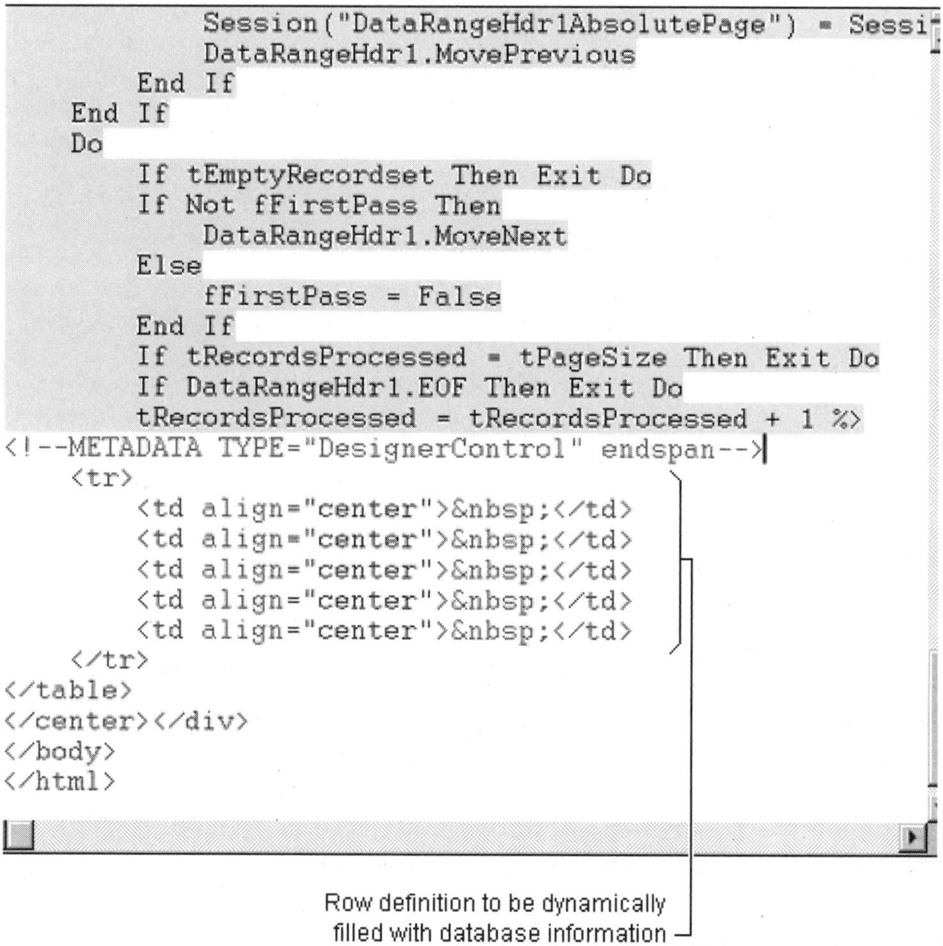

```
                Session("DataRangeHdr1AbsolutePage") = Sessi
                DataRangeHdr1.MovePrevious
            End If
        End If
        Do
            If tEmptyRecordset Then Exit Do
            If Not fFirstPass Then
                DataRangeHdr1.MoveNext
            Else
                fFirstPass = False
            End If
            If tRecordsProcessed = tPageSize Then Exit Do
            If DataRangeHdr1.EOF Then Exit Do
            tRecordsProcessed = tRecordsProcessed + 1 %>
<!--METADATA TYPE="DesignerControl" endspan-->
    <tr>
        <td align="center"> </td>
        <td align="center"> </td>
        <td align="center"> </td>
        <td align="center"> </td>
        <td align="center"> </td>
    </tr>
</table>
</center></div>
</body>
</html>
```

Row definition to be dynamically filled with database information ─┘

**Figure 2-6.** A data range header control.

Visual InterDev also includes a Query Designer that allows developers to visually build and test SQL statements against any ODBC database. While the Query Designer can be used stand-alone to build and test SQL statements within the development environment, special data-access controls called design-time ActiveX controls can be used with the Query Designer to generate server-side script that executes a query on the Web server and returns the results on a dynamic Web page.

Design-time ActiveX controls generate standard HTML and script that can be viewed in any browser on any platform. While Microsoft Visual InterDev includes a number of design-time ActiveX controls, third parties can build their own controls to extend Visual InterDev with new functionality.

An example of a design-time ActiveX Control is the Data Range Header control, which lets you build an SQL query in the Query Designer (figure 2-6), and then automatically builds the server script to display the returned records in HTML. This allows users to page forward and backward through the returned records.

Use of the Data Ranger Header and the Data Range Footer permits us to show live database records in a dynamically generated HTML page. The user can page through the records using the navigation bar at the bottom of the page. When a table contains hundreds or even thousands of records, paging through records is faster than having to wait for all the records to be displayed on a page.

### The Data Form Wizard

Web developers might also want to build HTML forms that allow users to modify database information directly through their Web browser, for example, inserting, updating and deleting database records in a table. Normally, building HTML forms bound to data is a complex task, but Visual InterDev's Data Form Wizard simplifies this task.

We can use the Data Form Wizard, which works with any ODBC database, to build a customized HTML form that allows Friendship Insurance agents to modify customer records stored in a SQL Server database.

Figures 2-7 through 2-11 graphically demonstrate how this is done:

The Data Form Wizard automatically generates three new Active Server Pages for  the customized Data Form:

    CustomerForm.asp
    CustomerList.asp
    CustomerAction.asp

You can customize the generated HTML and script in these files as desired.

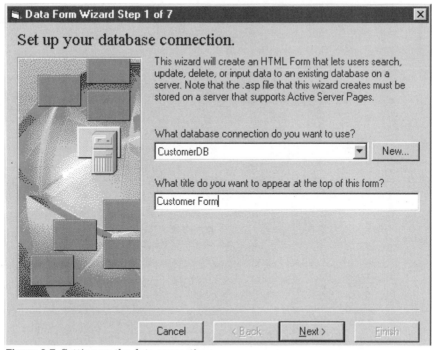

**Figure 2-7.** Setting up the data connection.

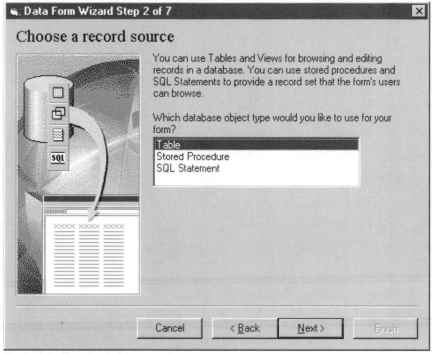

**Figure 2-8.** Choosing a data source.

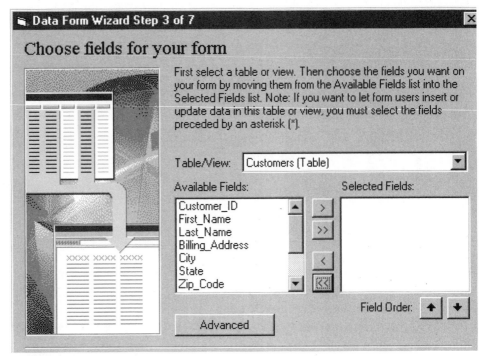

**Figure 2-9.** Choosing fields.

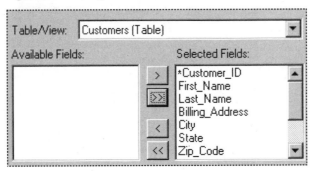

**Figure 2-10.** All the fields in the Customers table are moved to the Selected Fields box.

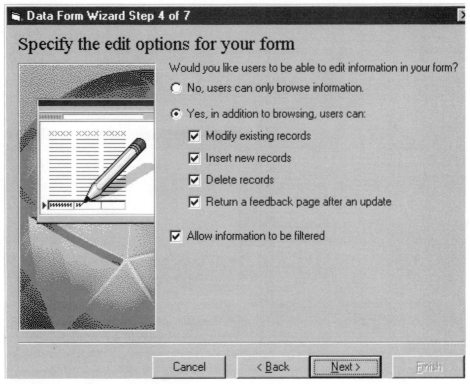

**Figure 2-11.** Specify all edit options.

## Working With Database Designer

The Visual InterDev Database Designer makes it easy to design, set up, and administer Microsoft SQL Server 6.5 databases. In this lesson, you'll use the Database Designer to create a new database design for the Friendship Insurance SQL Server database.

Note that this feature doesn't work with databases other than Microsoft SQL Server 6.5 and above databases.

In the past, setting up and managing client-server based database engines such as SQL Server, Oracle, and Sybase has been a fairly difficult and time-consuming task. The Database Designer brings the graphical ease-of-use features of Microsoft Access to the process of setting up and administering Microsoft SQL Server databases within the Visual InterDev development environment.

To create a new table with the Database Designer, as shown in figure 2-12, merely open the database in DataView; choose New Table in the Tables folder; choose a column as a primary key; now add new columns as per your database design as shown in figure 2-13.

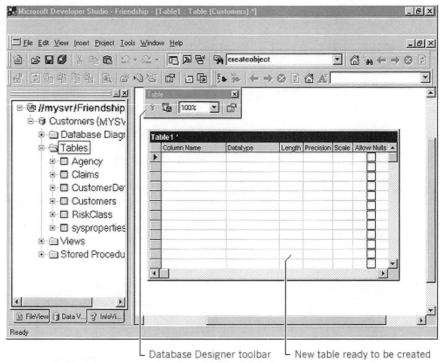

**Figure 2-12.** Creating a new table with Database Designer.

| | Column Name | Datatype | Length | Precision | Scale | Allow Nulls |
|---|---|---|---|---|---|---|
| 🔑 | Column1 | int | 4 | 10 | 0 | |
| ▶ | Column2 | varchar ▾ | 10 | 0 | 0 | ✓ |
| | | | | | | |
| | | | | | | |
| | | | | | | |
| | | | | | | |
| | | | | | | |

**Figure 2-13.** Creating a new table.

Ordinarily on a DBMS system such as SQL Server, making changes to the database would require many manual commands written in Data Definition Language (DDL). The Database Designer generates the DDL automatically as you work, and no changes are committed until you have completed making them. You can view the SQL change script to see the DDL generated.

The Database Designer is a great tool for doing "what-if" scenarios on large databases. If developers don't have permission to execute the changes, they can save the change script to a text file (DDL Change Script) and then give the file to an authorized database administrator to review and execute.

Besides creating and designing tables, the Database Designer also enables you to create sophisticated database diagrams (figure 2-14). For example, you can create a new diagram to establish relationships (figure 2-15) between tables. Microsoft's Visual InterDev is a fairly robust tool that goes a long way towards solving your Microsoft SQL connectivity problems.

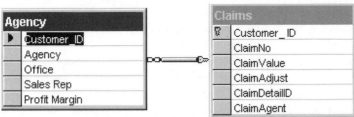

**Figure 2-14.** Graphically designing databases.

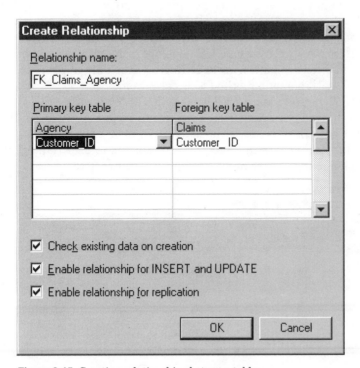

**Figure 2-15.** Creating relationships between tables.

## Information Builders' WebFOCUS

I've been in the IT business for over twenty years. For many of those years I've been involved, in one way or another, with building systems that use fourth generation languages (4GLs). A precursor, but with similarities, to SQL, the thrust of most of these 4GLs was to provide a way for end-users to get data out of corporate databases.

One of the leaders in this arena is Information Builders whose FOCUS 4GL is probably the most widely used end-user "programming language" today. So it's little wonder that IBI, as they've come to be called, has embarked on a path of connecting their FOCUS product to the Web. This they've done very ably with WebFOCUS.

Activated by a user's request to view information WebFOCUS runs the request, retrieves the data, formats it, and returns HTML output to the user's browser for display.

IBI is well-known for their middleware framework as well. Long before the advent of the commercial Internet, IBI embarked on a path towards a middle layer of software that would enable end-users to access enterprise data, no matter where or what format it was in. WebFOCUS uses this client/server middleware framework to access enterprise data needed for Web applications. Thus, developers and end users are shielded from the complexities and incompatibilities of using different proprietary operating systems, networks, and data sources. In sum, WebFOCUS developers do not need to worry about data residing on different platforms or DBMS's — the data appears to be from a single source, with a single method to access them.

WebFOCUS provides a CGI that enables Web pages to call WebFOCUS reporting procedures. Activated by a user's request to view information, the WebFOCUS CGI runs the request, and returns HTML output to the user's browser for display. When WebFOCUS responds to user requests for information, the following events happen (shown in figure 2-16):

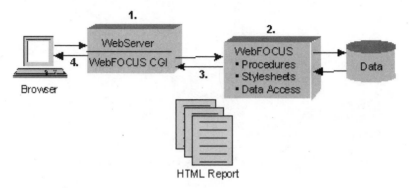

**Figure 2-16.** How WebFocus works.

1. The user request for information calls the WebFOCUS CGI, ibiweb.exe. Parameters from the calling HTML page is passed to the WebFOCUS CGI. The parameters can specify a FOCUS procedure to run, along with any other conditions.

2. The WebFOCUS CGI routes the request to WebFOCUS, which runs the request and retrieves information from the data sources.

3. WebFOCUS formats the answer set, and sends the HTML output back to the Web server.

4. The Web server delivers the report to the user's Web browser for display.

The data access, network communications, and server operations that support WebFOCUS are provided by Information Builders Enterprise Data Access (EDA) technology. EDA technology enables WebFOCUS to access heterogeneous enterprise data needed for Web applications, without concern about the complexities and incompatibilities of using different proprietary operating systems, networks, and data sources.

In addition to these components, WebFOCUS includes the FOCUS Six Power Edition as a development tool. You can create and prototype your applications using FOCUS Six, or any other FOCUS version that provides an application development environment, and then transfer the procedures and StyleSheet files to the WebFOCUS server for deployment.

You can use WebFOCUS Components in several configurations.

•If the Web server and the source data are on the same machine, you can use a two-tier configuration.

•If the Web server and the source data are on separate machines, you can use a three-tier configuration to access the data.

•If the source data is on several different machines, you can use EDA to access the remote data. The Web server and the WebFOCUS (EDA) server can be on the same or separate machines.

## Publishing Reports on the Web

Creating reports and deploying them with WebFOCUS consists of the following steps:

Step 1. Make the source data available for your report. WebFOCUS provides transparent access to local and remote data from 65 database formats on over 35 platforms, including relational databases and legacy hierarchical databases. To make data available to your reporting procedures, you must do the following:

1. Install and configure a WebFOCUS server and the Data Drivers required to access the specific data sources.

2. Identify the data sources available and provide the metadata required to access the data sources. This metadata includes the physical names and loca-

tions of the data, the tables in the data sources, and the column and attributes in the tables. WebFOCUS provides a Windows-based graphical tool to help you create metadata about your data sources.

3. If the WebFOCUS server and the Web server are on different machines, install the communications software provided by WebFOCUS on the Web server. This enables the Web server to communicate with the WebFOCUS server.

If the Web server and the WebFOCUS server are on the same machine, you do not need to install EDA/Client.

Step 2. Create styled reports that retrieve and format the data. WebFOCUS builds on the robustness and flexibility of the FOCUS Fourth-Generation Language (4GL) for data retrieval and report formatting and styling. After you create and style your reports with WebFOCUS you can choose whether to:

•Create pre-formatted or customized report pages that are stored as HTML files and are ready to be accessed via a client browser.
•Deploy your reports using a Web page that calls the WebFOCUS CGI and passes it the name of the report to run. WebFOCUS retrieves the report data at the user's request, and automatically displays the most up-to-date information.

To call the WebFOCUS CGI ibiweb.exe from a hyperlink, you use the HTML HREF tag. The syntax is

```
<A HREF=
"cgi-bin/ibi_cgi/ibiweb.exe?IBIF_ex=fex[&var=val[&var=val]...3]">text</A>
```

where

| | |
|---|---|
| IBIF_ex | Specifies the stored FOCUS procedure to run. |
| fex | Is the name of the FOCUS procedure to run. |
| var | Is the name of a variable you want to pass to the specified procedure. You can pass more than one variable. Do not include a space between variable-value pairs. |
| val | Is the value of the corresponding variable. If the value contains an embedded blank, enclose it in single quotation marks. |
| text | Is the text that appears on your Web page and serves as a hyperlink to execute the procedure when clicked. |

Step 3: Create a Web page from which to access your report. If you create procedures that store report pages as HTML files, ready to be accessed via a client browser, you can access these reports from a Web page using standard HTML commands.

If you create procedures designed to retrieve report data at a user's request and automatically display the most up-to-date information, you can deploy your reports using a Web page that calls the WebFOCUS CGI and passes it the name of the report to run. This page must contain either a hyperlink or a form.

You can use a hyperlink to run a report and pass it parameters that you specify. You can use a form to prompt the user for parameters to pass to the procedure.

### Calling WebFOCUS from a Hyperlink

The following FOCUS procedure, called CSALES, produces a report that shows total sales by category by region. In order to run, this procedure needs values for the fields CATEGORY and REGION:

```
TABLE FILE GGSALES
ON TABLE SET PAGE-NUM OFF
HEADING
"&CATEGORY Sales for &RGN Region"
SUM UNITS AND DOLLARS
BY REGION NOPRINT BY CATEGORY NOPRINT
WHERE (CATEGORY EQ '&CATEGORY') AND (REGION EQ '&RGN');
END
```

The following HTML file produces a page with four hyperlinks: Midwest, Northeast, Southwest, and West. Each of the HREF tags calls ibiweb.exe and passes it the name of the procedure to run, the value for CATEGORY, and the value for REGION.

```
<HTML>
<HEAD><TITLE> WebFOCUS Reports </TITLE></HEAD>
<BODY>
<H4 ALIGN=CENTER>Coffee Sales by Region</H4>
<HR><P><FONT SIZE=+2></FONT><BR>
<FONT SIZE=+1>Select a region:</FONT></P>
<UL TYPE=SQUARE>
<LI><A HREF="/cgi-bin/ibi_cgi/ibiweb.exe?IBIF_ex=csales&CATEGORY=
  Coffee&RGN=Midwest">Midwest</A>
<LI><A HREF="/cgi-bin/ibi_cgi/ibiweb.exe?IBIF_ex=csales&CATEGORY=
  Coffee&RGN=Northeast">Northeast</A>
<LI><A HREF="/cgi-bin/ibi_cgi/ibiweb.exe?IBIF_ex=csales&CATEGORY=
  Coffee&RGN=Southeast">Southeast</A>
<LI><A HREF="/cgi-bin/ibi_cgi/ibiweb.exe?IBIF_ex=csales&CATEGORY=
  Coffee&RGN=Northeast">Northeast</A>
</UL></BODY></HTML>
```

The resulting page is shown in figure 2-17. Clicking Midwest produces the report shown in figure 2-18.

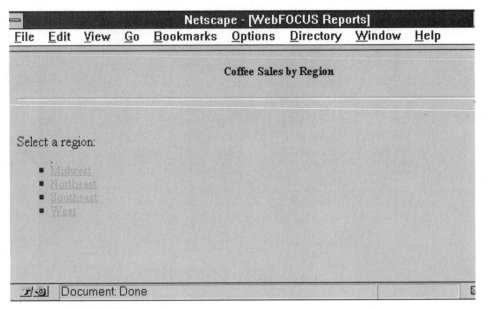

**Figure 2-17.** WebFOCUS example.

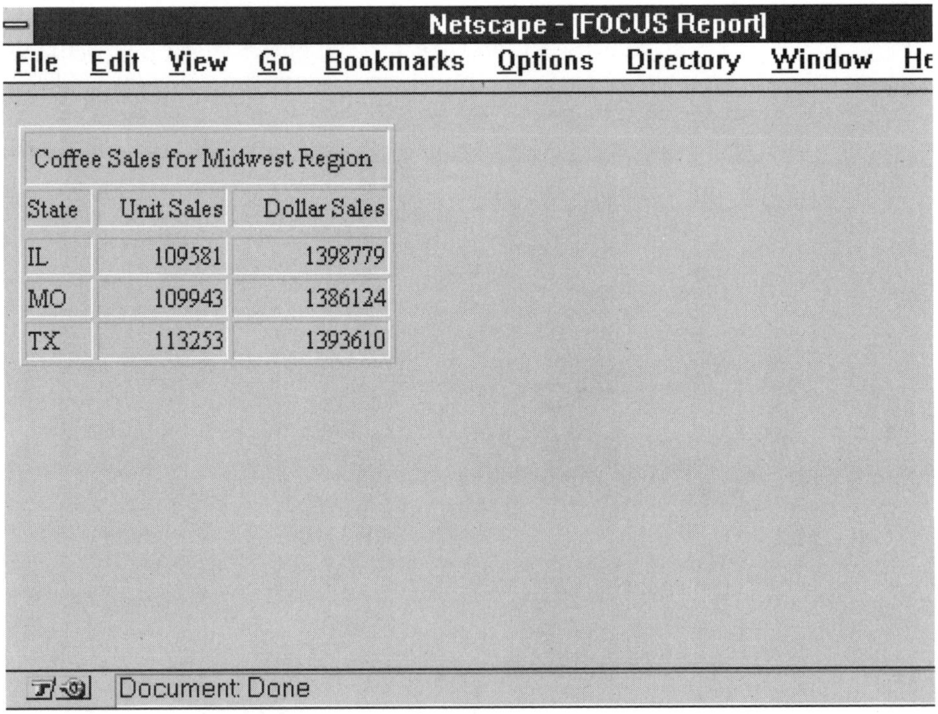

**Figure 2-18.** WebFOCUS report.

### Calling WebFOCUS from a Form

To call the WebFOCUS CGI ibiweb.exe from a form, you use the HTML FORM tags. You can use any available form tags, including text entry fields, selection lists, radio buttons, and check boxes. The syntax is

```
<FORM ACTION="/cgi-bin/ibi_cgi/ibiweb.exe" METHOD="get">
<INPUT NAME="IBIF_ex" VALUE="fex" TYPE="hidden" ...>
<INPUT NAME="variable" TYPE="text" SIZE="size" ...>
<INPUT NAME="variable" TYPE=RADIO VALUE=value>value
<SELECT NAME="variable"><OPTION>option_text</SELECT>
<INPUT NAME="variable" TYPE=CHECKBOX VALUE="check_value">MIS only
   .
   .
   .
</FORM>
```

where

| | |
|---|---|
| fex | Is the name of the FOCUS procedure to run. Note: To prompt the user for the name of the procedure to run, use TYPE=text in place of TYPE=hidden. |
| variable | Is the name of a variable you want to pass to the specified procedure. You can pass more than one variable. Create an input area for each variable. |
| text | Creates a text entry field on the Web page. The text that the user supplies in the input area is used as the value of the variable. |
| size | Is the number of characters you want the input area to be. The number you assign should accommodate the largest value the user can enter for the variable. |
| RADIO | Creates a radio button on the Web page. The value associated with the radio button is used as the value of the variable. |
| value | Is the value assigned to the variable specified with the RADIO tag and passed to the specified procedure. |
| SELECT | Creates a selection list field on the Web page. The option that the user selects is used as the value of the variable. |
| OPTION | Creates an option in the selection list on the Web page. One or more options can be included in a selection list. The option_text associated with the option is assigned to the variable specified with the SELECT tag and passed to the specified procedure. |
| option_text | Is the value assigned to the variable specified with the SELECT tag and passed to the specified procedure. |

CHECKBOX        Creates a check box field on the Web page. If the user checks
                the field, the value specified is used as the value of the vari-
                able.

check_value     Is the value assigned to the variable specified with the
                CHECKBOX tag and passed to the specified procedure.

The following FOCUS procedure, called CSALES, produces a report that shows total sales by category by region. In order to run, this procedure needs values for the fields CATEGORY and REGION:

```
TABLE FILE GGSALES
ON TABLE SET PAGE-NUM OFF
HEADING
"&CATEGORY Sales for &RGN Region"
SUM UNITS AND DOLLARS
BY REGION NOPRINT BY CATEGORY NOPRINT
WHERE (CATEGORY EQ '&CATEGORY') AND (REGION EQ '&RGN');
END
```

The following HTML file produces a form to run the FOCUS procedure CSALES. The form prompts the user for the category and region:

```
<HTML>
<HEAD>
<TITLE> WebFOCUS Reports </TITLE>
</HEAD>
<BODY>
<H4 ALIGN=CENTER>Sales Report by Category and Region</H4>
<HR>
<FORM ACTION="/cgibin/ibi_cgi/ibiweb.exe" METHOD="get">
<INPUT NAME="IBIF_ex" VALUE="csales" TYPE="hidden">
<P ALIGN=LEFT NOWRAP><PRE>
<B>Enter category: </B><INPUT NAME="CATEGORY" TYPE="text" SIZE="6">
</PRE></P>
<P><PRE><B>Select region: </B>
<INPUT NAME="RGN" TYPE=RADIO VALUE=Northeast>Northeast
<INPUT NAME="RGN" TYPE=RADIO VALUE=Southeast>Southeast
<INPUT NAME="RGN" TYPE=RADIO VALUE=Midwest>Midwest
<INPUT NAME="RGN" TYPE=RADIO VALUE=Western>Western
<INPUT NAME="RGN" TYPE=RADIO VALUE=Northwest>Northwest
<INPUT NAME="RGN" TYPE=RADIO VALUE=Southwest>Southwest
</PRE></P>
<P>
<INPUT NAME="submit" TYPE=SUBMIT VALUE="Run Report"> <INPUT NAME="reset"
TYPE=RESET VALUE="Clear Form">
```

```
</P>
</FORM>
</BODY>
</HTML>
```

The resulting page is shown in figure 2-19. Entering the category Coffee and the region Midwest produces the report shown in figure 2-20.

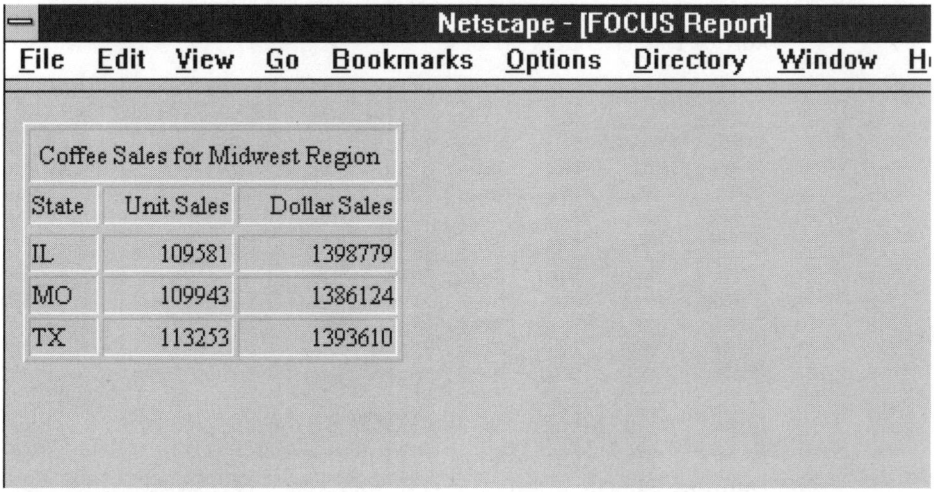

**Figure 2-19.** A WebFOCUS form

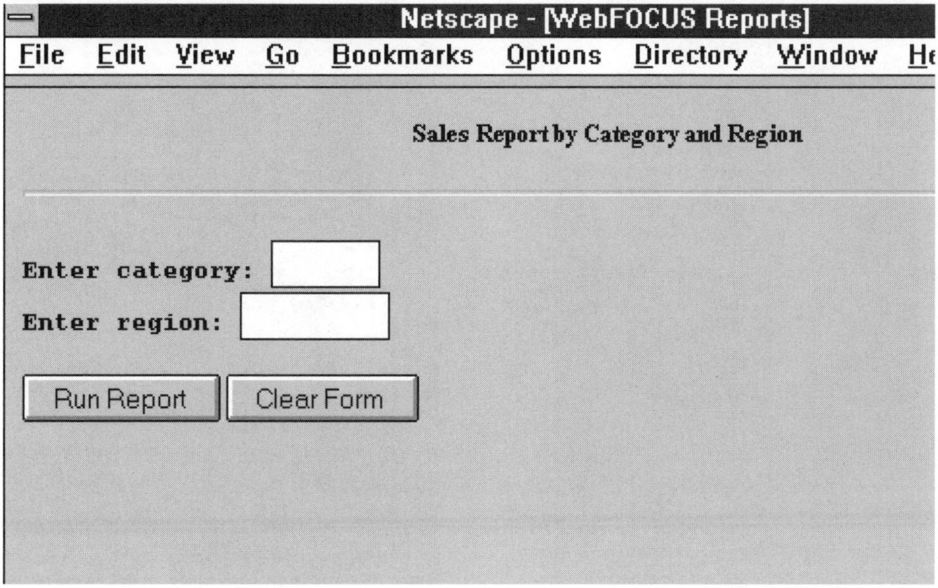

**Figure 2-20.** A WebFOCUS form generated page.

## Running Ad-hoc Reports

One of the strengths of any 4GL is that it permits end-users to create requests off the cuff. WebFOCUS also has this capability by permitting Internet users to create their own ad hoc requests.

You can design a form that calls the WebFOCUS CGI ibiweb.exe to run an ad-hoc report. The syntax is

```
<FORM ACTION="/cgi-bin/ibi_cgi/ibiweb.exe" METHOD="get">
<TEXTAREA NAME="IBIF_adhocfex" ROWS=rows COLS=columns ...>
</TEXTAREA>
        .
        .
        .

</FORM>
```

where

fex       Is the name of the FOCUS procedure to run.
rows      Is the number of rows in the text area.
columns   Is the number of columns in the text area.

The following HTML file produces a form to prompt the user for a report request:

```
<HTML>
<HEAD>
<TITLE> WebFOCUS Reports </TITLE>
</HEAD>
<BODY>
<H4>Enter report request:</H4>
<FORM METHOD="get" ACTION="/cgi-bin/ibi_cgi/ibiweb.exe">
<P ALIGN=LEFT NOWRAP><PRE>
<TEXTAREA NAME="IBIF_adhocfex" VALUE="" ROWS=12 COLS=48 ALIGN=LEFT>
</TEXTAREA>
</PRE></P>
<P>
<INPUT NAME="submit" TYPE=SUBMIT VALUE="Run Report"> <INPUT NAME="reset"
TYPE=RESET VALUE="Clear Form">
</P>
</FORM>
</BODY>
</HTML>
```

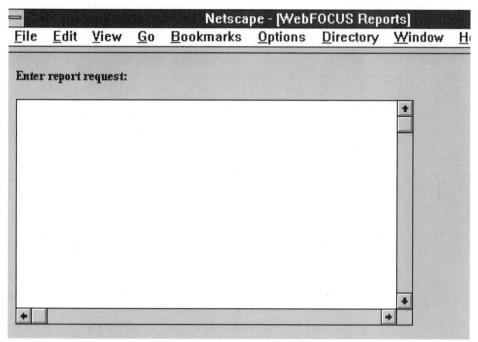

**Figure 2-21.** A WebFOCUS ad-hoc request screen.

| Coffee Sales for Midwest Region | | |
|---|---|---|
| State | Unit Sales | Dollar Sales |
| IL | 109581 | 1398779 |
| MO | 109943 | 1386124 |
| TX | 113253 | 1393610 |

**Figure 2-22.** The ad-hoc results.

Figure 2-21 shows what the resulting page looks like. Figure 2-22 shows the output of the following report request:

```
TABLE FILE GGSALES
ON TABLE SET PAGE-NUM OFF
HEADING "Coffee Sales for Midwest Region"
SUM UNITS AND DOLLARS BY REGION NOPRINT BY CATEGORY NOPRINT
WHERE (CATEGORY EQ 'Coffee') AND (REGION EQ 'Midwest');
END
```

## Special WebFOCUS Syntax

Like most robust Web development tools, WebFOCUS has its own HTML tags which it uses to provide formatting capabilities.

This example shows how some WebFOCUS tags are used to display two reports in the browser on a page that you have designed for that purpose. The numbers on the left refer to the notes that follow.  First you set up the Web page. The following file is called first.htm:

```
<HTML>
   <BODY>
1. Top report
2. <!— WEBFOCUS TABLE UPPER>
   <HR SIZE=5>
1. Bottom report
2. <!— WEBFOCUS TABLE LOWER>
   </BODY>
   </HTML>
```

Next you create your report request and send it to the Web page you have designed:

```
TABLE FILE GGORDER
   SUM QUANTITY BY PCD
   IF PCD EQ 'B$$$'
3. ON TABLE HOLD FORMAT HTMTABLE AS UPPER
   END
   TABLE FILE GGORDER
   SUM QUANTITY BY PCD
   IF PCD EQ 'F$$$'
3. ON TABLE HOLD FORMAT HTMTABLE AS LOWER
   END
   -RUN
4. -HTMLFORM first
```

1. Specifies text that will appear on the Web page to label the two reports.,
2. HTML comment format used to identify the two reports to be displayed. On the Web page, WebFOCUS will substitute the designated reports for the corresponding HTML comments. The report listed first will be appear on the page above the report listed second.
3. The FOCUS command that extracts report output into a temporary file, from which it can be sent to a Web page.
4. The Dialogue Manager command that runs the report requests and sends the output to first.htm, the HTML file that contains your Web page.

```
Netscape - [http://unxdemo/cgi-bin/...xec.wfs?focexec=+sa
File    Edit    View    Go    Bookmarks    Options    Directory    Window    He
```

Top report

| Product Code | Ordered Units |
|--------------|---------------|
| B141         | 100427        |
| B142         | 285689        |
| B144         | 61498         |

Bottom report

| Product Code | Ordered Units |
|--------------|---------------|
| F101         | 108792        |
| F102         | 136045        |
| F103         | 203076        |

**Figure 2-23.** A WebFOCUS Web page with two reports.

The Web page shown in figure 2-23 was generated from these files.

Since WebFOCUS has all the power of FOCUS 6, it has some pretty robust reporting capabilities including: temporary fields, sorting, tabular reporting, matrices, graphs, an SQL version translator, Cartesian products, joins, expressions, functions, subroutines, concatenation, and the list goes on.

# 3

# Maximizing the Efficiency of Your Web Database

## Introduction

Databases have been around the corporate enterprise for more than two decades. During that time we've honed our skills to the point of finally being able to deploy databases that are fast, stable and secure across corporate networks.

What disturbs me about datacasting is that all too frequently, databases are being created for use on the Web seemingly without benefit of the lessons we've learned across those two decades. Even accounting for slow modem speeds (the current average is still 28.8 kbps), I notice that many sites that make use of databases are painfully slow.

In a nutshell, the problem is that the majority of Web databases are just not maximized for efficiency. While some organizations are tapping into their primary databases for Internet/Intranet database access, many more are creating databases specifically for Web access. It's unclear whether these corporate database spinoffs are optimized for on-line use or even whether they have been created by folks knowledgeable in the black magic of efficient database administration.

This chapter is a bit of a departure from the rest of the book. I felt it necessary to spend a few minutes in discussing the ways and means to efficient databases. All relational databases share the same architecture so this DBMS efficiency primer, which stresses IBM's DB2 architecture, will be suitable for any database.

## The E-R Model

Although there are several different models for representing data and a multitude of methodologies for developing the design, the Entity-Relationship model is, by far, the most popular. Popularized by Peter Chen in the 1970s, interestingly the E-R model was originally associated with network structures. Today, this model has been tapped as the prime model for the relationship database table structure.

In this methodology, the first step taken is to identify the data objects. In relational terminology, these are called relations. In relational databases they are stored as tables. Examples of entities would include patients, admissions, services, drug orders, clinicians and employees as shown in figure 3-1. For each of the entities, you would then identify each of the attributes.

| Patient | Admission | Service |
|---|---|---|
| patient ID | patient ID | patient ID |
| last name | admit date | service date |
| first name | discharge date | type |
| sex | | clinician |
| birthdate | | |

**Figure 3-1.** An E-R table.

There are several steps that you can take to identify business information requirements:

Step 1.    The first phase of logical design is to understand the information needs of the business. In this step, we interview users and analyze manual and automated documents and reports. Our goal is to represent the business information structures and rules.

Step 2.    Identify the business entities. Let the users describe the business or application and what it does or is meant to do in their own terms. Obtain pertinent documents and files. Combine to produce appropriate lists of candidate entities. Review these lists with users and they will begin to understand the concept of a business entity, making it possible to refine our lists.

Step 3.    Describe the relationships between entities. Relationships are defined in terms of cardinality or how many. For example, the branch entity has one customer or the Branch entity has many customers. Figure 3-2 shows flowchart conventions for this process.

Step 4.    Distinguish between mandatory and optional relationships. Each side of the relationship will be one or the other. These distinctions alter the cardinality of the relationship.

Step 5.     Identify the data requirements. In this step, we translate these business entities and relationships into a logical data structure made up of data entities and relationships. Data entities are derived from business entities. In other words, we translate each business entity into a data entity. Each data entity will eventually correspond to a table. Most database systems do not support many to many relationships. To do so would require much of the same data appearing in each data entity. Instead, these relationships are resolved in the design process by creating an intersection record through which the two enti-

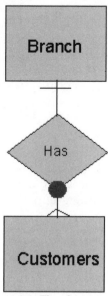

**Figure 3-2.** Flowcharting the database. An entity is represented by a box. A relationship is represented by a diamond between two entities. Relationships are defined in terms of cardinality or "how many" as shown by connecting lines. A mandatory relationship (between Branch and Has) is shown with a straight line. An optional relationship (between Has and Customers) is shown with a circle.

ties are connected. This is referred to as an associative data entity.

Define primary key data elements. A primary key is the minimal set of data elements that uniquely identifies an instance of an entity. A particular customer can be uniquely identified by one attribute, social security number. The key would remain unique if we added last name, but we would be violating the requirement that it be the minimal set of elements. In other words, last name is not required for uniqueness.

If a key consists of more than one attribute, it is a composite key. For example, the entity TRANSACTION requires a composite key. There may be many transactions for a given account number. Account number, transaction type and timestamp are the minimal set.

The primary key of our associative entity, CUST_ACCT, is the customer social security number plus account number. These are the primary keys of the two entities it associates.

Next, define foreign key data elements. A foreign key consists of those columns in a table that are the same as the columns making up the primary key in some other table.

Finally, define nonkey data elements. The nonkey data elements make up the content of the data structure while the key data elements make up the structure itself.

## Rules of Thumb for Easy Normalization

The purpose of normalization in database design is to reduce the redundant nonkey data held in a database, thereby reducing the inherent update problems that data redundancy can cause. Normalization in design involves a series of levels called normal forms. Each normal form has a set of criteria associated with it which a table (an entity) must satisfy to be considered in that normal form.

A relation is considered to be on first normal form if there are no repeating groups. In COBOL this would be an occurs clause. There are several problems with repeating groups:

1. Space is wasted when we allow for 5 occurrences but only store 3.
2. Some DBMS's do not directly support repeating groups. There are no array data types.
3. SQL statements that would be needed to process a repeating group would be extremely complicated.

```
SELECT MGR_ID FROM MANAGER
WHERE  MGR_BONUS1  =  100   OR
MGR_BONUS2 = 100 OR MGR_BONUS3
= 100   OR MGR_BONUS50 = 100
```

A table is in second normal form if it is in first normal form and if each non-key attribute represents a fact about the whole key rather than only a part of the key. A table with a primary key of a single column is automatically in second normal form.

The unnormalized TRANSACTION table is as follows:

```
TRANSACTION:
TR_TYPE
TR_TIMESTAMP
TR_AMT
TR_ACCT_NO
TR_VERIFY_CODE
Primary   key:   TR_ACCT_NO   +
TR_TYPE + TR_TIMESTAMP
Foreign Key: TR_ACCT_NO
```

Different types of transactions require different kinds of verification indicated in the verify code. The nonkey element, TR_VERIFY_CODE, represents a fact about a part of the key, TR_TYPE. This means that this table is not in second normal form.

A table is considered to be in third normal form if each nonkey attribute represents a fact about the whole key rather than another nonkey attribute. BRANCH table contains the following elements:

```
BRANCH:
BRANCH_ID
BRANCH_CITY
BRANCH_ADDR
BRANCH_GEO_RATING
Primary Key: BRANCH_ID
```

The geographic rating is generated by the marketing department based on the number of accounts in a city. This violates third normal form. A nonkey attribute (BRANCH_GEO_RATING) represents a fact about another nonkey attribute (BRANCH_CITY).

## Tricks For Using Denormalization to Speed Performance

Normalization results in more tables with smaller attribute sets. Retrieving data from more than one table requires a join operation, which means processing overhead. A completely normalized design is not always the optimal solution in practice. The process of selectively combining tables by inserting redundant nonkey data columns is called denormalization.

There are several advantages to denormalized tables: the cost is reduced if the data from the second table is needed most of the time when accessing the primary table; if the data is needed together, you do not need a join.

However, there are many disadvantages to denormalized tables as well: violating the rules of normalization can lead to inconsistency; and denormalized tables have larger rows. Therefore, access to sets of rows in the primary table will take longer; some SQL queries will be more difficult, unless you redundantly store the code, the expansion and the code table.

A rule of thumb here for denormalization is to start with a normalized design first and then denormalize.

Follow these steps when denormalizing:

Step 1. The first step in denormalization of data is to determine what processes represent the heaviest volume and on what tables those processes are operating. Figure 3-3 shows how a process/table usage matrix can be of great assistance:

| | TABLE A | TABLE B | TABLE C | TABLE D |
|---|---|---|---|---|
| Process 1 | | | | |
| Process 2 | | | | |
| Process 3 | | | | |

**Figure 3-3.** A process/table usage matrix.

Step 2.    After the number of executions has been placed in the appropriate cell in the matrix, the next step is to determine how many rows of the table will be needed by each execution. In other words when a process accesses a table, how may rows will it normally access? Do steps 1 and 2 on a 24-hour cycle over a week and average the results to account for variances.

The total number of rows needed for all processing is the sum of all row accesses going across the page.

Step 3.    We are now ready to determine two things: which tables to denormalize and which tables to cluster. Use these rules of thumb:
1. Combine the most heavily used tables.
2. Based on the usage determined via the matrix above, the analyst should question which two or more rows can be merged so that data used together is placed in the same row.
3. Rows that can be combined share part of a common key. For example, an employee base table, an employee education table and an employee job history table may be able to be combined. But an employee table and a parts usage table would not be good candidates.
4. Factor clustering in when the access mode is sequential.
5. Consider the deliberate introduction of redundancy into the system. The nonredundancy of data optimizes update of data at the expense of access to the data. The issue of denormalization now must address the question: Will the deliberate introduction of redundancy into the system significantly reduce the total amount of access that the system makes? Generally speaking, only a limited amount of data should be deliberately made redundant.
6. Add back internal arrays.
7. Sometimes splitting a table apart is the best route to denormalization.

## Keys to Separating and Consolidating Tables

Major performance gains are possible in the physical separation of the consolidation of data. For example, when two or more tables are accessed together by a majority of the programs in the system and where the data in the two logical tables can be physically merged together in a meaningful way, then it may make sense to merge the two tables together physically.

The physical merger of the two tables has the effect of allowing the data in the two tables to be accessed in the same I/O. If the two tables are not physically merged, then separate I/Os are required in their access, and performance suffers.

The main techniques for consolidation of data are:

- the simple merger of two or more tables
- the creation of redundant nonkey data
- the creation of arrays in the same row of data

Some of the trade-offs that must be considered are:

- the extra space that might be required
- the extra programming that might be required
- the extra maintenance of programs that might be required
- the additional complexity that is being introduced

As a rule, when there is a performance gain of 20% or more in terms of reduction of I/Os, the designer should seriously consider separating or consolidating tables.

In general, when nonkey data is spread redundantly across multiple tables at the moment of physical design:

- each redundant element should be considered individually
- redundancy should be minimized as much as possible
- there should be a single table where redundant nonkey data contains, by definition, the correct value for the contents of the data element.

Rules of thumb for when a logical design can be turned into a physical design:

- when there is a regularly occurring number of occurrences of data in the array
- when the occurrences of data in the array are created in an orderly fashion
- when the occurrences of data in the array are accessed in an orderly fashion
- when the occurrences of data in the array occupy only a small amount of space
- when the occurrences of data in the array occupy the same amount of space
- when the occurrences of data in the array are created and accessed, but not created and updated

Other than performance considerations, another reason why tables may need to be divided is how long the table will take to recover or reorganize or how long the table will take to have an index built on the rows in the table. In general, the smaller the table, the faster recovery and reorganization takes, and the quicker the indexes may be built.

Transaction separation requires that program specifications consider not just what function the transaction will accomplish, but also what resources the program will use in accomplishing the function.

## What Indexes Do, Don't Do and How They Can Slow You Down

Creating indexes for a table is an important part of the design and tuning of a relational database system. The main purpose of indexes is to help performance in finding rows.

The first basic rule about indexes is that indexes do not specify which columns can be used for selecting rows or in which order rows are returned.

```
SELECT * FROM CUSTFILE
WHERE AMTDATE BETWEEN '910202'
and '920909' ORDER BY CUSTNAME,
AMTDATE
```

This SQL statement will work the same regardless of whether or not there are any indexes:

The ORDER BY clause controls the order over which rows are retrieved. If there is no ORDER BY clause, then the rows will be returned in an order based on how the DBMS reads the data.

In general, you can't tell the database how to retrieve rows of a table. It will decide what it thinks is the best way. However, while programmers cannot tell the DBMS what to do, they can code their SQL statements to try to take advantage of the indexes.

The main purpose of indexes is for performance, but there are several other uses that affect the content of the database:

a. Uniqueness: It is often necessary to ensure that duplicate values are not allowed for a field in a table. An employee database would usually have a unique employee ID for each person. In a relational database, this is controlled by using an index on the columns that have this requirement. An index can be defined as being UNIQUE or NONUNIQUE. Usually, a CREATE command controls this option.

b. Primary keys: Most relational databases have implemented the concept of referential integrity. If a table is a parent table in a relationship, then it must have a primary key defined for it. This is done by using the keyword PRIMARY KEY in the CREATE TABLE command. A unique index must be created on these columns. There can only be one primary key for a table.

c. Clustering of data: There is one more way in which an index can affect the data, but in this case it is just the physical placement of rows — not their content.

## How to Manage Referential Integrity

Referential integrity is the capability of a system to keep the relationships between two occurrences of data synchronized in the face of change when data is interrelated by means of a foreign key. Depending on the database vendor and the release of the database itself, referential integrity may either be the responsibility of the application designer or maintained at the system level.

There are several rules governing how referential integrity works:

a. Uniqueness: A dependent can only have one parent row for each referential constraint. Therefore the primary key must be unique and not defined as NOT NULL. This rule is sometimes called Entity Integrity.

b. Insertion of dependent rows: This is sometimes called the Existence rule. With one exception, dependent rows must have a parent row already in the parent table. That is, there must be a parent table row with a primary key with the same value as the foreign key of the dependent row. The one exception is if the foreign key has a NULL value. In this case, the new row does not have a parent.

c. Deletion of parent (parameters to use when defining the dependent table): Parent row cannot be deleted if any dependent rows exist (default). When a parent row is deleted, all of its dependent rows are also deleted. When a parent row is deleted, the foreign key in any dependent is set to NULL.

Keep the following thoughts in mind with respect to performance issues and referential integrity:

a. When the DBMS does the checking, fewer SQL calls are needed.

b. The DBMS will do its checking every time but programmatic checks may be able to skip some steps.

c. All foreign keys should have indexes defined on them. Otherwise performance on deletes of the parent rows and updates of primary keys will be very poor.

d. Primary keys cannot be updated if the row has any dependents. The update process is as follows:

   •insert a new parent with the new primary key
   •update all dependents to have the new value as their foreign key
   •delete the old parent

From a performance perspective, there are several options on the management of referential integrity:

a. Delete all references to an object when the object is deleted as an integral part of the online transaction. The downside is that this might require too much I/O in the middle of the day.

b. Wait until the peak hours of processing have passed, then repair the inconsistency of the database.

c. The usage of application conventions can achieve significant savings in the implementation of referential integrity. An application convention is merely a means of coordinating the needs for referential integrity over an entire application.

d. Independent audits should occasionally be made. The frequency of the audit is determined by several factors including how sensitive the data is, how complex the relationship is, and how much data is contained in the relationship.

## Fixing the Control Database Bottleneck

While most relational tables contain data that is directly related to an application, it is frequently useful to put data that is considered auxiliary (or utilitarian) in a relational table as well. Such databases are called control databases. They often hold security data, audit data as well as terminal data.

Control databases are often candidates for performance bottlenecks. One of the online features of relational databases is locking. Data-locking prevents two online users from accessing and updating the same data at the same time. Locking occurs at two levels: the page level and the tablespace level. Further, locking can be done exclusively or shared. When locking is exclusive, no other program can access the data while the data is locked. When locking is shared, read-only access of the data is allowed. There are several solutions to the problems presented by control databases

a. Duplicate the data in the terminal security database.

b. Subdivide the terminal security data into small units of access and thus physically separate the data (i.e. create physically separate tables or separate different types of data into separate tables).

## Understanding Data Structures and Data Relationships

Indexes figure prominently in any discussion on performance. For each table you create one or more indexes. Indexes are used to implement the primary key and referential integrity concepts of the relational model, ensure uniqueness of rows within a table, and improve performance.

Indexes can be clustered or nonclustered. The difference has to do with how

they affect the tables with which they are associated. A clustering index causes the rows of the table to be stored in a physical order that approximates the
order of the index. A table can have only one clustering index because rows can
have only one physical order.

Although indexes improve performance, they are also expensive. They use
space, and increase operational overhead. On top of these costs, remember
that if a column that is part of an index is updated, performance degrades
because both the index and the table data have to be updated.

There are many ways to access data, all of which have an effect on the
amount of time it takes to get that data:

a. Sequential scan. This methodology takes the longest time as all records, up
to and including the record desired, must be read and processed.

b. Matching and nonmatching Index scans. A matching index scan reads the
index tree to find the required index entry.

```
SELECT  *  FROM  BRANCH  WHERE
BR_NO =300
```

In this example, a matching scan is used since BR_NO is an index and it can
be used to find the appropriate entry. But in this example:

```
SELECT  *  FROM  BRANCH  WHERE
BR_MGR = 'COLLINS'
```

a matching scan cannot be used since BR_MGR is not an index. However, since
(in this example) the page containing the index entry also contains BR_MGR,
a non-matching scan can be used.

When the DBMS knows it will have to retrieve a large number of pages
sequentially, it may use sequential prefetch. It retrieves many pages with one
I/O request in advance of those pages being required and stores them in the
bufferpool. This way, the wait for I/O will be reduced since the DBMS can
process already-retrieved rows while more rows are being fetched.

Another useful data structure that is built at the application level is that of
the secondary index or sparse index. When an index is created, if the table is
unclustered or not clustered along the column the index is created for, the
index is for all rows. For a large table there are correspondingly many index
entries. If the application developer is willing to build and maintain separate
tables, the size of the index can effectively be reduced.

Another design option is the sparse index. The sparse index is built and
maintained at the application level. For example, it is a table of ONLY
accounts that have a late payment. When a late surcharge is made, the application inserts a row into the table.

The creation of internal tables within a row can save considerable disk space because the key information for the row does not have to be repeated many times. In addition, performance can be enhanced in that only one I/O is needed to retrieve multiple activities. However, a burden of complexity is borne at the application level.

## Efficient Use of Joins and Subqueries

Joins and subqueries involve access to two or more tables. Actually, they may involve only one table that is accessed two or more times. There are several methods by which a relational database will join two tables, but the basic access paths to each one are the same as for the access in a simple SELECT from one table. The choices are:

- table scans
- index access
- nonmatching index access

Joins and subqueries can often be used interchangeably to access the same set of data. Usually, however, joins are more efficient.

```
SELECT PAT, PATID, LASTNAME,
ADMDATE
FROM THSPATO PAT, THSADMO ADM
WHERE PAT.PATID = ADM.PATID
```

When you join two tables you must tell the DBMS how to match up the rows. As shown above, this is done in the WHERE clause with predicates that involve columns from both tables.

If no join criteria are given, then every row of the first table will match every row of the second table. This is called a Cartesian product.

In the following example, we are joining patients with their admissions, but also want data from the characteristics and address tables. Other criteria limit the request to admissions in 1989 (there are 3000) and people who live in New York (80% of the patients).

```
SELECT  PAT.PATID,  LASTNAME,
ADMDATE, CITY, STATE,
EDUCATION
FROM THSPATO PAT, THSADMO ADM,
THSCHRO CHR, THSADDO ADD
WHERE ADMDATE BETWEEN '1989-
0101- AND '1989-12-31' AND
CITY = 'NEW YORK CITY' AND
PAT.PATID = ADM.PATID AND
PAT.PATID = CHR.PATID
```

There are several basic join methods:

a. Nested loop join. This involves one table being chosen as the outer table and the other as the inner table. The outer table is accessed to find all rows that meet the nonjoin criteria. This access may be a table space scan or may use an index. For each row select, the inner table will be accessed using the join criteria to find the matches. This access may also be via an index or a scan of the whole table space.

b. Merge scan join. This join takes both tables, sorts them into the order of the join columns (unless an index in that order is available) and then merges them.

Again, an outer and an inner table are chosen. A row from the outer table is read, then rows from the inner tables are chosen. If the join columns match, a row is selected and the next row from the inner table is read. This continues until an inner row with a higher value on the join columns is encountered. The next row of the outer table is read. And so on.

c. Hybrid join. This join is useful where the join columns of the inner table are in an unclustered index. The outer table will be scanned once in join column order (either through an index or after sorting). The inner table's index will be scanned. These partial rows will then be sorted. List prefetch will then be used to access the data rows of the inner table, to pick up the rest of the data that is needed. This method provides an efficient access path through an unclustered index of the inner table. With this method, the inner table rows are accessed only once, even if the outer table has duplicate rows.

d. Joining three or more tables. When three or more tables are joined, the DBMS may have to create an intermediate results table after joining the first two. The results will then be joined with the third table. However, if a nested loop join is used with indexes on the join columns, the DBMS will not create an intermediate table. The DBMS will do the three-way join, one row at a time.

The selection criteria for a column may depend on the data in another table or in other rows of the same table. This can be done with a subquery. A subquery can appear in either a WHERE clause or a HAVING clause.

To find the youngest patients, we ask for the patients whose birthdate is equal to the highest birthdate in the table:

```
SELECT PATID, LASTNAME, FIRST-
NAME FROM THSPATO
WHERE BIRTHDATE =
(SELECT  MAX(BIRTHDATE)  FROM
THSPATO)
```

There are four different types of subqueries, and each of these can be either correlated or noncorrelated. The four kinds differ in the number of values returned by the subquery, and the type of comparison used.

You can get the names of patients who have been in WARD 0100:

```
SELECT PATID, LASTNAME, FIRST-
NAME
FROM THSPATO
WHERE PATID IN
(SELECT  PATID  FROM  THSLOCO
WHERE WARD = '0100')
```

This is a noncorrelated subquery while the one below is a correlated subquery:

```
SELECT PATID, LASTNAME, FIRST-
NAME
FROM THSPATO PAT
WHERE PATID IN
(SELECT PATID FROM THSLOCO LOC
WHERE  WARD  =  '0100'  AND
PAT.PATID = LOC.PATID)
```

Here we are tying together (correlating) a row of the inner query with a specific row of the outer query. Both of these queries could also be done with a join of the two tables as

```
SELECT PATID, LASTNAME, FIRST-
NAME FROM THSPATO PAT, THSLOCO
LOC WHERE PAT.PATID =
LOC.PATID AND WARD = '0100'
```

The access path for a subquery depends on several things:

- Correlated or noncorrelated
- The type of subquery
- The presence of indexes on the comparison column
- Any other search criteria

In a join, the DBMS can choose any of the join methods, with either table as the outer table. With subqueries, there is less flexibility. For a noncorrelated query, the subselect is always evaluated first. For the qualifying rows, the values returned are sorted, duplicates eliminated and the values are placed in an intermediate results table. Then the outer SELECT is evaluated. Any row that meets the other search criteria is compared against this intermediate table to find a match.

For a correlated subquery, the outer table is evaluated first. For each qualifying row, the subquery is evaluated. The row from the outer table is then compared to the subquery result to determine if it will be selected. Generally, this means that the subquery will be evaluated many times.

Subqueries with IN and with EXISTS are often equivalent to a join. Generally, the join will perform better. With a join, the DBMS will choose either table as the outer table and will choose either of the join methods based on the cost estimates of the possible access paths. When there are no indexes on the join columns the merge scan join can provide reasonably good performance. With a subquery, there is less flexibility in the ways the DBMS will access the data, and the most efficient path may not be an available choice. Therefore, when possible, use a join.

## Reducing CPU Costs

Factors that affect CPU costs:

1. The large amount of CPU time each SQL statement uses.
2. The number of pages scanned — even if they are in buffers — and the number of rows scanned.
3. The amount of time it takes to sort. The sort time grows at a faster rate than the number of rows to be sorted.
4. The number of columns selected. Each selected column must be moved to a work area and ultimately placed in host variables.
5. The predicates of the WHERE clause.
6. The type of predicates used. BETWEEN is faster than >= and <=.
7. Referential integrity can either increase or decrease CPU time. If you do the same checking via a program, the costs will be higher because of the need for additional SQL statements.

Limit the number of selected columns to the ones that you really need. Fewer columns will mean less CPU processing to move them and quicker sorts. If the columns that are needed are in an index, then you also avoid having to read the data row. Other efficiency techniques:

1. Code the predicates well. Try to use indexable predicates.
2. Reduce the number of SQL calls.
3. Let the DBMS eliminate rows with predicates rather than returning the rows to the program and eliminating them with program logic. In both cases the same number of I/Os will be used (table scans). However, many fewer FETCHs and data transfers are needed.
4. Use a join where possible rather than two calls. The join eliminates at least one SQL call.

5. For frequently used code tables, substantial time can be saved if the table is kept in memory rather than in a table.

6. Denormalize.

7. Indexes can eliminate sorts as well as provide direct lookup.

## Considering View Performance Issues

A table is a collection of data organized into rows and columns. If a user is granted access to the table, he can request any of the data in the table. If he only wants to see part of it, he can limit the request to specific columns (SELECT) and specific rows (WHERE).

There is sometimes a need for a user to see the same subset of data at all times. To simplify and control this need, the DBA (Database Administrator) can define a view of the data. A view is a predefined way of looking at part of the data of a table, or a set of tables.

It is important to know what impact, if any, a view has on performance. Views can be harmful when the background work done by the system is factored into the view, particularly I/O intense Internet/Intranet servers. When a view spans two or more tables, a large amount of I/O may be required to service the view. On one hand, the view appears as a simple structuring of data to the user. On the other hand, the view may require large amounts of I/O to be consumed.

As a result, the designer should be careful in the assignment and usage of views. Generally speaking, the designer is safest with presenting data as it is defined in its table.

To access a relational table, a program must issue SQL statements. There are two modes of SQL — static and dynamic. Most application programs are written with static SQL. In this mode, the statements have a fixed format, but the particular values requested in WHERE clauses may vary:

```
EXEC SQL SELECT PATID, LAST-
NAME, FIRSTNAME
INTO :PATID, :LASTNAME,
:FIRSTNAME
FROM THSPATO
WHERE PATID=:PATIENT;
```

The example above demonstrates the use of static SQL in an application program. Dynamic SQL allows the statement format to be constructed at execution time.

There are several ways in which dynamic SQL is less efficient. The basic reason is that whatever work the DBMS must do to determine how to execute the statements must be done at execution time rather than at compile time. The DBMS must interpret the statement to see what it is doing (it only needs to be interpreted once even if it is executed many times). For static SQL, this is done by the preprocessor. The DBMS must then decide on an access path and then do authorization. These are normally done in the BIND process.

However, there are some times where dynamic SQL can provide improved performance. When a static SQL statement uses host variables in the predicates of the WHERE clause, the DBMS cannot always use the best access path because it does not know at compile time what values will be used in the host variables. The main example is the LIKE predicate. The DBMS can use an index with a LIKE provided that the value does not start with a wild card.

```
SELECT * FROM HSPAT WHERE LAST-
NAME LIKE 'JON%'
```

This query asks for patients whose last name starts with the letters JON and have any number of additional characters. We have an index on LASTNAME which is used to process the request.

```
EXEC SQL SELECT PATID, FIRST-
NAME
INTO PATID1 :FIRSTNAME
FROM THSPATO
WHERE LASTNAME=:LASTNAME;
```

In this query, the DBMS cannot use the index since it does not know at compile time what value the host variable will take.

With dynamic SQL, the comparison is also set at execution time, but the statement that the DBMS looks at to determine the access path already has the value of the variable filled into the statement. Therefore, it has more information available and can make a better choice of an access path. This can result in a significant savings in processing time.

## Minimizing Resources in the SQL Environment

SQL operates on sets of data, not on records of data. To achieve good performance, the designer must structure the usage of SQL so that only very limited sets of data can be retrieved or operated on.

Some of the techniques for minimizing the resources used by a transaction are the following:

1. Do not use language structures that will require a full or partial database scans such as AVERAGE, SUM, etc.
2. Do not use search criteria based on nonindexed fields.
3. Fully qualify every SQL query so that the absolute minimum of data is accessed. Ideally one row will satisfy every SQL call.
4. When multiple SQL rows are needed, access data as if it were clustered.

5. When multiple SQL rows are needed, retrieve no more than 10 rows per execution of the transaction.

6. When data must be accessed sequentially on a nonclustered field, access no more than 10 rows for each iteration of the transaction.

7. When views are used, do not use views that access data across multiple tables.

8. When foreign keys must be used to relate data, do not use the foreign key relationships more than 10 times in the execution of the transaction.

9. Do not use relational joins or projects during the online peak-period processing.

10. Do not do DDL processing during peak-period processing.

Consider this example:

```
SELECT PART, QOH, DESCRIPTION
FROM  PARTABLE  WHERE  PART  =
"123-x";
```

From a resource utilization perspective the question becomes, "What amount of I/O was required to process this simple transaction?" What we're really delving into here is the question, not of regular I/O, but of incremental I/O.

In the case of the example, one I/O is required to access the index looking for the key — part number 123-x (assuming the index has not been placed entirely in memory, which is not likely for an index for a large production database). The I/O to the index yields the page number needed, and another I/O is done to find the page that contains the row being sought. A total of two I/Os are needed.

Compare the example above with the following data-driven, undesigned transaction:

```
SELECT PART, QOH FROM PARTABLE
WHERE DESCRIPTION = 'NUT';
```

The amount of I/O needed to satisfy this request is indeterminate and potentially large. If there are 500 parts that satisfy the criteria and if three index pages must be read, then 503 I/Os will need to be done.

A third type of transaction is illustrated below:

```
SELECT COUNT(*) FROM PARTABLE
WHERE CLASS = 'p';
```

The number of I/Os required is the number of pages in the database. If the database is large and there are 1,500 pages, then 1,500 I/Os will be required.

To achieve good, consistent, on-line performance, none of the undesigned transactions must be allowed to execute during on-line, peak-period processing.

## Determining the Need for Tuning

Other than catalog statistics, there are other indicators of the need to tune:

1. Performance is not good. Perhaps the data was loaded in nonclustering order. The traditional DBMS LOAD utility loads the rows in the order they appear in the input file. Sort the data in clustering order before running LOAD. If the data was inserted with SQL INSERTs, it is quite possible that the table is not in clustering order. Do a REORG.

Poor design covers may things. The indexes could be inadequate — either not on the right columns or not in the order. The wrong index may have been chosen as the clustering index. Perhaps the tables are too normalized or too unnormalized.

2. Performance is getting worse. Volume increases will certainly affect table space scans. If there is twice as much data in a table, a table space scan will take twice as long. An increase in volume will also affect nonmatching index scans because the indexes will be bigger. Having a history file to store older data is a good way to limit growth of the tables.

Disorganized tables and indexes affect performance. As data is inserted into the database, the tables become less clustered and the indexes become less well-organized. REORGs help solve these problems.

Look at the catalog statistics. When performance problems occur, you can look at the statistics and try to find the cause. It is a good idea to look at the stats on a regular basis so you can monitor trends and anticipate potential problems. There are several things you will be looking for:

- Growth: How much data is being added.
- Changes in clustering indicators, index organization, percent of space used: They indicate a need for a reorg or for changes to the amount of freespace.
- Changes in the distribution of indexed columns.
- Non-uniformity of data.

During re-organization, there are several steps you can take to optimize DBMS performance. Any SQL statement can access any set of columns in the tables, regardless of any indexes present. One of the biggest limitations in table and index design is that there can be one clustering order to a table. If more than one order is needed, how do you design the tables and indexes for good performance for all transactions?

Weigh the transaction frequencies. It is most important to optimize the performance of the most frequently occurring transactions. The response time requirements for each must be determined. For each access order, you need to know the number of rows that will be accessed, both on average and the worst case. The analysis of these items gives you the basis for table and index design.

Separating rarely used columns into another table is a good means of reducing the row size. Larger rows mean longer table scans. If some of the columns are not usually needed with the other data, there is little performance penalty in accessing them, but a gain in accessing the other data.

In the case where many rows are needed, an alternative solution is to store duplicate data. The duplicate data has to be maintained by the application program. That has some disadvantages.

Most types of data can be compressed to save a lot of storage space. Textual data, for example, often has many consecutive blanks. These can be compressed down to a single blank plus a count of the number of spaces. Data compression is achieved by having an EDITPROC procedure defined for the table. This routine, written in assembler language, is automatically invoked everytime a row is inserted or updated (to compress) and every time a row is retrieved (to expand). There are costs to expand and compress the row but generally the savings far outweigh these costs.

When the DBMS reads a data or index page, it does an I/O and places the page into a storage area in memory. This storage area is called a buffer. Once a page is in storage it can stay there until the space is needed by something else. When the DBMS needs to read a page, it checks the buffer before doing any I/O.

A DBMS usually maintains more than one buffer for I/O operations. The set of buffers is called a buffer pool. There are many buffers in the pool. The pool is shared by all of the table spaces and indexes, or there can be several pools.

How many buffers should there be in a pool? Generally, the more buffers, the greater the chance of the page still being in memory, but there are some other factors.

The buffer pool is used for both random access and for table space scans using sequential prefetch and are usually kept separated. Table space scans quickly fill up the available buffers because many pages will be read in a very short time. If not separated, this could impact normal transaction processing (where a smaller number of pages are accessed at a time, but are often needed repeatedly).

Sequential prefetch will only be used if there are enough available pages in the buffer pool. Otherwise, a table space scan will be handled with synchronous I/Os of each page. A large pool, therefore, enables more concurrent table space scans with prefetch.

A large buffer pool also helps sort performance.

If a computer system does not have enough memory for its needs, too much paging would result as each of the tasks would be competing for the available real memory.

The following analysis should be done for every database that is large and requires a significant amount of uptime:

1. Question whether all the data is necessary.

2. Question whether the data will be used.

3. Determine the type of data that can be culled from the database (age of data, active data...).

4. Question whether the cost of storing the data on-line is worth it.

5. Has there been a conscious and deliberate split of primitive and derived data? Generally speaking primitive data is stored online and derived data is moved closer to the end-user.

6. Split administrative and operational data.

7. Separate and segregate one application from the next.

8. For large, single applications, consider splitting the application according to key values of the databases.

# 4

# Successfully Deploying Object Databases on the Web

### Mark Palmer

## Introduction

Stop. If you're a professional Web developer who's tired of marketing hype about the best way to build dynamic sites, continue reading. The software architectures in this chapter are based on production sites that scale to tremendous capacities; over five gigabytes of searchable meta data, active HTML generation from over 10 million user profiles, database transaction volume of over 500 million hits a week. These numbers can only be approached by software architects who have built them, messed them up, and finally done it right. The experience shared in this chapter comes from over 300 object-oriented development projects in 10 years — it will bring real competitive advantage to your business.

Stop. If you're saying to yourself: "Gee, my site doesn't have to handle that kind of volume or scale," read on. Andromedia Inc., an Internet company that specializes in Web site analysis tools, predicts that the activity level of the top 10 sites today will be only average levels in less than 18 months!

Stop. If you're not thinking about what it takes to build a dynamic site (which generates HTML based on a dynamically changing database or a user's input) or an active site (which actively constructs user-defined HTML pages, based on the user's preferences), get in the mood. If the Web is a strategic part of your business, you're really building a Web application, not just a Web site.

Start reading this chapter to learn how dynamic sites are being built with object-oriented database (ODBMS) technology today. No stopping from now on. First, we introduce the business problems that compel the technical solution, based on experience from top companies and the businesses they run on the

Web. Then we describe the Web site architecture used by these companies. Finally, we describe in detail how the technical solution solves the original business problems.

This experience comes from recent Internet and Intranet Web applications built with ObjectStore by Andromedia, AT&T, BOSE, GTE, Kodak, Lucent, Motorola, Prominet, Southwest Airlines, and Time-Warner. We've chosen three architectures to focus on in this article: Time-Warner's "Pathfinder" (www.pathfinder.com), GTE's "Superpages" (http://superpages.gte.com), and Southwest Airline's Reservation System (www.iflyswa.com).

## Business Problems, Technical Solutions

To establish a business on the Internet, you face unique challenges. A site must be interesting, dynamic, and meet the following business goals:

- Reduce time to market by an order of magnitude. Web sites must be developed in weeks, not months.
- Be prepared to add new features quickly. Once you are in business, the software architecture you put in place must keep you in business.
- Plan a high-performance, scalable site from day 1. You must plan for "success disaster." That is, if your Web site is successful, you'll have a disaster unless your system is designed to scale from the start.
- Leverage existing systems. Many corporations that have existing systems often feed content to the Web site. A Web site must leverage the investment made in existing systems.

These business goals can't be met by file-based, static HTML sites. They require a sophisticated Web application architecture. In the next section, we'll introduce the architecture of many leading dynamic sites today.

## The Anatomy of a Dynamic, Active Web Application

Web sites require a specialized database. They must perform well in a distributed architecture, support object-oriented applications, and store extended data types like images, spatial, and multimedia. Increasingly, Web sites use an ODBMS because they are optimized for distributed, object-oriented applications that store new data types. Relational DBMSs act as a data feed for the Web database. The RDBMS and ODBMS co-exist because they're optimized for different types of applications.

Let's take a detailed look at an ODBMS-powered Web server architecture, shown in figure 4-1.

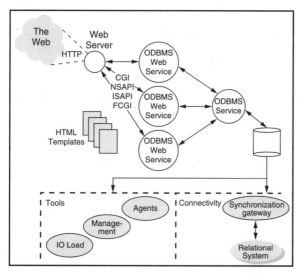

**Figure 4-1.** Common dynamic/active Web server architecture.

Some parts of it are pretty basic, but there are a few twists. The "Browser—>HTTP—>Web Server—>CGI—>Database client—>Database server—>Disk" path should be familiar to most developers. The key to this dynamic HTML architecture is the Web service. It performs HTML template processing and contains user code to produce data for the forms. The user code is a C++ or Java database client application. Application developers create methods that take arguments and CGI environment variables in and return values through variables. The template processing engine inserts the values into generated HTML statements. Finally, note the position of the relational database; GTE, Southwest, and Time-Warner have existing production systems that are integrated with the Web site's database.

To illustrate the flow of messages and data, let's follow a single browser request through the architecture. The Web browser sends a request for an HTML template to the Web server (e.g., Netscape's commerce server or Microsoft's IIS) via the HTTP protocol. The Web server receives the request and passes it to one of a "pool" of ODBMS Web service processes (a "Web service process" could also be one thread of a multi-threaded process), on the same machine or LAN as the Web server. The Web server and Web service communicate via a protocol (CGI, fast CGI, NSAPI, ISAPI, etc.). The Web service combines the HTML in the template file with variables returned from methods to form HTML dynamically. The browser receives standard HTML.

The ODBMS is synchronized with back-end relational systems by a "synchronization gateway." The gateway synchronizes the Web server database either in bulk at arranged points in time (nightly or hourly) or in response to an RDB event, which can be triggered asynchronously.

Tools, like agents that track user profile preferences, and database on-line backup utilities also interact with the database.

Now that we have the basic architecture down, let's see how this architecture addresses the original business problems.

What would you say about a guy who drives his car home every night, pulls into the garage, and takes the entire car apart, placing each part into a drawer? Nuts in one drawer, bolts in another, tires hung from the ceiling. After going to bed at 2 a.m., he wakes up at 2:30 a.m. to put the car back together, piece by piece. You'd probably call him crazy, and unemployed. Well, if you're building an object-oriented application with an relational database, you're doing the same thing.

Web applications use object-oriented programming languages: Java and C++. They store and manipulate complex objects like images, documents, and spatial data. Typically, 25–40% of analysis, design, coding, debug, and maintenance cycles are spent on a layer that flattens and rebuilds objects from relational tables or flat files; for complex data models, it can be higher.

ODBMS applications usually require little more than 2% of their application code to manage object storage. Why so much less code? An ODBMS stores data with a single-level store model; an RDBMS has a dual-level store model as shown in figure 4-2.

Specifically, an RDBMS stores and manipulates simple structures: rows and

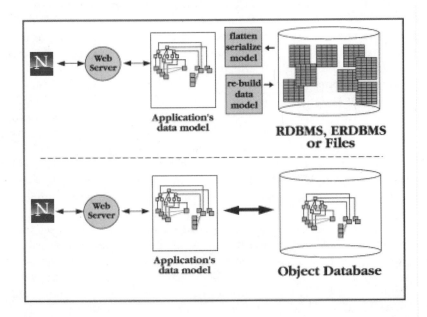

**Figure 4-2.** Single-level storage versus dual-level storage. An ODBMS stores objects on disk with the same representation they have in memory. The elimination of the application written code to translate between the two views of storage results in a simpler programming model and lowers runtime costs.

columns. The application and the database have different representations of the data — hence, the "dual-level" storage system. Who gets to bridge the gap? You do.

An ODBMS, in contrast, stores objects and the relationships between them on disk with the same representation as in-memory. The application and database have the same representation of the data. Therefore, anything you can represent in memory can be stored in the database. Multimedia data types, use reference information, and spatial data are sophisticated data types. They can all be stored in an ODBMS. Instead of taking the car apart, piece by piece, you drive it right in the garage — as is.

For example, at a high level, GTE's Superpages object model appears simple. Data elements such as business name, address, zip code, and phone number would appear to fit nicely into a relational database. However, a look deeper reveals that these simple attributes actually form a network of related objects. A business can have multiple phone numbers, multiple listings, and multiple addresses. A listing may be included in multiple categories. Spatial data stores the business location for reference to mapping data. The relationships in the objects are stored and managed by the ODBMS. In all, there are just a few (about 15) object types, but they are heavily interrelated. Not only are there many relationships, but there are five gigabytes worth of object instances.

The rapid construction and extension of this object-oriented application is enabled by the ODBMS engine. GTE releases a new version of Superpages every month or two partly because there's no database subsystem to rewrite with each change to the application. About a month after the initial release, a mapping feature was introduced. Since so little code exists to manipulate database objects and the relationships between them, the system can be extended quickly and new data types simply require the definition of a new class.

The result is simple: you don't have to build an object management layer at the start of your project or as it evolves over time.

The minute you link your site to the Net, you have access to millions of users. Time-Warner expects over a million subscribers to Personal Pathfinder in six months. Exponential growth in your user base creates exponential growth in user requirements. The developer must be prepared to add new features and functions rapidly to stay ahead on the Web.

Two pieces of the Web application architecture described enable rapid change. First, template-based HTML generation is implemented in an object-oriented way, separating the application layer (the Web service and its object methods) from the presentation layer (HTML templates). Second, as a result of the ODBMS architecture, the database storage system isn't reinvented with each change to the application's data model.

An effective HTML generation architecture isolates presentation from the application's operations. This isolation frees the two subsystems to evolve independently over time. Many developers fall into the trap of wiring HTML generation code into their application code. It's critical to allow editors to change the HTML independently of the application.

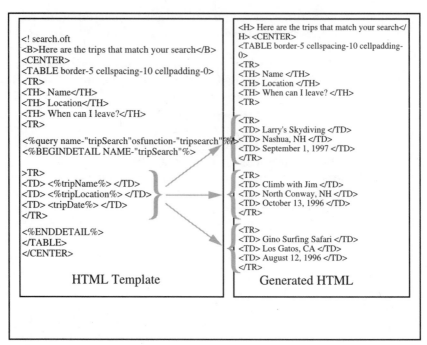

**Figure 4-3.** Dynamic object database template. An HTML template and the resulting generated HTML. The trip::search method returns appropriate trips based on the user's preferences. In this case, a cookie, passed by the CGI programming environment (not seen here), is used to generate HTML tailored to the user's interests — skydiving, climbing and surfing.

Figure 4-3 shows an example of a dynamic HTML template that works with a sample travel agency database. Here's how it works: the ODBMS template processor reads the template and looks for "query" tags. When a query tag (e.g., tripSearch) is found, an application method (e.g., trip::search) is invoked. The method executes application logic that searches for trips that match the user's interests: skydiving, climbing, and surfing. The method returns values through variables (e.g., tripName, tripLocation, tripDate), which are used to form generated HTML. The HTML generated by the code in figure 4-3 contains a simple table with a list of trip names, locations, and dates. The three trips that match the user's profile are wrapped with <TD> HTML tags.

To construct this template, the HTML editor only needs to know that a Web service has a method called "trip::search" that returns the variables "tripName," "tripLocation," and "tripDate." There isn't any SQL; the editor sees a simple, clean interface. Standard HTML authoring tools can be used to create the HTML for the template — tags are added for the dynamic sections.

The result? This site is now dynamic from three perspectives: the editors, the application developers, and the end user.

Editors alter the look and feel of the site without any change to the database methods or database subsystem. This is done without writing scripting code, SQL, C++, or Java code, and without stopping the Web service.

Application developers can extend the database and object methods without impacting the editors. Note that the logic involved in managing cookies is hidden from the template and, therefore, from the editor.

Most importantly, the end user will see a Web site customized to his or her interests. Each navigation reveals a page customized by the database. Instead of wading through endless links, this Web site delivers relevant information to the user, and makes the Web site more interesting.

## Extensibility in the Database Layer

Although the "holy grail" of object technology, reuse has proved difficult to achieve by many development organizations. However, encapsulation and abstraction capabilities of Java and C++ provide great benefit. These facilities allow abstract interfaces that evolve over time and leverage existing methods. However, you lose this benefit if the database subsystem needs to be rewritten, re-optimized, and reorganized to manage the data associated with the application's changing object model.

The single-level store architecture is why ODBMS vendors are so fast to extend the data types their systems support. Object Design has released support for eight "object managers," or classes, in the last four months: Text, Audio, Video, Image, Java Applets, HTML, Spatial, and Time Series.

Further, an ODBMS vendor's data types are fully extensible. You don't need a special software developer's kit (SDK) or a Ph.D. to extend the database system. The ODBMS classes are just that — C++ or Java classes that can be extended by inheritance or by encapsulating them in your own class (e.g., your own "business listing" object can contain a text object and a set of image objects).

Extensibility of the database subsystem means the ability to add more features faster and respond to new data types like VRML, image, audio, or the next multimedia type that we haven't even heard of yet.

If an ODBMS is so easy to use, why is the market still small compared to the RDBMS market? One reason could be that, although cumbersome, it is possible to write object-to-relational translation layers that work. Most application developers don't have to worry about the effects of a query that takes a second or two, or even a few hundred milliseconds. If you're building a Web application, start worrying. Hit rates of a million a day aren't rare any more, and will be commonplace tomorrow.

Scalability and high performance are separate issues, but depend upon one another. First we discuss Web application performance, then examine how the ODBMS architecture scales to handle large data sets and user hit volume.

## Performance and the Effect of Caching on
## Web Server Architecture

A high-performance Web server needs a caching mechanism. One reason Digital's AltaVista is so fast is its tremendous caching capacity; at this writing, it is powered by 10 64-bit Alpha processors with six gigabytes of RAM (RAM is cheap at DEC!). A cache provides enormous benefit, but at a cost. The problem with caching technology is that it's tricky to build; transaction consistency, scalability, distribution (two-phase commit), and cache synchronization are just a few of the challenges. The complexity of such a caching system, besides the fact that most implementers don't have in-house semiconductor foundries, puts custom, home-grown caching solutions out of reach for most organizations.

To achieve good performance for an interactive Web site, the database cache must be in the Web service layer (see Fig. 4-4). Sites that handle millions of transactions a day require direct access to cached data at in-memory speeds. Andromedia's product has a database component called "aria.Store." aria.Store is based on an ODBMS subsystem and utilizes this cache to capture HTTP requests data for over 10 million hits a day.

Relational databases have a cache, but in the wrong tier. The cache is in the

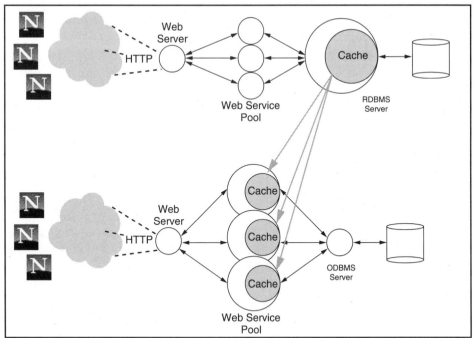

**Figure 4-4.** The Web application's cache moves forward to the second tier. This distributes the Web server cache to the point of processing; communication with the database server happens only when another client changes data in its cache. The client and server cooperate to keep the caches synchronized.

database server, and each HTTP request results in SQL query construction, transmission, optimization, execution, result construction, and the transmission of results back to the Web service before HTML can be generated. Only the lowest volume sites can afford the overhead. Remember, now you're taking the car apart a million times a day!

For comparison, as figure 4-4 shows, the ODBMS distributes the cache to the database client (the Web service) and eliminates the database server as a bottleneck. The service communicates with the ODBMS server only when objects change in the server. The Web service queries cached data at in-memory speed, on the order of machine instructions. To ensure cache coherency, an ODBMS implements a locking scheme called "callback locking." GTE, Southwest, and Time-Warner all leverage the ODBMS architecture in figure 4-4 to provide Web service caching. Each has configured the database and the cache for their own needs, which we'll discuss in detail in the next section.

Proper caching and distribution of data enable these dynamic sites to generate HTML in milliseconds, and produce responsive, engaging user interaction. It also allows on-line commerce-style transactions to execute at in-memory speeds, allowing for transaction volumes an order of magnitude faster than relational systems.

## The Scalability Challenge

Clustering and cache management are critical. As your site grows, your system's performance should remain constant. This is a simple goal, but a difficult technical challenge. And remember, Andromedia predicts: "The activity level seen on the top 10 sites of today will be only the average in less than 18 months." Simply having a Web service cache isn't enough. As a site provides more functionality and gets more hits, more demands are placed on the caching and storage mechanisms in the ODBMS. Clustering and cache management allow the system to deliver constant performance.

Clustering is an ODBMS feature that allows the application to group related objects of any type physically together on disk. The application can instruct the ODBMS to load an entire cluster into its cache. Figure 4-5 shows a simple clustering scheme utilized by Pathfinder. User profile information (which consists of over 30 different types including dynamic types to store interest lists, etc.) is physically clustered on disk according to last name.

Each service, when started, decides which methods it will handle, and loads the appropriate cluster of objects in cache. When a request for a given user profile comes to the Web server, the query is dispatched to the appropriate Web service, where the data is already cached.

Time-Warner's architecture will scale as more users subscribe. As subscribers are added, Web services are added. As services are added, the cache becomes more distributed and shared. As the cache becomes more distributed the system handles more users, but with the same performance as before.

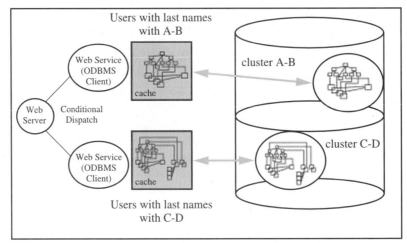

**Figure 4-5.** Web servers are ODBMS clients. As such, they take advantage of caching capabilities to provide high performance search-and-retrieval.

Common caching and clustering strategies include division, logical, and physical. Division is a technique where the cache is split among multiple members in the pool. Pathfinder's user profile scheme above is a good example: the cache is divided among multiple processes in the pool, according to the first letter of the last name. Each service performs the same logic, but the cache is optimized for the subset of those operations on a subset of the data.

Logical caching and clustering is useful for a service managing many different types of operations. For example, the Southwest Airlines Reservation System has a "Look up fare" operation. "Look up fare" includes a complex navigation of cities, fares, seat availability, and departure and arrival times to match the user's request. In contrast, the "Make Reservation" method is write-intensive. The object structure for the "Make Reservation" operation is very different than the "Look up fare" operation. One is complex in nature, the other, simple and time-based.

These two operations are implemented as separate services, each with their own cache optimized for the methods it supports.

Applications that handle geographical data typically use a physical partitioning strategy. GTE's scheme is a good example: all business listings for a geographic region in the country (e.g., all listings in Massachusetts, New York, etc.) are placed together in the database. Applications that perform queries for a region cache the appropriate objects for that region.

ODBMS caching and clustering prepares you for "success disaster," or the rapid change in performance and scalability requirements that occurs when you achieve even modest success on the Web. As your site grows, your system's performance remains constant.

## Leverage Existing Systems

Pathfinder uses relational tools for generating user reports and tracking accounts. GTE verifies new listing information in their customer service system, which contains a relational database to track customer account information. Southwest Airline's internal reservation system uses a relational database, so reservations made via the Web are staged in the ODBMS and pushed back to the older system.

All these systems need a gateway to keep the Web site synchronized with existing relational databases. A synchronization gateway is much more than a simple object-to-relational mapping layer. For example, when a record is updated in a relational database that the ODBMS needs, a trigger is sent to a gateway, which queries the relational database for the new record. The new data is migrated into the ODBMS.

Facilities in ODBMS synchronization gateways allow for numerous configurations: ODBMS to RDBMS; RDBMS to ODBMS; batch update nightly to live, asynchronously triggered update. The choice depends on the relationship between the two systems.

The use of an RDBMS synchronization gateway preserves investment in existing technology and meets the new business demands of the Web.

## Summary

Stop. You've got it now. How do you reduce time to market for a dynamic Web site? Don't waste your time taking your car apart each time you go home. Add new features quickly? Free editors so they can work without thinking about technology, and use a DBMS that was built to store objects, not punch cards.

Need a high-performance Web site? Either use an ODBMS, build the caching technology yourself, or go work for Digital. Scale that Web site? More of the same. All these business problems are solved while preserving the investment you have in existing systems.

Most importantly, your users see a snappy, interesting Web site that's different every time they visit. As the site gains popularity it will remain snappy and interesting. New data types will appear over time. Your users will want to come back to surf. Having customers come back, regardless of your business, is the number one goal.

Reprinted from WEB APPS Magazine with permission, Volume 1, issue 1, January 1997. Copyright Sigs Publications Inc.

## Author Bio

Mark Palmer is a Principal Consulting Engineer with Object Design's Professional Services organization. He has more than 10 years experience in developing large-scale object-oriented applications, and more than five years experience building object database-based distributed systems.

Mark can be be contacted at palmer@odi.com.

Object Design, Inc. (http://www.odi.com), the leader in object data management software, develops and markets the ObjectStore database management system and related tools. The company's products are used to build and deploy Internet, Intranet and other distributed computing applications, and are designed to handle the data types and data relationships found on the rapidly expanding World Wide Web. Headquartered in Burlington, Mass., Object Design sells and supports its products through branch offices across the U.S., international subsidiaries in the United Kingdom, France, Germany and Japan, and a worldwide network of distributors.

# 5

# Using Cold Fusion

## Introduction

This is another of what I like to call my mini-tutorials. I've chosen what I consider to be the most interesting of the Web to database products and have provided you with enough information to "get your feet wet." The first product up for review is (as of this writing) today's hot ticket item.

Cold Fusion is a Web application development tool for Windows NT and 95 servers. With Cold Fusion, you can create a wide variety of dynamic-page Web applications for commerce, collaboration, communication, interactive Web sites, and intranet systems. Cold Fusion provides an easy-to-understand server-side markup language, a powerful application server, and a complete framework for Web applications.

Developing applications with Cold Fusion does not require coding in a traditional programming language like Perl, C/C++, Visual Basic, Java, or Delphi. Instead, you build applications by combining standard HTML with a straightforward server-side markup language, the Cold Fusion Markup Language (CFML).

Cold Fusion is a Web application development tool for people who want to use the Web to create dynamic-page applications and interactive Web sites. Cold Fusion gives developers a way to quickly build powerful Web applications which integrate with key server technologies such as relational databases and SMTP e-mail.

Cold Fusion provides an easy-to-learn server-side markup language, a powerful application server, and a full Web application framework.

Cold Fusion 2.0 uses Netscape's server API (NSAPI), Microsoft's server API (ISAPI) and WebSite's API (WSAPI) to connect directly to the major Web servers supporting these standards. Cold Fusion also supports the Common

Gateway Interface (CGI) to communicate with other Web servers. It will work with a wide variety of Web servers running under Windows NT/95.

Cold Fusion uses 32-bit ODBC drivers to communicate with a wide variety of relational database systems. Bundled database drivers include

> Microsoft SQL Server
> Microsoft Access 1.0, 2.0 and 7.0
> Microsoft FoxPro 2.0, 2.5 and 2.6
> Oracle 7.0
> Borland Paradox 3.X and 4.X
> Borland dBase III and dBase IV
> Microsoft Excel 3.0, 4.0 and 5.0
> Plain Text Files

Developers running UNIX relational database servers such as Sybase, Oracle, or Informix can use ODBC drivers provided by the database vendor or one of many third-party ODBC-UNIX vendors (including Intersolv and Visigenic). ODBC also supports connectivity to dozens of other systems including AS/400, IBM mainframes, DB2 and Lotus Notes.

## Getting Started

This section contains a brief example designed to illustrate the basic operation of Cold Fusion. Creating dynamic Web pages with Cold Fusion is as straightforward as creating regular Web pages.

Example 1: Simple Dynamic Page (Hello World)

This first example shows you how to create two dynamic templates which work together to display text entered into an HTML form field.

1. Using a text editor create two files in the \cfdocs\ directory located in your Web server root document directory:

> hellopage1.cfm
> hellopage2.cfm

2. In the hellopage1.cfm file type the following code and save:

```
<HTML>
<HEAD>
<TITLE>Hello World Page One</TITLE>
</HEAD>
<BODY>
<H2>Enter Your Message</H2>
```

```
<HR>

<FORM ACTION="hellopage2.cfm" METHOD="post">
<INPUT TYPE="text" SIZE="30" NAME="HelloText">
<INPUT TYPE="submit" VALUE="Submit">
</FORM>

</BODY>
</HTML>
```

3. In the hellopage2.cfm file type the following code and save:

```
<HTML>
<HEAD>
<TITLE>Hello World Page Two</TITLE>
</HEAD>
<BODY>

<CFOUTPUT>
<H2>#Form.HelloText#</H2>
</CFOUTPUT>

</BODY>
</HTML>
```

4. Make sure that Cold Fusion and your Web server are running.

5. Open a Web browser and type the URL of the first page of your application:

6. In your browser enter text into the form and click "Submit." The page that appears will display the text you just entered.

In the first template, the form created a variable (Form.HelloText) Cold Fusion code used in the second template to display the information entered into the form.

Example 2: Database-driven Page (Department List)

The following example shows you how to create a database driven Web page using data from one of the example databases installed with Cold Fusion.

1. Using a text editor, create a filed called "courses.cfm" in the \cfdocs\ directory located in your Web server root document directory:

2. In the courses.cfm file type the following code and save:

```
<!-- Database Query --->
<CFQUERY NAME=CourseList DATASOURCE=CF 2.0 Examples>
SELECT * FROM Courses
</CFQUERY>

<HTML>
<HEAD>
<TITLE>Department List</TITLE>
</HEAD>

<BODY>

<H2>Course List</H2>
<HR>

 <!-- Output of database Query --->
<CFOUTPUT QUERY="CourseList">
<B>(#Number#)</B> #Description#<BR>
</CFOUTPUT>

</BODY>
</HTML>
```

4. Make sure that Cold Fusion and your Web server are running.

5. Open a Web browser and type the URL of your new application.

6. The page that appears should show a list of course numbers and courses.

In this example of a data-driven page, the CFQUERY tag used the SQL SELECT statement to retrieve the course list out of the CF 2.0 Examples database. Then the CFOUPUT tag returned the results of the query.

## Cold Fusion Technologies

In a normal Web site, pages are simple text documents marked with HTML. These pages are sent out to the user's browser by the Web server as they are requested.

A Cold Fusion Web application begins with a collection of dynamic-page templates instead of static HTML documents. A template is simply a text file that contains both HTML and the Cold Fusion Markup Language (CFML). Instead of being sent directly to the user's browser, templates are pre-processed by the Cold Fusion Application Server which generates an HTML page that is then sent to the user's browser.

Figure 5-1 shows what happens when a Web browser requests a Cold Fusion page. When a user clicks a "Submit" button on a form or a hypertext link, the user's Web browser sends an HTTP request to the Web server via the Internet or an intranet. The Web server passes the data submitted by the client and the appropriate template file to the Cold Fusion application server either through a server API or CGI. Cold Fusion reads the data from the client and

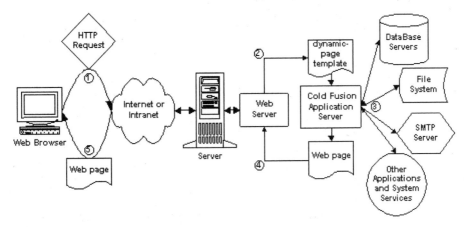

**Figure 5-1.** What happens when a Web browser calls Cold Fusion.

processes CFML commands used in the template. Based on the CFML commands the application server interacts with database servers, the file system, SMTP servers and potentially other applications and extensions.

Cold Fusion dynamically generates an HTML page and returns it to the Web server. The Web server then passes the page back to the user's Web browser.

## The Cold Fusion Markup Language

Like a normal Web page, a dynamic page template is simply a text file. The difference is that the dynamic page template is pre-processed by Cold Fusion and it contains commands in addition to HTML. Also, the template uses the CFM file extension. To create templates you need to understand Hypertext Markup Language (HTML), the Cold Fusion Markup Language (CFML), and the Structured Query Language (SQL).

The Cold Fusion Markup Language is a flexible server-side markup language. It has three parts: tags, expressions, and functions. CFML provides a number of tags you can use to interact with databases, send e-mail, build HTML output, manage files, and perform other Web application tasks. CFML tags look like HTML, but they are pre-processed on the server, not in the browser. Cold Fusion also includes an application programming interface that allows advanced developers to create their own custom tags.

Cold Fusion functions are predefined operations you can use to manipulate data. Functions can be used in expressions in a variety of places in templates.

CFML supports over 130 functions in the following categories:

1. Mathematical and trigonometric functions
2. Bit manipulation functions
3. Decision functions
4. String functions
5. Date and time functions
6. Administrative functions
7. System-level functions
8. Functions date, time, and number formatting
9. List functions

Most of the applications you create with Cold Fusion will use a relational database. A relational database stores information in a structured way. All of the information in a relational database is organized into tables. Creating and working with relational databases is straightforward. Cold Fusion is able to work with every major relational database because of ODBC. ODBC is a database access standard proposed and developed by Microsoft. It establishes a uniform interface for disparate database systems so that a single application (such as Cold Fusion) can easily communicate with all of them.

## Cold Fusion Administrator

The intent of this chapter is to provide an overview of the way Cold Fusion works in bridging the divide between the Web and the corporate database. Therefore, it is worthwhile to spend a few moments in explaining the administrative function of connecting a ODBC data source to Cold Fusion. This is done through the Cold Fusion Administrator.

You will need to create a data source for each database you wish to use with Cold Fusion.

To add an ODBC data source to Cold Fusion (see figure 5-2):

1. Open the Cold Fusion Administrator.
2. Click the Data Sources tab.
3. Click Add. The Add Data Source dialog appears.
4. Select the driver that corresponds with your data source.
5. Check the System DSN checkbox for every data source you create, since Cold Fusion applications use system data sources.
6. Click OK. At this point, a driver-specific dialog displays. As an example, the Microsoft Access 7.0 data source setup dialog is shown in figure 5-3.

Once you create your data source using the Cold Fusion Administrator, you can use Cold Fusion's data source verification feature to verify that your data source is configured properly and is ready to work with Cold Fusion.

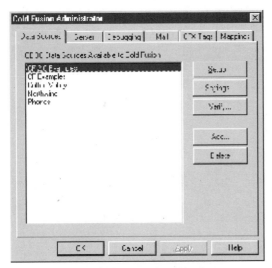

**Figure 5-2.** The Cold Fusion administrator.

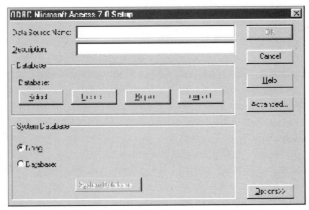

**Figure 5-3.** Connecting the Microsoft Access datasource to Cold Fusion.

## Selecting and Outputting Data

To select and output data from a database, you create a Cold Fusion template which includes both CFML and HTML. The template contains sections for selecting the data from a database and for outputting the results of the selection. The database query is done with the Structured Query Language (SQL) in a CFQUERY tag. The output is done with any one of a number of CFML tags.

The first step is to define the query that will run to select data from a database. Cold Fusion uses the CFQUERY tag to define queries. The full syntax for the CFQUERY tag is

```
<CFQUERY NAME="queryname"
         DATASOURCE="odbc datasource name"
         MAXROWS=n
         USERNAME="username"
         PASSWORD="password">
         TIMEOUT=n
         DEBUG >

    SQL statement here.

    </CFQUERY>
```

To illustrate, here is an example from a database called Company associated with an ODBC data source named "CompanyDB." To create a select query called EmployeeList that retrieves all of the records in the Employees table, use the following syntax:

```
<CFQUERY NAME="EmployeeList"
         DATASOURCE="CompanyDB">
         SELECT * FROM Employees
</CFQUERY>
```

Once you've created a CFQUERY in your template file, you can then reference its results within other CFML tags. The query results can be used to dynamically create an HTML page. Keep in mind that you can also use HTML tags and text in template files. Wherever you use standard HTML tags and text inside your template, Cold Fusion simply passes the tags and text directly back to the client browser.

The most flexible way to display data retrieved from a CFQUERY is to define a CFML output section in your template file using the CFOUTPUT tag. Output sections can be linked to a specific query or contain content from multiple queries. A CFOUTPUT tag can contain literal text, HTML tags, references to query columns, references to dynamic parameters like form fields, and functions.

Basic output sections have the following syntax:

```
<CFOUTPUT QUERY="queryname" MAXROWS=n >
        Literal text, HTML tags, and
        dynamic field references (e.g.
        #FullName#)
</CFOUTPUT>
```

If you execute a CFQUERY called EmployeeList and you want to use it to display the first name, last name, and phone number of each employee (separated by a horizontal rule), use the following CFOUTPUT section:

```
<CFOUTPUT QUERY="EmployeeList">
<HR>
#FirstName# #LastName# (Phone: #PhoneNumber#) <BR>
</CFOUTPUT>
```

If there were three records in the query result set, the HTML generated by the CFOUTPUT section would look like this:

```
<HR>
John Smith (Phone: 507-452-7224) <BR>
<HR>
Deborah Jones (Phone: 612-227-1019) <BR>
<HR>
Frank Wilson (Phone 612-831-9555) <BR>
```

The following shows a complete example of a template to select and output data.

```
<!-- Query to select customers -->

<CFQUERY NAME="EmployeeList" DATASOURCE="CF 2.0 Examples">
SELECT * FROM Employees
</CFQUERY>

<HTML>
<HEAD>
<TITLE>Employee List</TITL>
</HEAD>

<BODY>
<H2>Employee List</H2>
<CFOUTPUT QUERY="EmployeeList">
<HR>
#FirstName# #LastName# (Phone: #PhoneNumber#) <BR>
</CFOUTPUT>
</BODY>
</HTML>
```

You can call this template with a standard URL reference:

```
http://www.mycomputer.com/customers.cfm
```

The template reference can be in a standard hyperlink as well:

```
<A HREF="customers.cfm">Customer List</A>
```

Presenting the results of queries using CFOUTPUT sections is usually adequate if the number of records returned is small. However, you might need a more compact and structured display of query results. Because the CFOUTPUT tag can include any HTML, you can use the standard HTML table tags to dynamically build a table.

CFML also includes a pair of tags (CFTABLE and CFCOL) that work together to present query results in an attractive tabular format. This format uses the HTML <PRE> tag to precisely control the width and alignment of the columns displayed. The result is a clear, concise rendering of your query results. Below is an example use of the CFTABLE and CFCOL tags:

```
<CFTABLE QUERY="Messages" MAXROWS=10 >
<CFCOL HEADER="Subject" WIDTH=25 TEXT="<I>#Subject#</I>">
<CFCOL HEADER="User Name" WIDTH=15 TEXT="#UserName#">
<CFCOL HEADER="Date" WIDTH=15 ALIGN=RIGHT
TEXT="#DateFormat(DateSubmitted)#">
</CFTABLE>
```

This code creates a table with three columns labeled "Subject," "User Name, and "Date." These labels appear only if you specify at least one of the HEADER attributes. The table draws its data from the CFQUERY named "Messages" and shows no more than 10 rows. The columns display according to the HTML tags and dynamic parameters contained in their associated TEXT attribute.

Even though the preformatted tables produced by the CFTABLE tag are effective, HTML 3.0 tables are far more elegant and flexible. To make this transition easier, another CFTABLE attribute called HTMLTABLE is available. This attribute renders a CFTABLE as an HTML 3.0 table rather than as a preformatted table.

## Using Dynamic Parameters in SQL Statements

You can harness the real power of the CFQUERY tag when you dynamically customize the contents of the SQL attribute by using parameters passed to the template. The SQL statement is customized by embedding dynamic parameters within the SQL text. Dynamic parameters (also called variables) normally include form entries, parameters passed in the URL, and CGI environment information.

The convention for including a dynamic parameter inside a SQL statement is to enclose it in pound (#) signs (e.g., #State#). Whenever Cold Fusion sees text enclosed by # signs, it searches through all Form, URL, cookies, client and CGI variables looking for one that matches the specified name. When it finds the name, it substitutes the appropriate value for the parameter reference. There are several primary sources from which you can draw dynamic parameters for use in your SQL queries:

<u>Form Fields</u>: The most common way of passing parameters to a template. When a user enters data in a form field, a parameter bearing the name of the form field is passed to the template.

<u>URL</u> <u>Parameters</u>: Parameters are embedded on the end of a URL (e.g., /input.cfm?name=adam).

<u>CGI</u> <u>Environment</u>: Every request sent to a template has several environment variables sent to it that relate to the context in which it was sent. The variables available to you depend upon the browser and server software in use for a given request.

<u>Other</u> <u>Queries</u>: As soon as a query has been run you can use its results as dynamic parameters in other queries. For example, if you create a query named "LookupUser" that finds the ID for a user given their name, you might want to use this ID in another query. To do this, use the name of the query followed by a dot and the name of the field (e.g., #LookupUser.User_ID#).

<u>Cookies</u>: Cookies are a general mechanism for storing and retrieving information about the Web client (browser).

<u>Client</u> <u>Variables</u>: Can be used to store persistent client variables in the system registry on the Web server. These variables are specific to an individual browser accessing your Cold Fusion application.

If you created a form front end to search for employees by last name, you could use the following SQL statement with dynamic parameters:

```
SELECT * FROM Employees
WHERE FirstName = '#Form.LastName#'
```

If the user entered "Roger" for FirstName, the SQL statement sent to the database would be:

```
SELECT * FROM Employees
WHERE LastName = 'Roger'
```

## Creating an HTML Form Query Front End

The most common way to create dynamic parameters is with a query front end using an HTML form. HTML forms are easy to create and offer a number of flexible data input options. There a few steps that you must take to create an HTML form as a query front end to a Cold Fusion template:

### 1. Set the Form's ACTION and METHOD Attributes:

You must set the form's ACTION attribute. The ACTION attribute in your HTML form tells the browser "which template to call when the user clicks a submit button. You also must set the form's METHOD attribute to "post." In the following example, the EmployeeSearch.cfm template is executed when the user submits the form for processing.

```
<FORM ACTION="EmployeeSearch.cfm" METHOD="post">
```

### 2. Implement Data Query Fields:

Creating search fields for an HTML form is very simple. You need only implement the HTML form fields for each database column you want to search. To make your templates more legible, it is helpful to make the form field names identical to your database column names. For example, if you have a table called Employees with three columns called FirstName, LastName, and Department, your form fields might look like this:

```
Name: <INPUT TYPE="text" NAME="FirstName">
Phone: <INPUT TYPE="text" NAME="LastName">
E-Mail: <INPUT TYPE="text" NAME="Department">
```

You can use the full range of HTML input widgets, including list boxes, radio buttons, check boxes, and multi-line text boxes in your forms. The following example demonstrates a simple form:

```
<FORM ACTION="EmployeeSearch.cfm" METHOD="post">
<PRE>

Last Name: <INPUT TYPE="text" NAME="LastName">
Department: <SELECT NAME="Department">
<OPTION>Accounting
<OPTION>Administration
<OPTION>Engineering
<OPTION>Sales
</SELECT>

<INPUT TYPE="Submit" VALUE="Search">

</PRE>
</FORM>
```

The form above has two inputs: LastName and Department. The user can fill in the text area with a last name and select a department from the select list. When the submit button is clicked, the template specified in the form

ACTION is called, and all of the form fields are passed to the template as dynamic paramters.

Suppose the user enters the name "Peterson" and chooses "Sales". When she clicks the submit button, the form variables shown below will be sent to the template "EmployeeSearch.cfm":

```
LastName=Peterson
Department=Sales
```

## Using Parameters in CFOUTPUT Sections

CFOUTPUT sections are not used exclusively for outputting information returned from queries. You can also use CFOUTPUT sections to display Form, URL, Cookie, Client and CGI environment parameters. Like column names passed from a query, parameters must be enclosed in pound signs (#). For example, to report the  criteria a user entered into the employee search form, use the following syntax:

```
<CFOUTPUT>
<P>The search for #Form.LastName# in the #Form.Department# returned these
results:</P>
</CFOUTPUT>
```

You can use Form, URL, Cookie, Client, and CGI environment variables in CFOUTPUT sections associated with a query (e.g., those that have a QUERY attribute). In this case, the parameter's value is printed once for every row in the result set. If you do this, be sure to qualify references to the parameters with the appropriate prefix (Form, URL, or CGI) so that Cold Fusion is clear that the parameters are not referring to columns in the query result set.

The example template below (SearchForm.cfm) can be created as a query front end:

```
<HTML>
<HEAD>
<TITLE>Employee Search</TITLE>
</HEAD>

<BODY>
<FORM ACTION="EmployeeSearch.cfm" METHOD=POST>
<PRE>

Last Name: <INPUT TYPE="text" NAME="LastName">
Department: <SELECT NAME="Department">
          <OPTION>Accounting
          <OPTION>Administration
```

```
                <OPTION>Engineering
                <OPTION>Sales
                </SELECT>

<INPUT TYPE="Submit" VALUE="Search">

</PRE>
</FORM>

</BODY>
</HTML>
```

The example template below (EmployeeSearch.cfm) can be created to select and display the search:

```
<!-- CFML template to implement employee search -->
 <!-- Query database -->
<CFQUERY NAME="EmployeeList" DATASOURCE="CF 2.0 Examples">
     SELECT * FROM Employees
               WHERE LastName = '#LasName#'
               AND Department = '#Department#'
</CFQUERY>

<!-- Page header -->
<HTML>
<HEAD>
<TITLE>Employee Search Results</TITLE>
</HEAD>

<BODY>
<H2>Organization Search Results</H2>

<!-- Summarize search criteria for user -->
<CFOUTPUT>
<P>The search for #Form.LastName# in the #Form.Department# returned these
results:</P>
</CFOUTPUT>

<-- Display results -->
<CFOUTPUT QUERY="EmployeeList">
<HR>
#FirstName# #LastName# (Phone: #PhoneNumber#) <BR>
</CFOUTPUT>
```

```
<!-- Page footer -->
<P>
Thank you for searching the employee database!
<HR>

</BODY>
</HTML>
```

## Inserting, Updating, and Deleting Data

Inserting data into a database is usually done with two templates: an insert form and an insert template.

The insert form is created with standard HTML form tags. The insert form then calls an insert template. The insert template can contain either a CFINSERT tag or a CFQUERY tag with a SQL insert statement. The insert template should also contain a message for the end user.

When creating a form in HTML, recall that the ACTION and METHOD attributes must be specified. Generally, the METHOD attribute is always "post" and the ACTION attribute specifies the name of the Cold Fusion template (.CFM ) file you want to execute. The ACTION attribute in your HTML form tells the browser what to do when the user clicks a Submit button. In the following example, the INSDATA.CFM template is executed when the user submits the form data for processing.

```
<FORM ACTION="insdata.cfm" METHOD=post>
```

Creating data entry fields for an HTML form is very simple: you need only implement the HTML form fields for each database field into which you want to insert data. The names of your form fields must be identical with the names of your database fields. For example, if you have a table called Employees with three fields called FirstName, LastName, and Phone your form fields might look like this:

```
First Name: <INPUT TYPE="text" NAME="FirstName">
Last Name: <INPUT TYPE="text" NAME="lastName">
Phone: <INPUT TYPE="text" NAME="Phone">
```

You can use the full range of HTML input widgets, including list boxes, radio buttons, check boxes, and multi-line text boxes in your forms. When Cold Fusion reads the contents of the form submission, it uses the NAME attribute to map HTML form fields to the corresponding database fields and inserts the data entered by the user into the appropriate database fields. The following example demonstrates a simple form:

```
<FORM ACTION="insdata.cfm" METHOD="post">

<!- Data entry fields ->
<PRE>
First Name: <INPUT TYPE="text" NAME="FirstName">
Last Name: <INPUT TYPE="text" NAME="FirstName">
Phone: <INPUT TYPE="text" NAME="Phone">

<INPUT TYPE="Submit" VALUE="Enter Information">
</PRE>

</FORM>
```

The form above has three inputs: FirstName, LastName, and Phone. The user can fill these text areas in with data and click the submit button. When the submit button is clicked, the form action is carried out, and all inputs (including hidden inputs) are made available to the next template.

Suppose the user enters his first name as "William," his last name as "Burroughs," and his phone as "(212) 323-9734". When he clicks the Submit button, the form variables shown below are sent to the template:

```
FirstName=William
LastName=Burroughs
Phone=(212) 323-9734
```

This template might display these variables, insert them into the database, or perhaps do both.

The CFINSERT tag is the easiest way to handle simple inserts from a front end form. For example, the ODBC data source is named "Employees DB" and the table you want to insert data into is named "Employees." Given this information, the CFINSERT tag would be included in your template as follows:

```
<CFINSERT DATASOURCE="Employee DB" TABLENAME="Employees">
```

A Complete CFINSERT example using an HTML form to input data is shown below:

```
<!- Input data Form.  ->
<HTML>
<HEAD>
<TITLE>Example Insert</TITLE>
</HEAD>

<BODY>
```

```
<FORM ACTION="EmployeeInsert.cfm" METHOD="Post">
<PRE>
First Name: <INPUT TYPE="text" NAME="FirstName">
Last Name: <INPUT TYPE="text" NAME="FirstName">
Phone: <INPUT TYPE="text" NAME="Phone">

<INPUT TYPE="Submit" VALUE="Insert Information">
</PRE>
</FORM>

</BODY>
</HTML>
```

This is the template EmployeeInsert.cfm that inserts the Form data that was entered into the HTML Form:

```
<CFINSERT DATASOURCE="Employee DB" TABLENAME="Employees">

<HTML>
<HEAD>
<TITLE>Thanks!</TITLE>
</HEAD>
<BODY>

<CENTER><H2>Thank You!</H2></CENTER>
<HR>


<P>Thank you for entering your data into our database- please visit our
site often!<P>
<HR>
</BODY>
</HTML>
```

For more complicated inserts from a form submission you can use a SQL insert statement in a CFQUERY tag instead of a CFINSERT tag. The SQL insert statement is more flexible because you can selectively insert information or use functions within an insert statement. The syntax for a basic SQL insert statement is

INSERT INTO tablename (columnnames)
VALUES (values)

The VALUES keyword specifies the values for the columns in the new row. You have to type the values you want to add in the same order as the columns in the columnnames section of the statement. To insert the form data from the example above with a CFQUERY:

```
<CFQUERY NAME="AddEmployee" DATASOURCE="Employee DB"

INSERT INTO Employees (FirstName, LastName, Phone)
VALUES ('#Form.FirstName#', '#Form.LastName#', '#Form.Phone#')

</CFQUERY>
```

## Updating Data

Updating data in a database is usually done with two templates: an update form and an update template. The update form is created with standard HTML form tags. The update form calls an update template. The update template can contain either a CFUPDATE tag or a CFQUERY tag with a SQL update statement. The update template also usually contains a message for the end user.

An update form is similar to an insert form with two key differences. An update form contains a reference to the primary key of the record which is being updated. A primary key is a field or combination of fields in a database table that uniquely identifies each record in the table. For example, in a table of Employee names and addresses, only the Employee_ID would be unique to each record.

Because the purpose of an update form is to update existing data, the contents of an update form are usually populated out of a database. To populate the fields of an update form you must first select the record out of the database with a CFQUERY. Then put the form in a CFOUTPUT to reference the fields.

The easiest way to designate the primary key in an update form is to include a hidden input field with the value of the primary key for the record you want to update, for example:

```
<!- This is the Form that is used to input data.  ->

<!-- Query to select record -->
<CFQUERY NAME="EmployeeRecord" DATASOURCE="Employee DB">

SELECT * FROM Employees
WHERE Employee_ID = #URL.EmployeeID#

</CFQUERY>

<HTML>
<HEAD><TITLE>Example Update</TITLE></HEAD>
<BODY>
```

```
<CFOUTPUT QUERY="EmployeeRecord">

<FORM ACTION="EmployeeUpdate.cfm" METHOD="post">

<!-- Primary Key value indicating record to update -->
<INPUT TYPE="Hidden" NAME="Employee_ID" VALUE="#Employee_ID#">

<PRE>
Fname: <INPUT TYPE="Text" NAME="FirstName" VALUE=#FirstName#>
Lname: <INPUT TYPE="Text" NAME="LastName" VALUE=#LastName#>
Phone: <INPUT TYPE="Text" NAME="Phone" VALUE="#Phone#">

<INPUT TYPE="Submit" VALUE="Update Information">
</PRE>
</FORM>
</CFOUTPUT>
</BODY>
</HTML>
```

In this example, Employee_ID is the primary key of the Employees table, so a hidden field named Employee_ID is included in the HTML form. The hidden field indicates to Cold Fusion which record to update. In this case, the record ID was passed as the URL parameter 'EmployeeID' :

```
http://www.mysite.com/updateform.cfm?employeeid=2
```

The CFUPDATE tag is the easiest way to handle simple updates from a front end form. The CFUPDATE tag has an almost identical syntax to the CFIN-SERT tag. For example, the ODBC data source is named "Employee DB," and the table you want to update is named "Employees." With the form example above as the front end, the CFUPDATE tag would be included in your template as follows:

```
<CFINSERT DATASOURCE="Employee DB" TABLENAME="Employees">
```

**and this example:**

```
<!-- This is the template EmployeeUpdate.cfm -->

<CFUPDATE DATASOURCE="Employee DB" TABLENAME="Employees">

<HTML>
<HEAD>
<TITLE>Thanks!</TITLE>
```

```
</HEAD>

<BODY>

<H2>Thank You!</H2>
<HR>
<P>
Thank you for updating your data in our database - please visit our site
often!
</P>
<HR>

</BODY>
</HTML>
```

For more complicated updates you can use a SQL update statement in a CFQUERY tag instead of a CFUPDATE tag. The SQL update statement is more flexible for complicated updates. The syntax for a SQL update statement is

```
UPDATE tablename
SET columnname = value
WHERE condition
```

After the SET clause, a table column must be named. Then, you indicate a constant or expression as the value for the column. The WHERE clause is optional. If you do not specify a WHERE clause, then all records in the specified table are updated. It should, therefore, almost always be included. For example, to update the record with the front end form from the example above using a CFQUERY:

```
<CFQUERY NAME="UpdateEmployee" DATASOURCE="Employee DB">

UPDATE Employees
SET Firstname='#Form.Firstname#'
LastName='#Form.LastName#'
Phone='#Form.Phone#'
WHERE Employee_ID = #Employee_ID#

</CFQUERY>
```

## Deleting Data

Deleting data in a database can be done with a single delete template. The delete template contains a CFQUERY tag with a SQL delete statement. The syntax for a SQL delete statement is

```
DELETE FROM tablename
WHERE condition
```

The following example demonstrates deleting a single employee from the Employees table:

```
DELETE FROM Employees
WHERE Employee_ID = #URL.EmployeeID#
```

The following example demonstrates deleting several records from the Employee table. The example assumes that there are several Employees in the sales department:

```
DELETE FROM Employees
WHERE Department =  'Sales'
```

The following example demonstrates deleting all the records from the Employees table:

```
DELETE FROM Employees
```

A full delete template example is shown below:

```
<!-- Template to delete single employee record -->
<CFQUERY NAME=DeleteEmployee DATASOURCE=Employee DB>
DELETE FROM Employees WHERE Employee_ID = #URL.EmployeeID#
</CFQUERY>

<HTML>
<HEAD>
<TITLE>Delete Employee Record</TITLE>
</HEAD>
<BODY>
<H3>The employee record has been deleted</H3>
</BODY>
</HTML>
```

## The Cold Fusion Application Framework

The Cold Fusion Web Application Framework is based on several basic components. With these components you can easily combine your Cold Fusion Templates into sophisticated Web applications. Cold Fusion provides the ability to specify an application-level template file (Application.cfm) which is processed every time a template from the application is requested. The Application.cfm file can contain any CFML or HTML tags, so it can be used to set application level parameters, queries, or other functions.

Cold Fusion also provides the ability to maintain client state by seamlessly tracking variables for a browser as the user moves from page to page in an application. This easy-to-use feature can be used in place of other methods of tracking the client's state such as using URL parameters, hidden form fields, and HTTP cookies.

A Cold Fusion application is a collection of template files that work together. Applications can be as simple as a guest book or as sophisticated as a full Internet commerce system with catalog, shopping cart, and reporting. Individual applications can be easily combined in a number of different ways to create advanced Web systems.

There are a number of ways to configure Cold Fusion applications. The following section describes a basic approach that will work for most cases. But the flexibility of Cold Fusion allows for a number of different alternative strategies.

Once you have defined an application, you can use all of the application level features such as global settings and client state management in addition to all of the other features in Cold Fusion. The following are the basic steps for creating an application with the Cold Fusion Application Framework:

1. Establish an application root directory for all of the templates in the application. Templates may also be stored in subdirectories of the root directory.
2. Create an Application.cfm template in the root of the application directory for application level settings and functions.
3. Enable client state management with the CFAPPLICATION tag.
4. Set application level settings, error handling, and functions.
5. Enable any optional features you want.

The Application.cfm template file is a special template for application level settings and functions. Cold Fusion will automatically include an Application.cfm template in the beginning of every template in the same directory or a sub-directory. Each time a template is requested, the code in the Application.cfm file will be added to the beginning of the template. The Application.cfm template can be used to define potential application level settings and functions such as

- The application name
- Client state management
- Custom error pages
- Data sources
- Default style settings
- Other application level constants

The Web is a stateless system. Each connection that a browser makes to a Web server is unique in the eyes of the Web server. However, within an application it is important to be able to keep track of users as they move through the pages within the application. This is the definition of client state management.

Cold Fusion achieves client state management by creating a client record for each browser that requests a template in an application with client state management enabled. The client record is identified by a unique token which is stored in an HTTP cookie in the user's browser.

The application can then arbitrarily define variables within the client record. These variables are stored in the Windows registry. The variables are accessible as parameters in every template that the client requests within the scope of the application.

Each template in the application must contain a CFAPPLICATION tag which sets the name of the application and enables the client state management. In an application the best place to put this tag is at the beginning of the Application.cfm template. This way client state management is enabled for every page in the application.

To enable client state management for a Products application, add this CFAPPLICATION to the beginning of the Application.cfm template:

```
<CFAPPLICATION NAME="Products"
CLIENTMANAGEMENT="YES">
```

By adding this tag to the Application.cfm file all of the templates in the Products application will be able to use client state management. When client state management is enabled for an application you can use the system to keep track of any number of parameters associated with a particular client.

It is often useful to set default variables and application level constants in the Application.cfm file. For example you may want to designate

- A data source
- A domain name
- Style settings like fonts or colors
- Other important application level variables

The following example shows a complete Application.cfm template file for the Products application:

```
<!-- Set application name client variables option -->
<CFAPPLICATION NAME="Products" CLIENTMANAGEMENT="YES">

<!-- Install custom error pages -->
<CFERROR TYPE="REQUEST" TEMPLATE="RequestErr.cfm"
MAILTO="admin@company.com">
<CFERROR TYPE="VALIDATION" TEMPLATE="ValidationErr.cfm">
```

```
<!-- Set application constants -->
<CFSET #HomePage# = "http://www.mycompany.com">
<CFSET #PrimaryDataSource# = "CompanyDB">
```

Because the templates in your application are located in the Web server document directory you can use your Web server's native authentication and encryption to secure your Cold Fusion application.

Each Web server has a different way of configuring security settings, creating users, groups, and establishing privileges. Consult your Web server documentation for instructions on configuring your server's settings. When the Web server authenticates a user it returns a unique variable which is available within your template as the CGI Environment parameter "Auth_User." You can use this parameter to access additional information about a user out of a database. In general it is more straightforward to simply organize your security on a template level.

## Example Applications

This is a two-page application. The first HTML page contains a form with choices of bean types. The second template uses the selection on the form to retrieve and display the appropriate bean data. These templates are described below.

SelectBean.cfm:  This HTML page contains a form with a drop-down select box with the choices of bean types. The form is submitted to the BeanInfo.cfm template which processes the display of data related to the specific bean type.

BeanInfo.cfm: This template uses the bean type selected in the calling form to retrieve the appropriate bean record. It then generates a report displaying the data on the bean type selected.

SelectBean.cfm

```
<HTML>
<HEAD><TITLE>Coffee Valley: Beans Knowledge Base</TITLE></HEAD>
<BODY BGCOLOR="#FFFFFF">


<!------------ BANNER IMAGES ------------>
<A HREF="BTS.cfm"><IMG SRC="../images/BTS.gif" BORDER=0 ALIGN=Right></A>
<A HREF="../index.cfm">
<IMG SRC="../images/Back.gif" BORDER=0 ALIGN=Right></A>
<IMG SRC="../images/Banners/Beans.gif">


<!------------------------------------
```

Below is the form providing the user with a selection of the bean type they would like to view detail information on. This form calls the BeanInfo.cfm template which uses the value of the select box BeanName to retrieve the proper bean record from the database. See figure 5-4.

———————————————————————————>

```
<FORM ACTION="BeanInfo.cfm" METHOD=POST>
Bean Name: <SELECT NAME="BeanName">
      <OPTION VALUE="Kenya">Kenya
      <OPTION VALUE="Rwandan">Rwandan
      <OPTION VALUE="Cuban">Cuban
      <OPTION VALUE="FrenchRoast">French Roast
          </SELECT>

<INPUT TYPE="submit" VALUE="   Display Record   ">
</FORM>
</BODY>
</HTML>
```

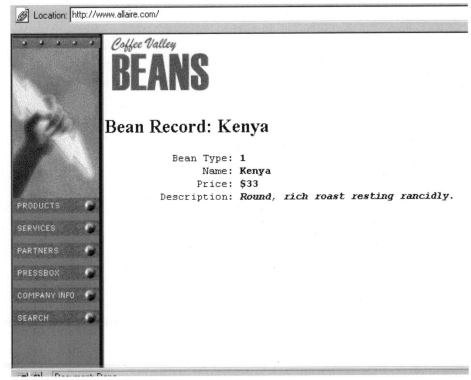

**Figure 5-4.** Cold Fusion Java Bean example application.

## BeanInfo.cfm

```
<!————————————————————
Below is the query which uses the value of the select box BeanName to
retrieve the corresponding bean record from the database. Notice the way
the value of the select box variable is used in the SQL statement driving
the logic of this database request.
————————————————————>


<CFQUERY NAME="GetBeanInfo" DATASOURCE="Coffee Valley">
SELECT * FROM Beans WHERE Name='#FORM.BeanName#'
</CFQUERY>


<HTML>
<HEAD><TITLE>Coffee Valley: Getting Started: SelectBox</TITLE></HEAD>
<BODY BGCOLOR="#FFFFFF">


<!——————— BANNER IMAGES ———————->
<A HREF="BTS.cfm">
<IMG SRC="../images/BTS.gif" BORDER=0 ALIGN=Right></A>
<A HREF="../index.cfm">
<IMG SRC="../images/Back.gif" BORDER=0 ALIGN=Right></A>
<IMG SRC="../images/Banners/Beans.gif">


<!————————————————————
Below is the script which displays the bean record within the HTML page
using the data retrieved in the GetBeanInfo query.
————————————————————>


<CFOUTPUT QUERY="GetBeanInfo">
<H2>Bean Record: #Name#</H2>
<PRE>
Bean Type: <B>#Bean_ID#                    </B>
Name: <B>#Name#                  </B>
Price: <B>$#Price#                </B>
Description: <B><i>#Description#</i></B>
</PRE>
</CFOUTPUT>


</BODY>
</HTML>
```

### Order Entry Example

The Order Entry example demonstrates the most basic use of the CFINSERT tag to append data to a database table. The form is used to enter records into the Orders table of the examples database. Each field in the Orders table has a like-named field in the input form. When the form is submitted, Cold Fusion matches the form fields with the appropriate database fields and inserts the data into the table. Besides the simple inserting of user-entered data, the example also demonstrates the entry of date/time and CGI environment information (using the DateEntered and ClientBrowser fields, respectively). The following templates are used:

<u>Main.cfm</u>: Allows the user to submit an order. See figure 5-5.

<u>Thanks.cfm</u>: Inserts the order and then thanks the user. See figure 5-6.

### Main.cfm

```
<HTML>
<HEAD><TITLE>Order Entry Example</TITLE></HEAD>
<BODY BGCOLOR="#FFFFFF">

<!—————— BANNER IMAGES ——————->
<A HREF="BTS.cfm"><IMG SRC="../images/BTS.gif" BORDER=0 ALIGN=Right></A>
<A HREF="../index.cfm"><IMG SRC="../images/Back.gif" BORDER=0
ALIGN=Right></A>
<IMG SRC="../images/Banners/OrderEntry.gif">

<CENTER><H3>WebDeveloper Subscription Order Form</H3></CENTER>

<FORM ACTION="thanks.cfm" METHOD="POST">
<!- Hidden fields for entering additional information about the submission
->

<INPUT TYPE="hidden" NAME="DateEntered" VALUE="CurrentDateTime()">
<INPUT TYPE="hidden" NAME="ClientBrowser" VALUE="CGI.HTTP_USER_AGENT">

<!- Data entry fields ->

<PRE>
<B>Subscription Options:</B>

<INPUT TYPE="radio" NAME="SubscriptionType" CHECKED
VALUE=1> 1 Year (12 months for $49.95)
<INPUT TYPE="radio" NAME="SubscriptionType"
```

```
VALUE=2> 2 Years (24 months for $69.95)
<INPUT TYPE="radio" NAME="SubscriptionType"

VALUE=3> 3 Years (36 months for $89.95)
<INPUT TYPE="checkbox" NAME="SendInfo"

VALUE="Yes"> Send me more information about products related to web devel-
opment.

<B>Mailing Address:</B>

Name:<INPUT NAME="FirstName" size=15> <INPUT NAME="LastName" size=28>
Company:<INPUT NAME="CompanyName" size=45>
Address:<INPUT NAME="Address1" size=45>
        <INPUT NAME="Address2" size=45>
City:<INPUT NAME="City" size=15> State:<INPUT NAME="State" size=5>
Zip:<input NAME="PostalCode" size=10>
Country:<INPUT NAME="Country" size=20>

<B>Credit Card Information:</B>

Type:<SELECT NAME="CreditCardType">
     <OPTION SELECTED>Visa
```

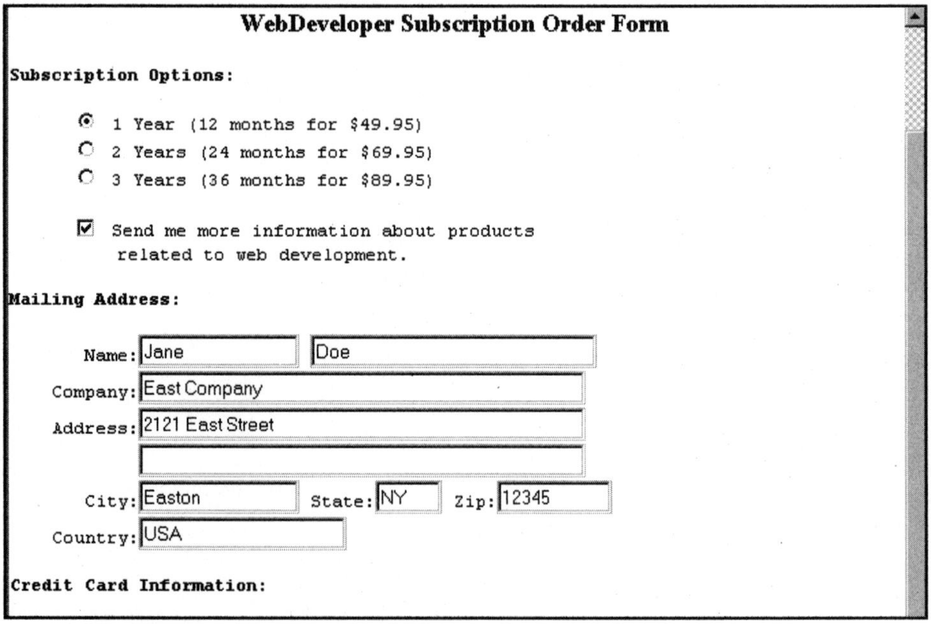

**Figure 5-5.** Cold Fusion order entry input form.

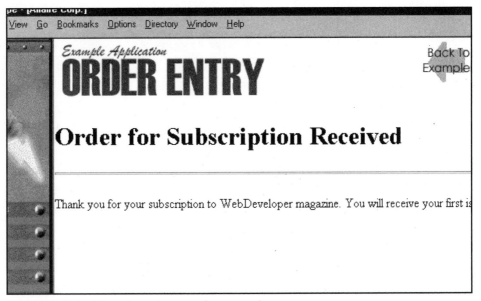

**Figure 5-6.** Output for order entry example.

```
    <OPTION>MasterCard
    <OPTION>Discover
    </SELECT> Name:<INPUT NAME="CreditCardName"
    size=25>
Number:<INPUT NAME="CreditCardNumber" SIZE=20> Expires:<INPUT
NAME="CreditCardExpDate" SIZE=7>
<INPUT Type="submit" Value="  Submit Order  "> <INPUT Type="reset"
Value="Clear Entries">
</PRE>
</FORM>
</BODY>
</HTML>
```

## Thanks.cfm

```
<!-- Insert the data passed from the form -->
<CFINSERT DATASOURCE="CF 2.0 Examples" TABLENAME="Orders">

<!-- Display a message to the user indicating that the order was received -
->

<HTML>
<HEAD><TITLE>Order for Subscription Received</TITLE>
</HEAD>
```

```
<!—————————— BANNER IMAGES ———>
ALIGN=Right></A>
<IMG SRC="../images/Banners/OrderEntry.gif">

<BODY BGCOLOR="#FFFFFF">
<H1>Order for Subscription Received</H1>
<HR>

<P>Thank you for your subscription to WebDeveloper magazine. You will
receive your first issue in 4-6 weeks.

</BODY>
</HTML>
```

# 6

# MiniSQL and the W3-mSQL Interface

## Introduction

What do you do if you don't have access to a database on your Web server but you still want to make use of its capabilities? If it's the high cost of one of the more popular RDBMS's that's preventing you from entering into the wonderful world of Internet databases, then a shareware relational database just might be right up your ally. MiniSQL was developed by David J. Hughes who is now Managing Director of Hughes Technologies Pty Ltd. located in Australia. He can be reached at bambi@Hughes.edu.au.

Mini SQL, or mSQL, is a lightweight (primarily UNIX) database engine designed to provide fast access to stored data with low memory requirements. As its name implies, mSQL offers a subset of SQL as its query interface. Although it only supports a subset of SQL (no views, sub-queries etc.), everything it supports is in accordance with the ANSI SQL specification. The mSQL package includes the database engine, a terminal "monitor" program, a database administration program, a schema viewer, and a C language API. The API and the database engine have been designed to work in a client/server environment over a TCP/IP network. The latest version of the software can be downloaded from http://hughes.com.au/software/msql2/current.htm.

## Mini SQL Specification

The mSQL language offers a significant subset of the features provided by ANSI SQL. It allows a program or user to store, manipulate and retrieve data in table structures. It does not support relational capabilities such as table joins, views or nested queries. Although it does not support all the relational operations defined in the ANSI specification, it does provide the capability of "joins" between multiple tables. Although the definitions and examples below depict mSQL key words in uppercase, no such restriction is placed on the actual queries.

### The Create Clause

The create clause as supported by mSQL can only be used to create a table. It cannot be used to create other definitions such as views. It should also be noted that there can only be one primary key field defined for a table. Defining a field as a key generates an implicit "not null" attribute for the field.

```
CREATE TABLE table_name (
    col_name col_type [ not null | primary key ] [ ,
    col_name col_type [ not null | primary key ] ]**
)
```

for example:

```
CREATE TABLE emp_details(
    first_name char(15) not null,
    last_name char(15) not null,
    dept char(20),
    emp_id int primary key ,
    salary int
)
```

The available types are

| | |
|---|---|
| char (len) | String of characters (or other 8 bit data) |
| int | Signed integer values |
| real | Decimal or Scientific Notation real values |

### The Drop Clause

Drop is used to remove a table definition from the database:

```
DROP TABLE table_name
```

for example:

```
.... DROP TABLE emp_details
```

### The Insert Clause

Unlike ANSI SQL, you cannot nest a select within an insert (i.e., you cannot insert the data returned by a select). If you do not specify the field names, they will be used in the order they were defined — you must specify a value for every field if you do this.

```
INSERT INTO table_name [ ( column [ , column ]** ) ]
VALUES (value [, value]** )
```

for example:

```
INSERT INTO emp_details ( first_name, last_name, dept, salary)
  VALUES ('David', 'Hughes', 'I.T.S.','12345')
  INSERT INTO emp_details
  VALUES ('David', 'Hughes', 'I.T.S.','12345')
```

The number of values supplied must match the number of columns.

### The Delete Clause

The syntax for mSQL's delete clause is

```
DELETE FROM table_name
WHERE column OPERATOR value
[ AND I OR column OPERATOR value ]**
OPERATOR can be <, >, =, <=, >=, <>, or LIKE
```

for example:

```
DELETE FROM emp_details WHERE emp_id = 12345
```

### The Select Clause

The select offered by mSQL lacks some of the features provided by the SQL spec:

No nested selects
No implicit functions (e.g. count( ), avg( ) )

It does, however, support

Joins — including table aliases
DISTINCT row selection
ORDER BY clauses
Regular expression matching
Column to Column comparisons in WHERE clauses

So, the formal syntax for mSQL's select is

```
SELECT [table.]column [ , [table.]column ]**
   FROM table [ = alias] [ , table [ = alias] ]**
   [ WHERE [table.] column OPERATOR VALUE
      [ AND | OR [table.]column OPERATOR VALUE]** ]
   [ ORDER BY [table.]column [DESC] [, [table.]column
   [DESC] ]

   OPERATOR can be <, >, =, <=, >=, <>, or LIKE
   VALUE can be a literal value or a column name
```

A simple select may be

```
SELECT first_name, last_name FROM emp_details WHERE dept = 'finance'
```

To sort the returned data in ascending order by last_name and descending order by first_name the query would look like this:

```
SELECT first_name, last_name FROM emp_details
WHERE dept = 'finance'
ORDER BY last_name, first_name DESC
```

And to remove any duplicate rows, the DISTINCT operator could be used:

```
SELECT DISTINCT first_name, last_name FROM
  emp_details
WHERE dept = 'finance'
ORDER BY last_name, first_name DESC
```

The regular expression syntax supported by LIKE clauses is that of standard SQL:

'_' matches any single character
'%' matches 0 or more characters of any value
'\' escapes special characters (e.g., '\%' matches % and '\\' matches \ )
all other characters match themselves

So, to search for anyone in finance who's last name consists of a letter followed by 'ughes,' such as Hughes, the query could look like this:

```
SELECT first_name, last_name FROM emp_details
WHERE dept = 'finance' and last_name like '_ughes'
```

The power of a relational query language starts to become apparent when you start joining tables together during a select. Let's say you had two tables defined, one containing staff details and another listing the projects being worked on by each staff member, and each staff member has been assigned an employee number that is unique to that person. You could generate a sorted list of who was working on what project with a query such as

```
SELECT emp_details.first_name,
    emp_details.last_name,
    project_details.project
FROM emp_details, project_details
WHERE emp_details.emp_id = project_details.emp_id
ORDER BY emp_details.last_name,
    emp_details.first_name
```

mSQL places no restriction on the number of tables "joined" during a query so if there were 15 tables all containing information related to an employee ID in some manner, data from each of those tables could be extracted, albeit slowly, by a single query.

One key point to note regarding joins is that you must qualify all column names with a table name. mSQL does not support the concept of uniquely named columns spanning multiple tables so you are forced to qualify every column name as soon as you access more than one table in a single select. mSQL-1.0.6 adds table aliases so that you can perform a join of a table onto itself. With this you could find out from a list of child/parent tuples any grandparents using something like the following:

```
SELECT t1.parent, t2.child from parent_data=t1, parent_data=t2
WHERE t1.child = t2.parent
```

The table aliases t1 and t2 both point to the same table (parent_data in this case) and are treated as two different tables that just happen to contain exactly the same data.

## The Update Clause

The mSQL update clause cannot use a column name as a value. Only literal values may by used as an update value.

```
UPDATE table_name SET column=value
[ , column=value ]**
WHERE column OPERATOR value
[ AND | OR column OPERA T OR value ]**
```

OPERATOR can be <, >, =, <=, >=, <>, or LIKE

for example:

```
UPDATE emp_details SET salary=30000 WHERE emp_id = 1234
```

## The Database Engine

The mSQL daemon, msqld, is a standalone application that listens for connections on a well known TCP socket. It is a single process engine that will accept multiple connections and serialize the queries received. It utilizes memory mapped I/O and cache techniques to offer rapid access to the data stored in a database. It also utilizes a stack based mechanism that ensures that INSERT operations are performed at the same speed regardless of the size of the table being accessed. Preliminary testing performed by a regular user of mSQL has shown that for simple queries, the performance of mSQL is comparable to or better than other freely available database packages.

The server may be accessed either via a well known TCP socket or via a UNIX domain socket with the file system (/dev/msqld ). The availability of the TCP socket allows client software to access data stored on machine over the network.

Use of the TCP socket should be limited to client software on remote machines as communicating with the server via a TCP socket rather than the UNIX socket will result in a substantial drop in performance. See the details on the programming API and also the command line options to standard programs for details on selecting the server machine.

The engine includes debugging code so that its progress can be monitored. There are currently 8 debugging modules available in the engine. Debugging for any of the available modules can be enabled at runtime by setting the contents of the MINERVA_DEBUG environment variable to a colon separated list of debug module names. A list of available debug modules is given below:

| | |
|---|---|
| cache | Display the workings of the table cache |
| query | Display each query before it is executed |
| error | Display error message as well as sending them to the client |
| key | Display details of key based data lookups |
| malloc | Display details of memory allocation |
| trace | Display a function call trace as the program executes |
| mmap | Display details of memory mapped regions |
| general | Anything that didn't fit into a category above |

For example, to make the server display the queries before they are processed and also show details of the memory allocation that takes place during the query execution, the following value would be set:

```
setenv MINERVA_DEBUG query:malloc
```

By default, the software is installed into /usr/local/Minerva and the server will use space within that directory for the storage of the databases and also temporary result tables during operations such as joins and ordering.

## C Programming API

Included in the distribution is the mSQL API library, libmsql.a, the API allows any C program to communicate with the database engine. The API functions are accessed by including the msql.h header file into your program and by linking against the mSQL library (using -lmsql as an argument to your C compiler). The library and header file will be installed by default into /usr/local/Minerva/lib and /usr/local/Minerva/include respectively.

Like the mSQL engine, the API supports debugging via the MINERVA_DEBUG environment variable. Three debugging modules are currently supported by the API: query, api, and malloc. Enabling "query" debugging will cause the API to print the contents of queries as they are sent to the server. The "api" debug modules causes internal information, such as connection details, to be printed. Details about the memory used by the API library can be obtained via the "malloc" debug module. Information such as the location and size of malloced blocks and the addresses passed to free( ) will be generated. Multiple debug modules can be enabled by setting MINERVA_DEBUG to a colon separated list of module names. For example:

```
setenv MINERVA_DEBUG api:query
```

### msqlConnect()

```
int msqlConnect(char * host)
```

msqlConnect( ) forms an interconnection with the mSQL engine. It takes as its only argument the name or IP address of the host running the mSQL server. If NULL is specified as the host argument, a connection is made to a server running on the localhost using the UNIX domain socket /dev/msqld. If an error occurs, a value of –1 is returned and the external variable msqlErrMsg will contain an appropriate text message. This variable is defined in "msql.h."

If the connection is made to the server, an integer identifier is returned to the calling function. This values is used as a handle for all other calls to the mSQL API. The value returned is in fact the socket descriptor for the connection. By calling msqlConnect( ) more than once and assigning the returned values to separate variables, connections to multiple database servers can be maintained simultaneously.

### msqlSelectDB()

```
int msqlSelectDB(sock,dbName)
    int sock;
    char *dbName;
```

Prior to submitting queries, a database must be selected. msqlSelectDB( ) instructs the engine which database is to be accessed. msqlSelectDB( ) is called with the socket descriptor returned by msqlConnect( ) and the name of the desired database. A return value of –1 indicates an error with msqlErrMsg set to a text string representing the error. msqlSelectDB( ) may be called multiple times during a program's execution. Each time it is called, the server will use the specified database for future accesses. By calling msqlSelectDB( ) multiple times, a program can switch between different databases during its execution.

## msqlQuery()

```
int msqlQuery(sock, query)
    int sock;
    char *query;
```

Queries are sent to the engine as plain text strings using msqlQuery( ). As usual, a returned value of –1 indicates an error and msqlErrMsg will be updated. If the query generates output from the engine, such as a SELECT statement, the data is buffered in the API waiting for the application to retrieve it. If the application submits another query before it retrieves the data using msqlStoreResult( ), the buffer will be overwritten by any data generated by the new query.

## msqlStoreResult()

```
m_result *msqlStoreResult()
```

Data returned by a SELECT query must be stored before another query is submitted or it will be removed from the internal API buffers. Data is stored using the msqlStoreResult( ) function which returns a result handle to the calling routines. The result handle is a pointer to a m_result structure and is passed to other API routines when access to the data is required. Once the result handle is allocated, other queries may be submitted. A program may have many result handles active simultaneously.

## msqlFreeResult()

```
void msqlFreeResult(result)
    m_result *result;
```

When a program no longer requires the data associated with a particular query result, the data must be freed using msqlFreeResult( ). The result handle associated with the data, as returned by msqlStoreResult( ) is passed to msqlFreeResult( ) to identify the data set to be freed.

## msqlFetchRow()

```
m_row msqlFetchRow(result)
    m_result *result;
```

The individual database rows returned by a select are accessed via the msqlFetchRow( ) function. The data is returned in a variable of type m_row which contains a char pointer for each field in the row. For example, if a select statement selected 3 fields from each row returned, the value of the 3 fields would be assigned to elements [0], [1], and [2] of the variable returned by msqlFetchRow( ).

A value of NULL is returned when the end of the data has been reached. See the example at the end of this sections for further details. Note, a NULL value is represented as a NULL pointer in the row.

## msqlDataSeek()

```
void msqlDataSeek(result, pos)
    m_result *result; in pos;
```

The m_result structure contains a client side "cursor" that holds information about the next row of data to be returned to the calling program. msqlDataSeek( ) can be used to move the position of the data cursor. If it is called with a position of 0, the next call to msqlFetchRow( ) will return the first row of data returned by the server. The value of pos can be anywhere from 0 (the first row) and the number of rows in the table. If a seek is made past the end of the table, the next call to msqlFetchRow( ) will return a NULL.

## msqlNumRows()

```
int msqlNumRows(result)
    m_result *result;
```

The number of rows returned by a query can be found by calling msqlNumRows( ) and passing it the result handle returned by msqlStoreResult( ). The number of rows of data sent as a result of the query is returned as an integer value. If a select query didn't match any data, msqlNumRows( ) will indicate that the result table has 0 rows.

## msqlFetchField()

```
m_field *msqlFetchField(result)
    m_result *result;
```

Along with the actual data rows, the server returns information about the data fields selected. This information is made available to the calling program via the msqlFetchField( ) function. Like msqlFetchRow( ), this function returns one element of information at a time and returns NULL when no further information is available. The data is returned in a m_field structure which contains the following information

```
typedef struct {
    char *name,    /* name of field */
        *table;    /* name of table */
    int type,      /* data type of field */
        length,    /* length in bytes of field */
        flags;     /* attribute flags */
} m_field;
```

Possible values for the type field are defined in msql.h as INT_TYPE, CHAR_TYPE and REAL_TYPE. The individual attribute flags can be accessed using the following macros:

IS_PRI_KEY(flags) /* Field is the primary key */
IS_NOT_NULL(flags) /* Field may not contain a NULL value */

## msqlFieldSeek()

```
void msqlFieldSeek(result, pos)
    m_result *result;
    int pos;
```

The result structure includes a "cursor" for the field data. Its position can be moved using the msqlFieldSeek( ) function. See msqlDataSeek( ) for further details.

## msqlNumFields()

```
int msqlNumFields(result)
    m_result *result;
```

The number of fields returned by a query can be ascertained by calling msqlNumFields( ) and passing it the result handle. The value returned by msqlNumFields( ) indicates the number of elements in the data vector returned by msqlFetchRow( ). It is wise to check the number of fields returned before, as with all arrays, accessing an element that is beyond the end of the data vector can result in a segmentation fault.

## msqlListDBs()

```
m_result *msqlListDBs(sock)
    int sock;
```

A list of the databases known to the mSQL engine can be obtained via the msqlListDBs( ) function. A result handle is returned to the calling program that can be used to access the actual database names. The individual names are accessed by calling msqlFetchRow( ) passing it the result handle. The m_row data structure returned by each call will contain one field being the name of one of the available databases. As with all functions that return a result handle, the data associated with the result must be freed when it is no longer required using msqlFreeResult( ).

## msqlListTables()

```
m_result *msqlListTables(sock)
    int sock;
```

Once a database has been selected using msqlInitDB( ), a list of the tables defined in that database can be retrieved using msqlListTables( ). As with msqlListDBs( ), a result handle is returned to the calling program and the names of the tables are contained in data rows where element [0] of the row is the name of one table in the current database. The result handle must be freed when it is no longer needed by calling msqlFreeResult( ).

## msqlListFields()

```
m_result *msqlListFields(sock,tableName);
    int sock;
    char *tableName
```

Information about the fields in a particular table can be obtained using msqlListFields( ). The function is called with the name of a table in the current database as selected using msqlSelectDB( ) and a result handle is returned to the caller. Unlike msqlListDBs( ) and msqlListTables( ), the field information is contained in field structures rather than data rows. It is accessed using msqlFetchField( ). The result handle must be freed when it is no longer needed by calling msqlFreeResult( ).

## msqlClose()

```
int msqlClose(sock)
    int sock;
```

The connection to the mSQL engine can be closed using msqlClose( ). The function must be called with the connection socket returned by msqlConnect( ) when the initial connection was made.

## The mSQL Terminal Monitor

Like all database applications, mSQL provides a program that allows a user to interactively submit queries to the database engine. In the case of mSQL, it is a program simply called msql. It requires one command line argument, being the name of the database to access. Once started, there is no way to swap databases without restarting the program. The monitor also accepts two command line flags as outlined below:

-h  Host        Connect to the mSQL server on Host.
-q              Process one query and quit returning an exit code.

Commands are distinguished from queries due to their being prefixed with a backslash. To obtain help from the monitor prompt, the \h command is used. To exit from the program, the \q command or an EOF (^D) must be entered.

To send a query to the engine, the query is entered followed by the \g command. \g tells the monitor to "Go" and send the query to the engine. If you wish to edit your last query, \e will place you inside vi so that you can modify your query.

If you wish to use an editor other than vi to perform query editing, msql will honor the convention of using the contents of the VISUAL environment variable as an alternate editor. When you have completed your editing, exiting the editor in the usual manner will return you to msql with the edited query placed in the buffer. The query can then be submitted to the server by using the \g "Go" command as usual.

The query buffer is maintained between queries to not only enable query editing, but to also allow a query to be submitted multiple times. If \g is entered without entering a new query, the last query to be submitted will be resubmitted. The contents of the query buffer can also be displayed by using the \p "Print" command of the monitor.

To enable convenient access to database servers running on remote hosts, the mSQL terminal monitor supports the use of an environment variable to indicate the machine running the server (rather than having to specify "-h some.host.name" every time you execute mSQL). Note that this is a function provided by the mSQL terminal monitor NOT the mSQL API library and as such is not available for use with other programs. To use this feature set the environment variable MSQL_HOST to the name or address of the desired machine.

## mSQL Database Administration

mSQL databases are administered using the msqladmin command. Several administrative tasks, such as creating new databases and forcing a server shutdown, are performed using msqladmin. Like all mSQL programs, msqladmin accepts the '-h Host' command line flag to specify the desired machine. The commands available via msqladmin are

| | |
|---|---|
| create DataBase | Create a new database called DataBase |
| drop DataBase | Delete the entire database called DataBase |
| shutdown | Tell the server to shut itself down |
| reload | Reload its access control information |
| version | Display various version information from the server |

It should be noted that the server will only accept create, drop, shutdown, and reload commands if they are sent by the root user (as defined at installation time) and are sent from the machine running the server. An attempt to perform any of these commands from a remote client or as a non-root user will result in a "permission denied" error. The only command you can execute over the network or as a non-root user is version.

## mSQL Schema Viewer

mSQL provides the relshow command for display the structure of a database. If executed with no arguments, relshow will list the available database. If it is executed with the name of a database, relshow will list the tables that have been defined for that database. If given both a database and table name, relshow will display the structure of the table including the field names, types, and sizes. Like all mSQL programs, relshow honors the '-h Host' command line flag to specify a remote machine as the database server.

## Access Control

Access control is managed by the msql.acl file in the installation directory. This file is split into entries for each database to be controlled. If the file doesn't exist or details for a particular database aren't configured, access reverts to global read/write. An example ACL entry is included below:

```
# Sample access control for mSQL
database=test
read=bambi,paulp
write=root
host=*.Bond.edu.au,-student.it.Bond.edu.au
access=local,remote
```

Using this definition, database 'test' can be accessed by both local and remote connections from any host in the Bond.edu.au domain accept for the machine student.it.Bond.edu.au. Read access is only granted to bambi and paulp. Nobody else is allowed to perform selects on the database. Write access is only available to root.

Control is based on the first match found for a given item. So, a line such as "read=-*,bambi" would not do the desired thing (i.e., deny access to everyone other than bambi) because -* will also match bambi. In this case the line would have to be "read=bambi,-*" although the -* is superfluous as that is the default action.

Note that if an entry isn't found for a particular configuration line (such as read) it defaults to a global denial. For example, if there is no "read" line (i.e., there are no read tokens after the data is loaded) nobody will be granted read access. This is in contrast to the action taken if the entire database definition is missing in which case access to everything is granted.

Another thing to note is that a database's entry _must_ be followed by a blank line to signify the end of the entry. There may also be multiple config lines in the one entry (such as "read=bambi,paulp" "read=root"). The data will be loaded as though it was concatenated onto the same "read" line (i.e. "read=bambi,paulp,root").

Wildcards can be used in any configuration entry. A wildcard by itself will match anything whereas a wildcard followed by some text will cause only a partial wildcard (e.g. *.Bond.edu.au matches anything that ends in Bond.edu.au). A wildcard can also be set for the database name. A good practice is to install an entry with database=* as the last entry in the file so that if the database being accessed wasn't covered by any of the other rules a default site policy can be enforced.

The ACL information can be reloaded at runtime using "msqladmin reload." This will parse the file before it sends the reload command to the engine. Only if the file is parsed cleanly is it reloaded. Like most msqladmin commands, it will only be accepted if generated by the root user (or whoever the database was installed as) on the localhost.

## W3-mSQL

w3-msql is an interface between the World-Wide Web and mSQL. It is a mechanism that can be used to greatly simplify the use of a Mini SQL database behind a web server. Using w3-msql, you can embed SQL queries within your pages and have the results generated on the fly. The w3-msql program is used as a CGI script that your w3-msql enhanced pages are passed through. It should be referenced as

```
/cgi-bin/w3-msql/Path/To/Your/Page.html
```

where /Path/To/Your/Page.html is a w3-msql enhanced html file within your WWW document tree. w3-msql will process the specified page and "fill in the blanks" by interpreting and processing the embedded mSQL commands.

A w3-msql directive is embedded within an html page using the following syntax:

```
<! msql command args >
```

The commands that are available are

<! msql connect [host] >

Connect to the mSQL database engine. An option hostname can be provided to indicate that the database is running on a remote machine, for example :

```
<! msql connect www.some.domain >
```

Unlike the C programming language API for mSQL, you can only have one connection to a database server from within your w3-msql page. You can access multiple databases from the one connection by using the database directive outlined below.

<! msql close >

Close the currently open mSQL database connection. You should call the close directive when you are finished with the database from within your page. Once you have closed the connection, you could open a new connection to another database server if your page requires data held in mSQL servers on different machines.

<! msql database DBName >

Choose the database that you wish to access from your queries, for example :

```
<! msql database test >
```

If you need to access data from multiple databases managed by the same mSQL server, you can simply issue the database directive again to select a new database to use. There is no limit to the number of times you can call the database directive in a single page so you can literally swap back and forth between databases at any time.

<! msql query "query text" QueryHandle >

Submit a query to the database. The query text is submitted to the database and any returned data is stored in the QueryHandle. You use the QueryHandle to access the data later in your page. For example:

```
<! msql query "select name from users" q1 >
```

Once the query has been processed, the first row of the returned data is fetched and stored in the query handle. The row of data currently stored in the query handle is called the current row. The fetch and seek directives are provided by w3-msql to allow you to use other data rows as the current row.

Another term used in association with the current row is the position of the data cursor. The data cursor is a logical pointer that indicates which row of the result table is the current row. The seek directive can be used to move the location of the data cursor and hence, change the current row.

<! msql free QueryHandle>

Frees the QueryHandle and any data associated with the query. For example:

```
<! msql free q1 >
```

<! msql print "format" >

Print the contents of variables from the current row of a query handle, the environment or from data passed to the page from a GET or POST (such as from a form). The format string is similar to a printf( ) format string in that escape characters such as \n and \t are understood. The contents of variables are accessed by embedding the variables within the format string (like Perl, ESL, or Shell scripts) rather than by using references to variables such as %s etc. in C.

The order of priority for variables is internal w3-msql variables followed by environment variables. That is, when a variable is accessed, w3-msql first looks for the variable in the w3-msql symbol table and if it can't find it, it then looks for an environment variable by that name. The first variable it finds that matches the name specified is used.

To simplify the processing of forms (and to enable data to be passed between pages) W3-mSQL loads all data passed to it in the URL into it's symbol table. If you have a form entry such as < INPUT NAME=user > then when you click the submit button, your browser will generate a URL like the following:

```
http://Your.Machine/Path/To/File.html?user=bambi
```

The ?user=bambi on the end of the URL reflects the name and contents of your form fields. W3-mSQL will see these values and load them into the symbol table  so you can access them as variables in your page. If you referenced the variable $user in this example it would evaluate to bambi.

As the example above indicates, variables are referenced using a $ sign.

This is the case for internal variables and environment variables. Accessing the contents of the current row from a query handle uses a difference format. Firstly, you have to indicate which query handle contains the information and secondly you have to indicate which field from the current row you want. The format used is @Handle.FieldOffset.

That is, you use a @ for database variables (not the $ sign used for internal and environment variables), followed by the name of the query handle, followed by a '.', followed by the numerical index of the desired field in the row. Fields are numbered from left to right starting at 0. To illustrate this further, if the following query

```
<! msql query "select name,age from people" result>
```

was submitted, @result.0 would correspond to the name field and @result.1 would correspond to the age field. You can reference any number of fields and other variables in a single format string. For example:

```
<! msql print "Hello @result.0, your path is $PATH" >
<! msql print_rows QueryHandle "format" >
```

The print_rows directive allows the entire contents of a Query Handle to be processed in one operation. The format specified is applied to each row of the remaining result data from the Query Handle, that is, all data from the position of the data cursor to the end of the result data is extracted and formatted.

If the data cursor has been moved from the first row of data by using either fetch or seek directives, only the remaining data will be displayed. Naturally, the seek directive can be used to return the data cursor to the initial row of the result data before calling the print_rows directive.

This facility can be used to easily create lists, tables and select menus from the contents of a query. An example of each is given below :

## Table Creation

```
<! msql query "select name, address from staff" result>
<TABLE>
<TH>Name <TH> Address <TR>
<! msql print_rows result "<TD> @result.0 <TD> @result.1 <TR>"
</TABLE>
```

## List Creation

```
<! msql query "select name, address from staff" result>
<UL>
<! msql print_rows result "<LI> @result.0 \n"
```

```
</UL>
```

## Select Menu Creation

```
<! msql query "select name, address from staff" result>
<SELECT NAME=menu>
<! msql print_rows result "<OPTION> @result.0 \n"
</SELECT>
```

## <! msql if ( condition ) >
## <! msql else >
## <! msql fi >

w3-msql provides an if-then-else construct for conditional inclusion of sections of an HTML page. If the condition evaluates to TRUE, the segment of the page between the IF and the ELSE or FI is processed. This may be normal HTML text or further w3-msql definitions. To enable complex pages to be created, w3-msql supports IF clauses nested to any level.

The structure of the condition statement is based on the syntax used by conditions in C. It supports the usual comparison operator, == != < <= > >= , as well as the C logical operators && and | | . Parentheses may be used within the condition to group sections of the expression to control the evaluation. Parentheses can be nested to any level. For example:

```
< ! msql if ( ($age < 50) && (($name == "fred") || ($name == "joe"))) >
```

The IF directive will try to interpret the data and variables within the condition in the manner you intend. For example, if you provided a condition such as

```
< ! msql if ( $age == 50 ) >
```

w3-msql would cast the value of $age to an integer value if possible because all w3-msql variables are text variables. If the variable in question does not contain a numeric string, the condition will abort and an appropriate error will be displayed. It should be noted that only the == and != operator may be used to compare string values. < <= > and >= can only be used on numeric values. Naturally, == and != can be used on numeric data too.

## <! msql fetch QueryHandle>

Fetches the next row of data from the query handle and updates the current row and the data cursor. For  example :

```
<! msql fetch q1 >
<! msql seek QueryHandle Position>
```

moves the data cursor for the specified query handle to the given position. Position 0 is the first row in the result data. If the value of position is negative, it will be replaced by 0. If the position is beyond the end of the table, the data cursor will be left pointing at the end of the table. The current row is replaced by the row of data located at the specified position. For example, to move to the 12th row of data returned in the query handle q1, you would call <! msql seek q1 12>

## The Lite Programming Language

W3-mSQL version 2.0 enables the development of entire programs within a WWW page while offering comprehensive access control and security features. W3-mSQL achieves this by providing a complete programming language embedded within an HTML document. The language, called Lite, is similar is style and syntax to the C programming language and the ESL scripting language.

Using W3-mSQL and the embedded Lite language, you can generate HTML code "on-the-fly" in the same way you do when you write custom CGI programs. What's more, you can mix normal HTML code with W3-mSQL code so that you only need to use the CGI styled approach where you actually have to.

To facilitate the W3-mSQL extensions to normal web pages, Lite code is included in your HTML code. It is differentiated from normal HTML code by including it inside <! > tags. As an example, a W3-mSQL version of the legendary Hello World program is provided below.

```
<HTML>
<HEAD>
<TITLE>Hello World from W3-mSQL</TITLE>
<HEAD>
<BODY>
<CENTER>
<H1>Introduction to W3-mSQL<H1>
<P>
<! echo("Hello World\n"); >
</CENTER>
</BODY>
</HTML>
```

As you can see, there is a line of code in the middle of the HTML page, enclosed in <! > tags. When the page is loaded through the W3-mSQL CGI program, anything enclosed in <! > tags is parsed and executed as an embedded program. Any output generated by the program is sent to the user's browser. In this case, the string "Hello World" would be sent as part of the HTML page to the browser. The remainder of the page is sent to the browser unmodified.

There can be any number of W3-mSQL tags within a single page and there can be any number of lines of code within a single W3-mSQL tag.

To execute the script listed above you must not just specify the path to the file in the URL as you would normally do. If you do that, your browser will just be sent the unprocessed HTML document. To execute the script you must specify a URL that executes the W3-mSQL binary and tells it to load and process your script.

The W3-mSQL binary is called w3-msql and will usually be located in the /cgi-bin directory (if it isn't there contact your system administrator). If the normal URL of a W3-mSQL enhanced Web page is /staff/lookup.html, you would load it using the following URL:

```
/cgi-bin/w3-msql/staff/lookup.html
```

This URL instructs the Web server to execute the W3-mSQL binary and tells it to load the /staff/lookup.html script file.

## Form Data

One thing virtually all CGI type programs have in common is that they process the contents of an HTML form. The form data is passed to the CGI program via either a GET or a POST method by the http server. It is then the responsibility of the CGI script to decipher and decode the data being passed to it. W3-mSQL simplifies this process greatly by converting any form data passed to a script into global Lite variables within the Lite Virtual Machine. These variables can then be accessed by your script code.

When an HTML form is defined, a field name is given to each of the elements of the form. This allows the CGI to determine what the data values being submitted actually mean. When the data is passed to W3-mSQL, the field names are used as the variable names for the global variables. Once a set of variables has been created for each form element, the values being passed to the script are assigned to the variables. This is done automatically during start-up of the W3-mSQL program.

As an example, imagine that the following form was defined in an HTML page:

```
<FORM ACTION=/cgi-bin/w3-msql/my_stuff/test.html METHOD=POST>
        <INPUT NAME=username SIZE=20>
        <INPUT NAME=password SIZE=20 TYPE=PASSWORD>
        <SELECT NAME=user_type>
        <OPTION VALUE="casual">Casual User
        <OPTION VALUE="staff">Staff Account
        <OPTION VALUE="guest">Temporary Guest Account
        </SELECT>
```

```
</FORM>
```

In the example we have defined 3 fields within the form, 2 text entry fields called username and password, and a menu called user_type. We have also specified that the action for the form is to call W3-mSQL and tell it to process /my_stuff/test.html passing the form data via the POST method. When the data is submitted, the values entered for the 3 form fields are passed to W3-mSQL. It then creates 3 global variables called $username, $password and $user_type, and assigns the user's data to those variables. The values can then be accessed within the Lite script code embedded in test.html by referencing the variables.

Lite has been designed to mimic the syntax and semantics of the C language while reducing some of the complexities and error prone features of C. This is intentional as most programmers working on UNIX machines have a working knowledge of C but look for a more "easy to use" language for scripting. The main changes from C are:

- All memory management (i.e., allocation and deallocation of memory for variables) is taken care of by the Lite Virtual Machine. Your script does not need to perform any memory management routines.

- A variable has no fixed type. It will contain whatever is stored in it (e.g. char value, numeric value). When you perform an operation on a variable, such as math or comparisons, the contents of the variable are checked to ensure they are of the correct type.

- There is a dynamic array type. Each element of the array is a variable as described above. The elements are accessed as they are in C, i.e., variable[offset], but they need not be declared before use. That is, the array element is created when a value is stored in it without any pre-definition of the array.

- Variables are not pre-declared. They are created when they are first used.

- Variable names must start with a $ character. This will be familiar to shell script programmers.

## Variables, Types and Expressions

Variables are constructed from a $ sign followed by alpha-numeric characters and the '_' character. The only restriction placed upon the name of a variable is that the first character of a user defined variable must not be an uppercase character. There is no need to pre-declare variables as you do in a language such as C. A variable is created the first time you assign a value to it. Similarly, the type of the variable is defined by the value that you assign to it. There are three types of scalar variables:

```
char
integer
real number
```

The example code below illustrates the creation of variables:

```
$int_value = 9;
$char_value = "Some text value";
$real_value = 12.627;
```

At any point in time, the type of a value can be changed by using the type cast notation from the C language. If, for example, you wished to include a numeric value from an integer variable in a text string, you would simply cast the integer value to the char type. For example, the code below would result in a char variable that contained the string "1234":

```
$int_val = 1234;
$char_val = (char) $int_val;
```

Array variables are supported by Lite but there is no fixed type for the array. Each element of the array can hold data from any of the available data types. An array is created by assigning a value to one of the array elements such as

```
$arrayval[3] = "Foo";
$arrayval[4] = 5;
$arrayval[6] = 1.23 + 5.38;
```

Lite expressions are formed from mathematical equations incorporating the values of variables and values returned from function calls. Lite is a little more flexible than other languages such as C. It will allow you to do math operations on all data types including the char type. Adding two char values together results in the concatenation of the two strings. You can also perform math on values of different types by casting the value to the correct type within the expression. Examples are given below:

```
$charval = "Hello" + " there!";
$intval = 8 + 1;
$charval = (char)$intval + " green bottles";
```

The first expression would result in the char value "Hello there!". The second would result in the integer value 9. The final expression would result in the char value "9 green bottles" using the text representation of the value of $intval from the previous line. Math expression of any complexity, including any number of subexpressions enclosed in ( ) characters, are supported.

A special operator supported by Lite is the count operator written as the # sign. The count operator is used to determine the size of certain variables. If you apply the count operator to a char value it will evaluate to the number of characters in the string. If you apply it to an array it will evaluate to the number of elements in that array. In the first example below, $intval would contain the value 5. In the second example, it would contain 3.

```
$charval = "Hello";
$intval = # $charval;

$array[0] = 0;
$array[1] = 1;
$array[2] = 2;
$intval = # $array;
```

## Conditions and Loops

Conditions are provided by Lite using the same syntax as C. That is, the conditional block is started by an 'if (condition).' The blocks of code are defined using the { and } character. Unlike C, you must always wrap code blocks in { } characters (in C you don't have to if the code block is only one line long). After the initial code block, an optional 'else' block may be defined.

Multiple parts of the conditional expression may be linked together using logical ANDs and ORs. Like C, the syntax for an AND is && while the syntax for an OR is | |. As you will see in the example below, Lite provides more flexibility than C in conditions containing text values. You can compare two text values using the '==' equality test or the '!=' inequality test rather than having to use a function such as strcmp( ).

```
if ($intval > 5 && $intval < 10)
{
    echo("The value is between 5 and 10\n");
}
else
{
    echo("The value is not between 5 and 10\n");
}
if ($charval == "")
{
echo("The variable contains no value!!!\n");
}
```

Lite supports only one form of looping — a 'while' loop. The syntax and operation of the while loop is identical the while loop offered by the C language. This includes the use of 'continue' and 'break' clauses to control the flow of execution within the loop.

```
while ($intval < 10)
{
     $intval = $intval + 1;
}
while ($charval != "")
{
     $charval = readln($fd); if ($charval == "Hello")
     {
          break;
     }
}
```

## User Defined Functions

As with most modern programming languages, Lite allows you to write functions. In a Lite script a function is defined as follows :

```
funct functName ( type arg, type arg ...)
{
          statements
}
```

As the definition dictates, a function must be started with the funct label. The remainder looks like a C function declaration in that there is a function name followed by a list of typed arguments. Any type may be passed to a function and any type may be returned from a function. All values passed to a function are passed by value not by reference. A few example functions are given below.

```
funct addition ( int $value1, int $value2 )
{
          $result = $value1 + $value2;
          return ( $value );
}


funct merge ( array $values, int $numVals)
{
          $count = 0;
          $result = "";
```

```
        while ( $count < $numValues)
        {
                $result = $result + $values [ $count ];
                $count = $count + 1;
        }
        return ( $result );
}


funct sequence ( int $first, int $last )
{
        $count = 0;
        while ( $first < $last )
        {
                $array [$count] = (char) $first;
                $first = $first + 1;
        }
        return ( $array );
}
```

It must be noted that function declarations can only be made before any of the actual script code of the file. That is, all functions must be defined before the main body of the script is reached.

### User Defined Libraries

To help provide an efficient programming environment, Lite (and W3-mSQL) allows you to build a library of functions and load the library into your script at run-time. This allows for effective re-use of code in the same way the languages such as C allow you to re-use code by linking against libraries. The main difference is that the library is not "linked" into the script, it is loaded on request at run-time (a little like a C shared library). If the functions that were defined in the previous section of this manual were placed into a library called "mylib," a script could access those functions by loading the library as shown below.

```
load "mylib.lib";
/*
** Now we can use the functions from the library
*/
$array = sequence(1,10);
$count = 0;
while ($count < # $array)
{
        printf("Value %d is '%s'\n", $count, $array);
        $count = $count + 1;
}
```

The power and convenience of Lite libraries is most obvious when writing large WWW based applications using W3-mSQL. Like any application, there will be actions that you will need to perform several times. Without the aid of libraries, the code to perform those actions would need to be re-coded into each W3-mSQL enhanced Web page (because each HTML file is a stand-alone program). By placing all these commonly used functions into a library, each Web page can simply load the library and have access to the functions. This also provides a single place at which modifications can be made that are reflected in all Web pages that load the library.

Library files are not like normal Lite script files. A Lite script file is a plain ASCII text file that is parsed at run-time by Lite. A library file contains pre-compiled version of the Lite functions that will load faster as they do not need to be re-parsed every time they are used. A Lite library file is created by using the –l flag of the Lite interpreter. If a set of functions was placed in a file called mylib.lite, a compiled version of the library would be created using the syntax shown below.

```
lite -lmylib.lib mylib.lite
```

The –l flag tells Lite to compile the functions and write the binary version of the functions to a file called mylib.lib. This is similar to the concept of using the C compiler to create an object file by using the –c flag of the compiler.

## More Information and Add-Ons

miniSQL FAQ:
It is recommended that you read this file before you download and install miniSQL. It is quite thorough. It discusses product limitations, requirements and problems with particular platforms.
ftp://bond.edu.au/pub/Minerva/msql/faq.txt

HTML archive of the mSQL mailing list:
http://www.tryc.on.ca/msql.html
http://tacyon.spectrum.com.au/mail/msql
http://cure.medinfo.org/lists/programming/index.html
 http://www.nexial.nl/cgi-bin/msql

Bug fix history file:
http://Hughes.com.au/product/msql/history.htm

Report a bug in mSQL:
msql-bugs@hughes.com.au
copy to mSQL mailing list at msql-list@bunyip.com.

Dbunk:
Dave Shevett <shevett@homeport.org> has written DBunk — a Java based graphical front end to mSQL. Source code is available from: http://www.home-port.org/~shevett/dbunk.tar.gz

Flat File Importer:
Pascal Forget <pascal@wsc.com> has contributed a program that will import flat file databases directly into mSQL databases. It supports both the version 1.x and 2.x releases of mSQL. It is available via anonymous ftp from: ftp://ftp.wsc.com/pub/freeware/msql/msql-import-0.1.4.tar.gz

Home Page Construction Kit:
Rasmus Lerdorf <rasmus@vex.net> has developed a package that allows users to create WWW sites with mSQL databases.
http://www.vex.net/php

Jate:
Josef <ht@aiace.lnf.infn.it> has developed Jate — a CGI program that builds HTML interfaces to mSQL databases. More details can be found at: http://aiace.lnf.infn.it/~ht/JATE.html

Java:
Darryl Collins <darryl@minmet.uq.oz.au> has developed a version of the mSQL API for the Java programming language. MsqlJava for mSQL version 1.x is available via anonymous ftp from:
ftp://dada.minmet.uq.edu.au/pub/MsqlJava-1.1.3.tar.gz

MsqlJava for mSQL version 2.x:
is available via anonymous ftp from:
ftp://dada.minmet.uq.edu.au/pub/MsqlJava-1.2.0.tar.gz
http://www.minmet.uq.oz.au/msqljava

JDBC:
George Reese <borg@imaginary.com> has developed a Java Database Connection (JDBC) class library using MsqlJava. It is available via anonymous ftp from:
ftp://ftp.imaginary.com/pub/Java/database/mSQL-JDBC.tar.gz
http://www.imaginary.com/Java

Meta-HTML:
Universal Access Inc has released a version of their Meta-HTML scripting language which has extensions for connecting to mSQL databases.
http://www.metahtml.com
ftp://ftp.metahtml.com/pub

mSQL CGI:
Alex Tang <altitude@petrified.cic.net> has written an mSQL front end as a
CGI program. For more details see:
http://petrified.cic.net/MsqlCGI

Perl:
Andreas Koenig <a.koenig@mind.de> has contributed a Perl 5 module which
allows perl to interface to mSQL databases. The latest version isavailable via
anonymous ftp from any of the CPAN archives, for example:
ftp://ftp.funet.fi/pub/languages/perl/CPAN/modules/by-
category/07_Database_Interfaces/Msql
ftp://ftp.funet.fi/pub/languages/perl/CPAN

Mailing List:
A mailing is operated to provide a place for common users of mSQL to discuss
the product. It is currently operated by Bunyip Information Systems in Canada
(a long-time user of Mini SQL). To subscribe to the mailing list, send an e-mail
message containing the word "subscribe" to msql-list-request@Bunyip.com.
Once you are subscribed you can send a message to the entire list by addressing it to msql-list@Bunyip.com. Please note that there are usually between 600
and 1,000 mSQL users subscribed to the mailing list at the time of writing so
it is an excellent forum for asking general mSQL user questions.

# A Natural Language Approach to Relational Data on the Internet

### Dr. Larry Harris

## Introduction

When I was in graduate school writing my computer science thesis on Natural Language there were but few luminaries in this particular field. One of the brightest stars was (and still is) Larry Harris. His work in the natural language arena was seminal to the proliferation of all artificially intelligent systems in the commercial arena.

This chapter is a bit of a departure from the rest. It is a combination of two chapters written by Dr. Harris — "Effective Use of Relational Databases on the Internet," and "Proliferating the Data Warehouse Beyond the Power User" — and a description of the latest entry into the natural language arena, English Wizard.

English Wizard is a natural language front end to relational databases and data warehouses both on and off the Web. What better way to provide end-users access to corporate information on the Internet than through the use of the English language.

## Effective Use of Relational Databases on the Internet

Search engines have a blind spot, a rather large blind spot. They can't see the contents of relational databases. While relational databases currently comprise a small percentage of the data available on the Internet, they make up the predominant portion of data available on corporate Intranets. This is one of the reasons it's hard to make effective use of relational databases using the

Internet protocol. It makes it hard for users to find the right information. Imagine how hard it would be to find relevant Web sites without the use of a search engine. As corporate Intranet sites become more complex, this is exactly the position we put users in when it comes to finding the right information they seek, particularly when it's in a relational database.

Even when the right database has been found, relational databases are hard to browse. Without knowledge of the database structure and the SQL language it can be virtually impossible to browse through a relational database to find the specific information you want. This problem is even worse using a Web browser because the query/reporting metaphors that have addressed this problem in the client/server arena are not available within the context of a Web browser. In addition, the mere existence of the Internet and Intranets place many more technically unsophisticated users in contact with a relational database. The combination of these factors places a real premium on the use of database browsing capability consistent with the Web browser protocol that does not require the user to know the database structure or the SQL language. This section describes how these two important problems, finding the right database and then browsing it, can be solved.

## Finding the Right Database

The problem of finding the right relational database can be solved by exposing relational databases to text search engines. This is the principle function of Linguistic Technology's Exposé product. Exposé generates a textual description of the database that contains words that relate to the contents of the database. Exposé automatically inserts this list of words, called the Magnet, as hidden text in the HTML file of your choosing, which we call the Database Home Page. Since the Database Home Page is an ordinary HTML file it will be indexed by the text search engine. Whenever a user searches using a word that is related to the database, the search engine will find the word in its index causing it to list the Database Home Page in its ranked list of relevant locations. For the first time, the user is now provided with the choice of exploring the database by transferring to the Database Home Page.

By using Exposé to expose all of your databases to the search engine, you effectively create a Universal Search Engine, an environment that allows users to search through both textual and relational data without even being aware of the distinction. You are free to use the text search engine of your choice to create this Universal Search Engine, since Exposé works with all search engines. Exposé uses the language processing technology of the English Wizard(tm) product to derive the list of relevant words that comprise the magnet. This list includes not only table and column names, but also intelligently selected data values and relationship words. In addition, synonyms of these words are automatically included using Exposé's built-in thesaurus. The result is a comprehensive, but relatively small, magnet that is inserted as hidden HTML within the Database Home Page. The creation of the magnet is a fully automatic process. The magnet itself is typically less than 100K for most databases.

In addition to inserting the magnet to attract users to the Database Home Page, Exposé will help you to construct the visible portion of the Database Home Page. The layout and the contents of the Database Home Page are completely under your control, but Exposé will help you add two very common components. First, Exposé will insert a hot link to the English Wizard Web/Server so that users can perform ad hoc query as described later. Second, Exposé will create HTML pages for answers to common questions that are automatically hot linked from the Database Home Page. This means that commonly asked questions can be answered directly from HTML that Exposé produces for you. You simply ask the common questions within Exposé. At the click of a button it will transform the answer to HTML and insert a hot link to the answer page in the Database Home Page. Figure 7-1 shows the system architecture.

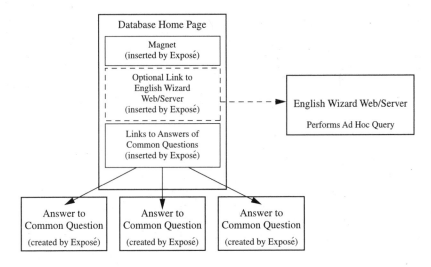

**Figure 7-1.** How Expose and English Wizard fit together.

In a typical Intranet environment in which a user is interested in product information, the use of Exposé will allow the user to simply mention a product name in his or her text search. The search engine will then present a list of choices that might include a textual description of that product, a database that contains product sales information for that product and perhaps a database that contains the inventory on hand for that product. In another case the mention of a benefit term will cause the search engine to list employee handbook pages related to benefits along with a database that might allow the employee to survey his or her particular benefit status. The use of Exposé to create a Universal Search Engine allows users to have convenient access to both textual and relational data, without even being aware of the difference!

## Browsing Relational Databases

Once the user has found the proper database, we must make it equally easy for them to browse the database. Textual pages can easily be browsed using the Web browser. Relational databases are too big and structurally too complex for such an approach. In addition, the query metaphors made popular in the client/server environment, such as Query-By-Example grids, are not available within the context of a Web browser. (In theory they could be provided as add-ins or applets running on the browser, but this adds complexity and variation to each client environment.)

The obvious approach is to simply continue the text search metaphor into the database browser itself. Let the user enter the ordinary English terms that describe the data they are interested in and hit the Submit button. The role of the English Wizard Web/Server is to translate this ordinary English input into the SQL required by the relational database, pass the SQL to the database and then dynamically generate the HTML to display the results of the query.

English Wizard is clearly in a better position to generate SQL than the user. It has a much more detailed knowledge of the database structure and much greater knowledge of the syntax and semantics of SQL than the user. Therefore, it should be no surprise that it can generate SQL better than the user. The surprise is that it can and must generate complex SQL from seemingly simple English input.

For example, the easily expressed English question "Who bought high margin products but not extended service plans?" will cause English Wizard to generate the following extremely complex SQL:

```
SELECT [CUSTOMERS].[LAST_NAME] as [Last Name], [CUSTOMERS].[FIRST_NAME] as
[First Name],
[CUSTOMERS].[COMPANY_NAME] as [Company Name]
FROM [CUSTOMERS]
WHERE exists(SELECT [CUSTOMERS].[LAST_NAME], [CUSTOMERS].[FIRST_NAME],
[CUSTOMERS].[COMPANY_NAME], [Product Name]  FROM [ORDERS], [LINE ITEMS],
[PRODUCTS]  WHERE ([Product_Margin]='High') and [CUSTOMERS].[CUST ID] =
[ORDERS].[CUST ID] and [ORDERS].[ORDER_ID] = [LINE ITEMS].[ORDER_ID] and
[PRODUCTS].[Product ID] = [LINE ITEMS].[PRODUCT_ID]) and
 not exists(SELECT [CUSTOMERS].[LAST_NAME], [CUSTOMERS].[FIRST_NAME], [CUS-
TOMERS].[COMPANY_NAME], [Product Name]  FROM [ORDERS], [LINE ITEMS], [PROD-
UCTS]  WHERE ([Product Name]='Extended Service') and [CUSTOMERS].[CUST ID]
= [ORDERS].[CUST ID] and [ORDERS].[ORDER_ID] = [LINE ITEMS].[ORDER_ID] and
[PRODUCTS].[Product ID] = [LINE ITEMS].[PRODUCT_ID])
```

The English Wizard Web/Server not only provides feedback of how it interprets a request, but it asks for clarification when necessary. The English descriptions entered by the user may be incomplete or ambiguous in terms of the database. The English Wizard Web/Server detects these situations and dynamically generates HTML-based clarification dialogs so that the user can clarify his or her intent.

## Embedding the English Wizard Web/Server in Web Applications

The English Wizard Web/Server is an ActiveX server control with Java wrapper functions. The Java wrapper functions allow the ActiveX control to be conveniently called from JavaScript. The product includes both Visual Basic and JavaScript scripts that run on the Microsoft and Netscape Web servers respectively. It is the Visual Basic or JavaScript script that ties together the English Wizard ActiveX control, the database and the dynamic generation of HTML.

Without any coding at all, the product provides an effective and attractive ad hoc query capability. You can have complete control of the HTML being generated by simply editing the template HTML within the script.

This approach also allows you to embed the English Wizard ActiveX server control within any program logic that you require. In this case, the Visual Basic and JavaScript scripts provide a sample of how to interact with the ActiveX control, which at a high level can be viewed as simply providing the SQL that corresponds to the English input provided.

## Architecture of the English Wizard Web/Server

The English Wizard Web/Server consists of 3 components: the ActiveX control, the Dictionary Administrator and the English Wizard DLL. The ActiveX control exists within an application, either the Visual Basic or JavaScript script we provide, or your own application. The Dictionary Administrator allows different users to use the same copy of the English Wizard dictionary. The Dictionary Administrator allows you to pre-load selected dictionaries on the server so that questions can be answered more efficiently. The English Wizard DLL is the component that actually stores the dictionaries and carries out the translation from English to SQL. Figure 7-2 shows the relationship of the 3 components.

Since the ActiveX control communicates via TCP/IP to the Dictionary Administrator, the application logic, which includes the ActiveX control, need not be running on the same processor as the Dictionary Administrator, although it typically is. Similarly, the database server need not be on the same processor as the English Wizard Web/Server.

## Conclusion

Exposé and English Wizard Web/Server work together to allow relational databases to be used in an ad hoc fashion on the Internet and corporate Intranets. Exposé exposes your relational databases to text search engines, allowing users to see relevant databases as well as textual data in response to their searches. Exposé also helps create standardized reports in HTML so that users can instantly hot link to the answers of common questions.

Once users have found the appropriate database, the English Wizard Web/Server allows them to browse the relational database by entering an ordinary English description of the data they are interested in. The English Wizard

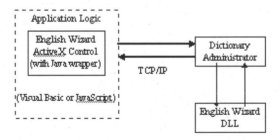

**Figure 7-2**. English Wizard components.

Web/Server automatically generates the corresponding SQL, passes it to the database and then dynamically generates the HTML to show the results.

The two products working together help turn an ordinary search engine into a Universal Search Engine that can search equally well across relational and textual databases.

## Proliferating the Data Warehouse Beyond the Power User

### Introduction

Data Warehouses are intended to deliver information derived from a variety of production systems to the entire business user community. While much of the challenge of building a successful data warehouse is in the design and population of the data warehouse, an equally important challenge arises in the deployment of the data warehouse. A handful of technically astute users will be capable of working with almost any tools they are given. But getting beyond this small group of power users has proven to be a significant challenge, one that has prevented data warehouses from meeting their original goals.

This section discusses in some detail, why usage of the data warehouse is difficult for the great majority of business users and the critical role that English Wizard's ability to translate ordinary English database requests into expert-level SQL can play in proliferating its usage. This section will also stress the additional issues raised by using the Internet or a private corporate Intranet to deliver data warehouse information to the business user community.

### Why Data Warehouses are Hard to Deploy

Data Warehouse databases are large. Since data warehouse databases are constructed by combining selected data from several operational databases, data warehouse databases are inherently large. They are often the largest databases within an organization. The very size of these databases can make them very difficult and expensive to query.

Data Warehouse databases are structurally complex. Because data warehouse databases are constructed by combining data from several operational databases, data warehouse databases are structurally complex. They have many tables with a variety of relationships existing between the tables. This complexity makes them particularly difficult to query, because a typical question will involve a number of tables and each table must be properly joined into the logic of the query. Most business users have difficulty even knowing which tables must be included, much less how they must be joined into a question. For example, a question as seemingly simple as "What customers bought high margin products" translates into the following imposing SQL, even when the notion of "high margin products" is directly coded in the database.

## Example 1

```
SELECT DISTINCT [CUSTOMERS].[LAST_NAME] as [Last Name],
[CUSTOMERS].[FIRST_NAME] as [First Name], [CUSTOMERS].[COMPANY_NAME] as
[Company Name]
FROM ((([CUSTOMERS] INNER JOIN [ORDERS] ON [CUSTOMERS].[CUST ID] =
[ORDERS].[CUST ID]) INNER JOIN [LINE ITEMS] ON [ORDERS].[ORDER_ID] = [LINE
ITEMS].[ORDER_ID]) INNER JOIN [PRODUCTS] ON [PRODUCTS].[Product ID] = [LINE
ITEMS].[PRODUCT_ID]
WHERE [Product Margin]='High'
```

Data Warehouse databases store historical data. Data warehouses not only store relatively current information, they also store historical information. This added time series dimension of the data adds to its complexity. In the simplest case it forces the user to explicitly select the desired timeliness of data. Unfortunately, expressing time and date related selection criteria is particularly difficult because it requires the use of complex built-in functions. For example, to ask "What were the sales of high margin products last month?" requires the following programming-like SQL.

## Example 2

```
SELECT [QUANTITY], [Product Name]
FROM (([LINE ITEMS] INNER JOIN [PRODUCTS] ON [PRODUCTS].[Product ID] =
    [LINE ITEMS].[PRODUCT_ID]) INNER JOIN [ORDERS] ON [ORDERS].[ORDER_ID] =
    [LINE ITEMS].[ORDER_ID]
WHERE [Product Margin]='High' and (Month([ORDER DATE])=7 and Year([ORDER
DATE])=1996)
```

## A Profile of Data Warehouse Queries

Analytical questions require sub-selects. In addition to the difficulties caused by the inherent size and complexity of the data warehouse itself, there are problems that arise due to the complexity of the analytical questions that are typical of the type of questions that the data warehouse was built to answer. The following sections will show the complex SQL required to express certain common analytical concepts. As we will see later, because all of these very common analytical concepts require sub-selects they are virtually inexpressible using the conventional point & click metaphors common to most query and reporting products.

Perhaps the most common analytical construct is the calculation of percentages. Because they require the selection of two sets, percentages always require sub-selects in SQL. A question as simple as "What percent of total sales are high margin products?" requires the following surprisingly complex SQL:

## Example 3

```
SELECT Sum([QUANTITY]) as [Sum Quantity],
   (100 * Sum([QUANTITY])) / (Select Sum([QUANTITY]) From LINE ITEMS Where
[Product Margin]='High') as [Percent]
FROM [LINE ITEMS] INNER JOIN [PRODUCTS] ON [PRODUCTS].[Product ID] = [LINE
ITEMS].[PRODUCT_ID]
WHERE [Product Margin]='High'
```

Other common percentage questions would be: "Show the percent of total sales of each product?" or "What percentage of customers bought extended service?".

Another class of common questions that require sub-selects and therefore are virtually inexpressible using point & click query interfaces, are questions that require selecting the best, worst, most recent or oldest. These questions require an inner select to find the extreme value and an outer select to display the desired information. For example, the question "What product sold the most last month?" requires the following SQL.

## Example 4

```
SELECT DISTINCT [Product Name]
FROM [EMPLOYEES], [ORDERS], [LINE ITEMS], [PRODUCTS]
WHERE ((Month([ORDER DATE])=7 and Year([ORDER DATE])=1996) and [QUANTI-
TY]=(SELECT Max([QUANTITY]) FROM [LINE ITEMS], [ORDERS] WHERE
((Month([ORDER DATE])=7 and Year([ORDER DATE])=1996)) and
[ORDERS].[ORDER_ID] = [LINE ITEMS].[ORDER_ID])) and [EMPLOYEES].[Employee
ID] = [ORDERS].[EMPLOYEE ID] and [ORDERS].[ORDER_ID] = [LINE
ITEMS].[ORDER_ID] and [PRODUCTS].[Product ID] = [LINE ITEMS].[PRODUCT_ID]
```

Perhaps the most interesting category of analytical questions are exemplified by questions such as "What customers bought both high margin products and support" or "Who bought high margin products but not extended service plans?" The extremely complex SQL for the latter example is shown below.

## Example 5

```
SELECT [CUSTOMERS].[LAST_NAME] as [Last Name], [CUSTOMERS].[FIRST_NAME] as
[First Name], [CUSTOMERS].[COMPANY_NAME] as [Company Name]
FROM [CUSTOMERS]
WHERE exists(SELECT [CUSTOMERS].[LAST_NAME], [CUSTOMERS].[FIRST_NAME],
[CUSTOMERS].[COMPANY_NAME], [Product Name]  FROM [ORDERS], [LINE ITEMS],
[PRODUCTS]  WHERE ([Product_Margin]='High') and [CUSTOMERS].[CUST ID] =
[ORDERS].[CUST ID] and [ORDERS].[ORDER_ID] = [LINE ITEMS].[ORDER_ID] and
[PRODUCTS].[Product ID] = [LINE ITEMS].[PRODUCT_ID]) and not exists(SELECT
[CUSTOMERS].[LAST_NAME], [CUSTOMERS].[FIRST_NAME],
[CUSTOMERS].[COMPANY_NAME], [Product Name]  FROM [ORDERS], [LINE ITEMS],
[PRODUCTS]  WHERE ([Product Name]='Extended Service') and [CUSTOMERS].[CUST
ID] = [ORDERS].[CUST ID] and [ORDERS].[ORDER_ID] = [LINE ITEMS].[ORDER_ID]
and [PRODUCTS].[Product ID] = [LINE ITEMS].[PRODUCT_ID])
```

## Limitations of Point & Click Query Metaphors

We have made several references to the difficulties using the conventional point & click metaphors to construct queries typical of a data warehouse. Since this is the most common metaphor used in nearly all query and reporting tools today, it is worthwhile understanding exactly where the point & click metaphor breaks down.

The first thing a user must specify when expressing a query to a point & click tool is which tables are to be included in the query. Most business users have trouble even specifying the complete list of tables, and for good reason. While some tables must obviously be included, others need to be included for navigational purposes only. This requires knowledge of not only the database structure, but also the joining requirements of SQL. If you look carefully at the SQL for Example 1 above, you will see that the question requires the inclusion of the Line Items table, which is not immediately obvious to many users. An unfortunate user that forgets to include this table initially can waste an arbitrary amount of time trying to express the query, without ever knowing why the correct answer perpetually eludes him.

As we have seen from our previous examples, it is common to require selections based on a date criteria. As common as these date criteria are, they are very difficult to express within the point & click metaphor. This is because dates require the use of built-in functions to be expressed. These are programming constructs that are not intuitive to most business users. For example, notice the amount of SQL that had to be generated to express the notion of "last month" in Example 2. The point & click metaphor only helps express these constructs in as much as it provides a list of all built-in functions. The burden remains on the user to know which functions to use and how to use them.

We have seen several surprisingly common examples of the need to generate

SQL sub-selects. Very few of the point & click implementations allow sub-selects to be generated by point & click means. This requires the user to actually type in the SQL making up the sub-select. Needless to say, there are very few business users who have the desire or the knowledge of SQL to actually perform this task. Therefore, it is fair to say that any question that requires a sub-select is effectively outside the scope of what can be expressed by all but the most technically sophisticated business users. This is particularly disappointing given that such common constructs as percentages and best and worst questions require sub-selects.

The Internet, or a private corporate Intranet, is a very attractive environment for deploying the data warehouse to the business user community. The most attractive aspect of using the Internet as a deployment mechanism is that it minimizes the cost and complexity of distributing query and reporting software on each user's computer. In many cases, the user need only have an Internet browser, such as Netscape Navigator, for accessing the data warehouse.

As attractive as this approach is, it limits users in the tools they have available to express queries. Without downloading, or otherwise installing additional software components, the user is limited to simple character input of queries. In particular, the common point & click metaphor is not available without extending the browser with a significant Java applet or browser plug. All this would be necessary to provide a query metaphor we have already shown is insufficient to meet the needs of the data warehouse.

## English Wizard and the Data Warehouse

Since business users are not in a position to generate SQL by themselves, it is important to provide them with a tool that will do it for them. English Wizard allows the business user to express even the difficult analytical questions required in the data warehouse in ordinary English. English Wizard will automatically ask for clarification if the question is ambiguously phrased. Once English Wizard is certain it understands what was intended, it will instantly generate the SQL needed to answer the question. English Wizard will then either pass the SQL to the DBMS and display the results, or it will work in conjunction with any ODBC-compliant reporting tool to display the results. English Wizard can also return the SQL to any application that invokes it. In addition, it can work in conjunction with a Web server and provide the results in HTML to be displayed by a Web browser.

By automating the critical step of generating the SQL, English Wizard makes even the most complex data warehouse accessible to the business user community. All of the examples shown above demonstrate both acceptable English input to English Wizard and the expert-level SQL that is generated in response to that question.

English Wizard allows for the full exploitation of the Internet as a deployment vehicle because the metaphor for query expression is a simple English question. This is consistent with the user's expectations in the Web from using text search engines such as Yahoo or Alta Vista. The user simply types in an English question and presses the submit button.

### The English Wizard Semantic Layer

In conceptual terms, English Wizard maps questions expressed in the User's conceptual view of the data into the formal SQL of the DBMS's logical view. This process is very similar to the function performed by the DBMS in mapping between the logical view and the hardware's physical view.

English Wizard does this translation by using a dictionary that defines what the relevant English words mean in the context of a particular database. This dictionary acts as a semantic layer that isolates the business user from the hard formalisms of the SQL. The beauty of this semantic layer is that by defining individual words, the users are allowed to use those words in literally thousands of different questions.

One of the critical functions that English Wizard performs is that it automatically builds the dictionary on its own by looking at the database. Once this process is complete you can modify and extend the dictionary as desired. In addition, dictionaries can be structured in a hierarchy so that changes made in an administrator's dictionary will automatically be propagated to other dictionaries that inherit from it. This allows users to personalize their terminology and still receive administrative improvements to the dictionary as the database changes.

### English Wizard Architecture

English Wizard can be implemented in the following five architectures:

1. As a Stand-Alone Query/Display Component. The English Wizard Client Version can be installed as a stand-alone Windows desktop query application. Users enter their database request, in plain English, into the Query Dialog Box and the answer is displayed in a spreadsheet workbook. Once displayed, the user can manipulate the data using the full power of the conventional spreadsheet including graphic display. There are no limitations as to where the data is physically located and there are no requirements for any other reporting/query software products to be installed on the user's desktop.

2. As an Add-in Component to Your Favorite Reporting/Query Tool. The English Wizard Client Version can be installed to English-enable your standard desktop reporting tool. Simply enter English where you would have normally defined the query request and English Wizard will generate the SQL and pass it off to your standard database driver. The data will be returned directly to your reporting tool's output report window. This way you have the ease of use offered by English Wizard and the full power and capability of your existing reporting tool. English Wizard works  with most ODBC compatible reporting/query tools including

| | |
|---|---|
| Microsoft Access | Forest & Trees |
| Microsoft Excel & Query | Intersolv Explorer |
| Crystal Reports | ReportSmith |
| Crystal INFO | InfoMaker |
| And More.... | |

3. As a Component Embedded Within Your Client/Server Application. Using the English Wizard Software Developer's Kit (SDK) you can embed English Wizard within your application. Your application can request that English Wizard interact directly with the user for entering the English question or your application can pass the English text string to English Wizard. In either case English Wizard will return the SQL directly to your application. English Wizard will return the SQL in either the ODBC, Microsoft Access, SQL Server, Oracle or INFORMIX dialects of SQL. When deploying an application, a copy of the English Wizard Client Version must be licensed for each desktop. Once a copy of the Client Version is licensed on the desktop it can be used to support any number of applications. Volume discounts are available for large scale deployments. English Wizard works with nearly all client/server development languages.

4. As Part of a Web Server Connected to the Internet. The English Wizard Web Server allows for English Wizard to be used by users accessing a server database attached to the Internet. All of the English Wizard software resides on an NT server and works directly with the Web browser running on the user's desktop to accept English requests and display the results. Support for Microsoft and Netscape Web server software is included, although English Wizard can be invoked from other Web servers.

5. As Part of a Server Connected to the Client/Server Network. The English Wizard Server allows for English Wizard to be used by users connected over a client/server network. This approach centralizes all the translation processing on the server machine, but still allows the user interface code to run on the client. The SQL returned can be in any one of several native dialects.

## Conclusion

Proliferating the use of the data warehouse beyond a handful of power users is a serious problem that is plaguing nearly all data warehouse installations. In this section we have discussed the reasons why business users find using the conventional query tools so daunting in a data warehouse context. In addition, we have discussed the important role that the Internet can play in proliferating the use of the data warehouse, and stressed the further restriction in query metaphor that is implicit in using the Internet.

Finally, we have highlighted the role that English Wizard can play in making the data warehouse available to the general business user community. We have presented a number of architectural choices of how English Wizard can fit

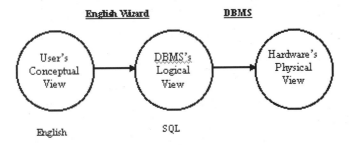

**Figure 7-3.** The English Wizard semantic layer.

into the data warehouse environment, whether working alone, along with your standard query and reporting tools or over the Internet. We have demonstrated the value of the English Wizard semantic layer (figure 7-3), discussed the Web to server connection (figure 7-4) and demonstrated the client/server connection (figure 7-5).

## A Tour Through English Wizard

The Structured Query Language (SQL) is the standard protocol for accessing relational databases. In order for users to construct a meaningful database query using SQL they need to understand SQL syntax, the database structure and the semantics of SQL. Few users care to master the idiosyncrasies of SQL. Traditional user interfaces such as Point & Click or Query By Example have made great strides in alleviating the need for users to know SQL syntax, however, these GUI metaphors still burden the user with the need to understand the database structure and the semantics of SQL.

Interestingly enough, users have no problem conceptually understanding their database information and are very capable of expressing their request in English. English Wizard insulates users from having to extrapolate from this basic understanding to a special language construct completely foreign to the way they think. Using English Wizard users continue to think about their data at a conceptual level and then simply express their query using ordinary English! English Wizard takes care of all the messy details of translating English into SQL!

English Wizard knows how to translate ordinary English questions into SQL by understanding the database structure, the expected vocabulary for accessing the data, English grammar rules and the structure and nuances of SQL. English Wizard examines the user's question, invokes its intuitive knowledge of English grammar, and then uses information stored in the English Wizard Dictionary to complete the translation to SQL.

The English Wizard Dictionary contains information necessary for supporting the translation of English to SQL. English Wizard includes an Automatic Dictionary Construction process that populates the dictionary with information obtained by processing the user's database. Once the automatic dictionary build is complete, English Wizard provides users the option of extending the dictionary by adding words or phrases unique to their business. The English Wizard dictionary contains

• A basic English vocabulary—supplied with the product
• A Thesaurus—supplied with the product
• Database Definitions—Database Names, Table Names, Column Names,
• Synonyms
• Data Values (Optional)
• Inflections
• Common Code Schemes
• Date Sensitive Definitions
• Joining Logic

For users of relatively small databases, the information obtained through the automatic dictionary build process is sufficient for a high level of English fluency. For users with larger databases containing many tables with complex relationships and presumably cryptic naming conventions, English Wizard provides a Dictionary Editor.

Using the Editor the application support staff can extend the information obtained as a result of the automatic build by customizing the dictionary to include additional synonyms, special business terms or phrases, a user's view of the database excluding sensitive or unnecessary data, defined data values, specific data groupings and more. You can do as much or as little dictionary customization as you wish. In the worst case, if English Wizard doesn't understand a word because the dictionary is lacking information, it will simply ask for clarification and then answer the user's question. Once clarification is given, English Wizard automatically updates the dictionary for all future reference. English Wizard learns as you use it!

English Wizard offers multi-tier Dictionary support for large organizations using English Wizard as part of implementing their Data Warehouse strategy. Often there is a need for a central dictionary to be made available on the network. Additionally, individual English Wizard users may want to create their

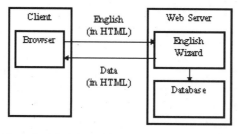

**Figure 7-4.** Web server connection.

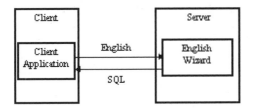

**Figure 7-5.** The client/server connection.

own personal dictionaries based on the central dictionary. English Wizard allows for multiple levels or extensions of the dictionary while providing the ability to synchronize these changes as necessary. Administrative control is provided to ensure the integrity of all dictionaries based on the central dictionary.

English Wizards works by users enter ordinary English questions. Using its inherent knowledge of English and SQL constructs along with information contained in the dictionary, English Wizard derives the complex SQL to express what is a seemingly simple English business question. If the question is ambiguous, English Wizard will work with the user for clarification and will even remember any new definitions for future reference.

The procedures for setting up and using English Wizard are straight forward and are shown as a series of illustrations in figures 7-6 through 7-10.

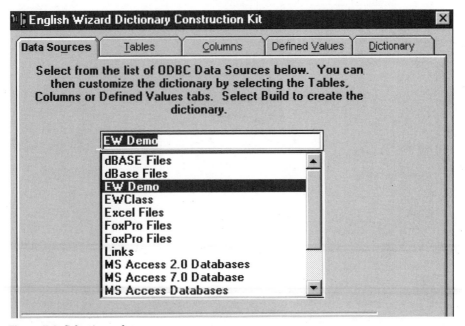

**Figure 7-6.** Selecting a data source.

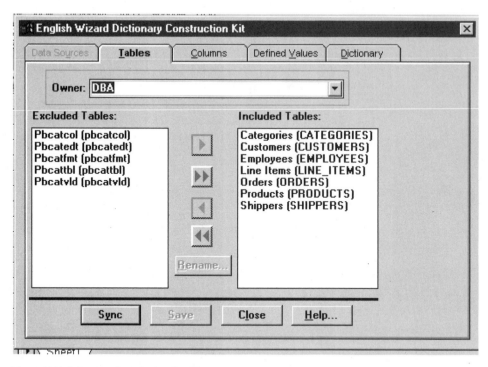

**Figure 7-7.** Selecting the relational tables.

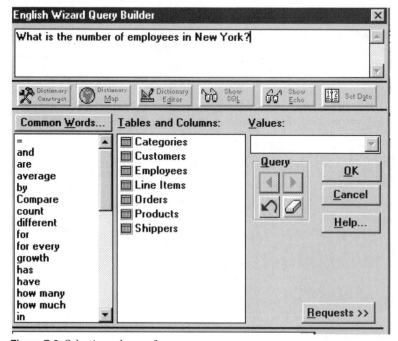

**Figure 7-8.** Selecting columns for a query.

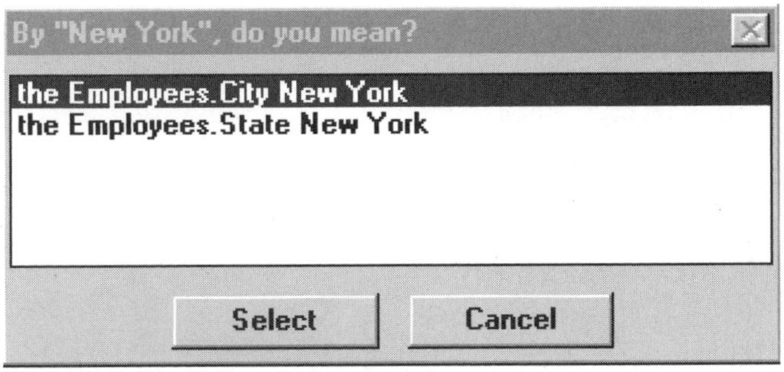

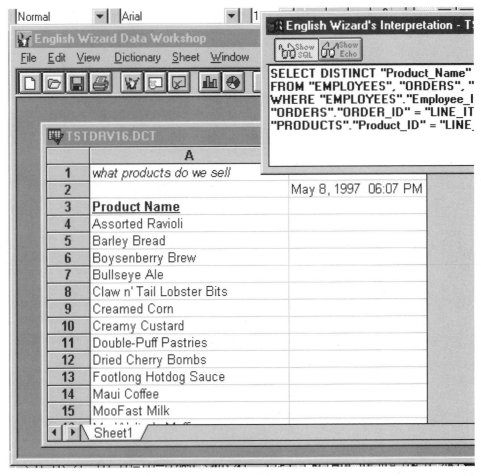

**Figure 7-9.** Clarifying what you want.

**Figure 7-10.** The result is displayed in a tabular form. One of the nice things about English Wizard is that it also displays the SQL command — a good way to learn the language.

## Author bio

Dr. Larry R. Harris is president and founder of Linguistic Technology Corporation, Littleton Massachusetts. Previous to starting Linguistic Technology he was the founder and chairman of AICorp, where commercial natural language products were first introduced. Dr. Harris is the author of Linguistic Technology Corporation's English Wizard and AICorp's mainframe natural language product, Intellect. He is an international authority on AI and natural language technology and has lectured on these topics throughout Europe, Russia, Japan and Australia. Dr. Harris received his Ph.D. in Computer Science from Cornell University. Linguistic Technology Corporation can be reached at 508-486-8860.

# 8

# Database Access from Java

## Dennis Minium

## Introduction

The Java programming language, developed at Sun Microsystems and promoted by its subsidiary, JavaSoft, offers some unique opportunities and interesting challenges to database access. It includes characteristics that make it an excellent language and execution environment for the Internet architecture, but many of those same characteristics make access to databases, particularly relational databases, more complex than you might expect.

## What's So Special About Java

Java is a robust, object-oriented, dynamically portable, semi-interpretive language that includes designed-in security facilities. While there is nothing particularly earth-shattering about any of its features in isolation, in combination they serve to create an excellent platform for executable, Web-based logic.

### Java Is Object-Oriented

Java is a truly object-oriented language, providing the benefits of software reusability, extensibility, and dynamic applications. It's based on C++, but its developers edited out C++'s most troublesome and confusing aspects. Pointers are gone, eliminating one of the biggest challenges to learning to program in C++ and a gaggle of typical programming errors. Java does automatic garbage collection, eliminating even more common and hard-to-find errors. A number of redundancies and holdovers from C included in C++ have also been omitted from Java.

That does not mean it is particularly easy to program in Java. It's a full-fledged programming language and requires a programmer to employ object-oriented approaches to gain its full benefit. However, Java is far simpler than C++, and learning it is well within reach of a competent COBOL or Visual Basic programmer.

### Java Is Platform Neutral

Java is designed to provide a "write once, run anywhere" mechanism for application development. While its detractors are openly skeptical, there is little argument that Java has been architected to meet the goal of platform neutrality. That is largely because Java is more than a language; it's also an environment that includes an execution architecture and a set of surrounding tools.

The Java language itself is semi-interpretive. As with most programming languages, Java programs must be compiled. However, instead of producing machine dependent object code, the Java compiler produces a platform-neutral form called bytecodes. At execution, these bytecodes as processed by a run time environment known as the Java Virtual Machine (JVM). The JVM specification ensures that the same bytecodes exhibit exactly the same behaviors on all platforms. This is the element of the architecture that makes Java platform independent.

### Java is Dynamically Portable

Java programs can execute in a standalone mode much as programs written in any language. Such programs are known as Java applications. More interesting for the Internet/Intranet world, though, are the mini-programs known as Java "applets."

Java applets are downloaded on demand, executed immediately, and dis-

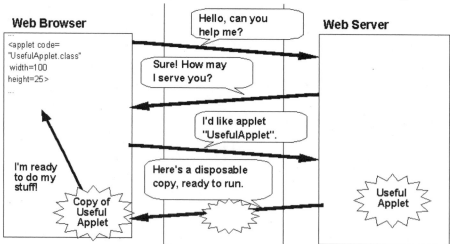

**Figure 8-1.** The short but fulfilling life of an applet.

carded. This process is depicted in figure 8-1. Whenever a Web page that includes a reference to an applet is opened using a Java-enabled Web browser, the bytecodes come with it and are handed off to the browser's JVM for execution. This behavior solves a configuration management problem that has long plagued the client/server environment: how to ensure that all of the client machines that use an application have the correct version of the client software. In a traditional environment in which client software is explicitly installed on potentially hundreds or even thousands of computers, upgrading to a new version is a major undertaking. In the Java environment, though, since Java applets are downloaded immediately prior to execution, a client machine will automatically have access to the latest version that is stored on the server.

## Java is Secure

The Java environment includes security features that make it difficult to craft "rogue applets" that do evil to their users. For example, because it includes no pointers and performs array bounds checking, the Java environment provides no mechanisms to allow programmers to stray into places they don't belong, either purposefully or accidentally. Java's run time environment also includes a bytecode verifier to ensure that the bytecodes conform to Java's rigorous constraints, so no one can build a bogus compiler that circumvents the language restrictions.

In addition to these features, the environments in which Java is supported, mostly Web browsers, sometimes add their own. For instance, it's common to describe Java applets as executing in a "sandbox," because of the rules that govern what they can do to permanent storage. In some cases, an applet is not allowed to write data on a client's machine, or at least is restricted to certain directories. It is also common to allow an applet to communicate only with the server from which it was downloaded. This way, an applet cannot be written that connects you to somewhere you don't want to be for some nefarious purpose.

With the latest version of the Java Development Kit (JDK) it is possible to "extend the sandbox" to allow circumvention of these constraints for specific trusted applets.

## Special Issues for Java-Based Data Access

Many of the features that make Java so appealing for use on the Internet and in corporate intranets present special problems when it comes to database access, particularly to relational and legacy databases. For instance, since Java is so heavily object oriented, it is well-suited to use with object databases for which Java bindings exist, but less well suited to the tabular structure of relational databases.

Another issue: in non-Java, non-Web environments, you would expect to see application software as well as any special data access software (for instance, ODBC drivers or native database drivers) installed on each client machine. This is not true in the world of Java, where application logic is stored in applets that are downloaded on demand. To insist that certain software for database access be pre-installed on each computer when the application logic is loaded and executed dynamically defeats the purpose of the platform neutrality inherent in Java architecture's. To conform to the Java environment, then, requires pure Java interfaces for applets.

Java's security constraints add another twist. Remember that it is generally unacceptable for an applet to connect to a server other than the one from which it was downloaded. However, it is frequently the case that the database to which a connection must be made is housed on a different machine from the Web server. It is therefore necessary to build data access software that lives within these security constraints.

As it happens, there are a number of solutions available to Java developers who require access to databases. In some cases obstacles are overcome, in others they are cleverly bypassed, and in a few they are simply apologized for. In no case, though, is database access as straightforward as you might expect in most other languages.

## JDBC — The Obvious Choice

JavaSoft has invented a Java application programming interface (API) called JDBC for executing SQL statements. While the JavaSoft points out that JDBC is actually a trademarked name and not an acronym, most folks assume it stands for "Java DataBase Connectivity." This is not surprising since JDBC is loosely modeled after Microsoft's Open DataBase Connectivity (ODBC) API, a programming interface based on the X/Open SQL CLI (Call Level Interface) that has gained wide acceptance for generalized access to relational databases. However, JDBC is not an implementation of ODBC; it is a similar but different API specifically geared for Java.

JDBC is a low-level API that makes it possible to connect to a data source, send commands across the connection, and process the results. This API interacts with a program known as a JDBC Driver, which is responsible for translating JDBC requests into a form recognizable by the target DBMS.

For a JDBC Driver to be designated "JDBC COMPLIANT™" it must support a certain level of SQL (ANSI SQL-2 Entry Level, to be precise.) However, a JDBC Driver may provide support for a great many additional features peculiar to a particular DBMS. The JDBC API allows any query string to be passed through to the underlying Driver, so SQL extensions can be exploited at will.

In some cases, application developers may not know which DBMS's their programs will be required to access. This is often true of packaged software vendors whose programs are required to run against whatever DBMS's their purchasers have in house. For such situations, JDBC includes a

"DatabaseMetaData" interface that allows characteristics of a DBMS to be interrogated at run time. These characteristics can be used to determine what SQL requests the DBMS can handle so the software package can configure the appropriate requests dynamically.

The Java Development Kit (JDK) from JavaSoft includes the JDBC Driver Manager (which connects Java programs to the correct JDBC Driver), the JDBC driver test suite, and the JDBC-ODBC Bridge.

## Differences Between JDBC and ODBC

While JDBC and ODBC share common roots, they do have their differences. These differences can be divided into two categories: changes JavaSoft made to JDBC in order to make it fit more cleanly into the Java environment, and features included in ODBC that are missing from JDBC.

A different interface from ODBC was necessary for Java simply because ODBC uses a C interface. JavaSoft could have done a literal translation of the ODBC API into Java, but they chose not to for a variety of reasons and, instead, developed an entirely new (but reasonably familiar) API. In JDBC, JavaSoft has attempted to simplify ODBC and to orient it more strongly towards object technology.

Since JDBC and ODBC are different, the driver programs each interface requires to translate their requests into the native protocol of a target DBMS are different, too. Thus, you cannot simply use your ODBC driver to access (say) Sybase from a JDBC-enabled Java program. You'll have to purchase a JDBC driver of some sort.

ODBC is a more mature interface than JDBC. It should come as no surprise, then, that ODBC includes some features that JDBC does not. In particular:

•Block read. ODBC allows a block of records to be retrieved with a single call. JDBC only supports the fetching of a single row at a time.

•Scrollable cursors. ODBC provides for backwards and forward movement (scrolling) through a result set, given that such a feature is supported by the subject database. JDBC allows only forward movement.

•Variable binding. ODBC supports the concept of binding database columns to program variables, thereby making the movement of data between program storage and database buffers very simple. JDBC does not and leaves the problem of mapping instance variables to database columns to the developer.

•Bookmarks. With ODBC it is possible to mark the location of a row of interest in a result set so that it can be easily located later. JDBC provides no similar features.

In addition, the ability to interrogate the specific capabilities of a DBMS is more advanced in ODBC than in JDBC.

While these deficiencies in JDBC are likely to be corrected over time, applications that have near term need of the omitted features might be well served to use one of the JDBC alternatives, described later in the chapter.

## Two-Tier versus Three-Tier JDBC Implementations

In a two-tier JDBC implementation (illustrated in figure 8-2), a Java application or applet communicates directly with a database through a JDBC driver. In the typical applet case, the applet is started by a Java-enabled Web browser. Using JDBC, the applet opens a connection to a database running on another machine. It sends its requests directly to the database and receives results directly from the database.

In order to employ this method of database access with an applet, you must take steps to extend the previously mentioned "Java sandbox." One of the constraints on the sandbox is that a Java applet can only directly communicate with the Web server from which it was downloaded unless special security measures are employed. Since it is unusual for the Web server and the database server to be located on the same machine, such security measures will almost certainly be required.

A three-tier JDBC implementation introduces a middle layer, sometimes called a "data access server." The Java application or applet sends requests to the middle layer, which in turn communicates with the database management system. After the DBMS processes the request, the result is returned to the data access server which immediately forwards it to the end user. In the case of applets, the data access server is usually located on the same physical machine as the server from which the applet was downloaded, thus avoiding the sandbox problem.

The three-tier implementation is often preferred because it provides a cen-

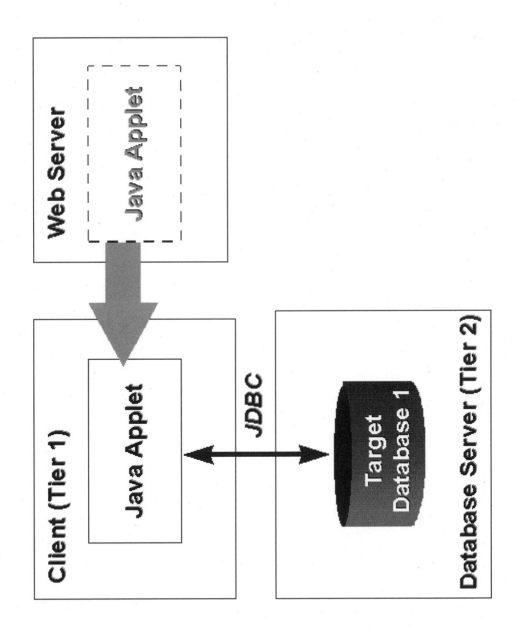

**Figure 8-2.** A two-tier JDBC implementation.

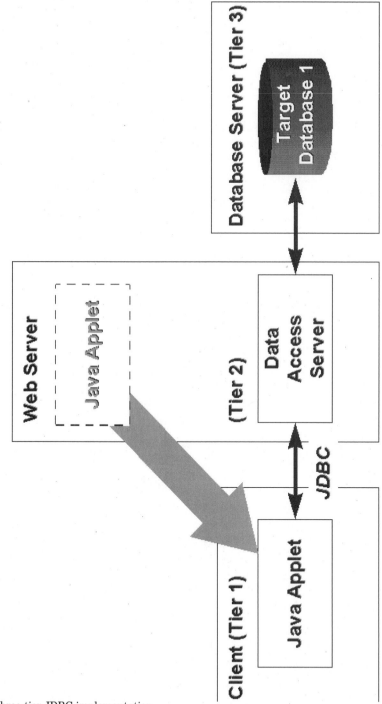

**Figure 8-3.** A three-tier JDBC implementation.

tral point of control through which data can enter and exit the enterprise. Also, there can be a performance advantage to concentrating database requests on a high-powered data access server.

## Types of JDBC Drivers

JavaSoft places JDBC drivers into one of four categories. Although they make clear that other kinds of drivers are possible, the driver types have already begun to be known as types 1 through 4.

JDBC-ODBC LOCAL BRIDGE (TYPE 1): The JDBC-ODBC local bridge is a temporary, two-tier solution offered by Sun in cooperation with Intersolv. It translates between JDBC and ODBC on the client. This requires the installation of native (i.e., non-Java) ODBC drivers on each client machine. This is, of course, directly contradictory to the whole aim of Java, seeing as how it makes an important part of the application environment permanently installed (instead of downloaded on demand) and platform dependent (instead of platform neutral). JavaSoft defends this implementation by arguing that data access is a problem mostly faced in corporate intranets, and that corporations usually have a small number of platform types to support, so platform independence is not critical. This argument is generally regarded as shallow, and the Type 1 implementation as sort of silly.

NATIVE API PARTLY-JAVA (TYPE 2): Another temporary solution, this is sim-

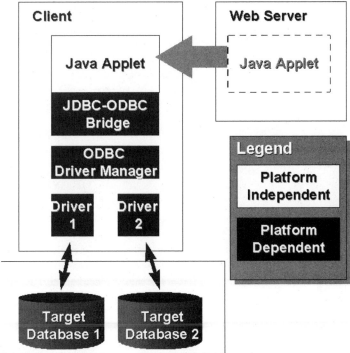

**Figure 8-4.** Type 1 JDBC Driver — JDBC-ODBC Bridge.

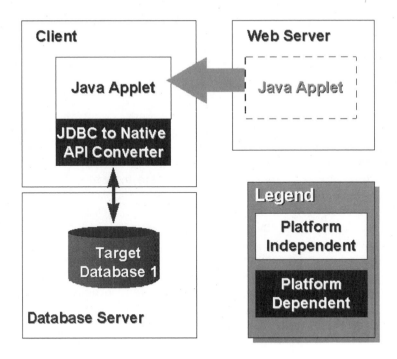

**Figure 8-5.** Type 1 JDBC Driver — Native API, partly Java.

ilar to the JDBC-ODBC Local Bridge. Where the JDBC-ODBC bridge translates between JDBC and ODBC, though, the Type 2 driver translates between JDBC and the client API for a specific DBMS. This alternative suffers the same drawbacks as the JDBC-ODBC bridge in that it requires the installation of non-Java executables on each client machine. Type 2 drivers for Oracle and Sybase are available from Intersolv, and a Type 2 driver for DB2/2 is available from IBM.

JDBC-NET (TYPE 3): Rapidly emerging as the most popular type of JDBC driver, Type 3 is a three-tier solution. It involves a pure Java client that communicates with a data access server using a DBMS-independent protocol. The data access server, in turn, handles the translation between JDBC and the database. There are a number of vendors that offer Type 3 drivers including Visigenic, Intersolv, Symantec, XDB Systems, and WebLogic. Most of these actually perform a function very similar to the JDBC-ODBC bridge (Type 1) except that all of the non-Java code is isolated to the data access server. Others translate from JDBC to native DBMS wire protocol. In any event, the distinguishing characteristics of type 3 are that

• The client side is pure Java, and

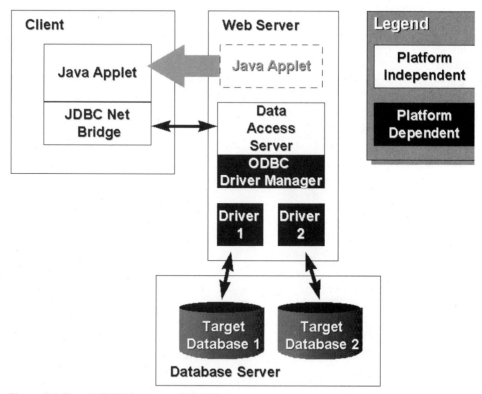

**Figure 8-6.** Type 3 JDBC Driver — JDBC Net.

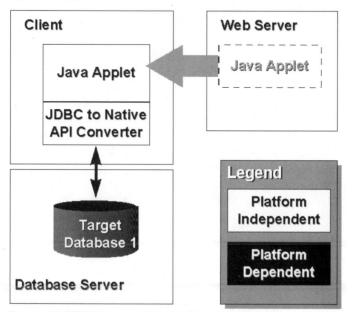

**Figure 8-7.** JDBC Driver — Fully JDBC native protocol.

•The translation between JDBC and the DBMS protocol takes place on the data access server.

FULLY-JAVA NATIVE PROTOCOL (TYPE 4): Finally, some database vendors (and others privy to the wire protocols of specific DBMS's) are creating direct, two-tier, Java-only JDBC drivers. These drivers convert JDBC into the DBMS's proprietary wire protocol. Sybase, Borland and some smaller database vendors have produced Type 4 drivers, and others are sure to follow suit.

In short, JDBC driver types 1 and 2 are destined for extinction. Types 3 and 4 will be supported increasingly well by DBMS vendors and are almost universally thought to represent the future of JDBC.

## Alternatives to JDBC

For generalized access to relational data sources, JDBC is your best bet. New JDBC drivers are popping out of vendors' development shops constantly and soon you will be hard pressed to find a database for which you cannot easily locate a JDBC driver.

Still, there are some alternatives to JDBC available. They fall into three categories: ODBC implementations for Java, native DBMS-specific API's, and object databases of various stripe.

### ODBC Implementations for Java

While JDBC and ODBC share a common heritage, there is no question that they are different from one another. For reasons explained earlier, it is clearly wrong to say that JDBC is a Java-based version of ODBC. In fact, JavaSoft has asserted that it would have been inappropriate to build JDBC as a literal translation of ODBC.

Despite that, some software vendors have successfully built products that directly expose ODBC functionality to Java applications and applets. Both JetConnect from XDB Systems and JAGG from BulletProof are examples of this type of product. While each provides access to ODBC-enabled data sources from JDBC, each also offers its own, unique interface that provides access to the more rich functionality of ODBC. JDBC may be adequate for most applications, but developers who need features like block fetches and scrollable cursors may find these direct ODBC implementations appealing.

### Native API'S

In most cases, the most efficient way to access a database is through a proprietary, native API offered by the DBMS vendor. Since DBMS vendors understand the wire protocol to their databases, they are in a position to build the highest performance interface to them. In addition, the native API is likely to expose all of the DBMS's proprietary extensions.

Unfortunately, a native API is specific to a particular DBMS, so you lose the DBMS independence of JDBC and ODBC. However, if you are confident that your application is destined to interact with a specific DBMS, using its native API may be a suitable alternative.

Informix offers a Java API at present, but few others have direct API's and instead rely on JDBC. Over time, though, you can expect to see more native API's emerging.

## The Object Route

Java aficionados are quick to point out that Java, being object oriented itself, is more suited to interaction with object-based storage mechanisms then relational ones. Unfortunately, Java applications that are forced to live in existing environments often have little choice but to find a mechanism by which to access the relational data stores that comprise the bulk of most organizations' information resource.

However, developers building applications for which access to legacy data stores is not an issue may find use of object-oriented storage mechanisms a quick and simple alternative to using JDBC. Vendors of object DBMSs provide language-specific bindings that make it incredibly simple to make an object persistent. In general, it is simply a matter of identifying a class as "persistable" and, at some point in the program logic, commanding an object defined on that class to become persistent.

There are several different mechanisms available for object storage. Object serialization, a process by which an object in a class marked "serializable" can be flattened out and written to disk, is available as part of the JDK and is appropriate for writing small amounts of data. Object Design Inc. has produced a lightweight object DBMS written completely in Java named the ObjectStore Persistent Storage Engine. GemStone offers a full function, multi-user object database written in Java. Finally, Java bindings to full-function ODBMS's including Versant, ObjectStore and GemStone are available.

While each object-based implementation is different from every other, it is generally true that reading and writing data from object-oriented languages is much easier and more straightforward with an ODBMS than an RDBMS. Conversely, it is generally true that the query language associated with RDBMS's is much more powerful than those supported by ODBMS's. In the end, the choice between ODBMS and RDBMS is entirely dependent on the specific needs of specific applications.

## Higher Level Interfaces

Like ODBC, its forebear, JDBC is a low-level interface. For everyday use by business application developers, operating at a higher level of abstraction is both appropriate and easier. There are several alternatives available that allow developers to take advantage of JDBC access to databases without having to write at the JDBC level.

### Embedded SQL-style API's

Embedded SQL is a mechanism for adding SQL capability to a programming language. Usually, it involves defining additional constructs or statements to the language that are translated by a program preprocessor into native language statements before the program is compiled. Embedded SQL hides quite a bit of the complexity associated with interacting with a database; the preprocessor generates code that handles routine housekeeping chores and such mechanistic tasks as retrieving results from the database buffer and moving them into the appropriate host variables.

This sort of capability is being added to Java by individual vendors in a variety of implementations. Typically, an embedded SQL style API provides method calls that translate high level requests into JDBC (or, in fact, ODBC or a native API) at execution time. JavaSoft indicates that at least one vendor is working on a "pure" embedded SQL interface that will involve a full precompiler that allows Java variables to be used directly in SQL statements.

In order to illustrate how much simpler the use of an embedded SQL interface is than native JDBC, figure 8-8 shows two code fragments that do exactly the same thing. One uses native JDBC and the other uses the embedded SQL-style API included as part of XDB's JetConnect product.

Object Relational Mappers

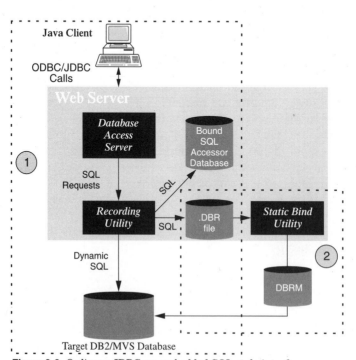

**Figure 8-8.** Ordinary JDBC vs. embedded SQL style interface.

Another option is a technology called "object-relational mapping" that attempts to bridge the gap between the object-ness of Java and the relational nature of the data with which it must deal. In a nutshell, an object-relational mapper converts an object graph into rows in tables. You can expect the interface employed to be similar to that of an object database. JavaSoft has announced an intent to create a general mapper of this sort, as have a number of other vendors.

As intriguing as this might sound, it is important to bear in mind that object structures and relational structures are fundamentally different. Relational structures are based on tables with fixed definitions, while object structures are composed of complex and flexible graphs. As a result, there is an impedance mismatch that inevitably leads to a mapping that is less than fully satisfying. For instance, if you choose a mapping product that creates Java classes based on relational database definitions, you're likely to end up with one class per table, hardly an object-oriented solution. If you choose an approach that builds relational tables based on Java class definitions, you're likely to end up with an overly complex, inefficient, and non-normalized database definition.

In any case, before you commit to a particular object-relational mapping product, be sure you understand exactly what sort of flexibility or capability you're giving up in order to gain an object-style interface.

## Optimizations for Enterprise Computing

In order to use Java in an enterprise computing environment, it is often necessary to employ special measures. Enterprise databases are frequently subject to strict performance and security constraints imposed to maximize throughput and minimize hanky-panky. The databases that compose the corporate information asset are carefully guarded by database administrators (DBA's) whose job it is to ensure that the integrity of that asset is not compromised.

There exists a natural tension between DBA's and the developers who wish access to data. Developers want unimpeded access, but the DBA's, by nature of their responsibility, must control access carefully. In order to resolve this conflict, DBMS vendors offer the DBA tools that can ensure that careless (or malicious) developers do no harm to the data resource. At the same time, these tools tend to be minimally intrusive and do not affect the way a developer writes code.

Unfortunately, in many cases certain access configurations, such as access from Java using JDBC, do not allow for the use of these tools. What, then, is a DBA to do when a Java developer asks for access to some vital corporate database for which she has obtained a JDBC driver? There are two obvious choices: either the DBA can either grant full, unrestricted access to the database and thereby place the data at risk, or it can deny the request entirely, thus preventing the developer from doing his job. Neither choice is very satisfying.

For some environments, though, there is also third choice: the use of specialized software that allows DBA's to protect and regulate access to databases from Java. Such software, called "data access middleware," is by nature DBMS-specific. Even so, properly implemented, data access software can provide the sort of performance optimization and security control that DBA's expect without requiring a developer to sacrifice the platform independence of the Java language or the DBMS independence offered by JDBC.

## Case in Point: JetExpress from XDB Systems

The remainder of this chapter is an example of a data access middleware approach that illustrates the sort of considerations that have to be taken into account in order to turn Java developers into solid corporate citizens. XDB's JetExpress, a product that helps Java developers access DB2/MVS databases running on IBM mainframe platforms within an installations performance and security guidelines, is used as a model for the discussion.

DB2/MVS gives DBA's control over data access through the "binding" of an application. In the case of an ordinary COBOL mainframe application, for example, each program is preprocessed before compilation. The SQL statements are segregated into a separate file called a Database Request Module, or DBRM, and the program source code is modified to make direct calls to DB2. The DBRM is submitted to a BIND process that does such things as determining optimal access paths. The result of this BIND process is an Application Plan which describes the "static SQL" it can execute.

DBA's can perform certain optimizations based on the contents of the DBRM and Application Plan. They can make changes to the access path and index usage that affects execution performance, for example.

More importantly, a DBA can control access to the database based on the Application Plan. That is, a user can be given authority to use a particular Application Plan without being given blanket authority to access the databases in the plan. This seemingly subtle distinction is extremely important. Consider the case of a user who is an order entry clerk who uses an order entry application. If the clerk is given access to each database in the order entry application (e.g., the Orders database, the Customer database, the Product database), it becomes possible for the clerk to access those databases using other means. For instance, the clerk can write a Visual Basic application that applies deep discounts to his own purchases; a practice that presumably would be disallowed by the order entry application.

On the other hand, if the clerk is given access to the databases only through the order entry application's Application Plan, he will be able to read and write to those databases only under the control of the order entry application software. This is an important aspect of the security of corporate data.

As it happens, assigning security at the Application Plan level also makes life easier for the DBA. The administrative effort associated with keeping lists of users who have EXECUTE privileges for a particular Application Plan is far easier than maintaining detailed lists of specific database access privileges on a user by user basis.

## The Problem with Dynamic SQL

The good news is that DB2/MVS provides some pretty sophisticated mechanisms for allowing DBA's to optimize application execution and safeguard corporate databases. The bad news is that the way in which JDBC is architected allows few of them to be used. That is because access using JDBC from a Java program typically employs "dynamic SQL." Dynamic SQL is SQL that has not been through the previously described BIND process. In other words, there is no predefined Application Plan to optimize or secure. Instead, at execution time the Java program simply presents whatever SQL its author coded directly to DB2 for processing dynamically.

This has several implications from the standpoints of performance and security. First, the DBA has no Application Plan to optimize, so she must trust the user to have coded efficient queries. Second, because there is no Application Plan, the DBA has to grant specific privileges to the specific databases referenced in the Java application or applet to each potential user. Third, the application will execute less efficiently. While BINDING is to SQL statements what compiling is to a program, dynamic SQL is interpretive. In effect, every time the application runs the equivalent of a BIND takes place.

As you might imagine, these shortcomings make DBA's very reluctant to grant access to DB2/MVS from Java applications and applets. In fact, many installations disallow the processing of dynamic SQL from any source as a matter of policy. Corporate databases are just too important to allow developers using Java (or, for that matter, any ODBC application environments, like Visual Basic or PowerBuilder) unrestricted access.

The obvious solution, then, is to allow the SQL presented to DB2 through JDBC to somehow be bound.

## The JetExpress Approach to Binding SQL

As mentioned earlier, in a typical MVS application development scenario, embedded SQL is extracted from the source application program by means of a precompiler that creates a DBRM file used as input to the BIND process. For Internet and intranet applications this approach is restrictive because such applications tend to include pre-built components, of either the ActiveX or Beans varieties. When a component includes SQL requests, the source may not be available and the precompiler will create a DBRM that is incomplete.

As a result, JetExpress approaches the BIND process for Java applications somewhat differently. Instead of extracting SQL during a precompile step, it is collected as the program executes in a test mode. During testing, a developer executes the Java program with JetExpress's RECORD utility activated. This utility listens for and collects the SQL requests being passed to DB2, creating a "DBR" file, a PC-based equivalent of a DBRM, in which each SQL statement is assigned a SECTION number. At the same time, a small database stored on the Web server (the Bound SQL Accessor database) is built to contain the mappings between specific SQL statements and the associated SECTION numbers.

This activity is shown in Box 1 of figure 8-9.

After the process of recording SQL statements is finished, the .DBR file is used as input to the BIND process. The SQL statements are subsequently bound to the DB2/MVS system. This results in DB2 creating an Application Plan and placing it in the Directory. This function is illustrated in Box 2 of figure 8-9.

At execution time, each time an SQL statement is presented to the middleware database access server by the Java program, the Bound SQL Accessor is consulted to identify the associated SECTION number as determined by the RECORD utility. When found, the SECTION number and host variables are

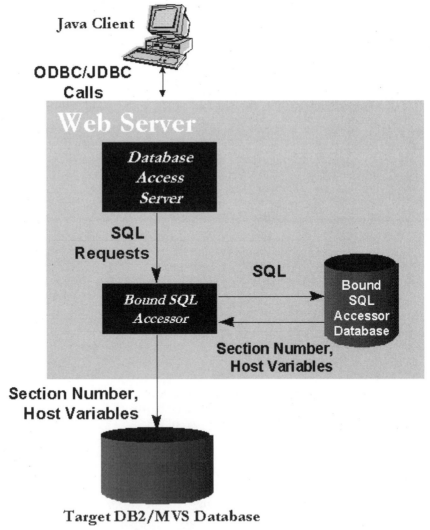

**Figure 8-9.** The static bind process for Java programs.

passed to DB2 in place of the original SQL statement using IBM's Distributed Relational Database Architecture (DRDA).

This example, while it may be a bit complex if you are not familiar with DB2, serves to illustrate how middleware can be used to bridge the gaps between different technologies. In the case of JetExpress:

> •The DB2 environment treats the Java application as though it were a native mainframe application with no modifications to any mainframe software required.
> •The Java applications and applets use JDBC just as they normally would to access any database.
> •The DB2 DBA can perform the same checks and enforce the same rules as for any ordinary mainframe application.
> •The Java developer gains access to the corporate information asset without having to worry about inadvertently compromising it.

In short, the middleware hides the incompatibilities between the access environment (in this case, Java) and the database environment (in this case, DB2/MVS) to enable them to interact in an enterprise setting.

## Author Bio

Dennis Minium, the Director of Product Strategies for XDB Systems, has been active in the research and development of software development tools and methodologies for the past nineteen years. A frequent speaker at industry events, he is responsible for establishing the short- and long-term strategic direction for XDB's growing line of software products with primary focus on the Java environment.

Prior to joining XDB, he led the architecture group responsible for the design of Texas Instruments' Composer product and authored the book *A Guide to Information Engineering Using the IEF: Computer Aided Planning, Analysis and Design*, published in several languages. He also wrote and hosted TI's CASE Satellite Seminar series and has authored several technical papers.

# Using OpenLink for Java Database Connectivity

**Kingsley Idehen**

## Introduction

The meteoric rise of the Internet to the global community it is today has totally eclipsed that of any other technology in the history of computing. Things change so quickly in the world of the Internet that it is now referred to in corporate circles in the same time-frame as that of the canine lifespan. The Internet is the arena where companies can spring up overnight and die just as quickly.

This unique environment of development has given birth to a unique programming language — Java. Java, a product of Sun Microsystems Inc., has been able to address many of the issues that have consistently plagued users and developers alike.

Whether Java lives on, or becomes another victim of corporate hype and fickleness among users and developers, it has laid the groundwork for the future of programming language technologies. It has already proven a fundamental functional requirement for the future of computing — platform independence. We are now at the beginning of an era where executable code can and must no longer rely on operating system and platform specific functionality. An executable compiled on a workstation should run with equal functionality on a Windows 95 PC — with no changes to the code or compiled binary.

Platform independence and connectivity are the new idols and corporate bodies will worship elsewhere at their peril. New programming languages will come and go, but in this new world of enterprise computing, the tenets that Java has introduced will live on for ever, and the world has just got that little bit smaller.

## The Java Language Environment

Java originated as part of a research project to develop advanced software for a wide variety of networked devices and embedded systems. The goal was to develop a small, reliable, portable, distributed, real-time operating environment. When the project started, C++ was the language of choice. But over time the difficulties encountered with C++ grew to the point where the problems could best be addressed by creating an entirely new language environment.

Design and architecture decisions drew from a variety of languages such as Eiffel, SmallTalk, Objective C, and Cedar/Mesa. The result is a language environment that has proven ideal for developing secure, distributed, network-based end-user applications in environments ranging from networked-embedded devices to the World Wide Web and the desktop.

The Java Language Environment is comprised of a number of dynamically linked "packages" that can be downloaded and linked dynamically at runtime. These packages contain the runtime classes that make up the Java programming interface. The interface to the native operating system from the Java Virtual Machine ("VM") is contained within the port of the Java VM to that particular operating system.

Some of the commonly used Java packages are java.awt (Abstract Window Toolkit), java.net (Java Networking), java.io (Java Input/output classes) and java.util (Utility classes).

The Java programming interface itself is being developed further along the lines of API's (Application Programming Interfaces). Some of the APIs that have already been developed and are currently under development are the Media API, Enterprise API and Security API.

## Java Database Connectivity Standard

The Java Database Connectivity Standard (JDBC) is part of the Java Enterprise API. JDBC is an SQL based database access interface. It provides Java Programmers with a uniform interface to a wide range of relational databases, and also provides a common base on which higher level tools and interfaces can be built.

The JDBC API defines classes to represent constructs such as database connections, SQL statements, result sets, and database metadata. JDBC allows a Java-powered program to issue SQL statements and process the results.

In conjunction with JDBC, JavaSoft is releasing an JDBC-ODBC bridge implementation that allows any of the dozens of available ODBC drivers to operate as JDBC drivers. The JDBC-ODBC bridge can run on the server rather than client side using a JDBC driver that translates to a DBMS-independent network protocol.

## JDBC Compared to ODBC

JDBC is the natural evolution of ODBC — ODBC has the same relationship to the 'C' language as JDBC has to Java in providing a standard API for access to data. ODBC, as a standard, is mature and proven, so it seemed sensible to design JDBC around some of the concepts of ODBC, but presenting the interface as a Java 'Package' with a number of embedded classes. The internal structure of the JDBC architecture relates very closely to the internal architecture of the ODBC standard as shown in figures 9-1 thru 9-3:

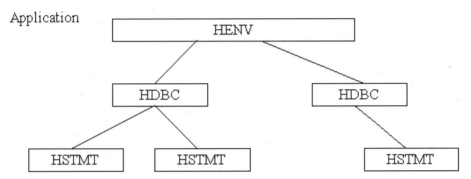

**Figure 9-1.** ODBC handle architecture.

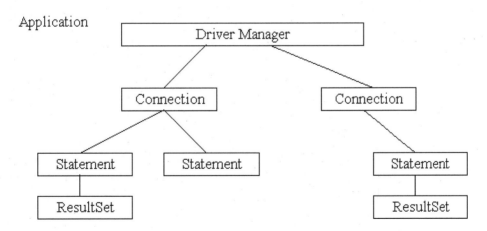

**Figure 9-2.** JDBC object architecture.

|  | JDBC | ODBC |
|---|---|---|
| Published Interface | Java Packages | 'C' function prototypes |
| Internal Architecture | Java Objects | C structures/C++ classes |
| Object Manipulation | Java Objects | Handles |
| Platform Dependency | Independent | Dependent |
| Communications Layer Platform Dependency | Independent | Dependent |
| Communications Layer Datasource Dependency | Independent | Dependent |
| Client code | Java | C/C++ |

[1] Unless the JDBC-ODBC Bridge is being used, in which case the Java application as a whole maintains the same platform dependency as the odbc driver being used.

[2] See Footnote 1, reading database dependency in for platform dependency.

[3] 'Single Tier' drivers are dependent on the database vendors communcations layer, whereas OpenLink 'Multipl' drivers use a database independent communcations layer.

**Figure 9-3.** Differences between JDBC and ODBC.

The other major architectural similarity that is common to both JDBC and ODBC is the use of a driver manager coupled with drivers. With an ODBC driver manager you would use an ODBC driver, and with the JDBC driver manager you would use a JDBC driver. Sun Microsystems has developed a JDBC/ODBC bridge which allows an ODBC driver to be used in place of a JDBC driver.

Where as ODBC is based around a C API, and defines a number of C function calls, JDBC defines a navigational API that is object based — as is Java. ODBC presents handles to its internal data structures to ODBC-enabled applications. This allows applications to manipulate the ODBC data structures and use the ODBC function calls correctly. They also provide an easily understood method of accessing the conceptual ODBC objects that are available —- Environment (HENV), Connection (HDBC) and Statement (HSTMT).

To allocate a Connection handle (HDBC) you first must have successfully allocated a single Environment handle, and must pass this handle to the function responsible for allocating the HDBC. In the same way, you must successfully allocate a connection handle before allocating a statement handle. In reverse, when deallocating ODBC object handles, you must free (drop) all statement handles before freeing the connection handles before freeing the environment handle.

The same concepts hold true for JDBC, except that instead of passing handles you pass the objects themselves. Java takes care of the object pointers.

Both JDBC and ODBC make use of a DriverManager, but these driver managers are in no way similar — you cannot use an ODBC driver with a JDBC driver manager and vice versa. It should also be noted that the above diagrams imply a similarity between the 'HENV' of ODBC and the 'Driver Manager' of JDBC. Although the 'Driver Manager' in ODBC and 'Environment Handle HENV' are normally seen as separate entities, they are in fact closely related. When an ODBC aware application allocates a HENV, this is signaling the ODBC driver manager to get ready for action.

ODBC and JDBC are both based on different language technologies, although they can be used to access the same data sources. The only way to use ODBC with Java is to use the JDBC-ODBC bridge which allows an ODBC driver to be used as a JDBC driver. There is no ODBC-JDBC bridge, nor is there ever likely to be.

## The OpenLink Multi-Tier ODBC Architecture

The OpenLink Multi-Tier Open Database Connectivity Architecture extends the commonly understood concept of an ODBC driver. The more commonly understood definition of ODBC, relating to client/server data sources, is in terms of an 'ODBC Driver.' This ODBC driver, more often than not will be 'data source dependent' in that when you want access to an Ingres database for instance, you go out and buy an 'Ingres ODBC Driver.' The software that you have purchased for your client computer cannot be used for anything more than accessing a particular type of data source, and, more often than not, a particular version of that data source. You have also bought software that is dependent on the availability of a particular version of a particular communications layer, and that can be only used to access the aforementioned data source.

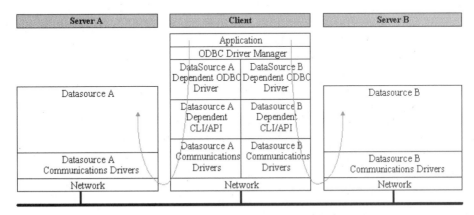

**Figure 9-4.** Single tier architecture to two databases on two servers.

This type of architecture is known as "Single-Tier" architecture. It is defined as an architecture implementing a data source dependent data communications protocol (see figure 9-4).

The OpenLink Multi-Tier Open Database Connectivity Architecture implements generic software at the client side, a generic data communications layer, with all the data source specific software residing on the server (figure 9-5). This means that if you have bought the OpenLink Multi-Tier ODBC software, your client software can be used to access any data source on any accessible server. You only need one client driver and access to a winsock-compliant network. All server data source configuration takes place in a single area of the server making for an easy, trouble-free installation and easily maintainable configuration for data access. License control is maintained at the server on a concurrent connections basis.

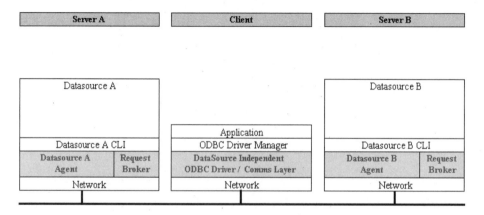

**Figure 9-5.** Multi-Tier ODBC architecture to two data sources on two servers.

Connection from the server side to the datasource is achieved by using a particular datasource 'Agent' and a 'Request Broker' to handle connections, security and licensing. The Database Agent is specific to the datasource, but the Request Broker will handle all agents that conform to the OpenLink Agent API (internal). Once the Request Broker has been satisfied that the connection request is valid, the Broker will spawn the Agent process and the agent will then communicate directly with the Client software.

## The OpenLink JDBC Architecture

The OpenLink JDBC driver architecture is based on the Multi-Tier architecture as described earlier. Generic Java-based client JDBC driver software is provided for the Web server site, which is downloaded when the Java applet or application is initialized. The Web server also implements an OpenLink Request broker, and a generic JDBC Agent. When a valid connection request for JDBC services is received at the Request Broker, the JDBC agent is spawned to handle direct connection between the Java client classes and the data source. The JDBC agent connects to the data source via another OpenLink Database Agent. This Database Agent can either be resident on the same machine as the Web server/JDBC agent (figure 9-6: Embedded server architecture), or on a completely different machine, providing a 3-tiered approach (figure 9-7: Separated-Server architecture). Each machine that utilizes the services of an OpenLink Database Agent must have a Request broker to control the agents.

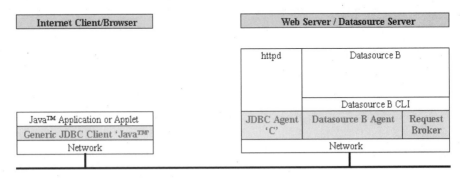

**Figure 9-6.** Embedded server JDBC implementation.

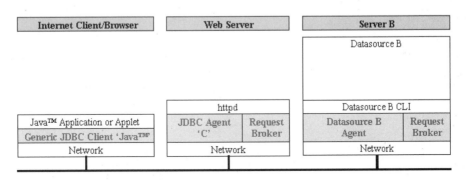

**Figure 9-7.** Separated server JDBC implementation.

The security constraints of the Java programming environment must be considered when implementing this architecture. A Java applet has a limitation in that it can only open a connection to the server that it was downloaded from. This constraint is not placed on Java applications. Thus, it is a requirement for the server to implement the JDBC agent. This cannot in any circumstances be placed on a different server. It is, however, possible to place the Database Agent on any accessible server, as the original Web server becomes responsible for the security of the system as a whole. The JDBC agent then behaves as a data source proxy.

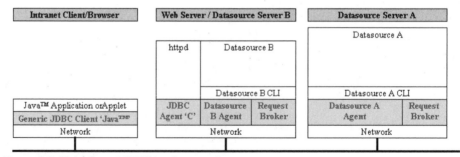

**Figure 9-8.** Multi-Server JDBC implementation.

The Multi-Server architecture, depicted in figure 9-8, outlines an architecture where the embedded server (figure 9-6) and separated server (figure 9-7) implementations are combined into a system that allows the JDBC client software to access two different datasources, one being on the Web server itself, and the other being on a completely different server.

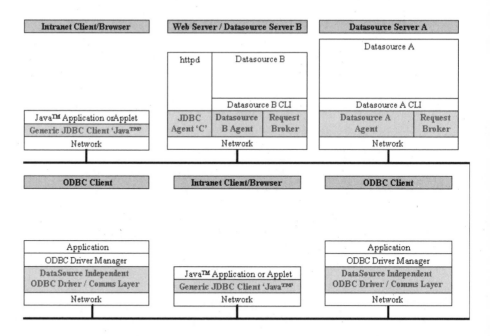

**Figure 9-9.** A Multi-Server Hybrid architecture, where both generic ODBC and JDBC clients are used to access a mixture of differing data sources within an intranet.

## Technical Guide to OpenLink JDBC

One or more JDBC compliant Java applications or applets are instantiated loading the JDBC Driver Manager classes in the process. The Driver Manager loads the appropriate JDBC Driver based on the URL presented by the relevant JDBC compliant application or applet.

OpenLink JDBC requests a JDBC Agent service via the OpenLink Request Broker, typically resident on a server machine. The OpenLink Request Broker in standard OpenLink fashion instantiates or reuses an OpenLink JDBC Agent, based on `Session Rules' depicted in the OpenLink `Session Rules' Book.

The JDBC agent requests Database Agent services via the OpenLink Request Broker. An OpenLink Request Broker instantiates or reuses an OpenLink Database Agent and then binds it to the OpenLink JDBC Agent that requested the service.

The OpenLink Request Broker returns to quiescent mode, while the OpenLink JDBC Driver, JDBC Agent, and Database Agent(s) in unison provide an OpenLink JDBC Session.

OpenLink JDBC URL Explained

| Configuration File Entry | JDBC Connection URL |
|---|---|
| [Accounts] | /DSN=Accounts |
| Host=<hostname> | /HOST=<hostname> |
| ServerType=<type> | /SVT=<type> |
| ServerOptions=<srvOptions> | {None Defined} |
| Database=<dbname> | /DATABASE=<dbname> |
| Options=<dboptions> | /OPTIONS=<dboptions> |
| UserName=<UserID> | /UID=<UserID> |
| Password=<Password> | /PWD=<Password> |
| ReadOnly=<Y|N> | /READONLY=<Y|N> |
| FetchBufferSize=<0-99> | /FBS=<0-99> |

**Figure 9-10.** Data Source Configuration File Section-Keys and OpenLink JDBC connection URL attribute correlation.

The URL for the OpenLink JDBC Driver has the following form (parameters are shown in figurte 9-10):

```
jdbc:openlink://<hostname>[:<port>][/<attribute>=<
value>]...
```

Hostname: The hostname parameter of the URL indicates the IP address or hostname of the machine that provides an OpenLink JDBC Agent service. There is a limitation imposed by the Java security model that states that applets cannot open a socket to any other machine besides the one from which the applet was downloaded. The consequences of this are that if the OpenLink JDBC drivers are being used within an applet, then the only valid value for the 'hostname' parameter is that of the server hostname. This restriction is not imposed on Java applications.

Port: For purposes of class size management and session initialization overhead reduction, the OpenLink JDBC Driver's client components require specific identification of the port number at which the OpenLink Request Broker is listening. The default TCP port for the OpenLink Request Broker is 5000.

The OpenLink 'Session Rules' Book provides for setting Request Broker port ranges via the PortLow and PortHigh section keys located in the '[Protocol TCP]' section of this file. A warning here: you should not assign identical section key-values to both section keys as the OpenLink Database Agents also make use of the port assignments within the ranges designated. The OpenLink Request Broker generally makes use of the lowest port number within the range.

Only the OpenLink Request Broker's port number needs to be specified in the OpenLink JDBC Drivers connection URL.

To determine the Request Broker port number log on to your server machine and then start the OpenLink Request Broker in debug mode.

Depicted below is the screen output that you will see:

```
$ oplrqb -d
OpenLink Request Broker
Version 2.4B (Release 1.5) as of Wed Jul 24 1996.
Compiled for Linux 2.0.0 (i486-linux)
Copyright (C) OpenLink Software.
Registered to OpenLink Internal Use
This is a 5 concurrent users license
oplrqb: using rulebook
/home/openlink/bin/oplrqb.ini
oplrqb: including rulebook jdbc_sv.book
oplrqb: including rulebook generic.book
oplrqb: bound UDP protocol to 127.0.0.1.60001
oplrqb: bound TCP protocol to 127.0.0.1.5000
```

                    The TCP port is 5000 ———-^

OpenLink URL Connection Attributes

Each connection attribute takes the form of a keyword and a value. The keyword and value are separated by an 'equals' sign, and each pair is preceded by a forward-slash

i.e.

```
/DSN=opltest/UID=scott/PWD=tiger
```

In the configuration examples shown below, it will be noted that each connection attribute has an 'INI-file' equivalent. The equivalent is the keyword used when setting up a JDBC data source on the server side.

DSN: DataSource Name. This attribute is an identifier associating an OpenLink JDBC Driver with a source of data, typically resident within an Database Management System. It is safe (on the surface at least) to deal with these values as being identical to ODBC Driver Manager Administered Data Sources in operating environments where an ODBC Driver Manager exists.

Host: This attribute identifies the network alias or IP address of the server machine hosting the OpenLink Request Broker, OpenLink JDBC agent, and OpenLink Database Agents.

SVT: Server Type. This attribute identifies the database type of the data source your OpenLink JDBC Driver will be connecting to, popular examples being Oracle, Informix, Sybase, MS SQL Server, etc.

Database: This attribute identifies the actual database name of a given database type (SVT attribute), typically accessible to JDBC application users via the logical data source name (DSN attribute) of an OpenLink JDBC connection URL.

ServerOptions: This attribute holds key database Session Initialization Parameters specific to the various database engines supported by OpenLink.

Options: This attribute holds database specific Connection Initialization Parameters (values are obtainable from the systems administrators guide of the relevant database used by your organization, OpenLink software provides acceptable defaults ).

FBS: Fetch Buffer Size. This attribute enables the optimization of record retrieval between the JDBC agent and the database agent. Greatest benefit will be seen here when a variation on the Separated-Server architecture is used. The number of rows applied to this attribute indicate the number of records transported over the network in a single network hop. Rows are fetched to the JDBC client software individually.

UID: User ID. This attribute identifies the user-name to be associated with an OpenLink JDBC session.

PWD: This attribute identifies the password of the associated user-name for an OpenLink JDBC session. Visually masking out the values associated with this attribute is the responsibility of the Java Application programmer. The OpenLink 'Session Rules' Book can be used to manage passwords remotely in a secure file accessible to your systems administrator only.

ReadOnly: The accepted values are either Y or N depending on if you want a read-only session or not.

## OpenLink JDBC Connection URL Examples

The two examples below provide examples of OpenLink JDBC connection URLs to an Oracle Database Engine:.

Example 1:

```
jdbc:openlink://localhost/DSN=dsn_oracle/
UID=scott/PWD=tiger
```

Example 2:

```
jdbc:openlink://test.open-
linksw.com:5000/SVT=Oracle
7/DATABASE=ora7/
UID=scott/PWD=tiger
```

Note: The OpenLink Request Broker enables partial JDBC connection URL attributes based on its ability to centrally store and enforce these values enterprise wide.

## Configuring OpenLink JDBC Connection Attributes

In operating environments where Microsoft's ODBC DriverManagers exists, OpenLink JDBC Agents leverage the Data Source Configuration elegance of the ODBC Administrator. As a result the OpenLink JDBC DSN attribute obtains its values directly from the pool of ODBC data sources configured via the ODBC Driver manager. The manner in which this is done is identical in mechanics to that of an ODBC compliant application operating within the same environment.

In operating environments where an ODBC Driver manager interface is unnatural or sporadically implemented, e.g., UNIX, VMS, and to a fair degree OS/2, OpenLink makes use of a text based Data Source Configuration file (located by the environment setting 'UDBCINI') or a special section of the OpenLink 'Session Rules' Book appropriately named '[UDBCINI]' for creating and managing OpenLink Data Sources. OpenLink Data Sources are responsible for linking OpenLink JDBC Drivers with the appropriate source of Attribute values should they not form part of the OpenLink JDBC connection URL, or should they be required for security and management purposes to reside on the server.

The examples below illustrate OpenLink 'Session Rules' Book (oplrqb.ini) or JDBC Agent Rule Book (jdbc.book) settings required for exposing OpenLink Data Sources to JDBC applications and applets.

Example 1: This example points the OpenLink JDBC Agent to an OpenLink Data Source configuration file called 'udbc.ini' located in the current directory (usually /usr/openlink/bin) for OpenLink JDBC Connection URL attribute mapping.

```
[java_client]
Program = jdbc_sv
CommandLine      =      +udbcini
udbc.ini
```

Example 2: This example points the OpenLink JDBC Agent to an '[Environment]' section named "[Environment JDBC]" located in host operating environment variable settings portion of the OpenLink 'Session Rules' Book, the section-key value of 'UDBCINI' instructs the OpenLink JDBC Agent to resolve the location of OpenLink Data Source Configuration file from the environment variable 'UDBCINI' (note: this variable must have been set within the user shell initializing the OpenLink Server components).

```
[Environment JDBC]
UDBCINI = udbc.ini

[java_client]
Program = jdbc_sv
CommandLine = +secure
Environment = JDBC
```

## OpenLink JDBC Connection URL
## Translation Explained

Scenario 1

If the OpenLink JDBC Connection URL contains a '/DSN=Accounts' Attribute, indicating a data source called Accounts. The OpenLink JDBC Agent during initialization looks for a section header called '[Accounts]' in the OpenLink Data Source Configuration file (located via the UDBCINI environment variable setting or configuration file section). Once located all other OpenLink connection URL attributes will be assigned values from section-key values situated within the section named [Accounts].

Scenario 2

If no DSN attribute is present in the OpenLink JDBC connection URL, then the "[Default]" section header within the OpenLink Data Source Configuration file is located and used to locate section-key values ultimately assigned to OpenLink JDBC Connection URL attribute values.

Scenario 3

You can place attributes in the OpenLink JDBC connection URL which by default override the attributes in the OpenLink Data Source Configuration file; on the other hand you can override OpenLink JDBC connection URL attributes originating from remote or local client machines by applying the option +secure as a startup parameter for the OpenLink JDBC Agent via the OpenLink Agent Configuration section of the 'Session Rules' Book (see example above). The OpenLink Request Broker can overrule some or all of the OpenLink JDBC Connection URL Attributes, depending on the rules you wish to enforce globally throughout your enterprise.

OpenLink JDBC Agent CommandLine Options:

+inifile <filename> - Use 'filename' for UDBC configuration
+secure - Ignore all connection attributes from the JDBC client connection URL except the data source name (DSN attributes vales).

## Java to C — The Bridge

In order to interface a platform and data source independent client module to a platform and language dependent data source, there must conceptually be a bridge, or a language mapping interface between the two technologies — the language of the client application, and the language of the data source interface. The data source API is, more often than not, presented as a set of 'C' function prototypes in a similar way to ODBC. For a totally platform and data source independent JDBC architecture, the client must retain no platform or data source dependent code. This means that the JDBC client must be written totally in Java, written to Java connectivity standards, and totally generic in its concept with regard to the underlying data source.

The position of the language bridge must therefore be carefully determined according to the concepts of the more stringent technology. So in order to retain the platform independent concept of Java, this bridging cannot therefore take place on the client, as this would involve bringing platform dependent code into the client environment.

The Java development tools provided by Sun Microsystems Inc. provide utilities and libraries for linking C code to Java, though bridging between C and Java in code limits the platform scope to platforms that both, a) have a valid port of the Java Virtual Machine and, b) can compile and Execute 'C' Code. This is a somewhat limited range of platforms, as the Java Virtual Machine has not yet been ported to the extent of C. This limitation too inhibits the implementation of the Java/C Bridge on the Web server.

The most logical and efficient place for the implementation of a Java/C Bridge in a Distributed Environment is the network itself. Both Java and C have standardized and common access to a networking environment, which permits easy implementation of networking applications between the two technologies. A network packet transmitted between C code and Java code will be handled natively by both technologies. Effectively the Network itself becomes the common link between both C and Java.

Therefore, the OpenLink JDBC Agent is a 'C' based utility that connects the OpenLink Multi-Tier architecture a Java-based JDBC client across a network. Implementing the language mapping across the network also removes the performance and 'overhead' issues that so often pervade software-based language mappings.

This chapter is reprinted with permission from OpenLink. © Copyright OpenLink.

## Author Bio

Kingsley Idehen is President and CEO of OpenLink. OpenLink database engines supported include: Oracle (6/7.x), Informix (5/6/7), Microsoft SQL Server (4/6.x), Sybase (4.2/10.x/11.x),  CA-Ingres (6.4, 7 CA-OpenIngres), Progress (6.3.x/7.x), Unify 2000 (2.4/2.5/3.0), Postgres95,   DB2 (4th Quarter 1996). It works in any operating environment with a working portation of the Java Virtual Machine (VM) or Java enabled Web Browser Support server operating systems include: Windows NT, Solaris (2.x), Linux, HP-UX, AIX, Open/VMS (VAX & AXP), SCO UNIX, Unixware, Digital UNIX, IRIX, DG-UX, Dynix/PTX.

http://www.openlink.co.uk/
E-mail Internet : oplodbc@openlink.co.uk
E-mail Compuserve : 72662,3403
(617) 273 0900

# 10

# A Brief Overview of Java's JDBC Database Access Protocol

## Introduction

Many Java application developers would like to write code that is independent of the particular DBMS or database connectivity mechanism being used, and a DBMS-independent interface is also the fastest way to implement access to the wide variety of DBMSs. So, JavaSoft decided it would be useful to the Java community to define a generic SQL database access framework which provides a uniform interface on top of a variety of different database connectivity modules. This allows programmers to write to a single database interface, enables DBMS-independent Java application development tools and products, and allows database connectivity vendors to provide a variety of different connectivity solutions. JavaSoft's immediate priority has been to define a common low-level API that supports basic SQL functionality. This API is called JDBC. This API in turn allows the development of higher-level database access tools and APIs.

Fortunately JavaSoft didn't need to design a SQL API from scratch. They based their work on the X/Open SQL CLI (Call Level Interface), which is also the basis for Microsoft's ODBC interface. The main task has been defining a natural Java interface to the basic abstractions and concepts defined in the X/Open CLI. It is important that the JDBC API be accepted by database vendors, connectivity vendors, ISVs, and application writers. JavaSoft believes that basing their work on the ODBC abstractions is likely to make this acceptance easier, and technically ODBC seems a good basis for their design.

ODBC is not appropriate for direct use from Java, since it is a C interface; calls from Java to native C code have a number of drawbacks in the security, implementation, robustness, and automatic portability of applications. Thus, JavaSoft has constructed an API that can easily be implemented on top of ODBC short-term, and that can be implemented in other ways longer term.

## A SQL-Level API

JDBC is intended as a "call-level" SQL interface for Java. This means the focus is on executing raw SQL statements and retrieving their results. It is expected that higher-level APIs will be defined as well, and these will probably be implemented on top of this base level. Examples of higher-level APIs are direct transparent mapping of tables to Java classes, semantic tree representations of more general queries, and an embedded SQL syntax for Java.

Database systems support a wide range of SQL syntax and semantics, and they are not consistent with each other on more advanced functionality such as outer joins and stored procedures. Hopefully with time the portion of SQL that is truly standard will expand to include more and more functionality. In the meantime, JavaSoft's position is:

•JDBC allows any query string to be passed through to an underlying DBMS driver, so an application may use as much SQL functionality as desired at the risk of receiving an error on some DBMS's. In fact, an application query need not even be SQL, or it may be a specialized derivative of SQL, e.g., for document or image queries, designed for specific DBMS's.

•In order to pass JDBC compliance tests and to be called "JDBC COMPLIANT" JavaSoft requires that a driver support at least ANSI SQL92 Entry Level. This gives applications that want wide portability a guaranteed least common denominator.

•The JDBC SQL API must be able to be implemented on top of common SQL level APIs, in particular ODBC. This requirement has colored some parts of the specification, notably the handling of OUT parameters and large blobs.

There has been a very strong positive response to Java. To a large extent this seems to be because the language and the standard runtimes are perceived as being consistent, simple, and powerful. JavaSoft's goal is to provide a Java database interface that builds on and reinforces the style and virtues of the existing core Java classes.

## Overview of the Major Interfaces

There are two major sets of interfaces. First there is a JDBC API for application writers. Second there is a lower level  JDBC Driver API.

The JDBC API is expressed as a series of abstract Java interfaces, as shown in figure 10-1, that allow an application programmer to open connections to particular databases, execute SQL statements, and process the results.

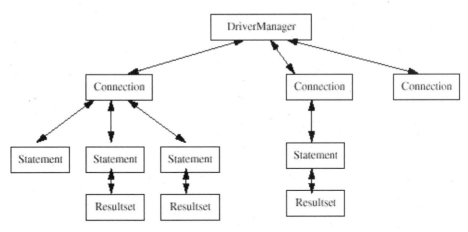

**Figure 10-1.** The JDBC API interfaces.

The most important interfaces are:

- •java.sql.DriverManager which handles loading of drivers and provides support for creating new database connections
- •java.sql.Connection which represents a connection to a particular database
- •java.sql.Statement which acts as a container for executing a SQL statement on a given connection
- •java.sql.ResultSet which controls access to the row results of a given Statement

The java.sql.Statement interface has two important sub-types: java.sql.PreparedStatement for executing a pre-compiled SQL statement, and java.sql.CallableStatement for executing a call to a database stored procedure.

## The JDBC Driver Interface

For the most part the database drivers simply need to provide implementations of the abstract classes provided by the JDBC API. Specifically, each driver must provide implementations of java.sql.Connection, java.sql.State-ment, java.sql.PreparedStatement, java.sql.CallableStatement, and java.sql.ResultSet. In addition, each database driver needs to provide a class which implements the java.sql.Driver interface used by the generic java.sql.DriverManager class when it needs to locate a driver for a particular database URL.

JavaSoft is providing an implementation of JDBC on top of ODBC, shown as the JDBC-ODBC bridge in the figure 10-2. Since JDBC is patterned after

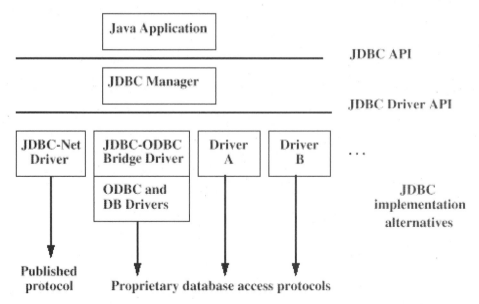

**Figure 10-2.** The JDBC driver interface.

ODBC, this implementation is small and efficient. Another useful driver is one that goes directly to a DBMS-independent network protocol. It would be desirable to publish the protocol to allow multiple server implementations, e.g., on top of ODBC or on specific DBMS's (although there are already products that use a fixed protocol such as this). Only a few optimizations are needed on the client side, e.g., for schema caching and tuple look-ahead, and the JDBC Manager itself is very small and efficient as well. The net result is a very small and fast all-Java client side implementation that speaks to any server speaking the published protocol.

## Database Connections

When you want to access a database, you may obtain a java.sql.Connection object by using the java.sql.DriverManager.getConnection method.

The DriverManager.getConnection method takes a URL string as an argument. The JDBC management layer will attempt to locate a driver that can connect to the database represented by the URL. The JDBC management layer does this by asking each driver in turn if it can connect to the given URL.

Drivers should examine the URL to see if it specifies a sub-protocol that they support, and if so, they should attempt to connect to the specified database. If they succeed in establishing a connection, then they should return an appropriate java.sql.Connection object. From the java.sql.Connection object it is possible to obtain java.sql.Statement, java.sql.Pre-paredStatement, and java.sql.CallableStatement objects that can be used to execute SQL statements.

JavaSoft also permits applications to bypass the JDBC management layer during connection open and explicitly select and use a particular driver.

It may sometimes be the case that several JDBC drivers are capable of connecting to a given URL. For example, when connecting to a given remote database it might be possible to use either a JDBC-ODBC bridge driver, or a JDBC to generic network protocol driver, or to use a driver supplied by the database vendor.

JDBC allows users to specify a driver list by setting a Java property "sql.drivers." If this property is defined, then it should be a colon separated list of driver class names, such as

```
acme.wonder.Driver:foobaz.openNet.Driver:vendor.OurDriver
```

When searching for a driver, JDBC will use the first driver it finds that can successfully connect to the given URL. It will first try to use each of the drivers specified in the sql.drivers list, in the order given. It will then proceed to try to use each loaded driver in the order in which the drivers were loaded. It will skip any drivers which are untrusted code, unless they have been loaded from the same source as the code that is trying to open the connection.

We need to provide a way of naming databases so that application writers can specify which database they wish to connect to.

The JDBC naming mechanism has to have the following properties:

1. Different drivers can use different schemes for naming databases. For example, a JDBC-ODBC bridge driver may support simple ODBC style data source names, whereas a network protocol driver may need to know additional information so it can discover which hostname and port to connect to.

2. If a user downloads an applet that wants to talk to a given database, then we would like to be able to open a database connection without requiring the user to do any system administration chores. Thus, for example, we want to avoid requiring an analogue of the human-administered ODBC data source tables on the client machines. This implies that it should be possible to encode any necessary connection information in the JDBC name.

3. A level of indirection in the JDBC name should be allowed, so that the initial name may be resolved via some network naming system in order to locate the database. This will allow system administrators to avoid specifying particular hosts as part of the JDBC name. However, since there are a number of different network name services (such as NIS, DCE, etc.) we do not wish to mandate that any particular network nameserver is used.

Fortunately the World Wide Web has already standardized on a naming system that supports all of these properties. This is the Uniform Resource Locator

(URL) mechanism. JavaSoft proposes to use URLs for JDBC naming, and merely recommend some conventions for structuring JDBC URLs. The JDBC URL's should be structured as

```
jdbc:<subprotocol>:<subname>
```

where a subprotocol names a particular kind of database connectivity mechanism that may be supported by one or more drivers. The contents and syntax of the subname will depend on the subprotocol. If you are specifying a network address as part of your subname, follow the standard URL naming convention of "//hostname:port/subsubname" for the subname. The sub-subname can have arbitrary internal syntax.

For example, in order to access a database through a JDBC-ODBC bridge, one might use a URL like

```
jdbc:odbc:fred
```

In this example the subprotocol is "odbc" and the subname is a local ODBC data source name "fred." A JDBC-ODBC driver can check for URLs that have subprotocol "odbc" and then use the subname in an ODBC SQLConnect.

If you are using some generic database connectivity protocol "dbnet" to talk to a database listener, you might have a URL like

```
jdbc:dbnet://wombat:356/fred
```

In this example the URL specifies that we should use the "dbnet" protocol to connect to port 356 on host wombat and then present the subsubname "fred" to that port to locate the final database. If you wish to use some network name service to provide a level of indirection in database names, then use the name of the naming service as the subprotocol. So for example one might have a URL like

```
jdbc:dcenaming:accounts-payable
```

In this example, the URL specifies that we should use the local DCE naming service to resolve the database name "accounts-payable" into a more specific name that can be used to connect to the real database. In some situations, it might be appropriate to provide a pseudo driver that performed a name lookup via a network name server and then used the resulting information to locate the real driver and do the real connection open.

In summary, the JDBC URL mechanism is intended to provide a framework so that different drivers can use different naming systems that are appropriate to their needs. Each driver need only understand a single URL naming syntax, and can happily reject any other URLs that it encounters.

JavaSoft will act as an informal registry for JDBC sub-protocol names. Send mail to jdbc@wombat.eng.sun.com to reserve a sub-protocol name.

The "odbc" sub-protocol has been reserved for URLs that specify ODBC style Data Source Names. For this subprotocol we specify a URL syntax that allows arbitrary attribute values to be specified after the data source name. The full odbc subprotocol URL syntax is

```
jdbc:odbc:< data-source-name>
[;< attribute-name>=< attribute-value>]*
Thus valid jdbc:odbc names include:
jdbc:odbc:qeor7
jdbc:odbc:wombat
jdbc:odbc:wombat;CacheSize=20;ExtensionCase=LOWER
jdbc:odbc:qeora;UID=kgh;PWD=fooey
```

When opening a connection, you can pass in a java.util.Properties object. This object is a property set that maps between tag strings and value strings. Two conventional properties are "user" and "password." Particular drivers may specify and use other properties.

In order to allow applets to access databases in a generic way, it is recommended that as much connection information as possible be encoded as part of the URL and that driver writers minimize their use of property sets.

A single application can maintain multiple database connections to one or more databases, using one or more drivers.

The JDBC management layer needs to know which database drivers are available. JDBC provide two ways of doing this. First, when the JDBC java.sql.DriverManager class initializes it will look for a "sql.drivers" property in the system properties. If the property exists it should consist of a colon-separated list of driver class names. Each of the named classes should implement the java.sql.Driver interface. The DriverManager class will attempt to load each named Driver class.

Second, a programmer can explicitly load a driver class using the standard Class.forName method. For example, to load the acme.db.Driver class you might do

```
Class.forName("acme.db.Driver");
```

In both cases it is the responsibility of each newly loaded Driver class to register itself with the DriverManager, using the DriverManager.registerDriver method. This will allow the Driver-Manager to use the driver when it is attempting to make database connections.

For security reasons the JDBC management layer will keep track of which class loader provided which driver and when opening connections it will only use drivers that come from the local filesystem or from the same classloader as the code issuing the getConnection request.

## Passing Parameters and Receiving Results

The result of executing a query Statement is a set of rows that are accessible via a java.sql.ResultSet object. The ResultSet object provides a set of "get" methods that allow access to the various columns of the current row. The ResultSet.next method can be used to move between the rows of the ResultSet.

```
// We're going to execute a SQL statement that will
//return a collection of rows, with column 1 as an int,
//column 2 as a String, and column 3 as an array of
//bytes.
java.sql.Statement stmt = conn.createStatement();
ResultSet r = stmt.executeQuery("SELECT a, b, c FROM
Table1");
while (r.next()) {
     // print the values for the current row.
     int i = r.getInt("a");
     String s = r.getString("b");
     byte b[] = r.getBytes("c");
     System.out.println("ROW = " + i + " " + s + " " +
     b[0]);
}
```

There are two alternative ways of specifying columns. You can either use column indexes (for greater efficiency) or column names (for greater convenience). Thus for example, there is both a getString method that takes a column index and a getString method that takes a column name.

For maximum portability, columns within a row should be read in left-to-right order, and each column should only be read once. This reflects implementation limitations in some underlying database protocols.

The ResultSet.getXXX methods will attempt to convert whatever SQL type was returned by the database to whatever Java type is returned by the getXXX method. For example, it is possible to attempt to read a SQL VARCHAR value as an integer using getInt, but it is not possible to read a SQL FLOAT as a java.sql.Date. If you attempt an illegal conversion, or if a data conversion fails (for example if you did a getInt on a SQL VARCHAR value of "foo"), then a SQLException will be raised.

## Mapping SQL Data Types Into Java

JavaSoft provides reasonable Java mappings for the common SQL data types. JDBC makes sure that we have enough type information so that we can correctly store and retrieve parameters and recover results from SQL statements.

However, there is no particular reason that the Java data type needs to be exactly isomorphic to the SQL data type. For example, since Java has no fixed length arrays, we can represent both fixed length and variable length SQL arrays as variable length Java arrays. Following are the default Java mapping for various common SQL data types. Not all of these types will necessarily be supported by all databases.

| SQL type | Java Type |
|----------|-----------|
| CHAR | String |
| VARCHAR | String |
| LONGVARCHAR | String |
| NUMERIC | java.lang.Bignum |
| DECIMAL | java.lang.Bignum |
| BIT | boolean |
| TINYINT | byte |
| SMALLINT | short |
| INTEGER | int |
| BIGINT | long |
| REAL | float |
| FLOAT | double |
| DOUBLE | double |
| BINARY | byte[ ] |
| VARBINARY | byte[ ] |
| LONGVARBINARY | byte[ ] |
| DATE | java.sql.Date |
| TIME | java.sql.Time |
| TIMESTAMP | java.sql.Timestamp |

Similarly the following shows the reverse mapping from Java types to SQL types:

| Java Type | SQL type |
|-----------|----------|
| String | VARCHAR or LONGVARCHAR |
| java.lang.Bignum | NUMERIC |
| boolean | BIT |
| byte | TINYINT |
| short | SMALLINT |
| int | INTEGER |
| long | BIGINT |
| float | REAL |
| double | DOUBLE |
| byte[ ] | VARBINARY or LONGVARBINARY |
| java.sql.Date | DATE |
| java.sql.Time | TIME |
| java.sql.Timestamp | TIMESTAMP |

## Asynchrony, Threading, and Transactions

Some database APIs, such as ODBC, provide mechanisms for allowing SQL statements to execute asynchronously. This allows an application to start up a database operation in the background, and then handle other work (such as managing a user interface) while waiting for the operation to complete.

Since Java is a multi-threaded environment, there seems no real need to provide support for asynchronous statement execution. Java programmers can easily create a separate thread if they wish to execute statements asynchronously with respect to their main thread.

JavaSoft requires that all operations on all the java.sql objects be multi-thread safe and able to cope correctly with having several threads simultaneously calling the same object.

Some drivers may allow more concurrent execution than others. Developers can assume fully concurrent execution; if the driver requires some form of synchronization, it will provide it. The only difference visible to the developer will be that applications will run with reduced concurrency. For example, two Statements on the same Connection can be executed concurrently and their ResultSets can be processed concurrently (from the perspective of the developer). Some drivers will provide this full concurrency. Others may execute one statement and wait until it completes before sending the next.

One specific use of multi-threading is to cancel a long running statement. This is done by using one thread to execute the statement and another to cancel it with its Statement.cancel( ) method.

New JDBC connections are initially in "auto-commit" mode. This means that each statement is executed as a separate transaction on the database. In order to execute several statements within a single transaction, you must first disable auto-commit by calling Connection.setAutoCommit(false). When auto-commit is disabled, the connection always has an implicit transaction associated with it. You can execute a Connection.commit to complete the transaction or a Connection.roll-back to abort it. The commit or rollback will also start a new implicit transaction.

The exact semantics of transactions and their isolation levels depend on the underlying database. There are methods on java.sql.DatabaseMetaData to learn the current defaults, and on java. sql.Connection to move a newly opened connection to a different isolation level.

## Cursors

JDBC provides simple cursor support. An application can use ResultSet.getCursorName( ) to obtain a cursor associated with the current ResultSet. It can then use this cursor name in positioned update or positioned delete statements.

The cursor will remain valid until the ResultSet or its parent Statement is closed. Note that not all DBMS's support positioned update and delete. The

DatabaseMetaData.supportsPositionedDelete and supportsPositionedUpdate methods can be used to discover whether a particular connection supports these operations. When they are supported, the DBMS/driver must insure that rows selected are properly locked so that positioned updates do not result in update anomalies or other concurrency problems.

## JDBC Interfaces

sql interfaces and classes are listed below:

java.sql.CallableStatement
java.sql.Connection
java.sql.DataTruncation
java.sql.Date
java.sql.Driver
java.sql.DriverManager
java.sql.DriverPropertyInfo
java.sql.PreparedStatement
java.sql.ResultSet
java.sql.SQLException
java.sql.SQLWarning
java.sql.Statement
java.sql.Time
java.sql.Timestamp
java.sql.Types

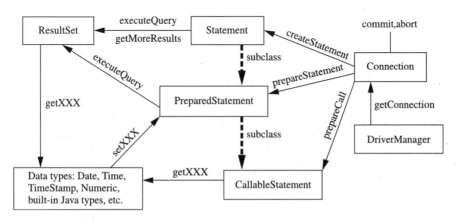

**Figure 10-3.** Relationships between interfaces.

The more important relationships between the interfaces are shown in figure

10-3 (with arrows showing functions and lines showing other methods):

## Dynamic Database Access

Most JDBC programmers will be programming with knowledge of their target database's schema. They can, therefore, use the strongly typed normal JDBC interfaces. However there is also another extremely important class of database access where an application (or an application builder) dynamically discovers the database schema information and uses that information to perform appropriate dynamic data access.

JDBC provides access to a number of different kinds of metadata, describing row results, statement parameters, database properties, etc., etc., JavaSoft originally attempted to provide this information via extra methods on the core JDBC classes such as java.sql.connection and java.sql.ResultSet. However, because of the complexity of the metadata methods and because they are likely to be used by only a small subset of JDBC programmers, JavaSoft decided to split the metadata methods off into two separate Java interfaces.

In general, for each piece of metadata information JavaSoft has attempted to provide a separate JDBC method that takes appropriate arguments and provides an appropriate Java result type. However, when a method such as Connection.getProcedures( ) returns a collection of values, JavaSoft has chosen to use a java.sql.ResultSet to contain the results. The application programmer can then use normal ResultSet methods to iterate over the results.

A number of metadata methods take String search patterns as arguments. These search patterns are the same as for ODBC, where a '_' implies a match of any single character and a '%' implies a match of zero or more characters. For catalog and schema values, a Java empty string matches an 'unnamed' value; and a Java null String causes that search criteria to be ignored.

The java.sql.ResultSetMetaData type provides a number of methods for discovering the types and properties of the columns of a particular java.sql.ResultSet object. The java.sql.DatabaseMetaData interface provides methods for retrieving various metadata associated with a database. This includes enumerating the stored procedures in the database, the tables in the database, the schemas in the database, the valid table types, the valid catalogs, finding information on the columns in tables, access rights on columns, access rights on tables, minimal row identification, and so on.

## Dynamically Typed Data Access

In order to support generic data access, JDBC also provides methods that allow data to be retrieved as generic Java objects. Thus there is a ResultSet.getObject method, a Prepared-Statement.setObject method, and a CallableStatement.getObject method. Note that for each of the two getObject methods you will need to narrow the resulting java.lang.Object object to a specific data type before you can retrieve a value.

Since the Java built-in types such as boolean and int are not subtypes of

Object, we need to use a slightly different mapping from SQL types to Java object types for the  getObject/setObject methods. This mapping is shown below:

| SQL type | Java Object Type |
|---|---|
| CHAR | String |
| VARCHAR | String |
| LONGVARCHAR | String |
| NUMERIC | java.lang.Bignum |
| DECIMAL | java.lang.Bignum |
| BIT | Boolean |
| TINYINT | Integer |
| SMALLINT | Integer |
| INTEGER | Integer |
| BIGINT | Long |
| REAL | Float |
| FLOAT | Double |
| DOUBLE | Double |
| BINARY | byte[ ] |
| VARBINARY | byte[ ] |
| LONGVARBINARY | byte[ ] |
| DATE | java.sql.Date |
| TIME | java.sql.Time |
| TIMESTAMP | java.sql.Timestamp |

The corresponding default mapping from Java Object types to SQL types is show below:

| Java Object | Type SQL type |
|---|---|
| String | VARCHAR or LONGVARCHAR |
| java.lang.Bignum | NUMERIC |
| Boolean | BIT |
| Integer | INTEGER |
| Long | BIGINT |
| Float | REAL |
| Double | DOUBLE |
| byte[ ] | VARBINARY or LONGVARBINARY |
| java.sql.Date | DATE |
| java.sql.Time | TIME |
| java.sql.Timestamp | TIMESTAMP |

Note that it is not possible to send or receive Java input streams using the  getObject  or  setObject  methods. You  must  explicitly  use PreparedStatement.setXXXStream or Result-Set. getXXXStream to transfer a value as a stream.

ResultSet.getObject returns a Java object whose type correspond to the SQL type of the ResultSet column, using the mapping specified above. So, for example, if you have a ResultSet where the "a" column has SQL type CHAR, and the "b" column has SQL type SMALLINT, here are the types returned by some getObject calls:

```
ResultSet rs = stmt.executeQuery("SELECT a, b FROM
foo");
while (rs.next()) {
    Object x = rs.getObject("a"); // gets a String
    Object y = rs.getObject("b"); // gets an Integer
}
```

For PreparedStatement.setObject you can optionally specify a target SQL type. In this case the argument Java Object will first be mapped to its default SQL type, then converted to the specified SQL type, and then sent to the database.

| Java Object | Type SQL type |
| --- | --- |
| String | VARCHAR or LONGVARCHAR |
| java.lang.Bignum | NUMERIC |
| Boolean | BIT |
| Integer | INTEGER |
| Long | BIGINT |
| Float | REAL |
| Double | DOUBLE |
| byte[ ] | VARBINARY or LONGVARBINARY |
| java.sql.Date | DATE |
| java.sql.Time | TIME |
| java.sql.Timestamp | TIMESTAMP |

Alternatively you can omit the target SQL type, in which case the given Java Object will simply get mapped to its default SQL type and then be sent to the database.

## Example JDBC Programs

### Using SELECT

```
import java.net.URL;
import java.sql.*;

class Select {
```

```
public static void main(String argv[]) {
  try {
  // Create a URL specifying an ODBC data source
  String url = "jdbc:odbc:wombat";

  // Connect to the database at that URL.
  Connection con =
  DriverManager.getConnection(url, "kgh", "");

  // Execute a SELECT statement
  Statement stmt = con.createStatement();
  ResultSet rs = stmt.executeQuery("SELECT a,
  b, c, d, key FROM Table1");

  // Step through the result rows.
  System.out.println("Got results:");
  while (rs.next()) {
    // get the values from the current row:
    int a = rs.getInt(1);
    Bignum b = rs.getBignum(2);
    char c[] = rs.getString(3).tocharArray();
    boolean d = rs.getBoolean(4);
    String key = rs.getString(5);

    // Now print out the results:
    System.out.print(" key=" + key);
    System.out.print(" a=" + a);
    System.out.print(" b=" + b);
    System.out.print(" c=");
    for (int i = 0; i < c.length; i++) {
      System.out.print(c[i]);
    }
    System.out.print(" d=" + d);
    System.out.print("\n");
  }
  stmt.close();
  con.close();
} catch (java.lang.Exception ex) {
  ex.printStackTrace();
                    }
                  }
              }
```

## Using UPDATE

```java
// Update a couple of rows in a database.
import java.net.URL;
import java.sql.*;

class Update {

    public static void main(String argv[]) {
        try {
        // Create a URL specifying an ODBC data source name.
        String url = "jdbc:odbc:wombat";

         // Connect to the database at that URL.
        Connection con = DriverManager.getConnection
        (url, "kgh","");

        // Create a prepared statement to update the "a" field of a
        // row in the "Table1" table.
        // The prepared statement takes two parameters.
        PreparedStatement stmt = con.prepareStatement(
                "UPDATE Table1 SET a = ? WHERE key = ?");

         // First use the prepared statement to update
         // the "count" row to 34.
         stmt.setInt(1, 34);
         stmt.setString(2, "count");
         stmt.executeUpdate();
         System.out.println("Updated \"count\" row OK.");

         // Now use the same prepared statement to update the
         // "mirror" field.
         // We rebind parameter 2, but reuse the other parameter.
         stmt.setString(2, "mirror");
         stmt.executeUpdate();
         System.out.println("Updated \"mirror\" row OK.");

         stmt.close();
         con.close();

    } catch (java.lang.Exception ex) {
         ex.printStackTrace();
    }
  }
}
```

## JDBC Downloadables

Users of JDK 1.0.2 can add support for JDBC by installing the JDBC 1.22. The functionality of this version is dentical to that of JDK 1.1 with the exception that java.math.BigDecimal precision is restricted to 18 digits.

A recent change to JDK 1.1 has resulted in a change to JDBC. The java.lang.Bignum class has been replaced with the combination of the java.math.BigDecimal and java.math.BigInteger classes. See the JDBC 1.2 release notes included in the distribution for more details. Drivers written for JDBC 1.1 will not work with this release. Contact your driver provider for a JDK 1.1 compatible version.

Download JDBC 1.22 as a compressed tar file or a zip file. This includes the .java and .html files for the API and also the .class files for the driver manager. Note that this does not include any database drivers.

> ftp://splash.javasoft.com/pub/jdbc-0122.tar.Z
> or
> ftp://splash.javasoft.com/pub/jdbc-0122.zip

Download the JDBC 1.2 API Documentation Part 1 as a postscript file or an acrobat file. This contains the JDBC interfaces in the documentation above.

> ftp://splash.javasoft.com/pub/jdbc-spec-0120.ps
> or
> ftp://splash.javasoft.com/pub/jdbc-spec-0120.pdf

Download the JDBC 1.2 API Documentation Part 2 as a postscript file or an acrobat file. This contains the JDBC classes and exceptions in the documentation above.

> ftp://splash.javasoft.com/pub/jdbc-api-1-0120.ps
> or
> ftp://splash.javasoft.com/pub/jdbc-api-1-0120.pdf

## The JDBC-ODBC Bridge Driver

The bridge driver translates JDBC method calls into ODBC function calls. It allows JDBC to leverage the database connectivity provided by the existing array of ODBC drivers. JDBC is designed to be efficiently implementable on ODBC, so the JDBC-ODBC bridge is the best way to use ODBC from Java. It is a joint development of JavaSoft and Intersolv.

If possible, use a Pure Java JDBC driver instead of the Bridge and an ODBC driver. This completely eliminates the client configuration required by ODBC. It also eliminates the potential that the Java VM could be corrupted by an error in the native code brought in by the Bridge (i.e., the Bridge native library, the

ODBC driver manager library, the ODBC driver library and the database client library).

The Bridge does not work with Microsoft's J++ (J++ uses a non-standard native calling convention). Use JavaSoft's JDK or Symantec's Cafe instead.

Download the Solaris JDBC-ODBC Bridge (1.2001) or the NT/Win95 JDBC-ODBC Bridge (1.2001). This is a beta version compatible with JDBC 1.20.

ftp://splash.javasoft.com/pub/jdbc-odbc-12001.tar.Z

# 11

# Sybase's web.sql

## Introduction

Not to be outdone by the competition, Sybase has developed its own middle-ware product that connects its own RDBMS to the Web. web.sql is a practical solution for those of you who are already on the Sybase track. The last time I looked the product was priced at $695. A 90 day free evaluation can be down-loaded from http://www.sybase.com/products/internet/websql/download.html. Make sure you read the frequently asked questions file (FAQ) at http://www.sybase.com/products/internet/websql/faq.html.

With Sybase web.sql, developers can insert database instructions such as SQL statements and Perl scripts into the text of HTML pages. Whenever the page is requested, these database queries are executed and the results are returned to the Web browser as pure HTML text. Developers can write Web pages that automatically generate personalized content for each user based on the user's preferences or previous behavior.

Sybase web.sql enables you to target specific Web users by generating high-ly personalized promotional and customer service materials. Integrating the Sybase Open Client technology, web.sql allows data from any of your data sources to be dynamically inserted into your Web pages, allowing you to make your Web pages unique for each user.

Sybase web.sql also represents a major innovation in database performance. Since it is directly linked with the Web server as shown in figure 11-1, web.sql is designed to support in-line scripting and scripting calls rather than the sep-arate scripting that is required for Common Gateway Interface (CGI) scripts. The result is dramatically improved database access and response time.

**Figure 11-1.** web.sql connects directly to the Web server.

web.sql also integrates perfectly into the Sybase enterprise architecture, with built-in capabilities to access:

> <u>Sybase IQ</u>, which delivers highly sophisticated data analysis features;
> <u>Replication Server</u>, Sybase's real-time replication engine;
> <u>SQL Server</u> support on massively parallel systems; and
> <u>Enterprise CONNECT</u>, which provides access to multiple data sources.

Sybase web.sql will run on Sun Solaris from Sun Microsystems, Microsoft Windows NT for Intel, IRIX from Silicon Graphics, Inc. and HP-UX from Hewlett Packard.

In London in the UK, the WebLink Group of Lombard Document Systems Ltd. (http://www.lombard-docsys.com/weblink/) utilizes the Sybase web.sql product to provide powerful Web-based document management features for the London Wandsworth Borough Council (http://www.wandsworth.gov.uk/)

They took the Image-Gen document management system, based around a Sybase database which holds images of current planning applications and decisions, and put it on the Web. The interface between the Web server and the Sybase database is web.sql as shown in figure 11-2.

Lombard believes that this is the first Sybase database in the UK to be directly interrogable on the Internet and also the first relational document management system to be placed directly on the Internet in the UK.

The WebLink Group of Lombard Document Systems Ltd. provides services in the following 3 key areas:

1. Provide Web-based document management systems
2. Provide services to integrate existing Sybase databases on Intranets
3. Provide services to place existing databases on the Internet and imple
   ment charging mechanisms if necessary.

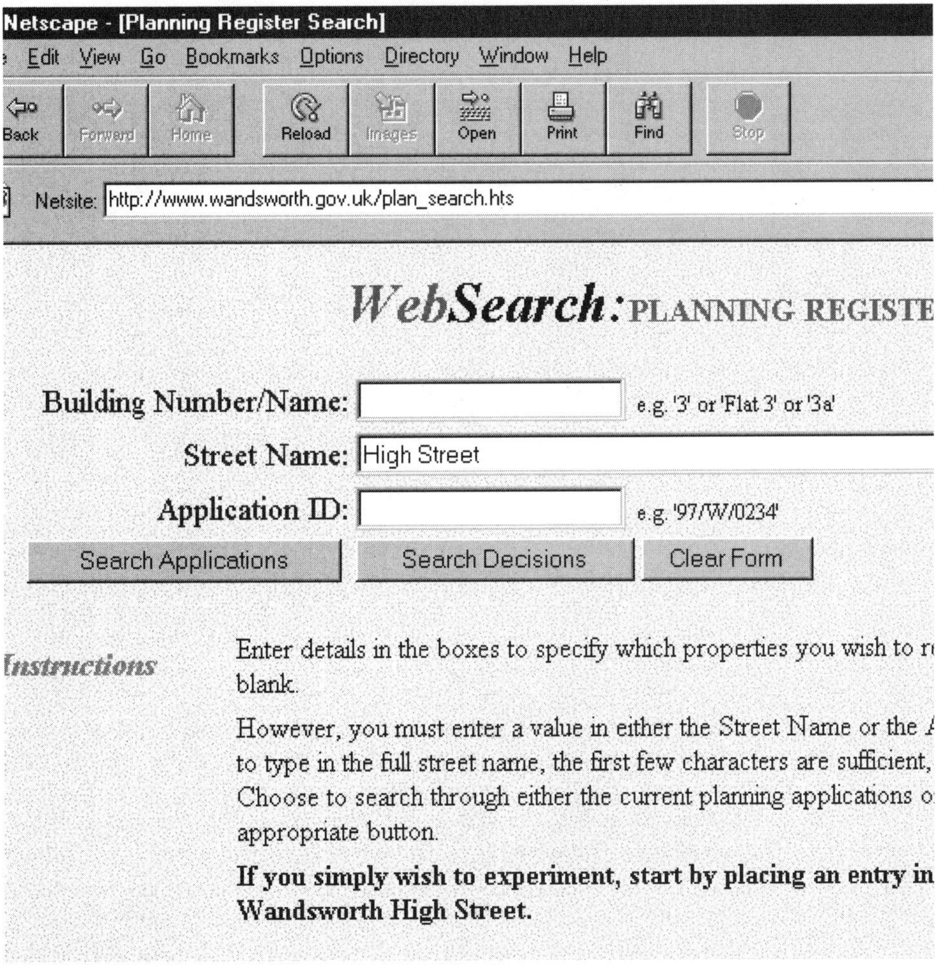

**Netscape - [Planning Register Search]**

Edit  View  Go  Bookmarks  Options  Directory  Window  Help

Back  Forward  Home  Reload  Images  Open  Print  Find  Stop

Netsite: http://www.wandsworth.gov.uk/plan_search.hts

*WebSearch:*PLANNING REGISTE

**Building Number/Name:** [                    ]   e.g. '3' or 'Flat 3' or '3a'

**Street Name:** [High Street]

**Application ID:** [                    ]   e.g. '97/W/0234'

[ Search Applications ]   [ Search Decisions ]   [ Clear Form ]

*Instructions*   Enter details in the boxes to specify which properties you wish to r
blank.

However, you must enter a value in either the Street Name or the /
to type in the full street name, the first few characters are sufficient,
Choose to search through either the current planning applications o
appropriate button.

**If you simply wish to experiment, start by placing an entry in
Wandsworth High Street.**

**Figure 11-2.** web.sql in action.

The people using web.sql in the WebLink Group claim that it is a powerful
product which allows them to develop applications much more quickly than
with other tools. They especially like the tight integration of the Perl scripting
language, which gives them very powerful string manipulation functionality.
Another favored feature is web.sql's ability to easily integrate both Sybase SQL
Server data and non-Sybase data sources.

## Sybase web.sql Overview

Sybase web.sql provides easy access to relational databases from the World Wide Web and allows you to dynamically generate customized Hypertext Markup Language (HTML) documents.

With web.sql extending your Web server, you can insert database instructions such as SQL statements and Perl scripts into the text of HTML pages. When a client browser requests these pages, web.sql runs the scripts and the resulting output is interpolated into the file.

web.sql recognizes two different file extensions: .hts and .pl. When your files have an .hts file extension, the client browser receives only pure HTML output, since the extensions supported by web.sql are processed on the server side.

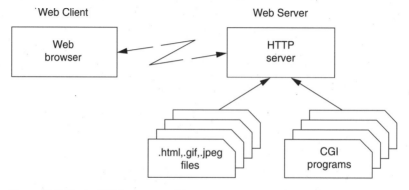

**Figure 11-3.** Typical Web server architecture.

However, if you want the client browser to receive other document types, such as .gif files, then you specify the content type of the document in the .pl file before sending the data to the browser.

Figure 11-3 shows the typical Web server architecture. The Web browser requests pages from the Web server by specifying a Universal Resource Locator (URL). The HTTP server translates this URL into a pathname for a file on the server's host machine. If the file is an .html, .gif, .jpeg, or another file type that the web server understands, the HTTP server sends the file directly to the browser. If the file is a program residing in an authorized directory, the HTTP server executes the program according to the Common Gateway Interface (CGI) and sends the output of the program to the Web browser.

Figure 11-4 shows the architecture of a Web server with web.sql. The Web server handles requests for simple HTML files just as it did in Figure 11-3. However, when a browser requests a URL that translates to an .hts (HyperText Sybase) file or a .pl (Perl) file (that is, a file with only Perl statements and no HTML), the HTTP server passes the request to the web.sql program.

The web.sql program reads the specified HTS file, processes the database

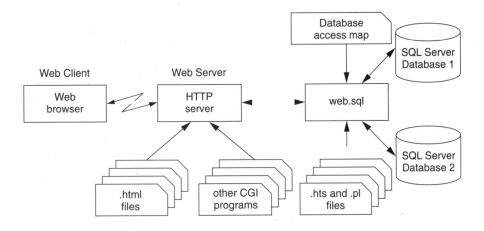

**Figure 11-4.** Web Server Architecture with web.sql.

and Perl requests contained in that file, and then composes HTML output for the HTTP server to pass to the browser.

### Using SQL in HTS Files

As discussed, in HyperText Sybase (HTS) File Format, you can include Transact-SQL statements in an HTS file by enclosing them between a set of <SYB> and </SYB> tags. To identify the block as Transact-SQL statements, the opening <SYB> tag must include the attribute TYPE=SQL.

The example below, which assumes that a database connection to the pubs2 database has been defined, shows how to include a simple select statement in an HTS file:

```
<SYB TYPE=SQL>
    select * from publishers
</SYB>
```

In this example, when a client browser requests the HTS file containing this code, the web.sql program sends the request to a SQL Server. The SQL Server evaluates the select statement and replaces the <SYB> block with the select output-in HTML format—in the HTML stream that it sends to the HTTP server. The client browser never actually sees the SQL statement that produced the output.

You can include multiple SQL statements in a single <SYB> block. You can also include multiple <SYB> blocks in a single HTS file, and even intersperse Perl <SYB> blocks with SQL <SYB> blocks. However, you cannot include both SQL statements and Perl statements within the same <SYB> block.

Querying a Database Using SQL

From within an HTS file you can use Transact-SQL statements to perform database queries. web.sql converts the results into a table in HTML 3.0 format. For example, the following simple select statement returns an HTML table containing the results of the query:

```
<SYB TYPE=SQL>
    select title, price
    from pubs2..titles
    where type = "business"
</SYB>
```

| title | price |
|---|---|
| The Busy Executive's Database Guide | 19.99 |
| Cooking with Computers: Surreptitious Balance Sheets | 11.95 |
| You Can Combat Computer Stress! | 2.99 |
| Straight Talk About Computers | 19.99 |

**Figure 11-5.** Example Table produced by a SQL select statement in an HTS File

The results are formatted into an HTML table as shown in figure 11-5.

A query returns an unlimited number of rows. To limit the number of rows returned as a result of a query, you call the ct_options routine with the appropriate settings from a Perl <SYB> block preceding your SQL <SYB> block. For example, to set the maximum number of rows to 200:

```
<SYB TYPE=PERL>
   ct_options($ws_db, CS_SET, CS_OPT_ROWCOUNT,
   200, CS_INT_TYPE);
</SYB>
<SYB TYPE=SQL>
   select * from hugetable
</SYB>
```

Performing Other Database Actions Using SQL

In addition to using the select command to query a database, you can use any other SQL command in an HTS file. As long as the database user for the HTS file (as specified in the web.sql database access map) has proper permission, the user can insert, delete, and modify rows, create tables, execute stored procedures, and so on.

If the SQL commands you execute in a <SYB> block do not produce row output, then the <SYB> block produces no output in the resulting HTML stream that web.sql sends to the HTTP server. In particular, web.sql does not print the status of commands such as insert, update, or delete.

For example, the following <SYB> block inserts a row into the publishers table of the pubs2 database:

```
<SYB TYPE=SQL>
     insert into pubs2..publishers
     values ("1622", "Jardin, Inc.", "Camden",
     "NJ")
</SYB>
```

As another example, the following block increases the price of all titles in the pubs2 database by 10%:

```
<SYB TYPE=SQL>
     update pubs2..titles
     set price = price * 1.1
</SYB>
```

When using the use statement, as in the example below, you must place the use statement in a separate <SYB TYPE=SQL> block preceding the SQL statements you want it to affect. The database you specify in the use statement is then in effect until the end of the HTS file or until the next use statement.

The following example includes a use statement so that it properly affects the SQL statements following it:

```
<HTML>
<HEAD>
<TITLE>Display All Titles</TITLE>
</HEAD>
<BODY>
<H1>Display All Titles</H1>
<SYB TYPE=SQL>
     use pubs2
</SYB>
<SYB TYPE=SQL>
     select * from titles
</SYB>
</BODY>
</HTML>
```

## Using Perl Variables and Form Data in HTS Files

web.sql allows you to define variables within a Perl <SYB> block and then use the value of those variables anywhere in your file. Also, web.sql automatically defines and sets some variables based on any form data passed to the HTS file.

In an HTS file, web.sql interprets any string preceded by a dollar sign ($) as a global Perl variable, even if that string appears outside of a Perl <SYB>

block. You can assign values to variables in a Perl <SYB> block and then use them later in your file.

The code below describes the syntax for accessing Perl variables from "plain" HTML and SQL <SYB> blocks. Note that web.sql supports only scalar values outside of Perl <SYB> blocks; you cannot access an entire array at once outside of a Perl <SYB> block.

| Format | Meaning |
| --- | --- |
| $foo or ${foo} | Scalar variable named "foo" |
| $values[2] | Third scalar element of array named "values" (arrays start with 0) |
| $assoc{"foo"} | Scalar element named "foo" of associative array named "assoc" |

The following example uses the value of a Perl variable in the HTML portion of an HTS file. Notice that the variable is assigned within a Perl <SYB> block but is referenced directly in the HTML code.

```
<HTML>
<BODY>
This example shows how to reference a Perl variable within HTML text in
Sybase web.sql.  Any Perl variable may be referenced in HTML text in an HTS
(web.sql) file, and the variable's value will be substituted into the text
before the document is sent to the browser.
<P><HR>

<SYB TYPE=PERL>
    # Assign the system date/time to a variable
    require "ctime.pl";
    $today = &ctime(time);
</SYB>

<STRONG>Today is: ${today}</STRONG>
<P>
</BODY>
</HTML>
```

## Accessing HTML Form Data in HTS Files

web.sql automatically parses HTML form data passed to the HTS file and assigns the values to Perl variables. (web.sql supports both the GET and POST methods for passing HTML form data.) You can then use these variables in your SQL statements. Variables can greatly simplify creating forms for database interaction.

The following code lists the predefined variables that web.sql provides. The format "$foo" is the simplest for use in a SQL statement; the other formats are more useful in Perl blocks where you can use a loop to process all the array values.

| Format | Meaning |
|--------|---------|
| $foo | The value of the form input field named "foo" if there is a single form input with this name. |
| @foo | Array of values of the form input fields named "foo" if there are multiple fields with that name. |
| %ws_form | Associative array of all form input fields and their associated values. |
| $ws_form{"foo"} | The value of the form input field named "foo." In the case of multiple input fields with the same NAME attribute, the value is the concatenation of all the values, separated by null characters. |
| %ws_multiple | An associative array indicating multiple form input fields with the same name. |

If $ws_multiple{"foo"} is true, then @foo is defined, and $ws_form{"foo"} contains the concatenation of all the values for the form input field "foo," separated by null characters. If $ws_multiple{"foo"} is false, then $foo is defined, and "foo" is a single-valued form input field name. $ws_multiple{"foo"} 1 if more than one field named foo, else 0.

As an example of using the Perl HTML form variables, consider a simple form allowing a user to search for stores by state. The following HTML file, stores.hts, displays a text field for the user to enter a state:

```
<HTML>
<BODY>
<H2>Search for a store by state</H2>
<FORM ACTION=stores.hts METHOD=POST>
Enter two-letter state abbreviation: <INPUT NAME=state>
<P>
<INPUT TYPE=SUBMIT VALUE=Search>
</FORM>
</BODY>
</HTML>
```

The ACTION attribute of the <FORM> tag causes the browser to send the form results to the server for the URL of stores.hts when the user clicks the Search button. The following HTS file, stores.hts, could then obtain the state name and use it in a select statement as shown below:

```
<HTML>
<BODY>
<H1>Stores</H1>
```

```
Stores found in $state:<P>
<SYB TYPE=SQL>
    select stor_name, stor_address, city, state
    from pubs2..stores
    where state = upper("$state")
    order by stor_name
</SYB>
</BODY>
</HTML>
```

The web.sql program can be used to return dynamic HTML pages to the browser with the help of the HTS file. web.sql can run a Perl script that returns text, pictures, sounds, movies, or other data that the Web browser can display or pass to a helper application. The Perl script can interact with a database just as an HTS file can. For example, you could use a Perl script to retrieve a picture from a database.

There are two versions of the web.sql program available: CGI and NSAPI (Netscape Server Application Programming Interface). In the CGI version web.sql runs as a CGI program. The HTTP server runs the program every time it receives a request for an HTS file.

On UNIX platforms, the NSAPI version of the web.sql program is linked directly into the Netscape HTTP server, which eliminates the overhead that results from starting the web.sql processor for every HTS or Perl request. This high-performance version also allows the web.sql program to cache database connections, further reducing overhead. It should be noted that the connection-caching feature is not available for the NT version of web.sql.

For more information about the differences between the Netscape Server API and the Common Gateway Interface, see the information provided by Netscape at http://home.netscape.com/newsref/std/nsapi_vs_cgi.html.

### HyperText Sybase (HTS) File Format

The HTS file format is an extension of the standard HTML format. You can include anything in an HTS file that you could in an HTML file. You can also include HTML extensions, such as Java or JavaScript (also known as LiveScript) tags. The web.sql program ignores these tags and passes them to the HTTP server.

HTS files support all HTML 3.0 tags and one additional tag, <SYB>, to provide for the additional web.sql functionality. The web.sql program interprets all lines between a <SYB> tag and its corresponding </SYB> tag as either Transact-SQL statements or Perl code. It inserts the output of those statements into the HTML stream that it sends to the HTTP server.

The <SYB> tag has one optional attribute, TYPE. Including "TYPE=SQL" indicates that the <SYB> block contains only Transact-SQL statements, whereas "TYPE=PERL" indicates that the <SYB> block contains Perl statements. (The Perl statements may contain function calls that execute Transact-SQL statements.) If you do not include a TYPE attribute, the web.sql processor assumes that the <SYB> block contains Perl statements.

The HTS file format returns only HTML content-type output. However, if you want to return output other than the HTML content-type, you need to use a Perl file (.pl) and specify the content type using ws_content_type( ). For example, in a Perl file called foo.pl, you could specify the file content as image/gif then print the file:

```
ws_content_type("image/gif")
print 'cat foo.gif';
```

The following listing shows a simple example of an HTS file. When a browser requests this file, the web.sql processor executes the lines appearing between the <SYB> and </SYB> tags, which fetch the current time and date on the server and print the results to standard output along with some HTML tags. The web.sql program executes the code within the <SYB> blocks and inserts the output into the HTML stream that it sends to the HTTP server.

```
<HTML>
<HEAD>
<TITLE>Sybase web.sql Perl Example</TITLE>
</HEAD>
<BODY>
<H2><CENTER> Perl Example</CENTER></H2>
```

This example shows how to include Perl constructs in an HTML document with Sybase web.sql. The example prints out the date and time on the machine by having Perl call a function that returns this information.

```
<P><HR>

<SYB TYPE=PERL>
    require "ctime.pl";
    print "<P>";
    print "Date: ", "<STRONG>", &ctime(time), "</STRONG>";
    print "<P>";
</SYB>
</BODY>
</HTML>
```

The resulting HTML file sent to the browser is

```
<HTML>
<HEAD>
<TITLE>Sybase web.sql  Perl Example</TITLE>
```

```
</HEAD><BODY>
<H2><CENTER> Perl Example</CENTER></H2>
This example shows how to include Perl constructs in an HTML document with
Sybase web.sql. The example prints out the date and time on the machine by
having Perl call  a function that returns this information.
<P><HR>
Date: <STRONG> Thu Feb 29 11:47:08 US/Pacific 1996 </STRONG>
<P>
<HR>
</BODY>
</HTML>
```

## Accessing HTS Files

You access HTS files through a Web browser using URLs, just as you would any other Web files. Open the web.sql welcome page by using one of the following platform-dependent URLs:

If you are using the NSAPI version of web.sql on a UNIX platform:

```
http://<servername>/<websql.dir>/welcome.hts
```

<servername> is the IP address (hostname) and the port number of the Web server,
<websql.dir> is the path to the web.sql subdirectory in the Web server's document root directory, and welcome.hts is the name of the HTS file that  welcomes you to Sybase web.sql.

If you are using the static (high-performance) CGI version of web.sql on a UNIX platform:

```
http://<servername>/<cgi-name>/ws.exe/<websql.dir>/welcome.hts
```

<servername> is the IP address (hostname) and the port number of the Web server,
<cgi-name> is the name of your Web server's CGI script directory, ws.exe is the name of the web.sql CGI program,
<websql.dir> is the path to the web.sql subdirectory in the Web server's document root directory, and welcome.hts is the name of the HTS file that welcomes you to Sybase web.sql.

If you are using the shared-library CGI version of web.sql on a UNIX platform:

```
http://<servername>/<cgi-name>/websql/<websql.dir>/welcome.hts
```

<servername> is the IP address (hostname) and the port number of the Web server,

<cgi-name> is the name of your  Web server's CGI script directory, websql is
the name of the web.sql CGI program,
<websql.dir> is the path to the web.sql subdirectory in the Web server's docu-
ment root directory, and welcome.hts is the name of the HTS file that welcomes you to Sybase web.sql.

If you are using the NSAPI version of web.sql on the NT platform:

```
http://<servername>/<websql>/welcome.hts
```

<servername> is the IP address (hostname) and the port number of the Web
server,
<websql> is the path to the web.sql subdirectory in the Web server's document
root directory, and welcome.hts is the name of the HTS file that welcomes you
to Sybase web.sql.

If you are using the CGI version of web.sql on the NT platform:

```
http://<servername>/<cgi-name>/ws.exe/<websql>/welcome.hts
```

<servername> is the IP address (hostname) and the port number of the Web
server,
<cgi-name> is the name of your Web server's CGI script directory, ws.exe is the
name of the web.sql CGI program,
<websql> is the path to the web.sql subdirectory in the Web server's document
root directory, and welcome.hts is the name of the HTS file that welcomes you
to Sybase web.sql.

## Using Perl in HTS Files

As discussed, you can include a Perl script in an HTS file by enclosing it
between a set of <SYB> and </SYB> tags. You can indicate that a <SYB> block
contains a Perl script by including the attribute "TYPE=PERL" in the opening
<SYB> tag; however, if you omit a TYPE attribute, the web.sql program
assumes that the block contains a Perl script. The following example shows
you how to include a simple Perl script in an HTS file:

```
<SYB TYPE=PERL>
require "ctime.pl";
print "<P>";
print "Date: ", "<STRONG>", &ctime(time), "</STRONG>\n";
print "<P>";
</SYB>
```

In this example, when a client browser requests the HTS file containing this
code, the web.sql program evaluates the Perl script and replaces the <SYB>

block with the printed output in the HTML stream that it sends to the HTTP server. The client browser never sees the Perl script that produced the output.

Note that in a Perl script, you must print anything that you want to include in the final HTML stream web.sql sends to the client browser. Also note that you can include HTML tags in the Perl output. You can use these tags to format the appearance of your output.

You can include multiple <SYB> blocks in a single HTS file. You can also intersperse SQL <SYB> blocks with Perl <SYB> blocks. You can use Perl variables in a SQL block. However, you cannot include both SQL statements and Perl statements within the same <SYB> block.

### APIs —Using Perl Variables and Form Data in HTS Files

web.sql allows you to define variables within a Perl <SYB> block and then use the value of those variables afterwards in your file. Also, web.sql automatically defines and sets some variables based on form data passed to the HTS file.

web.sql includes two Perl application programming interfaces (APIs) for database access: the web.sql "convenience" API and the web.sql Client-Library API. If you are new to Sybase Open Client, you may want to use the web.sql convenience API; it requires less programming.

All convenience functions are prefixed with "ws_". All Client-Library functions are prefixed with "ct_."

Use the web.sql convenience API to automatically generate HTML tables of the data returned by the SQL server. Use the Client-Library API to manipulate the data returned by the server on a row-by-row basis. The following sections describe the web.sql convenience and Client-Library APIs.

The web.sql convenience API provides a simple set of routines for accomplishing the most common tasks in an HTS file. You can use these routines individually to perform most database interaction, or you can combine them with routines described in Using the web.sql Client-Library API.

The following routines are made available by the convenience API.

| Function | Description |
| --- | --- |
| ws_connect | Connects to a SQL server and returns a connection handle. |
| ws_content_type | Sets the content type for the data returned by a .pl file. |
| ws_error | Prints an error message and an optional string, and terminates processing of the current page. |
| ws_fetch_rows | Fetches and prints rows returned by a call to ct_sql. |
| ws_print | Prints a string, expanding Perl variable references. |
| ws_sql | Executes one or more SQL commands and prints the results. |
| ws_rpc | Executes a stored and registered procedure, updates arguments, and prints the results. |

Sybase provides detailed documentation on the specifics of using this API, which is beyond the introductory scope of this chapter.

### Returning Non-HTML Data with web.sql

All HTS files are identified with the suffix .hts. When a Web browser requests an .hts file, the web.sql processor reads the file, processes the database requests contained in that file, and then composes HTML output for the HTTP server to pass to the browser. .hts files return HTML output in HTML format only.

You can also use web.sql to return data in other formats, such as JPEG graphics or WAV audio, by specifying the ws_content_type in a .pl file. web.sql can execute a Perl file that outputs any data format and then transmits the data to the Web browser.

Perl files that you want to execute through web.sql must have the extension .pl. To access Perl scripts, open the web.sql welcome page by using one of the following platform-dependent URLs:

If you are using the NSAPI version of web.sql on a UNIX platform:

```
http://<servername>/<doc-root-subdir>/<scriptname.pl>
```

If you are using the shared-library CGI version of web.sql on a UNIX platform:

```
http://<servername>/<cgi-name>/websql/<doc-root-subdir>/<scriptname.pl>
```

If you are using the static CGI version of web.sql on a UNIX platform:

```
http://<servername>/<cgi-name>/ws.exe/<doc-root-subdir>/<scriptname.pl>
```

If you are using the NSAPI version of web.sql on the NT platform:

```
http://<servername>/<doc-root-subdir>/<scriptname.pl>
```

If you are using the CGI version of web.sql on the NT platform:

```
http://<servername>/<cgi-name>/ws.exe/<doc-root-subdir>/<scriptname.pl>
```

When writing a Perl file to return non-HTML data, you can use

- Any of the predefined Perl variables described in Using Perl Variables and Form Data in HTS Files.

- Any of the web.sql convenience routines described in web.sql Convenience and Client-Library APIs.

•Any of the web.sql Client-Library routines described in Using the web.sql Client-Library API.

Perl files require one additional web.sql routine, ws_content_type, which indicates the type of data the script returns. (You do not need to use this routine in an .hts file because web.sql automatically includes an HTML data type identifier when it processes an .hts file.) You must call ws_content_type before your script outputs any data. The parameter you pass to ws_content_type should be a string containing a Multipurpose Internet Mail Extension (MIME) type. For example, the following line indicates that the script returns an image in .jpeg format:

```
ws_content_type("image/jpeg");
```

## Examples of Returning Data Using an HTS File and a Perl Script

The following examples contrast how return data using an HTS (.hts) file and a Perl file (.pl) would be created. Both examples return HTML data. The first example shows an HTS file that is used to call sp_who to obtain a list of the users logged on to a database server.

```
<HTML>
<BODY>
<H1><CENTER>
Example of web.sql using an .hts file
</CENTER></H1>
<SYB>
ws_sql($ws_db, "sp_who"); .
</SYB> .
<P>
</BODY>
</HTML>
```

The next example shows the same functionality implemented as a .pl script:

```
ws_content_type("text/html");
# Print HTTP header info
print qq!
<HTML>
<BODY>
<H1><CENTER>
Example of web.sql using a .pl file
</CENTER></H1>
!;
ws_sql($ws_db, "sp_who");
```

```
print qq!
<P>
</BODY>
</HTML>
!;
```

### Returning HTTP Header Information

web.sql provides a mechanism to output information that can be sent as an HTTP header to the Web browser, like Web server cookies and URL redirection. This section explains how to set a cookie value and URL redirection with web.sql.

A cookie is a small piece of information that a Web server can store with a Web browser and later read back from that browser. This is useful for having the browser remember specific information across several pages.

URL redirection is a mechanism to redirect the Web browser to a different URL from the current HTS file. When the HTS file is accessed, control is transferred to the redirected URL specified by the Location tag in the beginning of the current HTS file.

If you need further information about Web server cookies, see

http://home.netscape.com/newsref/std/cookie_spec.html

In order to set the HTTP headers from an HTS file you need to prefix the HTS file with the "wsh-" prefix. The wsh- prefix instructs web.sql to send the appropriate header information to the client, not the default header information. The application programmer should delimit headers in wsh- prefixed files with two line feed characters (\n\n) to indicate to the server which part of the file is the header and which is the body.

### Example of Setting the Cookie Value

In the following example, wsh-setcookie.hts sets the cookie value. The cookie value is read back from getcookie.hts.

```
wsh-setcookie.hts

<SYB>
print "Content-type: text/html\n";
print "Set-cookie: mycookie=my-cookie-value\n\n";
</SYB>

getcookie.hts

<SYB>
print $ENV{'HTTP_COOKIE'};
```

```
print "This is the value set in wsh_setcookie.hts.\n";
</SYB>
```

## Example of URL Redirection

The following example shows URL redirection. You only need to access the wsh-locate.hts. You are automatically redirected to newlocation.hts.

```
wsh-locate.hts

<SYB>
print "Content-type: text/html\n";
print "Location: http://hostname:port/newlocation.hts\n\n";
</SYB>


newlocation.hts

<SYB>
print "You were redirected to the new file.\n";
</SYB>
```

## Sybase web.sql Examples

This section contains examples of the types of Transact SQL statements and Perl scripts that you can include in an HTS file.

### Transact SQL Statements within an HTS File

Generally, you want to use SQL statements to create a table; insert, update, delete, or select data from a table; or execute a stored procedure. Sybase web.sql executes the statement; the results display on the client browser.

Any SQL statement can be used in an HTS file that has the attribute TYPE=SQL. This section contains examples of Transact SQL statements that you can include in an HTS file.

The following code is an example of a <SYB> block that contains a simple SQL select statement in which data is selected from the pubs2 database:

```
<SYB TYPE=SQL>
select au_lname, au_fname, title, price
from pubs2..authors a, pubs2..titleauthor ta, pubs2..titles t
where (a.au_id = ta.au_id
and t.title_id = ta.title_id)
and titles.type = "mod_cook"
</SYB>
```

The previous query yields the following results:

| au_lname | au_fname | title | price |
|----------|----------|-------|-------|
| del Castillo | Innes | Silicon Valley Gastronomic Treats | 19.99 |
| DeFrance | Michel | The Gourmet Microwave | 2.99 |
| Ringer | Anne | The Gourmet Microwave | 2.99 |

The following example includes two SQL statements within an HTS file. The first statement inserts values into the following columns in the publisher's table: pub_id, pub_name, city, and state. The second statement deletes information from the database.

```
<SYB TYPE=SQL>
insert publishers
values ("9934", "Long Horns", "Dallas", "TX")

delete titles
        from titles t, titleauthor ta, authors a
        where t.title_id = ta.title_id
        and ta.au_id = a.au_id
        and a.au_lname = "Panteley"
        and a.au_fname = "Sylvia"
</SYB>
```

## Perl Scripts within an HTS File

Perl is a flexible scripting language. You can use Perl scripts to access a database and manipulate SQL query results. This section provides examples of ways you can use Perl in your HTS file.

The following example enables users to select the database they want to query and enter the SQL statement. The ws_sql routine is used to execute the SQL statement.

```
<SYB TYPE=PERL>
#Send the SQL statement to the Server.
if ($ws_db && $sql)
{
        ws_sql($ws_db, "use $database");
        ws_sql($ws_db, $sql );
}
</SYB>
```

## Executing SQL Transaction Statements

The following example sends a SQL statement to the database that is a transaction rather than a query. The same procedure is used for insert, update, and delete statements. This example updates records in the pubs2 database discounts table, setting customer discounts to 6.0.

Such commands produce results from the server that you, the web.sql programmer, need to handle. For example, you may want to tell the user if the
command succeeded and if so, how many rows were affected.

```
<SYB TYPE=PERL>

my $sqlstmt = qq!
update pubs2..discounts
set discount = 6.0
where discounttype = "Customer Discount"!;

        print "Sending the following SQL statement to the
        server:<P>\n";
        print "<PRE>", $sqlstmt, "</PRE><P>\n";

        my $rc = ct_sql($ws_db, $sqlstmt);

        if ($rc != CS_SUCCEED) {
                ws_error("ct_sql() call to perform UPDATE
                failed.");
        }

        # Handle return values
        my $result_type = "";
        while (($rc = ct_results($ws_db, $result_type)) ==
        CS_SUCCEED)
        {
                RES_TYPE: {

                        if ($result_type == CS_CMD_SUCCEED) {

                         print "Command was successful.<BR>\n";
                         my $res_info = ct_res_info($ws_db,
                         ·CS_ROW_COUNT);
                         print "${res_info} row(s) affected by this \
                         command.<BR>\n";
                         last RES_TYPE;
                        }

                        if ($result_type == CS_CMD_FAIL) {
                         print "Command failed.<BR>\n";
                         last RES_TYPE;
                        }
```

```
                                if ($result_type == CS_CMD_DONE) {
                                        last RES_TYPE;
                                }

                                print "Unexpected result type returned.<BR>\n";
                        }
                }
        </SYB>
```

## Parsing Form Data

The following example contains multiple <SYB> blocks and illustrates how web.sql can parse form data passed to an HTS file. This example presents an online form in which users select the database to use from a list and then enter the SQL statement in an entry field. web.sql executes the SQL statement entered and displays the results in the client browser.

```
<FORM ACTION=isql_results.hts METHOD=POST>
<P><STRONG>Database: </STRONG>
<SELECT NAME=database>
<SYB TYPE=PERL>
        if ($database ne "") {
                print "<option selected>$database\n";
        }

# Send the T-SQL now.
ws_sql
($ws_db, qq!select name from master.dbo.sysdatabases
        where name <> "$database"!,
"<option>%s");
</SYB>
</SELECT>
<P>
<STRONG>SQL Command</STRONG>:
<TEXTAREA NAME=SQL ROWS=5 COLS=78>

# Print results.
<SYB TYPE=PERL>
    print $sql;
</SYB>
</FORM>
```

## Using Perl Variables in Form Data

The following example is from a document that is activated when a user enters data into a form and submits it. (This causes a "POST" to this document.) All the input data from the form document is received in the form of Perl variables.

For example, a user enters a state abbreviation into an entry field named "state" in the form, which posts to the following HTS file. The Perl variable called $state can be used to query the pubs2 database for all stores in that state.

```
<SYB TYPE=SQL>
   select stor_name,
   stor_address, city, state
   from   pubs2..stores where   state =
   upper("$state")
   order by stor_name
</SYB>
```

## Handling Error Messages

The web.sql routine ws_error specifies the text in an error message. When the ws_error routine is called, web.sql stops processing or executing the HTS file.

In the example below, a call is made to ws_sql. If an error occurs while web.sql is processing ws_error, then ws_error is executed, and the specified error message is executed. Also, when an error is encountered, all processing stops. In this case, web.sql does not process the stored procedure, nor does it print the remaining HTML text to the browser.

```
<HTML>
<HEAD>
<TITLE>Example of ws_error()</TITLE>
</HEAD>
<BODY>
ws_sql($ws_db, "sp_who");
ws_error("This is the text of my error.  Processing should stop now.");
</SYB>

<P>
This is more text after the sql block.  It should
not
appear in the output since the ws_error() call
should
stop processing of the HTS file.
<P>
</BODY>
</HTML>
```

The following example sets up subroutines to handle SQL Server or Open Client error messages. By default, these errors are routed to the default error-handling routines provided with web.sql. However, you can override the defaults and provide custom error-message handling by calling ct_callback to point to a custom error handler.

This example contains two custom handlers: one for client error messages and one for server error messages. An invalid SQL select statement is sent to activate the error handler.

```perl
<SYB TYPE=PERL>
#....code deleted....
        # Set up the callback routines for error messages
        # to point to the custom ones below.  Note that
        #these routines will also be used by any other
        #following <SYB> blocks in this document
ct_callback(CS_CLIENTMSG_CB, 'client_err');
ct_callback(CS_SERVERMSG_CB, 'server_err');

# Send an invalid ct_connect() call for an unknown server so we generate an
error

my $badconn = ct_connect("xxxxx","yyyy","ZZZZZXXX");

#....code deleted....

sub client_err
    {
        # This routine gets passed 6 arguments related to
        # the error
        local($layer, $origin, $severity,
        $errno, $msg, $osmsg)
            = @_;

        print "<P><HR><STRONG>CLIENT ERROR
        OCCURRED:</STRONG>\n";
        print "<P>Client error info: <BR>\n";
        printf "Error: Layer=%ld Origin=%ld Severity=%ld
                Number=%ld <BR>\n",
                $layer, $origin, $severity, $errno;
        printf "Message text: %s <BR>\n", $msg;

        if (defined($osmsg)) {
            printf "OS Message '%s' <BR>\n", $osmsg;
        }

        print "<P><HR>";
```

```
        CS_SUCCEED;
}


# Callback routine to handle server error messages
sub server_err
{
# This routine gets passed 8 arguments related to
#the error
local($cmd, $errno, $severity, $state, $line,
$server, $proc, $msg) = @_;

print "<P><HR><STRONG>SERVER ERROR
OCCURRED:</STRONG>\n";
print "<P>Server error info: <BR>\n";
printf "Cmd=%s <BR>\n", $cmd;
printf "Error: Number=%ld Severity=%ld State=%ld
Line=%ld <BR>\n",
     $errno, $severity, $state, $line;

if (defined($server)) {
  printf "Server '%s' <BR>\n", $server;
}

if (defined($proc)) {
  printf "Stored procedure '%s' <BR>\n", $proc;
}

  printf "Message text: %s <BR>\n", $msg;

print "<P><HR>";

CS_SUCCEED;
}


</SYB>
```

## Processing a Perl Script

Sybase web.sql can process a straight Perl file that contains valid Perl scripts and web.sql routines. If you do not need to interpolate Perl results into HTML code, you may want to use this approach.

web.sql expects Perl files to return the proper header information. The following call prints this header information, and in this case, it sets the MIME type to HTML. If you want to return data for a different MIME type, you can specify the type with the ws_content_type routine. This is useful if you want to query information from the database and return it to a special helper application that you "attached" to a browser. In that case, the helper application would not have to parse HTML. You could return any format of data to that helper application.

```
ws_content_type("text/html");
# Print HTTP header info

# Since we'll return HTML, let's print some of the
# standard info it
# expects.  We'll use the "qq" notation so that the
# carriage return
# characters get inserted into the strings that get
# printed...

print qq!
<HTML>
<HEAD>
<TITLE>Example of web.sql using a .pl file</TITLE>
</HEAD>
<BODY>
<H2><CENTER>
Example of web.sql using a .pl file
</CENTER></H2>
!;

# Do a simple web.sql query to get a list of who is
# logged on
# the database server by calling the "sp_who" stored
# procedure
# (Note that web.sql has already set up the $ws_db
# default
# connection for us, as it does for .hts files
# (assuming you have
# a valid default connection set up in .websql.pl).

ws_sql($ws_db, "sp_who");

# Now let's print the rest of the HTML

print qq!
<P><HR>
</BODY>
</HTML>
!;
```

Handling Server Results

This final chunk of code provides a comprehensive example that demonstrates how web.sql handles various result types returned after SQL queries. The following example uses a subroutine that includes a large switch statement to handle all types of results from different Transact-SQL statements. A number of different SQL statements are sent to show how web.sql handles the results.

```perl
<SYB TYPE=PERL>

   print "<P><BR><STRONG>First, point to the pubs2\
   database...</STRONG><P>\n";

   my $rc = ct_sql($ws_db, "use pubs2");

   if ($rc != CS_SUCCEED) {
      ws_error("ct_sql() call failed on 'use pubs2'
      command.");
   }

   process_results();

   print "<P><BR><STRONG>Try a simple SELECT \
        statement...</STRONG><P>\n";

   $rc = ct_sql($ws_db, qq!select type, price
           from    titles
           where   type in ("business","mod_cook")
           order by type!);

   if ($rc != CS_SUCCEED) {
      ws_error("ct_sql() call failed on first SELECT
      statement.");
   }

   process_results();


   print "<P><BR><STRONG>Now a SELECT statement with a
        COMPUTE...</STRONG><P>\n";

   $rc = ct_sql($ws_db, qq!select type, price
              from    titles
              where   type in ("business","mod_cook")
              order by type
              compute sum(price), avg(price) by
```

```
          type!);

if ($rc != CS_SUCCEED) {
   ws_error("ct_sql() call failed on SELECT
   statement with COMPUTE.");
}

process_results();

print "<P><BR><STRONG>Now send an UPDATE
statement...</STRONG><P>\n";

$rc = ct_sql($ws_db, qq!update pubs2..discounts
                set     discount = 6.0
                where   discounttype = "Customer
                Discount"!);

if ($rc != CS_SUCCEED) {
   ws_error("ct_sql() call failed on
   UPDATE statement.");
}

process_results();


print "<P><BR><STRONG>Execute a stored procedure
that returns\n"
"a status...</STRONG><P>\n";

# storename_proc expects one input argument,
# which is the starting letters of a store name.  It
# returns all stores that begin with that string and
# also sets its return status to the number of rows
# found.

$rc = ct_sql($ws_db, qq!exec storename_proc "B"!);

if ($rc != CS_SUCCEED) {
   ws_error("ct_sql() call failed on execution of
   stored procedure.");
}

process_results();
```

```
print "<P><BR><STRONG>Execute a stored procedure
(sp_help) that returns\n"
"results from several SELECT
 statements...</STRONG><P>\n";

$rc = ct_sql($ws_db, "exec sp_help");

if ($rc != CS_SUCCEED) {
    ws_error("ct_sql() call failed on execution of
    sp_help stored procedure.");
}

process_results();


print "<P><BR><STRONG>That's it for this example.
You may also want to \n"
"try executing a stored procedure that returns some
output \n"
"parameters to see how that result type is han
 dled.</STRONG><P>\n";

sub process_results {

# Define some local variables used only in this sub
#routine

my($ret, $result_type, $res_info, $num_cols, @row);

# ct_results() returns a $ret value to tell you if
# it executed ok or not and whether there are any
# more result types to get, and it also sets the
# argument $result_type to a valid result type
# that was passed from the server.

while (($ret = ct_results($ws_db, $result_type)) ==
CS_SUCCEED)
{
    RES_TYPE: {

        # CS_CMD_SUCCEED:
        # Returned when a SQL command that returns no
        rows
        # (i.e., INSERT/UPDATE/DELETE) is successful
```

```
if ($result_type == CS_CMD_SUCCEED) {
   print "<P>Last command executed was
   successful.<BR>\n";
   $res_info = ct_res_info($ws_db,
   CS_ROW_COUNT);
   if ($res_info >= 0) {
      print "<P>${res_info} row(s) were
      affected.\n";
   }
   print "<P>\n";
   last RES_TYPE;
}


# CS_CMD_FAIL:
# Returned when the last SQL command failed to
execute

if ($result_type == CS_CMD_FAIL) {
   print "<P>Execution of the last command
   FAILED.<P>\n";
   last RES_TYPE;
}


# CS_ROW_RESULT:
# Returned when there are regular data rows
# from a SELECT statement or stored procedure
# available to fetch from the server. You must
# fetch all these rows (or cancel the current
# result set) before you can retrieve addi-
# tional result info or execute more commands.
# The following code prints the resulting rows
# in HTML 3.0 tables, and also prints some
# header information.

if ($result_type == CS_ROW_RESULT) {

   print "<TABLE BORDER>\n";
   # First print the column heading
   # information
   print "<TR><TH>", join("<TH>",
   ct_col_names($ws_db)), "\n";

   # Then, print the row data
   $num_cols = ct_res_info($ws_db,
   CS_NUMDATA);
```

```
while (@row = ct_fetch($ws_db)) {
   print "<TR><TD>",
   join("<TD>", @row), "\n";
}
print "</TABLE>\n";
last RES_TYPE;
}


# CS_COMPUTE_RESULT:
# Returned in between batches of
# CS_ROW_RESULT rows if a SELECT
# statement containing a "COMPUTE" clause is
# being processed. If there is more than one
# item being computed (for example, "compute
# sum(price), avg(price) by type"), then each
#  computed item will be returned in a differ
# ent element of the returned array.  If you
# return the results into an associative
# array, you can receive information on what
# type of operation (i.e. sum(), avg()) was
# performed for the compute, and what column
# number the operation was performed on.  This
# information is used below to print informa
# tion related to the computer results for the
# current SELECT statement.  The data is
# printed in HTML 3.0 table format.

if ($result_type == CS_COMPUTE_RESULT) {

   print "<TABLE BORDER>\n";
   while (%row = ct_fetch($ws_db, 1))
   {  # fetch into assoc \
      array
      print "<TR><TD>COMPUTE info:<TD>",
      join("<TD>", %row),\
       "\n";
   }
   print "</TABLE>\n";
   last RES_TYPE;
}


# CS_STATUS_RESULT:
# Returned as a result of executing a stored
# procedure that returns a status value.  The
# status value is a single integer value.  In
```

```
# the code below, the information is fetched
# into the @row array, but only the first
# array element should be set to the status
# value.

if ($result_type == CS_STATUS_RESULT) {
   while (@row = ct_fetch($ws_db)) {
      print "<P>Stored procedure return
      status: ", $row[0],\
        "<P>\n";
   }
   last RES_TYPE;
}


# CS_PARAM_RESULT:
# Returned after calling a stored procedure
# has one or more of its parameters defined as
# an "output" parameter.  A single row of an
# array is returned, with each parameter value
# returned in a different array cell. In the
# code below, the information is fetched into
# the @row array, but only one row should be
# returned.

if ($result_type == CS_PARAM_RESULT) {
   print "<P>Stored procedure output parameter
     value(s):\n";
   while (@row = ct_fetch($ws_db)) {
      print join("<BR>", @row), "\n";
   }
   print "<P>\n";
   last RES_TYPE;
}


# CS_CMD_DONE:
# Returned after a SQL statement has been exe
# cuted and its results have been properly
# retrieved and processed by the client.
# Typically, you will just ignore this message
# and not print any information.  In this
# example, an informational message is printed
# so you can see when this result type is
# returned.

if ($result_type == CS_CMD_DONE) {
```

```
            print "<P>[CS_CMD_DONE result type
            returned]<P>\n";
            last RES_TYPE;
        }

        printf "<P>Unexpected result type returned:
        %s<P>\n", \
        $result_type;

    } # End of RES_TYPE
 } # end of ct_results() "while" loop

 return $ret;
}
</SYB>
```

# 12

# IBM Web Connectors for IMS and CICS

## Introduction

Like most other vendors, IBM has kept pace with the times by providing a plethora of offerings to connect their various products to the Web.

Their most exciting offering to date is something they call appropriately enough Net.Data. Net.Data is an application that allows Web developers to easily build dynamic Internet applications using "Web Macros." Net.Data Web Macros have the simplicity of HTML with the power of dynamic SQL. Net.Data provides database connectivity to a variety of data sources, including information stored in relational databases and flat files. Your data sources, such as DB2, Oracle, and Sybase, can be on a wide range of operating systems.

Net.Data is an upwardly compatible follow-on version of DB2 World Wide Web Connection (DB2WWW), building on its strong database access and reporting capabilities. In Net.Data, the functionality has been enhanced to become a comprehensive Web development environment for the creation of simple dynamic Web pages or complex Web-based applications.

Net.Data features macro capabilities, including conditional logic, for more flexible application development. Net.Data applications can contain INCLUDE files as well as Web URLs, allowing modularization and sharing of application components. For data persistence between Web pages and across Web applications, Net.Data supports HTML variable substitution and Netscape cookies which keep track of related visits to a Web site.

With Net.Data, you get full support for Java, the standard for exciting Web application development. You can use a Java applet to create a graphical chart, such as a pie chart, from the results of a Net.Data application. With Net.Data's support for JavaScripts, you can validate data entered at the client's Web browser. And to develop Java applications, you can use VisualAge for Java from IBM.

Net.Data is also compatible with NetObjects Fusion, a graphical template-based Web site authoring tool for generating Web pages. Together, Net.Data and NetObjects Fusion allow you to build visually rich Web pages, connecting your users to live business information.

While Net.Data may be IBM's future, it is worthwhile to note that they also realized that they had to come up with a solution for their past. The remainder of this chapter discusses solutions for connecting IBM's legacy solutions — IMS and CICS — to the Web.

## IMS Web

The IMS Internet Solutions (also called "IMS Connectors") are members of IBM's e-business Enterprise Connectors family. IBM Connectors are gateway products that enable you to easily access enterprise applications and data over the Internet using your Web browser!

IMS Web, one of the IMS Connectors, allows you to provide access to IMS applications across the Internet. Using information available from IMS, the tool generates the code necessary for mapping and communication between the Web and IMS.

This tool generates applications and classes (programs) for a number of server environments. It draws information from your IMS Message Format Services (MFS) definitions, allowing you to browse and download a set of MFS source files for a transaction. From the downloaded files, IMS Web generates a set of C++ classes (programs) for parsing and communication with IMS transactions. It builds the generated C++ files to generate a Common Gateway Interface (CGI) application for communicating from the Web to IMS. It also generates an input Hypertext Markup Language (HTML) form and the output HTML that displays the results of a transaction on the Web browser. Ultimately, this tool will make it easier for you to provide access to existing IMS applications from the Web.

To download IMS Web go to the IMS Web page at
http://www.software.ibm.com/data/ims/about/imsWeb/

### IMS Web Studio

IMS Web Studio is a GUI tool that runs on Windows NT or 95 and provides the following functions:

•Allows you to browse and download a set of MFS source files for a transaction

•Generates, from the downloaded files, a set of C++ and HTML files for the transaction

• Provides a makefile to compile and link the generated
C++ files to create an executable CGI-BIN program

You install the CGI-BIN program and input HTML form on your Web server to provide access to the IMS transaction.

## IMS Web Development

The following is a summary of the development process that you use to enable an IMS transaction to the Web:

1. Locate, on the host, the MFS source for the transaction.
2. Use IMS Web Studio to download the MFS source to your workstation.
3. Use IMS Web Studio to generate C++ and HTML files, and makefiles, for your transaction.
4. Build the executable form of the CGI-BIN program from the code and the makefile that IMS Web Studio generates.
5. Move the CGI-BIN executable and the generated input HTML form to your Web server.
6. From a browser, invoke the input HTML form, input the IMS transaction data, and then select the SUBMIT push button on the HTML form in order to run the transaction and receive its output.

## Creating a Project in IMS Web Studio

An IMS Web Studio project is a set of resources and information that is associated with building the CGI-BIN program and input HTML for an IMS transaction.

To create a new project, perform the following actions:

1. Select File from the IMS Web Studio window action bar. Select the New Project option from the pulldown menu.
2. Next, specify project-related information in the New Project dialog, as shown in figure 12-1.
   After you have created a project in IMS Web Studio, select and download the MFS source files that are associated with the transaction for which you want to generate code. To select and download these files, do the following:

1. Select File from the project window action bar.
2. Select the Insert Files into Project option from the pulldown menu as shown in figure 12-2.
3. The Logon dialog displays as shown in figure 12-3. IMS Web uses FTP to download MFS source files from the host to the workstation. You use this dialog to log on to the FTP server where the MFS source files are located. You don't have to use the FTP download function of IMS Web in order to transfer MFS

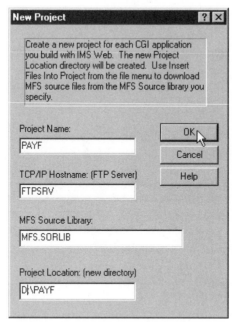

**Figure 12-1.** The New Project dialog.

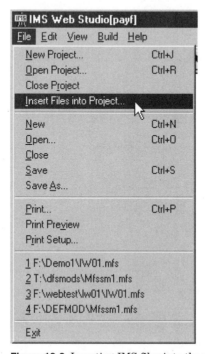

**Figure 12-2.** Inserting IMS files into the project.

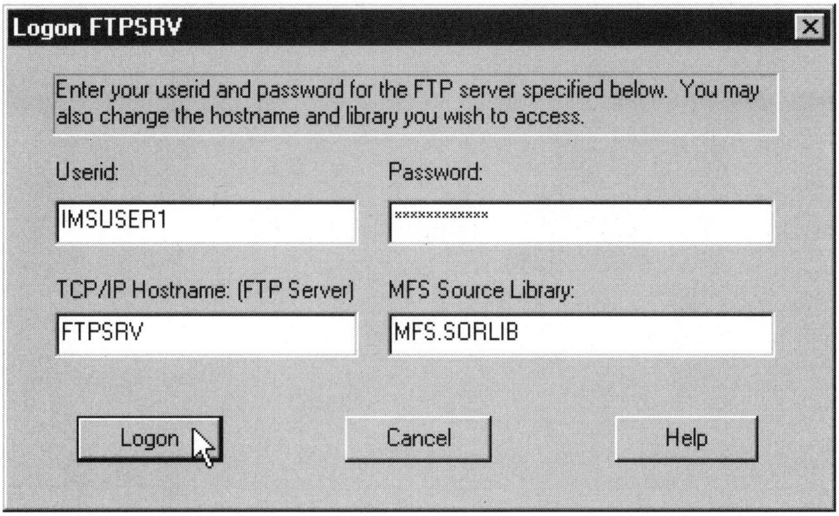

**Figure 12-3.** The Logon dialog.

source to your project directory, if you have another method for transferring it. Once the source is in the project directory, just use the Build > Generate option. Now enter the following information:

Userid
Your user ID for the FTP server where the MFS source files are located.

Password
Your password for the FTP server where the MFS source files are located.

TCP/IP Hostname (FTP Server)
The name of the FTP server where the MFS source files are located. This field displays the name that you specified when you created the project. You can change this default name, if necessary.

MFS Source Library
The name of the library where the MFS source files are located. This field displays the name that you specified when you created the project. You can change this default name, if necessary.

4. Select the Logon push button. The Insert Files into Project dialog displays a list of available MFS source files in the library you specified.

5. To select one or more files, select the file name or names in the Available list box, and then click on the right-arrow (>) push button located between the list boxes as shown in figure 12-4. The file name then disappears from the Available list box and appears in the Selected list box. To select all the available files, click on the double right-arrow (>>) push button.

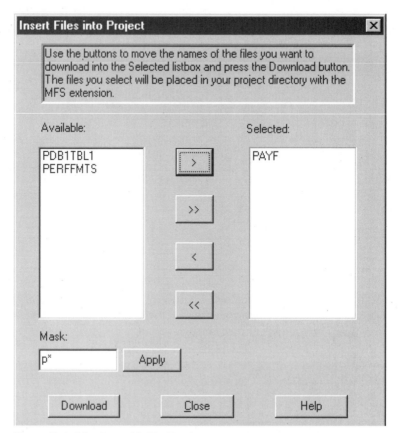

**Figure 12-4.** Selecting available files for your project.

6. To download the selected files, select the Download push button. The files are downloaded to the project directory with a file extension of .mfs.

Note: You must also download any COPY members that the MFS source uses for your transaction. If you only download base files, and if any of them contains COPY statements, the parser fails because the MFS source in the COPY member is not on the workstation.

## Customizing Generated Code

Because IMS Web does not use information in the MFS FMT statement that is associated with a transaction, the literal information that identifies fields on the original 3270 screen is not available. The appearance of the generated HTML differs from the 3270 display.

The input HTML is generated based on the message input descriptor of the MFS source. The HTML consists of an HTML form with the fields of the input message (MFLDs) arranged as text entry fields of an HTML table. MAXLENGTH is the defined length of the MFLD (that is, the LTH = value).

The rows of the table are arranged in the same order as the MFLD statements within the message input descriptor.

The POST method is used to transmit the user data, and the destination of the ACTION is the generated CGI-BIN executable on the Web server. IMS Web uses the path that you specify in IMS Web Studio to build the URL of the ACTION.

To submit the contents of the form to IMS, you select the SUBMIT push button. To reset fields to null, you select the RESET push button.

To modify the input HTML, edit the HTMproject_name.HTM file that IMS Web Studio generated where project_name is the name of the IMS Web Studio project you used to build your IMS Web application. You can tailor the input HTML for your environment.

Before you make any modifications note that because the generated code still contains the code that processes the corresponding attribute, removing a text input field from the input HTML is the same as not providing any data for the field. For example, if the corresponding input MFLD specifies a default literal, the literal value is used in the input message field. If the corresponding input MFLD does not specify a default literal, the field is padded as specified in the MFS source.

## IMS Web Legacy example

This example shows how you can use IMS Web to convert a legacy payroll application to a Web application. In Release 1, IMS Web applications are based on the MFS source of the legacy application. The application used in this example adds new employees to the payroll.

The following MFS source code shows the 3270 Model 1 screen format used in the legacy application, as well as the input and output message descriptors. First you type the employee information in the appropriate fields on the 3270 screen, and then press ENTER to send the input message to the IMS application program. The application program echoes the input data back to the user, and uses MSGFLD to present the status of the newly added employee. If the user needs to take special notice of the message in MSGFLD, the employee number displays in red. To cause the output data to display in red (which, of course, you can't see in this book), the application program dynamically sets the extended attribute bytes of the EMPNO output message field.

```
/**********************************************************************/
/*                                                                    */
/* (c) Copyright IBM Corp. 1996                                       */
/* All Rights Reserved                                                */
/* Licensed Materials - Property of IBM                               */
/*                                                                    */
/* DISCLAIMER OF WARRANTIES.                                          */
/*                                                                    */
/* The following [enclosed] code is generated by a software product  */
```

```
/* of IBM Corporation.                                              */
/* This generated code is provided to you solely for the purpose of */
/* assisting you in the development of your applications.           */
/* The code is provided "AS IS." IBM MAKES NO WARRANTIES, EXPRESS OR */
/* IMPLIED, INCLUDING BUT NOT LIMITED TO THE IMPLIED WARRANTIES OF   */
/* MERCHANTABILITY AND FITNESS FOR A PARTICULAR PURPOSE, REGARDING   */
/* THE FUNCTION OR PERFORMANCE OF THIS CODE.                        */
/* IBM shall not be liable for any damages arising out of your use   */
/* of the generated code, even if they have been advised of the     */
/* possibility of such damages.                                     */
/*                                                                  */
/* DISTRIBUTION.                                                    */
/*                                                                  */
/* This generated code can be freely distributed, copied, altered,  */
/* and incorporated into other software, provided that:             */
/*    - It bears the above Copyright notice and DISCLAIMER intact    */
/*    - The software is not for resale                             */
/*                                                                  */
/********************************************************************/

PAYF    FMT
        DEF     TYPE=(3270,1),FEAT=IGNORE,DSCA=X'00A0',
                SYSMSG=MSGFLD
        DIV     TYPE=INOUT
        DPAGE   CURSOR=((3,13))
        DFLD    '****EMPLOYEE PAYROLL ****',POS=(1,8)
        DFLD    'LAST NAME:',POS=(4,2)
LNAME   DFLD    POS=(4,13),LTH=10
        DFLD    'FIRST NAME:',POS=(5,2)
FNAME   DFLD    POS=(5,14),LTH=10
        DFLD    'EMPL NO:',POS=(6,2)
EMPNO   DFLD    POS=(6,11),LTH=5,EATTR=(NEUTRAL)
        DFLD    'SOC SEC NO.:',POS=(7,2)
SSN     DFLD    POS=(7,15),LTH=11
        DFLD    'RATE OF PAY:$',POS=(8,2)
RATE    DFLD    POS=(8,16),LTH=9
MSGFLD  DFLD    POS=(10,2),LTH=50
DATE    DFLD    POS=(10,55),LTH=8
        FMTEND
PAYIN   MSG     TYPE=INPUT,SOR=(PAYF,IGNORE),NXT=PAYOUT
        SEG
        MFLD    'SKS1 '
        MFLD    LNAME,LTH=10
        MFLD    FNAME,LTH=10
        MFLD    EMPNO,LTH=7,ATTR=(NO,1)
        MFLD    SSN,LTH=11
```

```
        MFLD    RATE,LTH=9,JUST=R,FILL=C'0'
        MSGEND
PAYOUT  MSG     TYPE=OUTPUT,SOR=(PAYF,IGNORE),NXT=PAYIN,
                OPT=1,FILL=NULL
        SEG
        MFLD    LNAME,LTH=10
        MFLD    FNAME,LTH=10
        SEG
        MFLD    EMPNO,LTH=7,ATTR=(NO,1)
        MFLD    SSN,LTH=11
        SEG
        MFLD    RATE,LTH=9
        SEG
        MFLD    MSGFLD,LTH=50
        MFLD    (DATE,DATE2)
        MSGEND
```

You use IMS Web Studio to generate the IMS Web application. After you have created an IMS Web Studio project and inserted the above MFS source file into the project, you are ready to generate and build your new IMS Web application. (Although the MFS source file contains both a FMT statement and MSG statements, IMS Web ignores the FMT statement and uses only the MSG statements in the generation process.)

For an IMS Web Studio project with the name HTMPAYF, IMS Web Studio generates the following files (note: source code for this files can be found in the Appendix to this chapter).

### HTMPAYF.HTM
This file contains the HTML form that you use to input data to the IMS application. The generated HTML uses the POST method to invoke the generated CGI-BIN program and the Web server path you provided to IMS Web Studio for its URL. Figure 12-5 is the generated input form.

### CGIPAYF.cpp
This is the CGI-BIN program. Its executable form runs on your Web server. The CGI-BIN program uses several C++ classes (described below) to parse the string from the HTML form, submit an input message containing the data from the HTML form to the IMS application, and then present the data in the output message from the IMS transaction to the Web browser. You only need to build its executable form using the generated MAKE file.

### HTMPAYF.hpp
This file contains the interface of the class that parses the string received from the input HTML form. The generated CGI-BIN program uses this class.

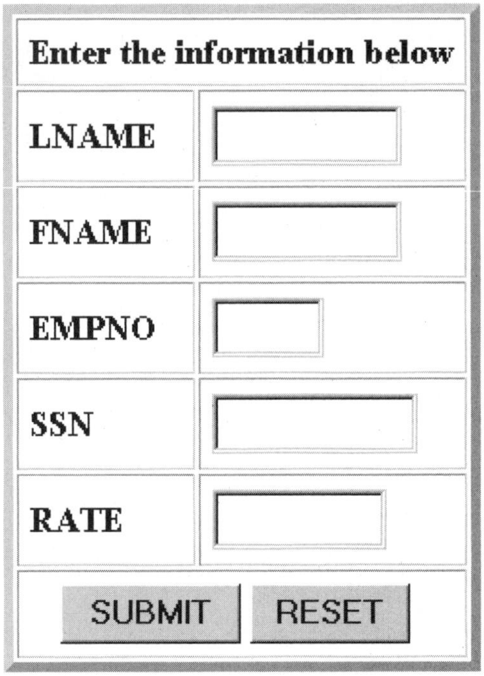

**Figure 12-5.** The generated IMS form.

HTMPAYF.cpp
This file contains the implementation of the class that parses the string received from the input HTML form.

HWSLPG01.hpp
This file contains the interface of the input logical page class. Because the MFS source does not include an input LPAGE statement, IMS Web generates a default logical page. The generated CGI-BIN program uses this class.

HWSLPG01.cpp
This file contains the implementation of the input logical page class.

HWSLPG02.hpp
This file contains the interface of the output logical page class. Because the MFS source does not include an output LPAGE statement, IMS Web generates a default logical page. The generated CGI-BIN program uses this class.

HWSLPG02.cpp
This file contains the implementation of the output logical page class.

CGIPAYF.MAK

This file is used to build the executable form of the CGI-BIN program, CGI-PAYF.EXE, for execution on a Windows NT Web server.

Modifying input HTML

IMS Web does not use information in the MFS FMT statement that is associated with a transaction. Therefore, the literal information that is used to identify fields on the original 3270 screen is not available for the generated HTML. To create an input HTML form (figure 12-6) that closely resembles the original 3270 display screen, modify the generated HTML as follows:

1. Left align the table.
2 .Replace the text preceding each text-entry field with the literal used in the MFS FMT statement.
3. Add a heading and horizontal rule.
4. Remove the IMS Web image.

Modifying output HTML

The CGI-BIN program uses the getHTML method of the output LPAGE to generate the output HTML. In this example, shown in figure 12-7, results are sent

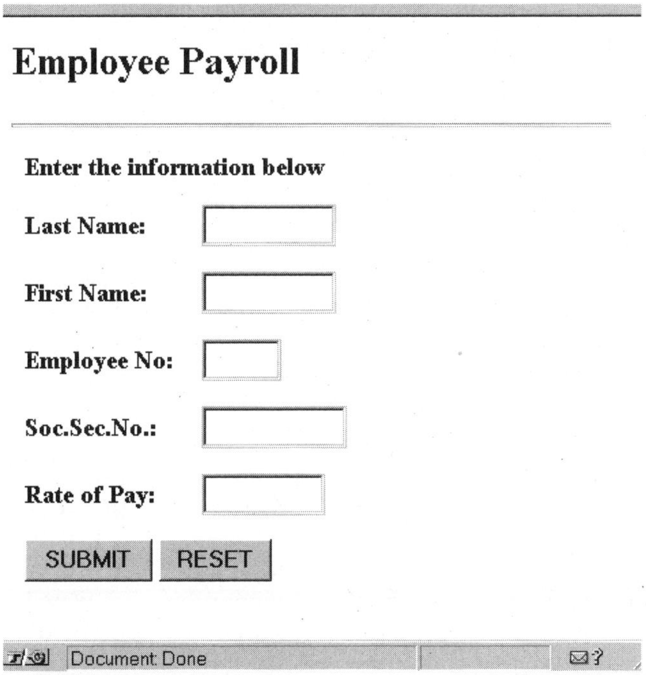

# Employee Payroll

**Enter the information below**

**Last Name:**

**First Name:**

**Employee No:**

**Soc.Sec.No.:**

**Rate of Pay:**

SUBMIT    RESET

Document Done

**Figure 12-6.** The modified form.

to the Web browser.

As is the case for input HTML, the output HTML is more meaningful if you modify it to resemble the original 3270 screen. Because the CGI-BIN program dynamically builds the output HTML, you must modify the code of the CGI-BIN program to get an output result that looks like the one in figure 12-8.

The CGIPAYF.cpp file was modified to replace the default Results heading with the heading Employee Payroll. In order to display the employee number

# Results

| LNAME | Hill |
| FNAME | Judith |
| EMPNO | 12345 |
| SSN | 999-88-7777 |
| RATE | 000000300 |
| MSGFLD | Employee is exempt. |
| DATE | 03/04/97 |

**Figure 12-7.** getHTML generates output.

in red, the genHTML method had to be modified to examine the attribute bytes associated with the output message field, and to add HTML to set the color of the data appropriately. Ordinarily, genHTML skips attribute bytes.

## IBM CICS Internet Connectors

The CICS Internet gateway is an IBM-provided CGI script that makes a Web browser appear like a 3270 terminal with a more appealing interface as shown in figure 12-9.

You can logon to a test CICS system, called patrick, using the userid guest and the password patrick. The CICS transaction to logon is called CESN. The CICS system is running in IBM Hursley, in the United Kingdom, and is the same CICS system used by the catalog demonstration (available on http://www3.hursley.ibm.com/www3/catalog.htm).

You can try the CICS transaction CEBR and browse the CEBR0000 temporary storage queue. (The catalog demonstration application writes records to

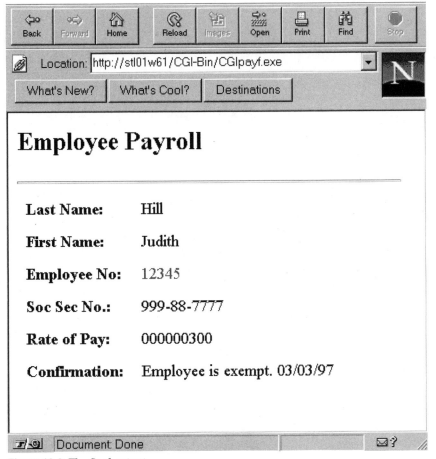

**Figure 12-8.** The final output.

the CEBR0000 temporary storage queue when you place orders.) If you browse to the end of the queue, by pressing the PF5 button, you may be able to see the records containing your name that you caused to be written. The PF5 button, along with the other buttons that represent keys, appear at the bottom of the appropriate pages.

Another CICS transaction to try is PA2 which provides summary statistics for the CICS system you are accessing. You will need to use the # key to select items, followed by the enter button.

A production example of using CICS on the Web is the State of Texas' job search facility as shown at http://www.twc.state.tx.us/joblists/gvjb.html and in figures 12-10 and 12-11.

The HTML code for figure 12-10 is shown below.

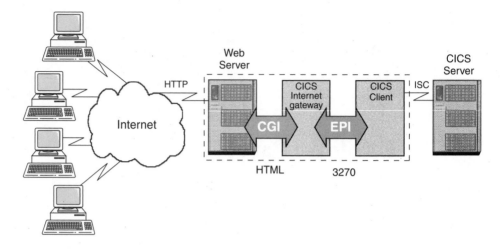

**Figure 12-9.** The CICS Internet gateway.

```
<!doctype html public "html2.0">

<HTML>
<HEAD>
<TITLE>Governor's Job Bank</TITLE>
</HEAD>
<BODY BACKGROUND="/icons/twcbkgd.gif">
<IMAGE SRC = "/icons/pagetopbanner.gif" hspace=6>
<form method="post" action="/cig-bin/route.pl/SendData">
<INPUT TYPE="hidden" NAME="CommData" VALUE="7">
<INPUT TYPE="hidden" NAME="SessionID" VALUE="21669">
<INPUT TYPE="hidden" NAME="SequenceNo" VALUE="1">

<h2> Social Security Number</h2>
The disclosure of your Social Security Number is voluntary.  TWC assesses
this system's effectiveness by matching social security numbers against
wage records maintained under the authority of 40 TAC section 301.20(3)
(A).
If you do not wish to disclose your SSN, please substitute nine zeros (0).

<p>SOCIAL SECURITY NUMBER: <INPUT TYPE="text" NAME="Inp506L3" VALUE=""
SIZE="3" MAXLENGTH="3"> - <INPUT TYPE="text" NAME="Inp512L2" VALUE=""
SIZE="2" MAXLENGTH="2"> - <INPUT TYPE="text" NAME="Inp517L4" VALUE=""
SIZE="4" MAXLENGTH="4">

<p>
<h2>Select Type of Job Desired:</h2>
<table>
```

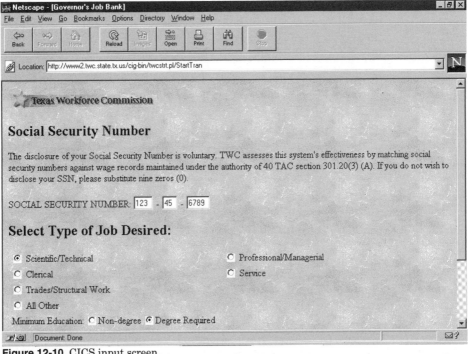

**Figure 12-10.** CICS input screen.

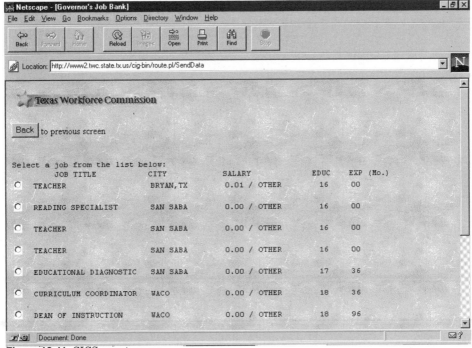

**Figure 12-11.** CICS ouput screen.

```
<tr>
<td>
<INPUT TYPE="radio" name="Inp746L1"" value="0"> Scientific/Technical
<td>
<td>
<INPUT TYPE="radio" name="Inp746L1"" value="1"> Professional/Managerial<br>
<tr>
<td>
<INPUT TYPE="radio" name="Inp746L1"" value="2"> Clerical
<td>
<td>
<INPUT TYPE="radio" name="Inp746L1"" value="3"> Service <br>
<tr>
<td>
<INPUT TYPE="radio" name="Inp746L1"" value="4"> Trades/Structural Work
<tr>
<td>
<INPUT TYPE="radio" name="Inp746L1"" value="5" checked> All Other<br>
<tr>
<td>
Minimum Education: <INPUT TYPE="radio" name="Inp1226L1" value="1"
checked>Non-degree <INPUT TYPE="radio" name="Inp1226L1" value="2">Degree
Required
</table>
(Optional) Enter Monthly Salary desired: $ <INPUT TYPE="text"
NAME="Inp1546L4" VALUE="" SIZE="4" MAXLENGTH="4">  (Enter dollars only, no
cents)

<HR ALIGN=center SIZE=4>
<INPUT TYPE="submit" NAME="FENTER" VALUE="Enter">
<HR ALIGN=center Width=50%>
<BR>
<I>
Texas Workforce Commission
<BR>
</I>
```

## What Does the CICS Gateway Do?

The CICS Gateway provides an interface between a Web server and a CICS application, allowing conversion of 3270 data streams into HTML (Hypertext Markup Language) format used by the World Wide Web. The CICS application can then be accessed by any Web browser with no change to either the browser or the CICS application.

The CICS Gateway enhances the functions of the Web server by exploiting a standard Web server mechanism known as the Common Gateway Interface

(CGI). It dynamically builds Web pages containing the CICS data and transmits them to the Web browser.

The CICS Gateway provides automatic translation between CICS 3270 data streams and HTML using the CICS External Presentation Interface which is part of the CICS Client.

The CICS Gateway interfaces between a Web server and a CICS EPI client to provide a connection from a Web browser to a CICS system.

The security from the Web browser to the Gateway (via the Web server) is provided by the Web server. The security from the Gateway (via the CICS client) to CICS hosts is whatever CICS authorization and access control that has been set up for the CICS client to CICS hosts connections. There is no specific security code in the Gateway.

The first interaction with a CICS system involves the "creation" of a terminal on that system and establishment of communications. This optimization continues until the terminal is explicitly "ended."

## Configuring the Web Server

In order to use the CICS Gateway with your Web server, the server has to be configured to access the CICS Gateway programs and files and also be configured to run CGI scripts.

The /cig-admin/ directory allows users to perform administration tasks on your CICS Gateway but it is recommended that you restrict access to this directory to authorized users only.

## Starting the CICS Gateway

The CICS Internet Gateway runs as a Windows NT service. To start it, open the Windows NT Control Panel application and start the Services program. The CICS Internet Gateway should appear as a startable service. Select Start to start the CICS Internet Gateway service running. Alternatively, select Startup and change the Startup Type to Automatic to cause the CICS Internet Gateway service to start up automatically every time the machine is started.

To use the CICS Gateway, view the cigstart.htm page from IBM WebExplorer or any other Web browser. The Uniform Resource Locator (URL) is

http://hostname.domain.name/cig/cigstart.htm

where hostname.domain.name is your server's host name.

The cigstart.htm page can be used as-is, or can be customized to an individual's or organization's needs. From here you can perform a number of tasks, including:

•list the CICS servers known to the CICS Client

•start a CICS transaction running on a specific CICS server

•switch the CICS Gateway internal tracing on or off.

That's all there's to it. Given the fact that the vast majority of corporate systems are already IMS and/or CICS ready, these two IBM Connectors will provide an easy way to connect a goldmine of information to the Internet.

## Appendix

HTMPAYF.HTM

```
/**********************************************************************/
/*                                                                  */
/* (c) Copyright IBM Corp. 1996                                     */
/* All Rights Reserved                                              */
/* Licensed Materials - Property of IBM                             */
/*                                                                  */
/* DISCLAIMER OF WARRANTIES.                                        */
/*                                                                  */
/* The following [enclosed] code is generated by a software product */
/* of IBM Corporation.                                              */
/* This generated code is provided to you solely for the purpose of */
/* assisting you in the development of your applications.           */
/* The code is provided "AS IS." IBM MAKES NO WARRANTIES, EXPRESS OR */
/* IMPLIED, INCLUDING BUT NOT LIMITED TO THE IMPLIED WARRANTIES OF  */
/* MERCHANTABILITY AND FITNESS FOR A PARTICULAR PURPOSE, REGARDING  */
/* THE FUNCTION OR PERFORMANCE OF THIS CODE.                        */
/* IBM shall not be liable for any damages arising out of your use  */
/* of the generated code, even if they have been advised of the    */
/* possibility of such damages.                                     */
/*                                                                  */
/* DISTRIBUTION.                                                    */
/*                                                                  */
/* This generated code can be freely distributed, copied, altered,  */
/* and incorporated into other software, provided that:            */
/*    - It bears the above Copyright notice and DISCLAIMER intact   */
/*    - The software is not for resale                             */
/*                                                                  */
/**********************************************************************/


<!- ******************************************************** ->
<!- *                                              *   ->
<!- *   IMS Web generated HTML input form.          *   ->
```

```
<!- *                                                    * ->
<!- *   This form :                                      * ->
<!- *                                                    * ->
<!- *    - has a table with label-entry fields pair for  * ->
<!- *       each input field for the associated transaction. * ->
<!- *    - upon clicking on SUBMIT button, will POST the * ->
<!- *       corresponding CGI-Bin program.               * ->
<!- *                                                    * ->
<!- *   You may modify this form as long as the names for * ->
<!- *   each entry fields are not changed.               * ->
<!- *                                                    * ->
<!- ************************************************************* ->
<HTML>
<HEAD>
<TITLE>IMS.Web.</TITLE>
</HEAD>
<BODY TEXT="000000">
<form method="POST" action="/CGI-Bin/CGIpayf.exe">
<center>
<table border="5" cellpadding="6">
<tr>
<td colspan=2 align="center" valign="center">
<strong>Enter the information below</strong><br>
<tr>
<td>
<strong>LNAME</strong>
<td>
<INPUT TYPE="text" NAME="LNAME" SIZE=10 MAXLENGTH=10 VALUE="">
<tr>
<td>
<strong>FNAME</strong>
<td>
<INPUT TYPE="text" NAME="FNAME" SIZE=10 MAXLENGTH=10 VALUE="">
<tr>
<td>
<strong>EMPNO</strong>
<td>
<INPUT TYPE="text" NAME="EMPNO" SIZE=5 MAXLENGTH=5 VALUE="">
<tr>
<td>
<strong>SSN</strong>
<td>
<INPUT TYPE="text" NAME="SSN" SIZE=11 MAXLENGTH=11 VALUE="">
<tr>
<td>
```

```
<strong>RATE</strong>
<td>
<INPUT TYPE="text" NAME="RATE" SIZE=9 MAXLENGTH=9 VALUE="">
</strong>
</td>
<tr>
<td colspan=2 align="center" valign="center">
<input type="submit" value="SUBMIT">
<input type="reset"  value="RESET">
</td>
</table>
</center>
</form>
<P>
<CENTER>
<img src="ims1.gif" align="center" hspace="5"
alt="Another Web Site Powered by IMS.Web" border=0>
</CENTER>
</BODY>
</HTML>
```

CGIPAYF.CPP

```
/***********************************************************************/
/*                                                                   */
/* (c) Copyright IBM Corp. 1996                                      */
/* All Rights Reserved                                               */
/* Licensed Materials - Property of IBM                              */
/*                                                                   */
/* DISCLAIMER OF WARRANTIES.                                         */
/*                                                                   */
/* The following [enclosed] code is generated by a software product  */
/* of IBM Corporation.                                               */
/* This generated code is provided to you solely for the purpose of  */
/* assisting you in the development of your applications.            */
/* The code is provided "AS IS." IBM MAKES NO WARRANTIES, EXPRESS OR */
/* IMPLIED, INCLUDING BUT NOT LIMITED TO THE IMPLIED WARRANTIES OF    */
/* MERCHANTABILITY AND FITNESS FOR A PARTICULAR PURPOSE, REGARDING    */
/* THE FUNCTION OR PERFORMANCE OF THIS CODE.                         */
/* IBM shall not be liable for any damages arising out of your use   */
/* of the generated code, even if they have been advised of the      */
/* possibility of such damages.                                      */
/*                                                                   */
/* DISTRIBUTION.                                                     */
```

```
/*                                                           */
/* This generated code can be freely distributed, copied, altered,   */
/* and incorporated into other software, provided that:              */
/*    - It bears the above Copyright notice and DISCLAIMER intact     */
/*    - The software is not for resale                               */
/*                                                           */
/*********************************************************************/


#include <iostream.h>
#include <stdio.h>
#include <string.h>
#include <stdlib.h>
#include <process.h>
#include "hwsutil.hpp"
#include "HTMpayf.hpp"
#include "HWSLPG01.hpp"
#include "HWSLPG02.hpp"


/*********************************************************/
/*                                                    */
/*   IMS Web generated CGI-Bin executable source code.   */
/*                                                    */
/*   INPUT : string generated by input HTML from STDIN   */
/*   OUTPUT: generated HTML to STDOUT                 */
/*                                                    */
/*   This routine :                                   */
/*                                                    */
/*    - parses the input for associated IMS transaction  */
/*      by using the constructor of HTML parsing class,  */
/*    - invokes the transaction by calling the execute    */
/*      method of the transaction input class,           */
/*    - and generates the output HTML from the output of  */
/*      the IMS transaction by using the transaction      */
/*      output class.                                  */
/*                                                    */
/*********************************************************/


/********************/
/*   MAIN PROGRAM   */
/********************/

int main (int argc, char *argv[])
{
        // The length of the following arrays must be changed to
```

```
// reflect the actual possible length calculated during GEN
char input[1024];
char ruName[9];

HtmIn *request;

HWSUtil *util;

HWSLPG01In tranObj;

HWSTranOut *pLpg = NULL;
HWSTranOut *qLpg = NULL;

/*******************************************************/
/* input comes from POST action of the input HTML file */
/*******************************************************/
cin >> input;
request = new HtmIn (input);

util = new HWSUtil;

cout << "Content-type: text/html\n\n";
cout << "<html><head><title>IMS.Web</title></head>\n";
cout << "<BODY TEXT=\"000000\">\n";

cout << "<h2>Results</h2>\n";

tranObj.setUser("GOFISHIN");
tranObj.setGroup("HARRY");
tranObj.setHost("CSDMEC13");
tranObj.setPort("9999");
tranObj.setIMS("SOCKEYE");
tranObj.setRUname(util->getRUname(ruName));

tranObj.setLNAME(request->LNAME);

tranObj.setFNAME(request->FNAME);

tranObj.setEMPNO(request->EMPNO);

tranObj.setSSN(request->SSN);

tranObj.setRATE(request->RATE);

pLpg = tranObj.execute();
```

```
        if (!pLpg) {
                cout << "Error Occurred in the Server CGI-BIN program con
                        tact the WEB.Master<p>\n";
        } else {
                while (pLpg) {
                        cout << "   " << pLpg->genHTML() << "<p>";
                        qLpg = pLpg;
                        pLpg = qLpg->getNext();
                        free(qLpg);
                } /* end while */
        } /* end if */

        cout << "</body></html>\n";

        delete request;
        return 0;

}
```

HTMPAYF.HPP

```
        /*********************************************************************/
        /*                                                                 */
        /* (c) Copyright IBM Corp. 1996                                    */
        /* All Rights Reserved                                             */
        /* Licensed Materials - Property of IBM                            */
        /*                                                                 */
        /* DISCLAIMER OF WARRANTIES.                                       */
        /*                                                                 */
        /* The following [enclosed] code is generated by a software product */
        /* of IBM Corporation.                                             */
        /* This generated code is provided to you solely for the purpose of */
        /* assisting you in the development of your applications.          */
        /* The code is provided "AS IS." IBM MAKES NO WARRANTIES, EXPRESS OR */
        /* IMPLIED, INCLUDING BUT NOT LIMITED TO THE IMPLIED WARRANTIES OF  */
        /* MERCHANTABILITY AND FITNESS FOR A PARTICULAR PURPOSE, REGARDING  */
        /* THE FUNCTION OR PERFORMANCE OF THIS CODE.                       */
        /* IBM shall not be liable for any damages arising out of your use */
        /* of the generated code, even if they have been advised of the   */
        /* possibility of such damages.                                   */
        /*                                                                 */
        /* DISTRIBUTION.                                                   */
        /*                                                                 */
```

```
/* This generated code can be freely distributed, copied, altered,   */
/* and incorporated into other software, provided that:              */
/*   - It bears the above Copyright notice and DISCLAIMER intact      */
/*   - The software is not for resale                                 */
/*                                                                    */
/**********************************************************************/

#ifndef HTMpayf_HPP
#define HTMpayf_HPP

#include <stddef.h>
#include <ctype.h>


/**********************************************************/
/*                                                        */
/*  IMS Web generated HTML input parsing class defintion.*/
/*                                                        */
/*  This class :                                          */
/*                                                        */
/*   - parses the input for associated IMS transaction    */
/*     passed in the constructor and populates its        */
/*     attributes with the parsed value.                  */
/*                                                        */
/**********************************************************/

class HtmIn
{
        public:
                HtmIn  (char * req);
                ~HtmIn ();

                char LNAME[11];

                char FNAME[11];

                char EMPNO[6];

                char SSN[12];

                char RATE[10];

};


#endif
```

HTMPAYF.CPP

```
/********************************************************/
/*                                                    */
/*   IMS Web generated HTML input parsing class.      */
/*                                                    */
/*   This class :                                     */
/*                                                    */
/*    - parses the input for associated IMS transaction */
/*      passed in the constructor and populates its   */
/*      attributes with the parsed value.             */
/*                                                    */
/********************************************************/

#include <stdlib.h>
#include <stdio.h>
```

```
#include <string.h>
#include "hwsutil.hpp"
#include "HTMpayf.hpp"

/***************/
/* Constructor */
/***************/

HtmIn::HtmIn (char * req)
{
        int i;
        char *preq, *key, *value, *posamp, *poseq;
        HWSUtil util;

        /************************************/
        /* Change all plusses back to spaces */
        /************************************/

        for(i=0; req[i]; i++) {
                if(req[i] == '+') req[i] = ' ';
        } /* end for */

        poseq = strchr(req,'=');
        if (poseq) {
                *poseq = '\0';
                key = req;
                preq = poseq+1;
        } else {
                key = NULL;
        } /* end if */

        while (key) {
                posamp = strchr(preq,'&');
                value = preq;
                if (posamp) {
                        *posamp = '\0';
                        preq = posamp+1;
                } else {
                        preq = NULL;
                } /* end if */
                if (*value) {
                        util.unper(value) ;
                } else {
                        value = NULL;
                } /* end if */
```

```c
if (!strcmp(key,"LNAME")) {
        if (value) {
                strcpy(LNAME,value);
        } else {
                memset(LNAME,'\0',sizeof(LNAME));
        } /* end if */
} /* end if */
if (!strcmp(key,"FNAME")) {
        if (value) {
                strcpy(FNAME,value);
        } else {
                memset(FNAME,'\0',sizeof(FNAME));
        } /* end if */
} /* end if */
if (!strcmp(key,"EMPNO")) {
        if (value) {
                strcpy(EMPNO,value);
        } else {
                memset(EMPNO,'\0',sizeof(EMPNO));
        } /* end if */
} /* end if */
if (!strcmp(key,"SSN")) {
        if (value) {
                strcpy(SSN,value);
        } else {
                memset(SSN,'\0',sizeof(SSN));
        } /* end if */
} /* end if */
if (!strcmp(key,"RATE")) {
        if (value) {
                strcpy(RATE,value);
        } else {
                memset(RATE,'\0',sizeof(RATE));
        } /* end if */
} /* end if */

if (preq) {
        poseq = strchr(preq,'=');
} else {
        poseq = NULL;
} /* end if */
if (poseq) {
        *poseq = '\0';
        key = preq;
```

```
                              preq = poseq+1;
                } else {
                              key = NULL;
                } /* end if */


        } /* end while */


}


/*************/
/* Destructor */
/*************/


HtmIn::~HtmIn ()
{
}
```

HWSLPG01.HPP

```
/*    - The software is not for resale                            */
/*                                                                */
/******************************************************************/


...


#ifndef HWSLPG01_HPP
#define HWSLPG01_HPP

#include "HWSTIn.hpp"

#define HWSLPG01IN_MAX_HWSMF001        5
#define HWSLPG01IN_MAX_LNAME          10
#define HWSLPG01IN_MAX_FNAME          10
#define HWSLPG01IN_MAX_EMPNO           5
#define HWSLPG01IN_MAX_SSN            11
#define HWSLPG01IN_MAX_RATE            9


/**********************************************************/
/*                                                        */
/*   IMS Web generated transaction input class definition.*/
/*                                                        */
/*   This class :                                         */
/*                                                        */
/*    - provides the execute method which compiles a      */
/*      list of all attribute values and calls the server */
/*      DLL for building and passing the message to IMS.  */
/*                                                        */
/**********************************************************/

class HWSLPG01In : public HWSTranIn {

        public:

                // LifeCycle
                HWSLPG01In();
                ~HWSLPG01In();

                // Overloaded Method
                virtual HWSTranOut * execute();

                // Access Methods for Fields
                void setLNAME(char *);
                inline char * getLNAME()    {return(LNAME);};
                void setFNAME(char *);
```

```
            inline char * getFNAME()     {return(FNAME);};
            void setEMPNO(char *);
            inline char * getEMPNO()     {return(EMPNO);};
            void setSSN(char *);
            inline char * getSSN()     {return(SSN);};
            void setRATE(char *);
            inline char * getRATE()     {return(RATE);};

    private:

            virtual HWSDList * export();

            char HWSMF001[HWSLPG01IN_MAX_HWSMF001+1];
            char LNAME[HWSLPG01IN_MAX_LNAME+1];
            char FNAME[HWSLPG01IN_MAX_FNAME+1];
            char EMPNO[HWSLPG01IN_MAX_EMPNO+1];
            char SSN[HWSLPG01IN_MAX_SSN+1];
            char RATE[HWSLPG01IN_MAX_RATE+1];

    };

    #endif
```

HWSLPG01.CPP

```
/**********************************************************************/
/*                                                                    */
/* (c) Copyright IBM Corp. 1996                                       */
/* All Rights Reserved                                                */
/* Licensed Materials - Property of IBM                               */
/*                                                                    */
/* DISCLAIMER OF WARRANTIES.                                          */
/*                                                                    */
/* The following [enclosed] code is generated by a software product  */
/* of IBM Corporation.                                               */
/* This generated code is provided to you solely for the purpose of  */
/* assisting you in the development of your applications.             */
/* The code is provided "AS IS." IBM MAKES NO WARRANTIES, EXPRESS OR */
/* IMPLIED, INCLUDING BUT NOT LIMITED TO THE IMPLIED WARRANTIES OF    */
/* MERCHANTABILITY AND FITNESS FOR A PARTICULAR PURPOSE, REGARDING    */
/* THE FUNCTION OR PERFORMANCE OF THIS CODE.                          */
/* IBM shall not be liable for any damages arising out of your use    */
/* of the generated code, even if they have been advised of the      */
/* possibility of such damages.                                       */
/*                                                                    */
```

```
/* DISTRIBUTION.                                                    */
/*                                                                  */
/* This generated code can be freely distributed, copied, altered,  */
/* and incorporated into other software, provided that:            */
/*    - It bears the above Copyright notice and DISCLAIMER intact    */
/*    - The software is not for resale                             */
/*                                                                  */
/********************************************************************/

#include <stdio.h>
#include <string.h>
#include <stdlib.h>
#include "HWS.h"
#include "HWSTran.hpp"
#include "HWSMFSF.hpp"
#include "HWSMsgF.hpp"
#include "HWSLPGF.hpp"
#include "HWSSegF.hpp"
#include "HWSFldF.hpp"
#include "HWSDMod.hpp"
#include "HWSDList.hpp"
#include "HWSLNode.hpp"
#include "HWSLPG01.hpp"
#include "HWSLPG02.hpp"


/***********************************************************/
/*                                                         */
/*   IMS Web generated transaction input class.            */
/*                                                         */
/*   This>class :                                          */
/*                                                         */
/*    - provides the execute method which compiles a       */
/*      list of all attribute values and calls the server */
/*      DLL for building and passing the message to IMS.   */
/*                                                         */
/***********************************************************/

// LifeCycle
HWSLPG01In::HWSLPG01In():
        HWSTranIn("CGIpayf")
{

        HWSMFSFormat     *aFmt;
        HWSMsgFormat     *aMsg;
        HWSLPageFormat   *aLpg;
```

```
HWSSegFormat      *aSeg;
HWSFldFormat      *aFld;
Condition         *aCond;

aFmt = new HWSMFSFormat();

aMsg = new HWSMsgFormat("PAYIN",OPT1,HWSIN);
aFmt->addMID(aMsg);

aCond = NULL;
aLpg = new HWSLPageFormat("HWSLPG01",NOCOND,aCond);
aMsg->addLPage(aLpg);

aSeg = new HWSSegFormat("HWSSEG01");
aLpg->addSeg(aSeg);

memcpy(HWSMF001,"SKS1 ",5);
memset(HWSMF001+5, '\0', 1);

aFld = new HWSFldFormat("HWSMF001",FLDLIT,5);

aFld->pp = 0;
aFld->justify = HWSLEFT;
aFld->fillType = HWSCHAR;
aFld->fill = ' ';
aFld->A3270Attr = NO3270;
aFld->eAttr = 0;
aFld->literalLen = 5;
aFld->literalVal = (char *) malloc (5+1);
memcpy(aFld->literalVal,"SKS1 ",5);
memset(aFld->literalVal+5, '\0', 1);

aSeg->addFld(aFld);

LNAME[0] = '\0';

aFld = new HWSFldFormat("HWSMF002",STANDARD,10);

aFld->pp = 0;
aFld->justify = HWSLEFT;
aFld->fillType = HWSCHAR;
aFld->fill = ' ';
aFld->A3270Attr = NO3270;
aFld->eAttr = 0;
aFld->literalLen = 0;
```

```
aFld->literalVal = NULL;

aSeg->addFld(aFld);

FNAME[0] = '\0';

aFld = new HWSFldFormat("HWSMF003",STANDARD,10);

aFld->pp = 0;
aFld->justify = HWSLEFT;
aFld->fillType = HWSCHAR;
aFld->fill = ' ';
aFld->A3270Attr = NO3270;
aFld->eAttr = 0;
aFld->literalLen = 0;
aFld->literalVal = NULL;

aSeg->addFld(aFld);

EMPNO[0] = '\0';

aFld = new HWSFldFormat("HWSMF004",STANDARD,7);

aFld->pp = 0;
aFld->justify = HWSLEFT;
aFld->fillType = HWSCHAR;
aFld->fill = ' ';
aFld->A3270Attr = NO3270;
aFld->eAttr = 1;
aFld->literalLen = 0;
aFld->literalVal = NULL;

aSeg->addFld(aFld);

SSN[0] = '\0';

aFld = new HWSFldFormat("HWSMF005",STANDARD,11);

aFld->pp = 0;
aFld->justify = HWSLEFT;
aFld->fillType = HWSCHAR;
aFld->fill = ' ';
aFld->A3270Attr = NO3270;
aFld->eAttr = 0;
aFld->literalLen = 0;
```

```
aFld->literalVal = NULL;

aSeg->addFld(aFld);

RATE[0] = '\0';

aFld = new HWSFldFormat("HWSMF006",STANDARD,9);

aFld->pp = 0;
aFld->justify = HWSRIGHT;
aFld->fillType = HWSCHAR;
aFld->fill = '0';
aFld->A3270Attr = NO3270;
aFld->eAttr = 0;
aFld->literalLen = 0;
aFld->literalVal = NULL;

aSeg->addFld(aFld);

aMsg = new HWSMsgFormat("PAYOUT",OPT1,HWSOUT);
aFmt->addMOD(aMsg);

aCond = NULL;
aLpg = new HWSLPageFormat("HWSLPG02",NOCOND,aCond);
aMsg->addLPage(aLpg);

aSeg = new HWSSegFormat("HWSSEG02");
aLpg->addSeg(aSeg);

aFld = new HWSFldFormat("HWSMF007",STANDARD,10);

aFld->pp = 0;
aFld->justify = HWSLEFT;
aFld->fillType = HWSNULL;
aFld->fill = '\x3F';
aFld->A3270Attr = NO3270;
aFld->eAttr = 0;
aFld->literalLen = 0;
aFld->literalVal = NULL;

aSeg->addFld(aFld);

aFld = new HWSFldFormat("HWSMF008",STANDARD,10);

aFld->pp = 0;
```

```
aFld->justify = HWSLEFT;
aFld->fillType = HWSNULL;
aFld->fill = '\x3F';
aFld->A3270Attr = NO3270;
aFld->eAttr = 0;
aFld->literalLen = 0;
aFld->literalVal = NULL;


aSeg->addFld(aFld);

aSeg = new HWSSegFormat("HWSSEG03");
aLpg->addSeg(aSeg);

aFld = new HWSFldFormat("HWSMF009",STANDARD,7);

aFld->pp = 0;
aFld->justify = HWSLEFT;
aFld->fillType = HWSNULL;
aFld->fill = '\x3F';
aFld->A3270Attr = NO3270;
aFld->eAttr = 1;
aFld->literalLen = 0;
aFld->literalVal = NULL;


aSeg->addFld(aFld);

aFld = new HWSFldFormat("HWSMF010",STANDARD,11);

aFld->pp = 0;
aFld->justify = HWSLEFT;
aFld->fillType = HWSNULL;
aFld->fill = '\x3F';
aFld->A3270Attr = NO3270;
aFld->eAttr = 0;
aFld->literalLen = 0;
aFld->literalVal = NULL;


aSeg->addFld(aFld);

aSeg = new HWSSegFormat("HWSSEG04");
aLpg->addSeg(aSeg);

aFld = new HWSFldFormat("HWSMF011",STANDARD,9);

aFld->pp = 0;
```

```
        aFld->justify = HWSLEFT;
        aFld->fillType = HWSNULL;
        aFld->fill = '\x3F';
        aFld->A3270Attr = NO3270;
        aFld->eAttr = 0;
        aFld->literalLen = 0;
        aFld->literalVal = NULL;

        aSeg->addFld(aFld);

        aSeg = new HWSSegFormat("HWSSEG05");
        aLpg->addSeg(aSeg);

        aFld = new HWSFldFormat("HWSMF012",STANDARD,50);

        aFld->pp = 0;
        aFld->justify = HWSLEFT;
        aFld->fillType = HWSNULL;
        aFld->fill = '\x3F';
        aFld->A3270Attr = NO3270;
        aFld->eAttr = 0;
        aFld->literalLen = 0;
        aFld->literalVal = NULL;

        aSeg->addFld(aFld);

        aFld = new HWSFldFormat("HWSMF013",SLITDAT2,8);

        aFld->pp = 0;
        aFld->justify = HWSLEFT;
        aFld->fillType = HWSNULL;
        aFld->fill = '\x3F';
        aFld->A3270Attr = NO3270;
        aFld->eAttr = 0;
        aFld->literalLen = 0;
        aFld->literalVal = NULL;

        aSeg->addFld(aFld);

        formatObj = aFmt;

    }

HWSLPG01In::~HWSLPG01In()
    {
```

```
        }

// Overloaded Method
HWSTranOut * HWSLPG01In::execute()
{
        HWSTranOut * aMod = NULL;
        HWSTranOut * pMod = NULL;
        HWSTranOut * qMod = NULL;
        HWSTran     aTran(this);
        HWSDList    * pList;
        HWSDList    * qList;
        int errNum = 0;

        pList = aTran.doIMS(export(),formatObj);

        if (pList) {
                while (pList) {
                        if (strcmp(pList->MDName,"HWSErrOut") == 0) {
                                pMod = new HWSErrOut(pList);
                        } else if (strcmp(pList->MDName,"PAYOUT&HWSLPG02")
== 0) {
                                pMod = new HWSLPG02Out(pList);
                        } else if (strcmp(pList->MDName,"DFSMO1&HWSMO1") ==
0) {
                                pMod = new HWSMO1(pList);
                        } else if (strcmp(pList->MDName,"DFSMO2&HWSMO2") ==
0) {
                                pMod = new HWSMO2(pList);
                        } else if (strcmp(pList->MDName,"DFSMO3&HWSMO3") ==
0) {
                                pMod = new HWSMO3(pList);
                        } else if (strcmp(pList->MDName,"DFSMO4&HWSMO4") ==
0) {
                                pMod = new HWSMO4(pList);
                        } else if (strcmp(pList->MDName,"DFSMO5&HWSMO5") ==
0) {
                                pMod = new HWSMO5(pList);
                        } else if (strcmp(pList->MDName,"DFSDSPO1&HWSD-
SPO1") == 0) {
                                pMod = new HWSDSPO1(pList);
                        } else {
                                pMod = new HWSErrOut(1000,"AN UNKNOWN MOD
RETURNED BY HOST");
                        } /* end if */
                        if (!aMod) aMod = pMod;
```

```
                              if (qMod) qMod->setNext(pMod);
                              qMod = pMod;
                              qList = pList;
                              pList = qList->getNextList();
                      } /* end while */
              } else {
                      pMod = new HWSErrOut(1001,"SEVERE ERROR NULL RETURNED FROM
      DLLs");
              } /* end if */

              return (aMod);

      }


      // Private Method Export
      HWSDList * HWSLPG01In::export()
      {
              HWSDList  * expList;
              HWSLNode  * aFld;
              char    * iStr;
              int      iStrLen;

              expList = new HWSDList(formatObj->firstMID->name);

              iStrLen = strlen(HWSMF001);
              if (iStrLen > 0) {
                      iStr = (char *)malloc(iStrLen + 1);
                      strcpy(iStr,HWSMF001);
              } else {
                      iStr = NULL;
                      iStrLen = 0;
              }
              aFld = new HWSLNode("HWSMF001",iStrLen,iStr);
              expList->addNode(aFld);

              iStrLen = strlen(LNAME);
              if (iStrLen > 0) {
                      iStr = (char *)malloc(iStrLen + 1);
                      strcpy(iStr,LNAME);
              } else {
                      iStr = NULL;
                      iStrLen = 0;
              }
              aFld = new HWSLNode("HWSMF002",iStrLen,iStr);
              expList->addNode(aFld);
```

```
iStrLen = strlen(FNAME);
if (iStrLen > 0) {
        iStr = (char *)malloc(iStrLen + 1);
        strcpy(iStr,FNAME);
} else {
        iStr = NULL;
        iStrLen = 0;
}
aFld = new HWSLNode("HWSMF003",iStrLen,iStr);
expList->addNode(aFld);

iStrLen = strlen(EMPNO);
if (iStrLen > 0) {
        iStr = (char *)malloc(iStrLen + 1);
        strcpy(iStr,EMPNO);
} else {
        iStr = NULL;
        iStrLen = 0;
}
aFld = new HWSLNode("HWSMF004",iStrLen,iStr);
expList->addNode(aFld);

iStrLen = strlen(SSN);
if (iStrLen > 0) {
        iStr = (char *)malloc(iStrLen + 1);
        strcpy(iStr,SSN);
} else {
        iStr = NULL;
        iStrLen = 0;
}
aFld = new HWSLNode("HWSMF005",iStrLen,iStr);
expList->addNode(aFld);

iStrLen = strlen(RATE);
if (iStrLen > 0) {
        iStr = (char *)malloc(iStrLen + 1);
        strcpy(iStr,RATE);
} else {
        iStr = NULL;
        iStrLen = 0;
}
aFld = new HWSLNode("HWSMF006",iStrLen,iStr);
expList->addNode(aFld);
```

```
                return (expList);


}


// Access Methods for Fields
void HWSLPG01In::setLNAME(char * value)
{
        memset(LNAME,'\0',HWSLPG01IN_MAX_LNAME+1);
        if (*value) {

memcpy(LNAME,value,(strlen(value)<=HWSLPG01IN_MAX_LNAME)?strlen(value):HWSL
PG01IN_MAX_LNAME);
        } /* end if */
}


void HWSLPG01In::setFNAME(char * value)
{
        memset(FNAME,'\0',HWSLPG01IN_MAX_FNAME+1);
        if (*value) {

memcpy(FNAME,value,(strlen(value)<=HWSLPG01IN_MAX_FNAME)?strlen(value):HWSL
PG01IN_MAX_FNAME);
        } /* end if */
}


void HWSLPG01In::setEMPNO(char * value)
{
        memset(EMPNO,'\0',HWSLPG01IN_MAX_EMPNO+1);
        if (*value) {

memcpy(EMPNO,value,(strlen(value)<=HWSLPG01IN_MAX_EMPNO)?strlen(value):HWSL
PG01IN_MAX_EMPNO);
        } /* end if */
}


void HWSLPG01In::setSSN(char * value)
{
        memset(SSN,'\0',HWSLPG01IN_MAX_SSN+1);
        if (*value) {

memcpy(SSN,value,(strlen(value)<=HWSLPG01IN_MAX_SSN)?strlen(value):HWSLPG01
IN_MAX_SSN);
        } /* end if */
}
```

```
void HWSLPG01In::setRATE(char * value)
{
        memset(RATE,'\0',HWSLPG01IN_MAX_RATE+1);
        if (*value) {

memcpy(RATE,value,(strlen(value)<=HWSLPG01IN_MAX_RATE)?strlen(value):HWSLPG
01IN_MAX_RATE);
        } /* end if */
}
```

HWSLPG02.HPP

```
/*********************************************************************/
/*                                                                 */
/* (c) Copyright IBM Corp. 1996                                    */
/* All Rights Reserved                                             */
/* Licensed Materials - Property of IBM                            */
/*                                                                 */
/* DISCLAIMER OF WARRANTIES.                                       */
/*                                                                 */
/* The following [enclosed] code is generated by a software product */
/* of IBM Corporation.                                             */
/* This generated code is provided to you solely for the purpose of */
/* assisting you in the development of your applications.          */
/* The code is provided "AS IS." IBM MAKES NO WARRANTIES, EXPRESS OR */
/* IMPLIED, INCLUDING BUT NOT LIMITED TO THE IMPLIED WARRANTIES OF  */
/* MERCHANTABILITY AND FITNESS FOR A PARTICULAR PURPOSE, REGARDING  */
/* THE FUNCTION OR PERFORMANCE OF THIS CODE.                       */
/* IBM shall not be liable for any damages arising out of your use  */
/* of the generated code, even if they have been advised of the    */
/* possibility of such damages.                                    */
/*                                                                 */
/* DISTRIBUTION.                                                   */
/*                                                                 */
/* This generated code can be freely distributed, copied, altered,  */
/* and incorporated into other software, provided that:           */
/*    - It bears the above Copyright notice and DISCLAIMER intact   */
/*    - The software is not for resale                            */
/*                                                                 */
/*********************************************************************/

...

#ifndef HWSLPG02_HPP
#define HWSLPG02_HPP
```

```
#include "HWSTOut.hpp"

#define HWSLPG02OUT_MAX_LNAME           10
#define HWSLPG02OUT_MAX_FNAME           10

#define HWSLPG02OUT_MAX_EMPNO           5
#define HWSLPG02OUT_MAX_EMPNO_ATTR      2
#define HWSLPG02OUT_MAX_SSN             11

#define HWSLPG02OUT_MAX_RATE            9

#define HWSLPG02OUT_MAX_MSGFLD          50
#define HWSLPG02OUT_MAX_DATE            8


/***********************************************************/
/*                                                         */
/*   IMS Web generated transaction output class definition.*/
/*                                                         */
/*   This class :                                          */
/*                                                         */
/*    - provides the genHTML method which generates the    */
/*      HTML output based on the result of IMS tran.       */
/*                                                         */
/***********************************************************/

class HWSLPG02Out : public HWSTranOut {

        public:

                // LifeCycle
                HWSLPG02Out(HWSDList * fldList);
                ~HWSLPG02Out();

                // Overloaded Method
                virtual char    * genHTML();
                virtual HWSLNode * genList();

                // Access Methods for Fields
                inline char * getLNAME()     {return(LNAME);};
                inline char * getFNAME()     {return(FNAME);};
                inline char * getEMPNO()     {return(EMPNO);};
                inline char * getEMPNO_Attr()    {return(EMPNO_Attr);};
                inline char * getSSN()    {return(SSN);};
                inline char * getRATE()     {return(RATE);};
```

```
           inline char * getMSGFLD()     {return(MSGFLD);};
           inline char * getDATE()     {return(DATE);};

       private:

           HWSDList * fList;

           char LNAME[HWSLPG02OUT_MAX_LNAME+1];
           char FNAME[HWSLPG02OUT_MAX_FNAME+1];
           char EMPNO[HWSLPG02OUT_MAX_EMPNO+1];
           char EMPNO_Attr[HWSLPG02OUT_MAX_EMPNO_ATTR+1];
           char SSN[HWSLPG02OUT_MAX_SSN+1];
           char RATE[HWSLPG02OUT_MAX_RATE+1];
           char MSGFLD[HWSLPG02OUT_MAX_MSGFLD+1];
           char DATE[HWSLPG02OUT_MAX_DATE+1];

   };

   #endif



HWSLPG02.CPP


   /**********************************************************************/
   /*                                                                  */
   /* (c) Copyright IBM Corp. 1996                                     */
   /* All Rights Reserved                                              */
   /* Licensed Materials - Property of IBM                             */
   /*                                                                  */
   /* DISCLAIMER OF WARRANTIES.                                        */
   /*                                                                  */
   /* The following [enclosed] code is generated by a software product */
   /* of IBM Corporation.                                              */
   /* This generated code is provided to you solely for the purpose of */
   /* assisting you in the development of your applications.           */
   /* The code is provided "AS IS." IBM MAKES NO WARRANTIES, EXPRESS OR */
   /* IMPLIED, INCLUDING BUT NOT LIMITED TO THE IMPLIED WARRANTIES OF   */
   /* MERCHANTABILITY AND FITNESS FOR A PARTICULAR PURPOSE, REGARDING   */
   /* THE FUNCTION OR PERFORMANCE OF THIS CODE.                        */
   /* IBM shall not be liable for any damages arising out of your use  */
   /* of the generated code, even if they have been advised of the    */
   /* possibility of such damages.                                     */
   /*                                                                  */
   /* DISTRIBUTION.                                                    */
   /*                                                                  */
```

```
/* This generated code can be freely distributed, copied, altered,    */
/* and incorporated into other software, provided that:               */
/*    - It bears the above Copyright notice and DISCLAIMER intact      */
/*    - The software is not for resale                                 */
/*                                                                     */
/***********************************************************************/

...

#include <stdio.h>
#include <string.h>
#include <stdlib.h>
#include "HWS.h"
#include "HWSTran.hpp"
#include "HWSMFSF.hpp"
#include "HWSMsgF.hpp"
#include "HWSLPGF.hpp"
#include "HWSSegF.hpp"
#include "HWSFldF.hpp"
#include "HWSDMod.hpp"
#include "HWSDList.hpp"
#include "HWSLNode.hpp"
#include "HWSLPG02.hpp"

/********************************************************/
/*                                                     */
/*  IMS Web generated transaction output class.        */
/*                                                     */
/*  This class :                                       */
/*                                                     */
/*    - provides the genHTML method which generates the */
/*      HTML output based on the result of IMS tran.    */
/*                                                     */
/********************************************************/

// LifeCycle
HWSLPG02Out::HWSLPG02Out(HWSDList * fldList):
        HWSTranOut("HWSLPG02Out")
{

        HWSLNode * aFld;

        fList = fldList;

        aFld = fldList->getFirst();
```

```
        memset(LNAME,'\0',HWSLPG02OUT_MAX_LNAME+1);
        memcpy(LNAME,aFld->data,(aFld->length <=
HWSLPG02OUT_MAX_LNAME)?aFld->length:HWSLPG02OUT_MAX_LNAME);
        aFld = aFld->next;

        memset(FNAME,'\0',HWSLPG02OUT_MAX_FNAME+1);
        memcpy(FNAME,aFld->data,(aFld->length <=
HWSLPG02OUT_MAX_FNAME)?aFld->length:HWSLPG02OUT_MAX_FNAME);
        aFld = aFld->next;

        memset(EMPNO_Attr,'\0',HWSLPG02OUT_MAX_EMPNO_ATTR+1);
        memcpy(EMPNO_Attr,aFld->data,(aFld->length <=
HWSLPG02OUT_MAX_EMPNO_ATTR)?aFld->length:HWSLPG02OUT_MAX_EMPNO);
        aFld = aFld->next;
        memset(EMPNO,'\0',HWSLPG02OUT_MAX_EMPNO+1);
        memcpy(EMPNO,aFld->data,(aFld->length <=
HWSLPG02OUT_MAX_EMPNO)?aFld->length:HWSLPG02OUT_MAX_EMPNO);
        aFld = aFld->next;

        memset(SSN,'\0',HWSLPG02OUT_MAX_SSN+1);
        memcpy(SSN,aFld->data,(aFld->length <= HWSLPG02OUT_MAX_SSN)?aFld-
>length:HWSLPG02OUT_MAX_SSN);
        aFld = aFld->next;

        memset(RATE,'\0',HWSLPG02OUT_MAX_RATE+1);
        memcpy(RATE,aFld->data,(aFld->length <= HWSLPG02OUT_MAX_RATE)?aFld-
>length:HWSLPG02OUT_MAX_RATE);
        aFld = aFld->next;

        memset(MSGFLD,'\0',HWSLPG02OUT_MAX_MSGFLD+1);
        memcpy(MSGFLD,aFld->data,(aFld->length <=
HWSLPG02OUT_MAX_MSGFLD)?aFld->length:HWSLPG02OUT_MAX_MSGFLD);
        aFld = aFld->next;

        memset(DATE,'\0',HWSLPG02OUT_MAX_DATE+1);
        memcpy(DATE,aFld->data,(aFld->length <= HWSLPG02OUT_MAX_DATE)?aFld-
>length:HWSLPG02OUT_MAX_DATE);
        aFld = aFld->next;

}


HWSLPG02Out::~HWSLPG02Out()
{
}
```

```cpp
// Overloaded Method genHTML
char * HWSLPG02Out::genHTML()
{
        char      * buf;
        HWSLNode * aFld;

        buf = (char *)malloc(sizeof(HWSLPG02Out)*10);
        strcpy(buf,"<table border=5 cellpadding=6>\n");

        aFld = fList->getFirst();
        strcat(buf,"<tr><td><strong>");
        strcat(buf,"LNAME");
        strcat(buf,"</strong>\n");
        strcat(buf,"<td>");
        strncat(buf,(char *)aFld->data,aFld->length);
        strcat(buf,"\n");
        aFld = aFld->next;
        strcat(buf,"<tr><td><strong>");
        strcat(buf,"FNAME");
        strcat(buf,"</strong>\n");
        strcat(buf,"<td>");
        strncat(buf,(char *)aFld->data,aFld->length);
        strcat(buf,"\n");
        aFld = aFld->next;
        /* skipping the extended attribute data*/
        aFld = aFld->next;
        strcat(buf,"<tr><td><strong>");
        strcat(buf,"EMPNO");
        strcat(buf,"</strong>\n");
        strcat(buf,"<td>");
        strncat(buf,(char *)aFld->data,aFld->length);
        strcat(buf,"\n");
        aFld = aFld->next;
        strcat(buf,"<tr><td><strong>");
        strcat(buf,"SSN");
        strcat(buf,"</strong>\n");
        strcat(buf,"<td>");
        strncat(buf,(char *)aFld->data,aFld->length);
        strcat(buf,"\n");
        aFld = aFld->next;
        strcat(buf,"<tr><td><strong>");
        strcat(buf,"RATE");
        strcat(buf,"</strong>\n");
        strcat(buf,"<td>");
        strncat(buf,(char *)aFld->data,aFld->length);
```

```
        strcat(buf,"\n");
        aFld = aFld->next;
        strcat(buf,"<tr><td><strong>");
        strcat(buf,"MSGFLD");
        strcat(buf,"</strong>\n");
        strcat(buf,"<td>");
        strncat(buf,(char *)aFld->data,aFld->length);
        strcat(buf,"\n");
        aFld = aFld->next;
        strcat(buf,"<tr><td><strong>");
        strcat(buf,"DATE");
        strcat(buf,"</strong>\n");
        strcat(buf,"<td>");
        strncat(buf,(char *)aFld->data,aFld->length);
        strcat(buf,"\n");
        aFld = aFld->next;
        strcat(buf,"</table>\n");
        return buf;


}


// Overloaded Method genList
HWSLNode * HWSLPG02Out::genList()
{
        HWSLNode * fldList   = NULL;
        HWSLNode * aNode     = NULL;
        HWSLNode * newNode   = NULL;
        HWSLNode * prevNode  = NULL;
        if (fList) {
                for (aNode = fList->getFirst();
                    aNode != NULL;
                    aNode = aNode->next) {
                    newNode = new HWSLNode(aNode->name,aNode-
>length,aNode->data);
                    if (prevNode) {
                            prevNode->next = newNode;
                    } else {
                            fldList = newNode;
                    } /* end if */
                    prevNode = newNode;
                } /* end for */
        } /* end if */
        return fldList;


}
```

CGIPAYF.MAK

```
/**********************************************************************/
/*                                                                    */
/* (c) Copyright IBM Corp. 1996                                       */
/* All Rights Reserved                                                */
/* Licensed Materials - Property of IBM                               */
/*                                                                    */
/* DISCLAIMER OF WARRANTIES.                                          */
/*                                                                    */
/* The following [enclosed] code is generated by a software product  */
/* of IBM Corporation.                                                */
/* This generated code is provided to you solely for the purpose of  */
/* assisting you in the development of your applications.             */
/* The code is provided "AS IS." IBM MAKES NO WARRANTIES, EXPRESS OR */
/* IMPLIED, INCLUDING BUT NOT LIMITED TO THE IMPLIED WARRANTIES OF    */
/* MERCHANTABILITY AND FITNESS FOR A PARTICULAR PURPOSE, REGARDING    */
/* THE FUNCTION OR PERFORMANCE OF THIS CODE.                          */
/* IBM shall not be liable for any damages arising out of your use    */
/* of the generated code, even if they have been advised of the      */
/* possibility of such damages.                                       */
/*                                                                    */
/* DISTRIBUTION.                                                      */
/*                                                                    */
/* This generated code can be freely distributed, copied, altered,   */
/* and incorporated into other software, provided that:              */
/*    - It bears the above Copyright notice and DISCLAIMER intact     */
/*    - The software is not for resale                               */
/*                                                                    */
/**********************************************************************/
#######################################
# IMS.Web Studio Generated NMAKE File #
#######################################

!IF "$(CFG)" != "HWSRel" && "$(CFG)" != "HWSDbg"
!MESSAGE Invalid configuration "$(CFG)" specified.
!MESSAGE You can specify a configuration when running NMAKE on this make-
file
!MESSAGE by defining the macro CFG on the command line.  For example:
!MESSAGE
!MESSAGE NMAKE /f "CGIpayf.mak" CFG="HWSDbg"
!MESSAGE
!MESSAGE Possible choices for configuration are:
!MESSAGE
!MESSAGE "HWSRel" : build a PRODUCTION version
```

```
!MESSAGE "HWSDbg" : build a DEBUG version
!MESSAGE
!ERROR An invalid configuration is specified.
!ENDIF


!IF "$(OS)" == "Windows_NT"
NULL=
!ELSE
NULL=nul
!ENDIF


!IF "$(CFG)" == "HWSRel"
CFLAGS= /nologo /MD /W3 /GX /O2 /D "WIN32" /D "NDEBUG" /D "_CONSOLE" /D
"HWSNT4" /YX /c
LFLAGS= /nologo /subsystem:console /incremental:no /machine:IX86
/out:".\CGIpayf.exe"
!ENDIF
!IF "$(CFG)" == "HWSDbg"
CFLAGS=/nologo /MDd /W3 /Gm /GX /Zi /Od /D "WIN32" /D "_DEBUG" /D "_CON-
SOLE" /D "HWSNT4" /YX /c
LFLAGS= /nologo /subsystem:console /incremental:no /debug /machine:IX86
/out:".\CGIpayf.exe"
!ENDIF
!IF "$(CFG)" == "HWSTrap"
CFLAGS=/nologo /MDd /W3 /Gm /GX /Zi /Od /D "WIN32" /D "_DEBUG" /D "_TRAP"
/D "_CONSOLE" /D "HWSNT4" /YX /c
LFLAGS= /nologo /subsystem:console /incremental:no /debug /machine:IX86
/out:".\CGIpayf.exe"
!ENDIF


##########################################################################
#####
# Begin Project

ALL : ".\CGIpayf.exe"

LINK_OBJS= \
        "HWSLPG01.obj"\
        "HWSLPG02.obj"\
        "HTMpayf.obj"\
        "CGIpayf.obj"


LINK=link.exe
COMPILE=cl.exe
```

```
LINK_LIBS= \
 HWSTran.lib HWSCom.lib HWSUtil.lib HWSFMT.lib HWSMFS.lib

.CPP.obj:
 $(COMPILE) $(CFLAGS) %s

".\CGIpayf.exe" : \
    $(LINK_OBJS)
    $(LINK) @<<
     $(LFLAGS)
     $(LINK_LIBS)
     $(LINK_OBJS)
<<


############  END OF FILE  ############
```

# 13

# INFORMIX-Universal Web Connect

## Introduction

Informix is one of the leading enterprise-level RDBMS vendors. As can be expected, they've been working diligently to provide an assortment of Web connecting solutions to users of their databases. While this chapter is about Informix's Universal Web Connect solution, I don't want you to leave here with the impression that this is all Informix offers. They also provide a set of Webkits that extend existing Informix products to enable you to build Web-based applications that interact with databases.

The Webkits set includes

> A class library for INFORMIX-NewEra.
> A function library for INFORMIX-4GL.
> A function library for INFORMIX-ESQL/C.

Each library provides the capability to write scripts that process CGI environment variables and form entry values, use those values to interact with databases, and send output back to a Web page. All are provided on an "as is" basis and can be downloaded from the following INFORMIX Web site: http://www.informix.com/informix/products/dlprod/webkits/docentry.htm.

And now on to the main topic.

Unlike all other Web solutions which store Web applications as flat files and scripts in the operating system directory, Informix Universal Web Architecture stores the entire Web application content — including HTML files, application

templates, and multimedia content such as images, maps, and photos within the Informix database. By storing all the Web application content within the database, developers can manage the application as it grows
in size and complexity, ensuring the dynamic delivery of information to users.

A critical component of the Informix Universal Web Architecture is the ability to generate database applications that can dynamically access the information stored within any Informix database. This capability is provided by INFORMIX-Universal Web Connect. INFORMIX-Universal Web Connect provides development and run-time components that integrate the Web server with any Informix database server. By utilizing this interface, developers can quickly and easily generate Web applications that incorporate data retrieved dynamically from an Informix database server.

## Web-Enabled Database Application Architecture

To build a Web-enabled database application, the following components as shown in figure 13-1 are necessary:

- Web client
- Web server
- Middleware
- Database server

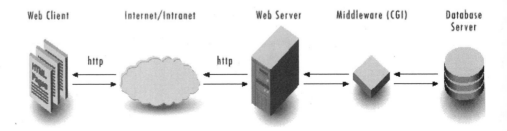

**Figure 13-1.** Components of a Web-enabled database application.

The Web client is a Web browser such as Netscape Navigator or Microsoft Internet Explorer. The Web server is any HTML-based server such as Netscape FastTrack or Enterprise Server or Microsoft Internet Information Server. Database applications typically reside on the Web server. An end user can spawn a database application through the Web browser that communicates with the Web server through the Internet via hypertext transport protocol (HTTP).

The middleware is responsible for managing communication and providing application services between the Web server and the database server. Residing on the Web server, the middleware software calls external programs or "scripts" that act as the "transport mechanism" between the Web server and the database server. This script constructs the query, passes the query to the database, and formats the output as an HTML page. The Web server then returns the HTML page to the Web browser to display the information to the end user. The database server manages the data residing within the database.

There are a number of middleware solutions in the market today. The most popular middleware used today is the common gateway interface (CGI). Other solutions include ISAPI from Microsoft and NSAPI from Netscape.

CGI is an interface used for interfacing external applications with a Web server. Applications can use CGI as a vehicle to communicate with the database, transmit information to the server, and receive results for display on the client.

This technique provides a simple mechanism for basic database connectivity. While CGI offers a simple way to connect to a database, it does have some limitations. First, CGI applications are not persistent. Each time the CGI program is accessed through the Web server the CGI program starts up, performs its processing, then exits. Because the CGI application is restarted with each request, the database connection must be re-established each time. As a result, applications that require a persistent database connection have to use complicated techniques to maintain state between client requests.

CGI also suffers from performance problems, especially in multiuser applications where multiple database connections are required. In addition to the persistence problem discussed above, CGI applications cannot be shared by multiple client requests. Even if a CGI application is running when a new request comes in, a new copy of the CGI application is started. As more concurrent requests are made, more concurrent processes are created on the server. Creating an application process for every request is time-consuming and requires a large amount of memory. Additionally, it restricts the resources available for the application itself, thereby slowing down performance and increasing wait time.

Another problem with CGI is the fact that there is no language associated with it. To provide a Web application with access to a database, a developer must write a script using languages such as Perl, Tcl, or C, or in HTML files. Many application developers simply do not have the knowledge or the time to create these CGI scripts and HTML files.

Finally, manageability is a key concern with CGI. Since developers have to write separate scripts and/or HTML files in order to connect to the database, these scripts and files may be spread out across the network; hence they become very difficult to manage and control. Additionally, security is of a special concern. Since a CGI program is executed on a company's Web server, special precautions are needed to ensure security. These precautions may include moving CGI programs to a special directory. This creates additional work for both programmers and Web masters.

To overcome the limitations described above, both Microsoft and Netscape came out with their own middleware solutions: Microsoft with ISAPI and Netscape with NSAPI. These APIs provide better performance, enable developers to more easily develop complex applications, and offer better protection and security.

However, ISAPI and NSAPI are not compatible with each other. The lack of an industry standard governing these interfaces makes it difficult for companies to choose the right interface for their environments or customers. Additionally, these APIs work on specific Web servers and operating systems. As a result, many companies choose to develop with CGI, which is supported by most Web servers.

## Solution Overview

To address the limitations and the incompatibilities of CGI, NSAPI, and ISAPI, Informix has developed INFORMIX-Universal Web Connect. INFORMIX-Universal Web Connect lets customers maximize the potential of the Web by allowing them to create intelligent database applications.

INFORMIX-Universal Web Connect lets developers create Web applications that incorporate data retrieved dynamically from Informix databases. The type of data retrieved by the application can be any datatype supported by Informix database servers, including traditional alpha-numeric datatypes, as well as HTML pages, images, documents, spreadsheets, presentations, maps, audio, or any user-defined datatypes.

INFORMIX-Universal Web Connect provides a set of session and connection management services to maintain a persistent database connection. When the user starts a session by requesting the first HTML page of the application, INFORMIX-Universal Web Connect generates a session identifier and forks the application. When the HTML page is returned to the Web browser, the session identifier is also returned. This session identifier is then used when the user requests the second and subsequent HTML pages from the application. With INFORMIX-Universal Web Connect, Web authors and developers do not have to resort to creating complicated scripts in order to maintain state between client requests.

Unlike CGI, a copy of the application does not have to be invoked with each client request. INFORMIX-Universal Web Connect applications can be shared among multiple client requests to spare the system overhead of restarting the application. The number of IUWC applications started is configurable by the administrator to meet the needs of the user load. To ensure performance and scalability, INFORMIX-Universal Web Connect provides a load-balancing algorithm to distribute the client requests across all the available applications.

Tightly integrated with the Informix database server, INFORMIX-Universal Web Connect takes advantage of Informix's multithreaded database architecture and its parallel processing capabilities. Therefore, as the number of Web database application users and the amount of multimedia processing increases, the Informix database server will automatically scale across all available system resources to deliver the highest performance possible.

Unlike CGI that requires developers to write proprietary scripts to create Web applications, IUWC offers two industry-standard development methods to address the different needs of Web application developers.

The first development method is ideal for Web masters and other HTML-proficient authors that create applications for the publishing market. Through a collection of Informix-specific HTML tag extensions, Web authors can create applications that dynamically retrieve HTML data and multimedia content from a database and present it to the end users. INFORMIX-Universal Web Connect also lets users create their own customized tag extensions to perform specialized tasks. Through the use of HTML tag extensions, Web authors are able to create powerful applications quickly and easily without resorting to programming.

The second method is for applications that are more transaction-based or client/server oriented. To extend the functionality of the application, this method lets developers create customized Web applications through a programmatic API. The API offers a collection of basic services, such as connection and session management, that is automatically incorporated within any customized Web applications created by the developers to ensure performance and persistency.

INFORMIX-Universal Web Connect supports applications developed in all programming languages, including C, C++, and Java. This flexibility lets developers port existing database applications to the Web, as well as develop new Web-enabled applications using more sophisticated languages.

INFORMIX-Universal Web Connect stores the entire Web application content inside the Informix database. This ensures that developers can gain easy access to all the content associated with the Web application, allowing them to efficiently manage the application as it grows in size and complexity.

## Technical Overview

This section provides a detailed discussion of the INFORMIX-Universal Web Connect architecture and its product components. As mentioned in the previous section, the CGI architecture requires a developer to write scripts in PERL, Tcl, or C. These scripts construct the query, pass the query to the database, and format the output into an HTML page.

INFORMIX-Universal Web Connect eliminates the need for creating tedious scripts. Instead, developers are provided with tools for creating intelligent HTML pages directly within the database. These HTML pages, called Application Pages (or AppPages), execute SQL statements dynamically, format the results, and return the resulting HTML to the end users. Figure 13-2 illustrates CGI implementation of INFORMIX-Universal Web Connect. While based on CGI, INFORMIX-Universal Web Connect addresses the shortcomings of CGI previously identified. The key architectural distinction is that INFORMIX-Universal Web Connect has two middleware application components-the WebDriver and the IUWC Web Application.

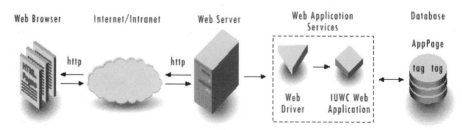

**Figure 13-2**. INFORMIX-Universal Web Connect architecture.

Recall that a new CGI application must be spawned for each client/browser connection. Typically, this extreme overhead is detrimental to performance. To minimize this overhead, INFORMIX-Universal Web Connect creates a featherweight CGI process called the WebDriver. It is invoked when a URL request is sent from the Web browser to the Web server. Upon receiving the request, the WebDriver generates a unique session identifier and sends the request to the IUWC Web Application.

The IUWC Web Application is a persistent application that does not terminate after each request. Developed using the INFORMIX-Universal Web Connect API, the IUWC Web application provides important Web application services such as connection and session management. Companies that need specialized application services can create customized Web applications through the INFORMIX-Universal Web Connect API. To ensure that all customized Web applications deliver a persistent application environment and the highest performance possible, the INFORMIX-Universal Web Connect API automatically incorporates all Web application services provided by the IUWC Web Application within all customized Web applications.

When the IUWC Web Application receives a request from the WebDriver, it connects to the database and executes a function called WebExplode. WebExplode executes the queries within the SQL statements, expanding the tag extensions embedded within the AppPages as necessary, and formats the subsequent results. WebExplode then returns the resulting HTML output to the WebDriver, which forwards the results to the Web browser. The WebDriver and the IUWC Web Application combined offer a collection of Web application management services. These services include connection and session management, and application management.

The WebDriver and IUWC Web Application ensure application persistency by offering a collection of connection and session management services. Since the IUWC Web Application is a shared application, multiple client requests are funneled into one or more IUWC Web Applications. The number of IUWC Web

Applications is configurable to meet the scalability needs of applications. To track relationships between users and applications, the WebDriver generates a unique, secure session identifier for each client. This session identifier is used for the entire session to recognize new requests from the same client and provide that information to the IUWC Web Application.

Based on the application, the IUWC Web Application will maintain the value of application variables and database connections from one browser request to the next. The WebDriver and IUWC Web Application share the session information using a shared memory segment.

The IUWC Web Application provides a wide range of application management services. INFORMIX-Universal Web Connect lets developers customize their Web applications using information stored within a wide range of sources, including the configuration file, the Web server environment, URLs, HTML forms, and Web application variables. This flexibility enables customers to easily customize applications to their businesses without any CGI programming. As discussed earlier, the behavior of the IUWC Web Application is configurable.

For example, the state information for client requests should not be maintained infinitely. There is a default time-out value for browser sessions which can be changed by an administrator. For scalability purposes, administrators can define the number of IUWC Web Applications to run. The WebDriver will distribute client requests across the available IUWC Web Applications utilizing a load-balancing algorithm. This load-balancing architecture provides the basis for an extremely scalable and high-performance solution. To further promote high performance, frequently accessed pages and objects are cached in memory. Additionally, the WebDriver and the IUWC Web Application provide error handling and logging capability as well as event management.

The WebExplode function within the IUWC Web Application provides the services to manage the AppPages. These services include the retrieval of AppPages and objects from the database and expanding the AppPages from the embedded tags to perform special tasks. Additionally, it also provides services for interpreting AppPage macro language and using the AppPage schema to manage application content such as HTML pages, documents, images, user-defined tags, etc.

## Components of INFORMIX-Universal Web Connect

INFORMIX-Universal Web Connect provides several components for building Web applications.

The Web-DB Publisher is a simple wizard which end users or administrators can use to create Web-based reports of Informix database data. The wizard consists of a small number of screens which walk the user through creating a report. When executed, the report will be written in HTML format and made available through the Web server. These reports can be static or dynamic. Dynamic reports will actually fetch values from the database when the user accesses the report via its URL. Also, the Web-DB Publisher includes a scheduling mechanism so that reports can be executed without user intervention.

Within the AppPages, developers and sophisticated Web authors can incorporate HTML tag extensions to create dynamic Web applications without resorting to programming. These HTML tag extensions give Web authors a simple, nonprogrammatic way to access application logic and content stored in the Informix database. The content can include dynamically constructed or static HTML documents and associated multimedia content.

Developers can use a set of special tags provided by Informix, as well as create their own tags to perform customized tasks. For example, Informix offers an HTML extension tag that allows Web authors to temporarily return control from the AppPage to the application so developers can execute specialized code in order to achieve specific functionality. In this way, developers have the flexibility to use the AppPage to generate some parts of the page and use code for other parts of the page.

High performance OLTP applications that cannot be implemented using AppPages and HTML tag extensions alone can use the INFORMIX-Universal Web Connect API library of C functions to ease development efforts. This set of API services provides a framework for programmers to easily port or develop client/server database applications on the Web. It provides a core set of services to enable session and connection management, minimize overall development time, and encapsulate the process of building HTML. Through this interface, applications can establish connectivity with other distributed object brokers such as IIOP, DCOM, and CORBA. Applications developed with the INFORMIX-Universal Web Connect API library can utilize any programming language such as C, C++, and Java.

## Using Universal Web Connect

INFORMIX-Universal Web Connect provides the following set of services to build Web applications:

URL interface
AppPage tags
INFORMIX-Universal Web Connect API

The URL interface allows Web developers a single point of access to application logic and content stored in the database. This content can include dynamically constructed or static hypertext markup language (HTML) documents and associated multimedia content. Users gain advantages of a database-driven Web application because INFORMIX-Universal Web Connect passes URL requests directly into the database for fast, personalized content delivery, all transparent to the user.

An INFORMIX-Universal Web Connect application uses AppPages as templates for these HTML pages. An AppPage is an HTML file that can include special tags, variables, and functions. INFORMIX-Universal Web Connect provides special AppPage tags, which are SGML-compliant tags and attributes that you place in AppPages to accomplish special tasks.

Use the INFORMIX-Universal Web Connect AppPage tags to create HTML pages that dynamically execute SQL statements and format the results, eliminating the need for you to develop a CGI application. AppPages provide a powerful HTML scripting technique which you can use to easily develop sophisticated database-aware HTML documents. AppPages support Netscape by enabling you to drop Java script or Java applets in the AppPage.

AppPage tags include

| | |
|---|---|
| <?MIBLOCK> | Delimits a logical block of HTMKL to be executed on the basis of a variety of conditions. |
| <?MIEVENT> | Temporarily stops processing of the AppPage and returns control to the calling program. |
| <?MICONNECTION> | Sets up a database connection. |
| <?MISQL> | Executes a SQL statement and displays the result of that statement in an HTML page. |
| <?MIVAR> | Assigns and displays variables in an HTML page. |

One of the AppPage tags, MIEVENT, allows you to temporarily return control from the AppPage to the application so you can execute specialized code in order to achieve specific functionality. In this way, you have the flexibility to use the AppPage to generate some parts of the page and use code for other parts of the page, increasing the power of the application/AppPage architecture.

In the following AppPage, the MIEVENT tag passes control to the application code. The application parses a file and calculates a value for the ParseVar variable, then returns control to the AppPage. ParseVar is then used in the MIVAR tag later in the AppPage.

```
<HTML>
<BODY>
...
<?MIEVENT NAME="ParseFile">;
<?MIVAR>The value is: $ParseVar<?/MIVAR>
...
</HTML>
</BODY>
```

The following code shows how the ParseFile event is handled in the application:

```
/* Declare the event handling function */
int parser(controlHandle)
```

```
                void *controlHandle;
        {
                int valOut;
                ...
                /* Code to read a file and calculate a value */
                /*for valOut */
                /* Set ParseVar=valOut */
                wcSetVariable(controlHandle,"ParseVar",
                valOut);
        }


        int requestLoop(controlHandle)
                void *controlHandle;
        {
                char *pageText;
                wcConOpen(controlHandle, 0);

                /* Associate parser( ) with the "ParseFile" */
                /* event */
                wcSetEventHandler
                (controlHandle, "ParseFile", parser);

                /* Load and explode the AppPage */
                wcLoad(controlHandle, "page", &pageText);
                WebExplode(controlHandle, pageText, NULL);
                wcConClose(controlHandle);
        }
```

The parser( ) function is called when WebExplode( ) encounters the MIEVENT tag in the AppPage.

In the following example, the MIEVENT tag triggers a function that runs a query to populate a list box in the HTML page.

```
/* Declare the event handling function */
int nameList(controlHandle)
        void *controlHandle;
{
        WebSelectList(cntrlHandle, "select last_name
        from customers",
        "NAME=last&VALUE=selectList1", NULL);
}


int requestLoop(controlHandle)
        void *controlHandle;
{
```

```
char *pageText;
wcConOpen(controlHandle, 0);

/* Associate nameList() with the "List" event*/
wcSetEventHandler(controlHandle, "List",
nameList);

/* Load and explode the AppPage */
wcLoad(controlHandle, "page", &pageText);
WebExplode(controlHandle, pageText, NULL);
wcConClose(controlHandle);
}
```

## INFORMIX-Universal Web Connect API

If you need to develop an extremely high-performance OLTP application which cannot be implemented using AppPages alone, use the INFORMIX-Universal Web Connect API library of C functions to ease your development efforts. This set of API services provides a framework for programmers to easily port or develop client/server database applications on the Web. It provides a core set of services that enable state and connection management. Through this interface, connectivity with other distributed object brokers (IIOP and CORBA) is achieved . You can use any language to create applications (C, C++, Active X, or Java).

A typical application written with INFORMIX-Universal Web Connect API performs the following basic tasks:

1. Loads an AppPage from file or from the database.
2. "Explodes" the AppPage, performing dynamic queries and getting updated values for variables embedded in the AppPage.
3. Returns the resulting HTML page to the end user.

The following skeleton pseudo-code shows how the major INFORMIX-Universal Web Connect API functions are used together in a typical application:

```
int main(argc, argv)
        int     argc;
        char    **argv;

{

        void    *wcp;
        char    *pageId;

        /* Initialize and synchronize application: */
        wcInit(argc, argv, &wcp);
```

```
      /* Connect to AppPage repository: */
      wcDBOpen(wcp, "APP_PAGES", "admin", "pass4545",
      "apps@venus");

      while (1)
      {
          /* Open connection to browser and wait for*/
          /* user request: */
          wcConOpen(wcp, 0);

          /* Get ID of AppPage requested by user: */
          wcGetVariable(wcp, "MIval", &pageId);

          /* Get handle to the AppPage: */
          wcLoad(wcp, pageId, &pagePtr);

          /* Expand variables and perform queries to*/
          /* add data to AppPage: */
          WebExplode(wcp, pagePtr, NULL);

          /* Return page to browser & close browser*/
          /* connection: */
          wcConClose(wcp);

      /* Return to top of loop, re-open browser */
      /*connection, and wait for next request */
      }

      wcDBClose(wcp);

return wcExit(wcp);
}
```

The application starts up, opens a connection to the browser, and waits for the user to request the next HTML page in the application. When the request is received, the page is returned to the user and the browser connection is closed. The loop repeats immediately and re-opens the browser connection, then stops and waits again for the next user request.

The application exits if the connection times out while waiting for a user request. The timeout is set in the MI_WEBTIMEOUT parameter in the configuration file (wcconfig.std). If the browser session times out, wcConOpen( ) returns the error message ERR_MSGSHUTDOWN. This message notifies the application so it can perform cleanup tasks and exit. If you do not include cleanup code in your application to respond to this error message, Universal

Web Connect will terminate the application process automatically with no cleanup.

## Component Details

INFORMIX-Universal Web Connect consists of the following components:

- Web browsers
- Web server
- Web driver module
- End user applications
- Shared memory
- Configuration file
- Log files
- The Universal Web Connect service
- The wcstat program

### Web Browsers

A Web client is any generally available, HTML-based Web browser such as Netscape or Mosaic. INFORMIX-Universal Web Connect provides a solution independent of vendor-specific browser/server HTML extensions. Although you can embed these extensions in the application, they are not required.

The use of standard Web browsers allows you to provide a more open solution that does not rely on the use of specific browsers or servers. This ability is critical when developing applications for use on the Web, because the user's browser is not under your control.

### Web Server

INFORMIX-Universal Web Connect works with any HTML-based Web server such as CERN or Netscape. Again, INFORMIX-Universal Web Connect provides a solution that is independent of any specific vendor's product. This allows you to change Web servers without affecting your application code. In an enterprise environment, this ability is important if you have not standardized on a specific Web server.

### Web Driver Module

The Web driver is a lightweight process that runs on the server. It initiates and manages the connection from the end user's Web browser to your application. The Web driver is spawned using the common gateway interface (CGI) protocol. For more information about CGI, see About CGI.

When the user starts a session by requesting the first HTML page of the application, the Web driver executes. It attaches to shared memory and allocates a block in the shared memory for the client. It generates a session ID and forks the application.

The application generates the first HTML page for the user and returns it to the Web driver, which returns it to the Web browser. The session ID is also returned to the Web browser. The Web driver process is terminated after the HTML page is returned to the user.

When the user requests the second and subsequent HTML pages from the application, the Web driver module is involved only if you are using the Managed Connect type of browser connection.

## End User Applications

End user applications are the Web applications you develop using the INFORMIX-Universal Web Connect API, which includes several standard library functions designed to minimize overall development time and encapsulate the process of building HTML. These applications perform whatever tasks you desire, but typically they access an INFORMIX database and return dynamic data to the end user.

Once spawned, applications stay resident until the user exits the application or the browser connection times out. This persistence allows the application to maintain state and reduces the overhead of continuously reopening the connection to the database. Shared memory is used to track the relationships between users and applications.

## Shared Memory

INFORMIX-Universal Web Connect uses shared memory to maintain system information, application-specific configuration, and session-related data. The shared memory is allocated when the Universal Web Connect service starts. This service uses the configuration file to set up the shared memory area. For details about the shared memory area, see Shared Memory Layout.

As users launch applications, each session is allocated an entry in the session table in shared memory. The session table tracks client-specific information such as the following:

- Session ID
- Process ID of the application
- Time and date the session was created
- Time and date the application was last accessed

To display the contents of shared memory, use the wcstat program.

## Configuration File

The configuration file is used to allocate the shared memory segment and set system parameters. It is similar to the INFORMIX OnLine configuration file. You can use this file to set system defaults for parameters such as timeout or error log location. You can also override some of the configuration parameters on a application by application basis.

## Log Files

INFORMIX-Universal Web Connect has a general log file similar to the INFORMIX OnLine log file. Problems and errors encountered are recorded in this file. The INFORMIX-Universal Web Connect API includes a function, wcLogPrintf( ), that writes to the log so that you can record application problems.

You specify the location of the log file using the MI_WEBLOGFILE parameter in the configuration file.

## The Universal Web Connect Service

The Universal Web Connect service is used to initialize and remove the shared memory segment. When called, it either allocates or deallocates the segment and then terminates.

You can start, stop, and pause the Universal Web Connect service through the Services manager in Windows NT. The service provides an interface with the following features:

- •Double-click the red light to stop, the yellow light to pause, or the green light to start the service.
- •Click the pencil button to edit the configuration file. After editing this file, you typically stop and restart the service to put the new configuration parameters into effect.
- •Click the right mouse button to display a popup menu when the service is displayed as an icon in the service tray.

## The wcstat Program

The wcstat program is a command line utility that displays the overall status of INFORMIX-Universal Web Connect. To get details about this utility, type "wcstat" at the command line.

For example, you can use wcstat to display the session table and track user sessions. You can also find out the amount of free memory in the shared memory area by using the following command:

```
wcstat -f
```

If the total free shared memory available gets close to 0, set the MI_WEB-VARSPACE configuration parameter to a higher value.

Types of Browser Connections

You can choose from two different ways to make the connection between the end user's Web browser and your application:

- Managed Connect uses a Web driver module to manage the connection.
- Direct Connect uses the Web driver module only for the initial user request. Subsequent requests bypass the Web server and connect your application directly with the end user.

Use Managed Connect when you want:

- Portable architecture that works with more browser/server combinations
- Secure HTTP
- More informative messages when application times out

Use Direct Connect when you want:

- Improved performance and less use of machine resources because of direct communication between browser and application with no CGI driver application in between

The type of connection used does not affect how you write application code. You can use either type of connection with any application without making any changes to the code files. The wcConOpen( ) and wcConClose( ) functions, which you call in your application, manage the connection type automatically.

Therefore, you do not need an in-depth understanding of how Managed Connect and Direct Connect work. To specify which type of connection you want:

1. Set the MI_WEBDRIVER configuration parameter in the configuration file to one of the following values:
     Y for Managed Connect
     N for Direct Connect
2. To set different connection types for individual applications, place multiple MI_WEBDRIVER parameters within APP...ENDAPP tags in the configuration file.

When you use Managed Connect, all communications between the client and the applications go through a Web driver, using the following sequence of events:

1. The user starts the session by sending a URL from the Web browser to the Web server using HTTP protocol. For example, the following URL is used to

request the Web driver wcdrvr.exe and the application myapp.exe:

http://server/cgi-bin/wcdrvr.exe/myapp.exe

Rather than give this URL to users, you would typically embed it in a more user-friendly opening application screen. For example, you might provide the user with an opening screen with a Start button that sends this URL.

2. The Web server starts the specified Web driver process, in this example wcdrvr.exe. The Web driver attaches to shared memory and assigns a global session ID, which is used to track the user's Web browser session with the application.

3. The remaining path information in the URL specifies which application the user has requested. In the example URL above, the application myapp.exe is specified. The Web driver checks the shared memory to find the location of that application's binary file and get the values of variables and any other configuration information about the application. Then the Web driver forks the application, allocates a TCP port to it, and waits.

4. When the application starts, it attaches to the same TCP port. Now the Web driver and application are able to communicate with each other.

5. The application performs its tasks. Typically, it opens a connection to the database, generates the first page of HTML, and returns it to the Web driver. The Web driver returns this page, with the session ID embedded, to the browser.

6. The Web driver terminates. The application stays resident, listening on the TCP port.

7. Subsequent calls to the application begin by starting the Web driver again. Instead of the application name, the session ID and any parameters are encoded in the URL. For example, the following URL shows how the second page of an application might be requested when you are using Managed Connect:

http://server/cgi-bin/wcdrvr.exe/WCID=0503?MiVal=menu&lastName=Smith

This URL is constructed for you automatically through the use of the $WEB_HOME variable. Use this variable in an AppPage wherever you need a URL like the one above. This variable automatically expands to the following portion of the URL:

http://server/cgi-bin/wcdrvr.exe/WCID=0503?

The rest of the URL consists of parameter names and values being passed from the HTML page to the application. In this example, the parameters are MiVal and lastName. This portion of a URL is called a query string.

8. The application uses the session ID to find its area in the shared memory, then generates the next HTML page and returns it through the Web driver.

9. Steps 7 and 8 are repeated for each subsequent page of the application until the application times out or is exited normally.

When you use Direct Connect, the first connection between the client and the application uses a Web driver module. However, subsequent communications go directly from the browser to the application. The function wcConOpen which is called from the application can handle HTTP requests and so enables your application to act in place of the Web server.

The first six steps in a Direct Connection are the same as a Managed Connection. The difference is in how subsequent pages of the application are handled. When you use Direct Connect, the following sequence of events occurs:

1. The user starts the session by sending a URL.

2. The Web server starts the Web driver, which attaches to shared memory and allocates a session ID.

3. The Web driver gets the location and configuration of the application from shared memory, then forks the application, allocates a TCP port to it, and waits.

4. The application starts and attaches to the same TCP port.

5. The application performs its tasks. The Web driver returns the resulting HTML page to the browser.

6. The Web driver terminates. The application stays resident.

7. Subsequent calls to the application begin with a URL sent from the browser. Instead of the Web driver name, the server and TCP port number are encoded in the URL. For example, the following URL shows how the second page of an application might be requested when you are using Direct Connect:

http://server:8000/WCID=0503?MiVal=menu&lastName=Smith

This URL is constructed for you automatically through the use of the $WEB_HOME variable. This variable expands differently depending on whether you are using Managed or Direct Connect. In Direct Connect, $WEB_HOME automatically expands to the following portion of the URL:

http://server:8000/WCID=0503?

The rest of the URL consists of parameter names and values being passed from the HTML page to the application. In this example, the parameters are MiVal and lastName.

8. The application uses the session ID to find its area in the shared memory, then generates the next HTML page and returns it directly to the Web browser.

Steps 7 and 8 are repeated for each subsequent page of the application until the application times out or is exited normally.

# 14

# Progress Software's WebSpeed: Securing Transactions on the Internet

## Introduction

Now that the Internet has become a normal part of the business environment more than just a few organizations are considering its use in deploying large amounts of transactional data to customers, employees and vendors. Given the enormous amount of publicity given to hacker and saboteur problems on the Internet, however, Progress Software's decision to develop a secure Internet Transaction Processing environment is noteworthy and timely. This chapter first delves into the thorny issues of Internet security and then discusses Progress's WebSpeed solution to the problem. More information on this product can be obtained from www.progress.com.

The original purpose of the Internet was to give government and academic researchers an easy way to collaborate and share information. To ensure easy access, the Internet was designed to be available to all computers connected to it, not to be a secure place for confidential or private information. This has made the IS community very reluctant to use the Web for business transactions. Much concern has been focused on credit-card authorizations, while many IS professionals are worried about business transactions in general.

Fortunately, secure transaction processing is a reality, with many standards already in place to address these concerns. A number of products today offer secure transaction processing mechanisms on the Internet for business data processing. In this chapter we will explore challenges to Internet security, and discuss the solutions to those challenges that are available to developers today.

The creation of a robust security model for Internet/Intranet applications is a major concern among application developers. Database access over the Web involves a variety of users who may have access privileges to different data-bases on the Intranet. The major benefit that the Internet provides is universal access, which presents opportunities to serve a different class of user. Figure 14-1 illustrates some of the common scenarios for Web-based database applications in the future.

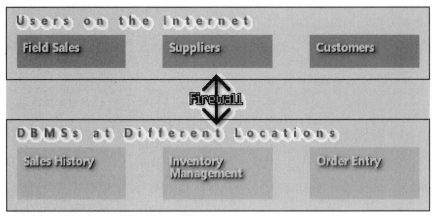

**Figure 14-1.** Database applications of the future.

•A corporate user such as a field sales representative may need to read a customer's sales history, check current inventory levels, or enter new orders.

•A customer may be able to check his or her own sales history, but not other customers' histories, and may submit new orders, but not view inventory levels.

•A supplier may need to check the inventory levels of parts that he or she provides to the company, but is not permitted access to competitors' parts data.

In many cases, these databases will reside on different DBMSs, at different physical locations, and will belong to different divisions within the company. In this environment, identifying not only who is a valid user but also enforcing specific permissions for that user becomes a requirement.

## The Challenge

Given the scenarios for database access described in figure 14-1, what are the threats to the security and integrity of your system? We will discuss four major areas of concern for developers implementing business applications on the Web:

Client authentication — to verify clients' identity
Channel security — to allow private information transfer
Access control — to enforce user permissions on data
Data consistency — to ensure database integrity

Authentication offers a guarantee of identity. Business transactions require that both parties offer a guarantee of their identities, that is, to authenticate themselves. Client authentication means that a server can identify and authenticate users. Standard Web protocols, such as TCP/IP and HTTP, make impersonating a person or an organization relatively simple. Conversely, how does the user connecting to site http://www.yourbusiness.com know that he or she is really talking to that site?

An example of how impersonation can circumvent security is a spoofing attack. This occurs when intruders create packets with false (spoofed) source Internet Protocol (IP) addresses. The intruders transmit packets from outside the corporate Intranet that claim to be from a trusted machine. If the corporate network is not set up to filter incoming packets with source addresses that are in the local domain, it forwards the traffic, potentially compromising the targeted system. This type of attack exploits applications that use authentication-based IP addresses, and may lead to unauthorized access.

Another major concern of developers of Internet/Intranet applications is that information traveling over the public Internet can be intercepted, compromising channel security. For example, information passed along the Internet sometimes gets cached temporarily on other people's computing equipment (such as routers), during which time it can be collected by someone and examined. People wishing to capture this information can do so relatively easily by using a program called a sniffer or protocol analyzer to collect packets as they go in and out of a site.

Access control refers to determining who is given access to a computer resource. In the case of Internet Transaction Processing (ITP), this often means determining which users have permissions to access specific databases. This problem is well understood in client/server DBMS applications, but on the Web it is complicated by the fact that the viewer may be drawing information from a wider variety of sources and presenting the data to a wider audience. Much of the data presented to users of the ITP application may come from confidential documents, sequential files, record-oriented data management systems, and older DBMS systems (see figure 14-2). Many existing schemes for accessing SQL-based relational databases are specific to a particular vendor's product and therefore cannot address the issue of data coming from heterogeneous sources.

Finally, business data processing often requires work to be performed as an

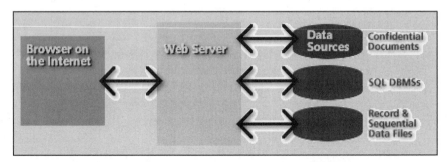

**Figure 14-2:** Access control is required over a variety of data sources.

atomic unit to maintain data consistency in all areas that may be affected by the transaction. Most Web RDBMS interfaces available today do not have a notion of traditional transaction consistency across multiple database commands. Furthermore, the ability to maintain consistency across multiple databases using standard algorithms, such as two-phase commit, is not readily available.

## Security and Integrity Solutions

Fortunately, a broad range of security measures is available today that deals effectively with the common challenges discussed above. Choosing the appropriate security model for ITP applications depends greatly on the value and confidentiality of the data. In many cases, very simple measures are all that are required to effectively safeguard your application. In this section, we will discuss:

Basic security measures
Advanced security measures
Transaction processing systems

Most HTTP servers have built-in security features that are configurable by the Webmaster. These features provide the basis for a security model. We will discuss each of these measures briefly in the sections that follow.

Document directories allow the Webmaster to specify to which directory the Web server is allowed access. All public information is placed under a specific directory, while access to other files on the server can be limited, using the operating system's access control list mechanism. Since the Web server process is only allowed to access files in that directory, other files on the server are protected from view.

Authentication allows the Webmaster to limit access to specific files or directories based on a user ID/password pair. When users attempt to access a file that has been restricted in this way, they are prompted for a userID and password. This is effective for low-security situations, but since the information is not encrypted, it is vulnerable to sniffing attacks. Using the user ID and password is very effective in keeping casual browsers from accessing data not appropriate for the general public. It is easy to implement and maintain.

IP filtering allows the Webmaster to restrict access to a site-based IP address. (IP filtering can also be done by your routing hardware; this type of filtering is discussed in the next section.) Access to a file or directory can be restricted based on the remote user's network address in one of two ways:

Permit type: Anyone within a certain address range can access a file or directory
Deny type: No one from a specific range of addresses can access a file or directory

The combination of IP filtering and authentication is adequate for most low- to medium-security situations, but will not repel a determined hacker. Since IP addresses can spoofed, IP filtering can be defeated.

## CGI Scripts

Common Gateway Interface (CGI) scripts are programs that the Web server executes to respond to a user query. They provide a gateway to other information that is invoked by the server in response to a user action. CGI scripts are an area of security concern, since anytime that a networked client is interacting with an executing program, there is a possibility that the program will be attacked by the client to gain unauthorized access. Because of this, it is important that the Web server's user account be limited to access only those areas required for its function. Furthermore, all CGI scripts must be confined to a specific directory. To learn more about the possible hazards of CGI scripts you may want to view the National Center for Supercomputing Applications (NCSA) archive on this subject at the URL:
http://hoohoo.ncsa.uiuc.edu/cgi/security.html.

The good news is that well-administered sites using proper scripting techniques can develop CGI scripts to increase security in areas such as user authentication. More information can be found at the NCSA Web site, http://hoohoo.ncsa.uiuc.edu/docs/tutorials/user.html; this URL contains sample scripts that can be used to strengthen security.

All Web servers log data which provides useful information about who and what people are doing on your site. These logs maintain a record of domains, or at least, IP addresses and files accessed on your Web site. Logs of errors and script execution are also created. To be useful, these logs need to be reviewed on a regular basis.

## Advanced Security Features

To achieve higher levels of security, more sophisticated solutions may be required. In this section, we will talk about two basic areas, firewalls and cryptographic solutions.

A firewall is simply a defensive mechanism that allows a network administrator to protect a network from an untrusted network. The mechanism for doing this varies widely, but, in principle, the firewall can be thought of as a pair of mechanisms: one that exists to block traffic, and another that exists to permit traffic.

A firewall includes one or more of the following components: screening routers; host-based gateways; proxy applications.

A router is a special computer or hardware device responsible for routing packet traffic in and out of a local network. The router is the first line of defense in a firewall. A router can filter network traffic by applying rules to the traffic it is routing. These rules may include:

The IP addresses of the connecting and accepting addresses
The service or protocol used, such as SMTP, HTTP, Telnet, etc.
The direction of flow

These rules can be used to eliminate or restrict traffic between two networks. Using a router as a screening firewall is convenient because the routing hardware is usually already in place.

A gateway is a mechanism that centralizes security, access control, and logging. Gateways can be configured to provide security by controlling user access to the resources of the network. There are two types of gateways:

A Bastion host is a firewall that is located at the local connection to the Internet. This machine is the central point for Internet services provided to the outside.

Dual homed is a firewall in which the host is configured with two network adapters. No default routing takes place between the secure internal network and the unsecure external network. Proxy applications (see below) are configured to provide a secure flow of data between the two networks.

A proxy application mediates traffic between a protected network and the Internet. Proxies are often used instead of router-based traffic controls to prevent traffic from passing directly between networks. Many proxies contain extra logging capabilities and support for user authentication. Since proxies "understand" the application protocol being used, they can implement protocol-specific security. (For example, for Web service, an HTTP proxy might be configured to allow internal incoming Web traffic, but restrict outgoing HTTP.) Application proxies provide much higher levels of security than simple screening router techniques. The key advantages are

•Application-level proxies hide internal addressing of packets. The address of the firewall is the only one visible to remote clients.

• Outside users must go through the firewall, giving it an internal host name, and provide authentication information to the application proxy.

• Proxies often provide comprehensive logging of information and monitoring of suspicious activity for all connection attempts.

• IP packet forwarding is disabled. If a hacker somehow learns the IP address of, and attempts to ping a host behind the firewall, the ping will fail.

Cryptography is a general technology that provides the highest levels of security for applications when combined with the measures that we have already discussed. It directly addresses the issues of channel security and authentication. Cryptography includes the following technologies:

Encryption: Transforming data into an unreadable form to ensure privacy.
Decryption: Transforming encrypted data back to a readable form.
Authentication: Identifying as authentic an entity, such as an individual, a machine on the network, or an organization.
Digital signatures: Binding a document to the possessor of a particular key or signature.
Signature verification: Verifying that a particular signature is valid.

A number of standards have evolved to perform these functions. These standards form the foundation for secure transaction processing solutions. The key standards in this area are

X.509: ITU standard for digital certificates or public key certificates that allow a user of a system to establish identity.
SSL: Secure Sockets Layer is an industry-standard protocol that uses public-key technology.
SET: A secure message protocol for credit-card transactions.
S/MIME: A secure messaging protocol for electronic mail.

The details of how cryptography works are extremely complex. However, the principle behind these standards is easy to understand, and the tools that use these standards are designed to be straightforward to the implementer and transparent to the end user. Figure 14-3 shows how an SSL handshake works:

1. At the user's request, the SSL client and Web server establish communication and proceed to exchange X.509 certificates. Certificates are verified by checking for valid dates and for the signature of a trusted certification author-

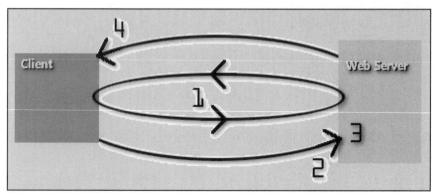

**Figure 14-3.** An SSL handshake establishes secure communications.

ity (CA).

2. The client generates a random set of keys that is used for encryption. Multiple keys are needed, since separate keys are used for client-to-server and server-to-client communication.

3. The server uses its private key to decrypt the keys.

4. Message encryption algorithms and integrity checks are negotiated. The SSL session is now in place.

### Certification Authorities

In order to verify the authenticity of the X.509 certificate, there must be an entity that issues electronic certificates for authenticating user and server identities. Companies may set up their own certification infrastructure, or they may purchase this service from external organizations such as VeriSign, BBN, GTE, or AT&T, among others.

SSL-based security solutions are a cornerstone for secure transaction processing, because they can be effectively deployed in both Intranet and Internet networks. Unlike many proprietary solutions, SSL works both inside and outside the firewall. The technology is broadly deployed in a wide range of commercial Web servers and browsers from the predominant suppliers including Netscape, Microsoft, IBM, Spyglass, and OpenMarket, as well as public domain NCSA-based products such as Apache-SSL.

SSL addresses three major issues for ITP applications.

1. Channel security: All traffic between the SSL server and SSL client is encrypted. SSL communications are not vulnerable to "sniffing" attacks.

2. Communication integrity: SSL integrity checks ensure that communications are not vandalized by tampering with the message contents.

3. Mutual authentication: The SSL handshake procedure validates both parties involved in the communication.

## Internet Transaction Processing Systems

As we have discussed, the Internet brings its own unique challenges in the area of security and integrity. Internet Transaction Processing (ITP) systems perform a strategic role in mediating between the security and integrity features offered by DBMSs and those offered by the technologies discussed above. In addition, ITP products enable developers to create applications that provide:

- Data integrity with two-phase commit across multiple DBMSs
- Access control to data across multiple data sources
- Data context for sessions which span multiple forms
- Load-balancing capabilities to deliver consistent response times
- Reliability through support for rollback and restart of applications

Figure 14-4 illustrates the role played by ITP systems. While client identification is guaranteed by the interaction between the browser and the Web server, that information must be translated by the Internet Transaction Processor to obtain access to one or more DBMSs and non-DBMS data sources. Likewise, while the server is concerned with the integrity of the communication between

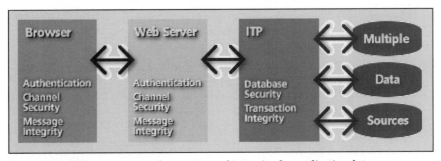

**Figure 14-4.** ITP systems provide security and integrity for application data.

the browser and Web server, the ITP is responsible for DBMS transaction consistency across all DBMSs used by the application.

## The WebSpeed Approach

WebSpeed (tm) is Progress' Internet Transaction Processing system for delivering multiuser database Internet/Intranet applications. In this section, we will discuss WebSpeed's open architecture and the WebSpeed approach to providing greater security and data integrity.

The WebSpeed application model is composed of a development environment, WebSpeed Workshop, and the deployment environment, WebSpeed Transaction Server. Figure 14-5 shows the components of the WebSpeed application model and how they interact.

WebSpeed Workshop is a Windows-based development environment that provides the developer with a tool kit for building commercial online transac-

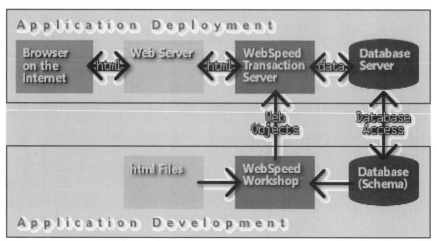

**Figure 14-5.** The WebSpeed application model.

tion processing applications for the Web. WebSpeed's open approach to creating applications allows developers to use any HTML authoring environment to build Web pages, and use JavaScript or Java to enhance the user interface. Business logic and database manipulation are handled using a powerful interpreted language, the WebSpeed 4GL. An application module constructed with the WebSpeed 4GL is called a Web object. Web objects process input from and output to data-driven Web pages. As illustrated in figure 14-5, applications are deployed by moving these Web objects to the WebSpeed Transaction Server.

From the Web user's perspective, a WebSpeed application looks like any other Web site. The user specifies a URL, using a Web browser. That triggers the execution of a CGI program which calls the WebSpeed Messenger that resides on the server system. The Messenger process calls the WebSpeed Transaction Server to service the request for a particular Web object. Web objects may be requested to execute business logic and/or process database commands. The interaction with the user is through HTML documents sent by the Web server and viewed by the browser. A WebSpeed application may consist of several Web objects accessing one or more databases.

The WebSpeed Transaction Server executes the Web object in a separate process called a transaction agent. If a Web user initiates a session with a transaction agent, that agent may remain dedicated to that browser, perhaps servicing several requests until the application ends. In this case, the WebSpeed agent maintains the data context between the browser and a single transaction agent.

Anyone who has used a search engine to find information realizes how important this context can be. For example, when you conduct a large query on a search engine such as AltaVista, Infoseek, or Lycos, you are presented with a screen of ten hits. When asked for the next page of hits, the server maintains a context of what your query was and where you are in the session. If you wait too long to request the next page, the server drops your session, and you have to resubmit your query. The technology for implementing this context differs from engine to engine, but from the user's perspective, it operates on the same principle.

A WebSpeed transaction may consist of one or more database transactions. A WebSpeed database transaction is an atomic unit of work done by one or more database commands. WebSpeed supports transactions across distributed databases. WebSpeed provides two-phase commit support across the PROGRESS DBMS and any of the many RDBMSs supported. This means that DBMS transactions accessing data residing on multiple DBMSs in a distributed environment will be synchronized. This transaction support is unique to the WebSpeed Transaction Server.

## WebSpeed and Security

WebSpeed was designed to be an open environment, allowing WebSpeed applications to take advantage of innovations in Web security. Likewise, as an ITP system, WebSpeed can enhance the database integrity and transaction consistency of applications running on one or more databases. The combination of these capabilities provides a robust model for implementing applications on the Web.

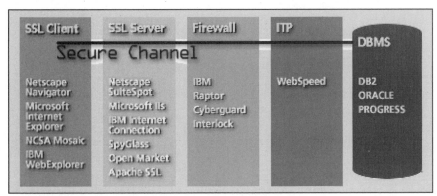

**Figure 14-6**. Security on the Internet.

Figure 14-6 shows some of the products that are available on the market today to create a secure application. Basic security measures can provide a good foundation for a robust security model. For example, for applications that need user authentication for access to DBMS data, the Webmaster can associate a user ID/password combination with the execution of the CGI script which launches the WebSpeed Messenger and communicates with the Transaction Server.

A Webmaster can screen out unauthorized WebSpeed users by allowing only certain IP addresses to execute the WebSpeed Messenger. To use this IP screening function, the IP addresses of all valid users must be known. This measure, combined with password authentication, is simple and will screen out most unauthorized users from entering your corporate databases. To protect from a sniffing attack, communications between the client could be encrypted, using SSL and digital certificates. Some servers will allow you to associate a digital certificate with an entry in the server's access control database. This allows users to present certificates to enter the application rather than user IDs and passwords.

On the WebSpeed side, once a valid user has started a WebSpeed transaction, the user can be queried for more security information. The Web object can use that information to apply standard database security to allow read, write, and modify permissions at the record, table, or database levels.

Since many corporate databases reside on internal corporate networks, in most cases, the database itself will reside behind a firewall mechanism. Since the communication between the Web server and the WebSpeed Transaction Server follows special protocols, the Transaction Server acts as a type of application proxy which restricts traffic to very specific high-level protocols communicating between the WebSpeed messenger and the Transaction Agents.

## WebSpeed Security Summary

Below is a brief summary of the way WebSpeed handles security and integrity on the Internet:

Directory permissions: WebSpeed Messenger program and CGI script files can have restricted access.

Authentication/password: WebSpeed Messenger program and CGI script files can be password protected.

CGI scripting: CGI Scripts may be customized to add security features.

Web server logging review: Complementary measure will record the occurrence of WebSpeed transactions along with time, date, size of transfer, and domain name of client.

SSL encryption/X.509 certificates: WebSpeed Messenger program and CGI script can be access-controlled by mapping client signatures to these files in the access control database (not available on all servers).

Database security: WebSpeed 4GL controls connect logic for entering databases and record management systems. Capabilities depend on the type of DBMS used. Custom security logic may be added, using WebSpeed 4GL.

WebSpeed in the Future

In a business transaction, it is important that both parties to that transaction have proof that the transaction actually occurred. Both parties need to know the time that the transaction occurred and the information regarding payment, including taxes, shipping charges, quantities purchased, and the like.

Progress Software is exploring the use of transaction certificates as a means to provide a record of a business transaction. These certificates would be processed in a way that is similar to how mutual authentication is provided today using X.509 and SSL protocols. The natural place for these certificates to reside would be within the existing certification authority. In this scheme, the certification authority would be a neutral third party that would retain an audit trail of all transactions that occurred (see figure 14-7).

With transaction certificate enabled applications, hooks for providing transaction details would be provided by both the Web server and by WebSpeed in order to supply the necessary information to create a transaction certificate. Progress Software is working closely with certification authorities and standards organizations to ensure that WebSpeed will support these capabilities as standards evolve.

One problem that currently exists with doing business on the Internet is the unpredictability of available bandwidth for conducting transactions. At key times, the speed of communications can grind to a standstill. Many businesses are ready and willing to pay extra for a guarantee of Bandwidth on Demand (BoD), also known as Quality of Service (QoS). Many Internet service providers (ISPs) are looking to address this issue through a protocol called RSVP.

The Resource ReSerVation Protocol (RSVP) is a protocol for reserving bandwidth to implement an integrated service, such as a mission critical business

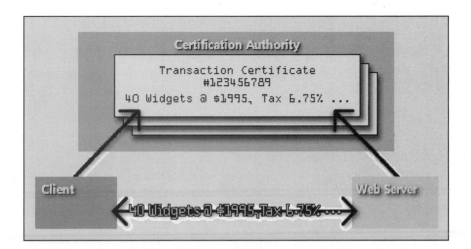

**Figure 14-7.** Certification Authorities can provide a crucial service.

application. RSVP allows particular users to obtain preferential access to network resources, under the control of an admission control mechanism. Permission to make a reservation depends upon both the availability of the requested resources along the path of the data and the adherence to policy rules.

A system that controls bandwidth must be very secure. To protect the integrity of this admission-control mechanism, RSVP requires the ability to protect its messages against corruption and spoofing. Standards for providing these protections are currently being defined. Progress Software intends to support these standards as they evolve.

As RSVP becomes more broadly used by ISPs to create different levels of service, WebSpeed will provide mechanisms to request this bandwidth within the user's application logic. These mechanisms will allow the user to dynamically pay for better service. Changing the bandwidth allocation may be triggered by the type of transaction, the class of customer, or the quantity of product being sold. Within WebSpeed, a natural complement to requesting higher classes of service will be changing the priority of execution of certain processes within the CPU which services the transaction. These combined measures will guarantee fast and reliable execution of mission-critical transactions.

Today, most commercially available encryption solutions involve communications between the Web browser and Web server. Other uses for encryption technology in ITP applications also exist. Progress Software is working closely with Security Dynamics, Inc. and RSA Data Security, Inc. to create additional security options for WebSpeed applications. One area of cooperation involves end-to-end encryption for WebSpeed applications. End-to-end encryption would involve encrypting all data communications flowing in and out of the WebSpeed Transaction Server. This would include communications between the database server and the WebSpeed Transaction Server as well as the data flowing from the Web server to the Transaction Server. The encrypted data could move safely over public communications channels like the Internet. This would provide more flexibility in the physical placement of databases and Web servers relative to where the WebSpeed application is being executed. It may also include encryption of stored database data.

## Glossary of Internet Security Terms

Access control: The process of determining who is given access to a computer resource, such as database information, and how much information he or she can receive.

Authentication: The process of verifying that users are who they say they are. An example of authentication is requiring users to identify themselves with a password.

Authorization: The process of granting access to a local or remote computer system, a network, or online information.

CA (Certification authority): An entity or service that distributes electronic keys for encrypting information and electronic certificates for authenticating user and server identities used to create the encryption pattern.

Digital certificate: A public-key directory entry that has been "signed," or validated, by a certification authority. Digital certificates are used to verify digital signatures.

Digital signature: A coded message added to a document or data that guarantees the identity of the sender.

Electronic commerce: The use of an electronic information infrastructure through which businesses can speed the exchange of information, improve customer service, reduce operating costs, and increase global competitiveness.

Encryption: Encoding of information to prevent anyone, other than the intended recipient, from reading the information.

Firewall: A defensive mechanism that allows a network administrator to protect a network from an untrusted network.

Public-key security: Also known as asymmetric-key security or public-key encryption technology, this is a security mechanism for securely distributing encryption keys that are used to "lock" and "unlock" data across an unsecure path. Public-key security is based on encryption key pairs, in contrast to private-key security, which is based on a single, shared key.

Recovery: Restoring the database to a consistent state after a hardware or software failure.

RSA: Generic name for an encryption mechanism developed by RSA Data Security that uses both a private and a public key. RSA is also used to verify user and/or server authenticity.
SSL (Secure sockets layer): A security protocol developed by the Netscape Communications Corporation to encrypt sensitive data and verify server authenticity.

TCP/IP (Transmission control protocol/Internet protocol): The suite of protocols developed by the U.S. Department of Defense in the 1970s to support the construction of world-wide Internetworks. Today, millions of users are connected to the Internet through software that uses the TCP/IP protocol suite.

Transaction: A mechanism for ensuring that a group of actions is treated as a single unit of work.

Transaction management (DBMS): Ensuring that transactions are either completed or canceled so that the database is left in a consistent state.

Two-phase commit: Protocol used by database management systems to guarantee that transactions which span databases on multiple servers are properly committed as a group.

X.509: An ITU standard for digital certificates or public-key certificates that allow users of a system to establish their identity.

## For More Information

The following Web sites contain valuable information concerning Web security.

Cryptography

Excellent FAQ on cryptography:
http://www.rsa.com

Overview of security issues, cryptographic solutions, and how Netscape products fit:
http://home.netscape.com/newsref/ref/128bit.htm

Detailed specifications for SSL 3:
http://home.netscape.com/eng/ssl3/3-SPEC.HTM

Overview of security issues, solutions, and Microsoft's plans for the future:
http://2 07.68.137.40/intdev/security/

Compendium of technical references:
http://www.yahoo.com/Science/Mathematics/Security_and_Encryption

Firewalls

FAQ on firewalls:
http://www.greatcircle.com/firewalls/FAQ

Futures

RSVP Bandwidth Reservation Protocol Specifications:
ftp://ftp.ietf.org/internet-drafts/draft-ietf-rsvp-spec-13.txt

Security Guidelines and Policies

Resource page on cryptography policy:
http://www.crypto.com

Internet Engineering Task Force security working group's Site Security
Handbook, currently in draft stage but comprehensive nevertheless:
http://www.cert.dfn.de/eng/resource/ietf/ssh/draft-02.txt

Security Tools

List of http sites providing security tools and services:
http://www.commerce.net/jump/techno/sectools.html

Transaction Processing

Overview of WebSpeed and Internet transaction processing issues:
http://webspeed.progress.com

# 15

# Using NetObjects Fusion

## Introduction

NetObjects Fusion™ is a smart Web site production application that combines automated site building, database publishing, and professional-quality design features. Its visual, site-oriented approach to Web site authoring offers unprecedented efficiency and ease of use for users of all levels.

You can use NetObjects Fusion to design and create an entire site without any HTML knowledge. When you preview or publish a site, NetObjects Fusion automatically generates the necessary HTML code. You can use NetObjects Fusion to design and prototype sites that will later be completed using other tools, and you can import sites created in other tools to NetObjects Fusion. NetObjects Fusion's open architecture and HTML standards support let you create sites that can be integrated with scripts, Java applets, Shockwave, digital video, and other rich media plug-ins.

In this chapter we will discuss the database publishing aspect of NetObjects Fusion in detail while providing a short summary of the product's other integrated development features. Additional product information and downloads can be obtained from www.netobjects.com.

## NetObjects Fusion Primary Views

NetObjects Fusion uses five different views to let you design, create, and manage the various aspects of your site. They are arranged to guide you through the main steps of building a Web site. Changes made in one view are reflected in the others.

1. Use the Site view to create the overall site structure.

2. Use the Page view to add content to your pages.
3. Use the Style view to apply a site-wide visual theme.
4. Use the Assets view to manage your files, links, data objects, and variables.
5. Use the Publish view to stage or publish your completed site.

The NetObjects Fusion Site view is a visual site-structure editor, where you create the hierarchy of your site's sections and subsections. You can drag a page or section to any location in a site, and NetObjects Fusion updates its links to other pages automatically. The Site view lets you focus on organizing and updating the information of your Web site, freeing you from the details of files and links.

In the Site view, the pages of your Web site are represented by page icons. When you want to add content to a particular page, you use the Page view. When you construct a site, you typically go back and forth between the Site view and the Page view. In the Site view, you work on all the pages and their relationships. In the Page view, you work on one page at a time.

The NetObjects Fusion Page view is a graphical, draw-based layout editor. This view gives you drag-and-drop control to author your pages with pixel-level accuracy. You can place elements anywhere on a page and NetObjects Fusion will generate an HTML Web page that preserves its precise position.

Components controllable through the Page view include:

- MasterBorders
- frames
- navigation controls
- page layouts
- text and pictures
- drawn shapes
- tables
- forms
- rich and interactive media
- NetObjects Components
- advanced scripting
- scripted frames
- HTML pages created with other tools

The Style view is where you view, apply, edit, and create the look and feel of your entire site. SiteStyles are sets of thematic elements that are included with NetObjects Fusion. Some style elements are graphical, and others affect the text colors used in your Web pages. NetObjects Fusion 2.0 comes with a gallery of brand-new, professionally designed SiteStyles that take advantage of GIF 89a transparency to blend seamlessly with any background color you choose. You can use these new SiteStyles as they are, edit them, or create your own styles to give your site a distinctive look.

## The Assets View

This component is the reason why I included NetObjects Fusion in this book. Most Web application development tools have all the bells and whistles you need for tweaking the graphical and textual component of a Web site. The problem is that these tools, for the most part, fall short of providing the ability to connect "real live data" to your site.

NetObjects Fusion provides functionality for

- managing files
- managing links
- managing data objects
- managing variables

When you open the Assets view, you can choose which kind of asset to see. For each file in your site, the Assets view lists

- name
- type
- in use
- location
- size
- date
- verify status

For each link used in your site, the Assets view lists name, link to type and verify status. For each data object used in your site, the Assets view lists its name. For each variable, the Assets view lists name, type and contents.

When you click the Files button, the Assets view displays a list of all the files associated with your site, both external files and those generated by NetObjects Fusion. File types include images, sound, video, and applets/plugins.

Data objects are collections of fields of data. You can use a data object to publish data without using CGI scripts or database programming.

When you click the Data Objects button in the secondary control bar, the Assets view displays a list of all the data objects used in your site.

You can edit the name of an internal data object, as well as its field names, and add new fields. Assets view will display these values for an external data object, but you cannot change them because they are taken from the external data file.

## The Publish View

When you've completed your site, you're ready to publish it as a series of HTML pages and associated assets. Publishing is similar to previewing. Previewing is when you click the Preview button in the control bar to test how your site looks using your local browser. During publishing, NetObjects Fusion takes the site file (.nod) and creates the following on a server that you specify:

• a home page in HTML format
• a folder containing all the other HTML pages
• a folder containing all the associated assets (i.e., pictures, applets, auto-generated images)

To publish a site:

1. Open the completed site file in NetObjects Fusion.
2. Switch to the Publish view.
3. Click the Publish button in the Publish view window. NetObjects Fusion generates the HTML and associated files, places them in an organized folder structure, and uploads the finished site to your server by means of FTP. Unless you've unselected the Publish changed assets only option, publishing generates all HTML pages and updates only the assets you modified since the last time you published.
4. When your site is in place, access it with your Web server.

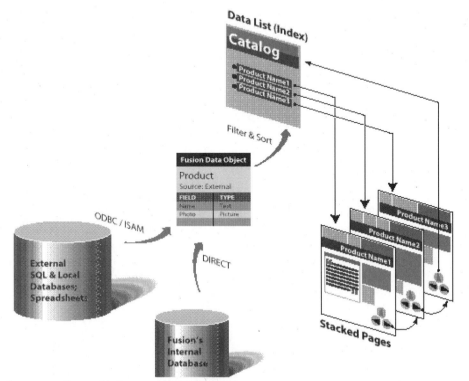

**Figure 15-1.** Data publishing with NetObjects Fusion.

NetObjects Fusion makes it easy to publish listings of information such as employee directories, product and service catalogs, and event schedules. You can enter, manage, and store this information as records either in an external application such as a database or spreadsheet or in your NetObjects Fusion site file. To publish the data, you specify its source and create a master layout for data-based pages. Then NetObjects Fusion uses your layout to create a separate page for each record, and automatically provides your site visitor with buttons to navigate between them. Figure 15-1 shows the key elements of data publishing with NetObjects Fusion.

You can publish data from internal and external sources. NetObjects Fusion lets you present your data to the site visitor in a data list and a series of associated stacked pages. Once you've chosen a source, NetObjects Fusion automatically creates the appropriate number of stacked pages. Each stacked page corresponds to a record in the data source.

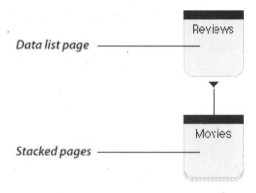

**Figure 15-2.** Data List Page and its child stacked pages.

For example, suppose you publish a shirt catalog on the Web. Each row in the shirt data list lets the site visitor navigate to the stacked page that contains the corresponding shirt.

At the heart of data publishing is the data object, which is simply a collection of data fields. You use a data object to define what information you want to publish. To create your shirts catalog, your first step is to create a shirts data object. A data object can be defined once and used in different filtered data lists. For example, using the shirts data object, you can create one data list of all the shirts in your database. With the same data object, you can create another data list of just button-down shirts. And with the same data object, you can create still another data list of all the shirts on sale (and so on).

If the data object is created from an external source (for example, a Microsoft Access Database), and the source is updated, a site containing this data object will be updated when you publish again. For example, suppose your shirts data object references 50 records originally and the external database is updated with 25 new records. After republishing, the data object references 75 records, the shirt data list contains 75 rows and there are 75 stacked pages. After you create a data list on a page, NetObjects Fusion generates a stacked page as its child. When you create the layout of the first stacked page, the remaining stacked pages automatically inherit the same layout.

In the Site view, the page icon for the data list page and the page icon for its child stacked pages appear as shown in figure 15-2.

A data list acts as an automatic table of contents for the stacked pages. Links between the data list icons and the stacked pages are automatically created.

Publishing Data

In general, when you work with data publishing, you follow a three-step process:

1. Create a data object: When you create a data object, you identify the fields you want to use in your site. When you store records internally, you must specify the data fields you want to store. When you store records externally, NetObjects Fusion assumes you want to use all fields available in the source.

2. Create a data list: When you create a data list, you prepare a display of the data in a row-and-column format. The display serves as a table of contents, typically summarizing the data that appears in the stacked pages. You select the fields you want to display as column headers in the list. Each row of data that appears in the data list represents information available on a single stacked page. The field data from either the internal or external source populates the data list when you publish.

3. Create a set of stacked pages: When you create a data list, NetObjects Fusion automatically creates the first of your stacked pages, where you create the layout to be used for all the pages in the stack. When you design a stacked page, you create or identify the field data you want to display on the page. If you are storing data internally, you enter the field data on the stacked page itself. Data can also be drawn from an external database, spreadsheet, or ASCII text file.

Creating a Data Object

You create a data object in the Page view or in the Assets view. If you create a data object in the Page view, you can continue immediately to create stacked pages to contain the data. If you create a data object in the Assets view, you must return to the Page view to create stacked pages.

To create a data object from the Page view:
1. In the Page view, click the Data List tool. If you plan to store data internally, use the default secondary Data List tool.
2. Draw an area on the page. NetObjects Fusion displays the Data Publishing dialog box. From this dialog box, you can select an already existing data object,

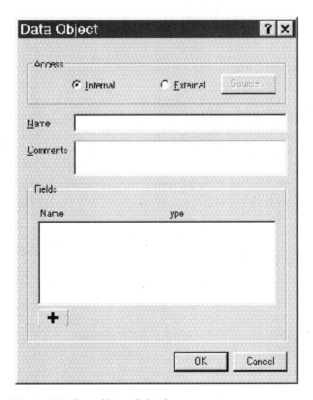

**Figure 15-3.** Data Object dialog box.

or you can create a new one.

3. To create a new data object, click the New... button. NetObjects Fusion displays the Data Object dialog box as shown in figure 15-3.

4. Choose whether to create an internal or external data object.

5. When you have finished creating the data object, click OK. NetObjects Fusion displays the data list placeholder showing the column headings and the Data List icon for the first row.

To create a data object from the Assets view:

1. To display the list of data objects in the Assets view, click the Data Objects button in the secondary control bar.

2. Click the New Object button in the control bar. NetObjects Fusion displays the Data Object dialog box.

3. Choose whether to create an internal or external data object.

4. When you have finished creating the data object, click OK. The data object is added to the list of data objects in the Assets view. The next time you create a data list, the data object will appear in the list of data objects in the Data Publishing dialog. You can also create a Data Object for Internal Data. This is information that you enter directly into a stacked page, either by typing text, or numbers, or by placing a picture. When you create a data object for internal

data, you specify a name for the data object and create the fields you want to use to store and display information.

To create a data object for internal data:
1. Create a data object. NetObjects Fusion displays the Data Object dialog box.
2. In the Data Object dialog box, verify that the Internal radio button is selected, then enter a name for the data object and any comments. NetObjects Fusion uses the data object name to identify the data object later, when you create a data list and in the Assets view list of data objects. Now you can add fields to this object. The fields will contain data when you create stacked pages.
3. Click the "+" button to add a field. NetObjects Fusion displays the Data Field dialog box.
4. To specify a field, type its name and select the data type for the field, then click OK. Data fields can store the following data types: formatted text, plain text, image file,
5. Add all the fields you want to use in the data object.
6. When you have finished, click OK.

## Creating a Data Object for External Data

External data exists in a database, spreadsheet, or text file. NetObjects Fusion lets you draw information directly from the external file with a data object. You can use data from local desktop databases or from SQL data sources. NetObjects Fusion uses ISAM drivers to draw data directly from desktop databases such as Access, Paradox, dBASE, FoxPro, Excel, or delimited text files. NetObjects Fusion uses standard ODBC drivers to draw data from SQL files.

Note: ODBC is an Open Data Base Connectivity standard supported by Microsoft and is in general use. ODBC drivers for specific types of data files, including database files, spreadsheet files, and text files, are available from Microsoft Corporation. If you are a user of MS Office or MS Office Professional for Windows 95, you already have a set of ODBC drivers that enable you to bind to the data files created by those products. If you do not use those products, you will need to obtain the drivers elsewhere. Contact Microsoft for more information. When you create a data object for external data, you specify a name for the object, the data source, and the data file you want to use. NetObjects Fusion 2.0 automatically gives you access to all the fields available in the external file. It can import pictures stored in the external file either as BLOBs in GIF or JPG format, or as image file paths.

NetObjects Fusion offers three ways to initiate the creation of a new external object. You can use the standard Data List tool in Page view or the New Object button in the Assets view or you can use the New External Data Object secondary tool in Page view, as described in the following procedures.

To create a data object from a desktop database:
1. In Page View, select the Data List tool and click the New External Data Object secondary tool as shown in figure 15-4.

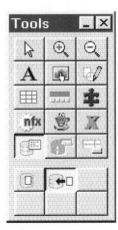

**Figure 15-4.** Selecting the Data List tool.

2. Draw a rectangle for your data list. NetObjects Fusion displays the Data Source Type dialog box.
3. In the Type panel, select the data file type from the pull-down menu of desktop database types as shown in figure 15-5.

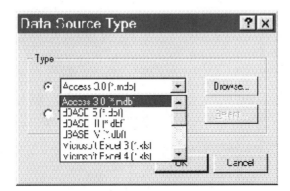

**Figure 15-5.** Selecting the database type.

NetObjects Fusion always provides access to Access 3.0 database files. Additional data types are available if Index Sequential Access Method (ISAM) drivers have been installed. ISAM drivers are automatically installed when you install Microsoft FoxPro, Microsoft Visual FoxPro, Paradox, Microsoft Excel, or dBASE.
4. Click the Browse button, locate the database you want to use, and open it. If the file is a multiple-file database or a spreadsheet with multiple tabs, NetObjects Fusion displays the Select dialog box as shown in figure 15-6.

**Figure 15-6.** The Select dialog box.

Choose the file or tab you want to use and click OK. NetObjects Fusion displays the Data Publishing dialog with your new data object selected. There you can see that the data object contains all fields present in the external source, and that it has taken the name of the file or tab you selected.

To create a data object from a SQL data source:
1. In Page View, select the Data List tool and click the New External Data Object secondary tool.
2. Draw a rectangle for your data list. NetObjects Fusion displays the Data Source Type dialog box.
3. In the Type panel, click the ODBC button. The SQL Data Sources dialog box appears as shown in figure 15-7. This dialog displays all the ODBC data

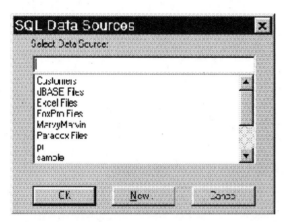

**Figure 15-7.** The SQL Data Sources dialog.

sources stored on your computer. You can either select one that you have previously created or you can create a new one.

4. To create a new data source, enter a name and click New...NetObjects
Fusion displays the Add Data Source dialog box. This is the same dialog that
is available through the ODBC control panel. Click the Help button to bring
up the standard Microsoft ODBC help topic for more information.

5. Select the driver type in the list. The driver type must be the same as the
type of data file you want to use because to create the source, the system must
bind the driver to the data file.

6. Click OK. The system displays a dialog box appropriate to the driver you
selected so that you can locate and select the data file you want to use. For
example, if you selected a SQL database driver, the system displays the ODBC
SQL Server Setup dialog box.

7. Select the data file you want to use and click OK. If the file is a multiple-file
database, NetObjects Fusion will ask you to select the one you want. Then
NetObjects Fusion displays the Data Publishing dialog with your new data
object selected. There you can see that the data object contains all fields present in the external source, and that it has taken the name of the file or tab
you selected. You can now finish creating the data list as described in the next
section.

## Creating a Data List

Once you have created a data object, you can create a data list on any page.
The data list, in turn, allows you to create stacked pages, one page for each row
in the list. When you have finished, NetObjects Fusion automatically adds
data list icons to the first column in the data list. The data list thus acts as a
table of contents—each row contains data for, and is linked to, a single stacked
page.

To create a data list:

1. In the Page view, display the page on which you want to place the data list.

2. Click the Data List tool and verify that the standard secondary Data List
tool is selected.

3. Draw a rectangle in the page body as shown in figure 15-8. The Data
Publishing dialog box appears as shown in figure 15-9. It displays the available data objects and the fields of the selected data object.

4. Select the data object you want to use for this data list. The fields that data
object contains appear.

5. Choose a field to sort by. Records in your data list will appear in ascending
order by that field.

6. Click Set... to select a filter. By default, NetObjects Fusion displays all available records in the data list and on stacked pages. A filter selects a subset of
the available records to display. You can create selection criteria that isolates
exactly the records you want to appear in your data list. When you click Set...,
NetObjects Fusion displays the Query dialog box as shown in figure 15-10.

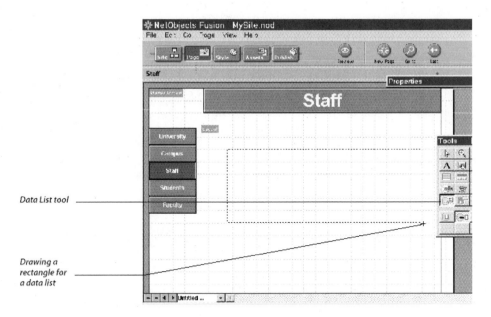

Data List tool

Drawing a
rectangle for
a data list

**Figure 15-8.** Creating a data list.

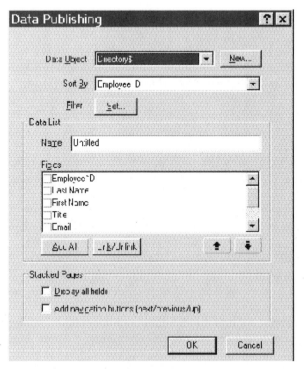

**Figure 15-9.** The Data Publishing dialog box.

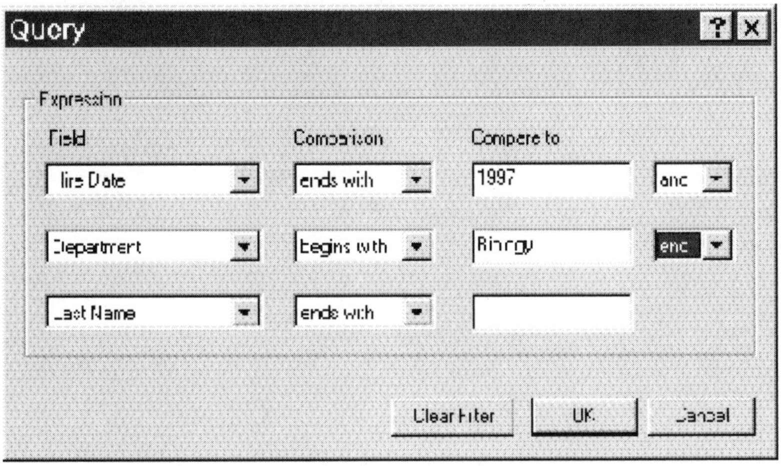

**Figure 15-10.** The Query dialog box.

Enter your selection criteria and click OK.

7. In the Data List area, enter a name for the data list.

8. In the Fields list, select fields to include in the data list by clicking the check box to the left of the field name. As a shortcut, you can click the Add All button, which marks all fields for display. Typically, however, you display only a subset of fields in the data list and display all fields on stacked pages.

9. To link a field to its stacked page, select the field and click the Link/Unlink button. A data list automatically includes a navigation button at the left of each row that links to the record's stacked page. When you link a field, your site visitor can click either the button or the linked field to jump to the record's stacked page.

10. To change the order in which fields appear left to right in the data list, select the field you want to appear first and click the up-arrow button until it appears at the top of the field list. Continue to select fields and press the up- and down-arrow buttons until the list is in the order you want.

11. If you wish, set options for the creation of stacked pages. When you select the Display all fields option, NetObjects Fusion automatically places all fields available in the data object in a simple layout when it creates the first stacked page. This shortcut can save you the effort of placing fields individually.

12. Click OK. NetObjects Fusion displays the data list placeholder, which presents as column heads the names of the fields you selected for display and a data list button at the left of the first row. This is enough information for you to use the Properties palette to specify the appearance of your data list. NetObjects Fusion populates the data list only when you preview or publish the page. Data never appears in the data list in Page view.

13. Click the data list to see the Data List tab in the Properties palette.

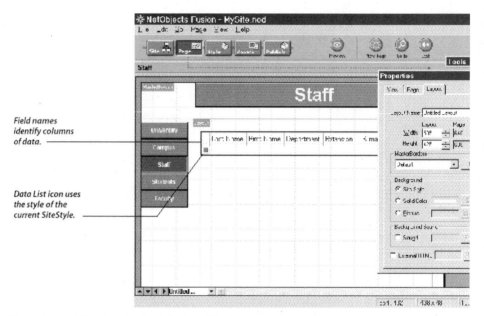

*Field names identify columns of data.*

*Data List icon uses the style of the current SiteStyle.*

**Figure 15-11.** Adjusting the data's look and feel.

As shown in figure 15-11, you can adjust the settings on the Data List tab to change the bullet type, background color, border size, and spacing of the data. You can also mouse over the column heading borders and drag them to set column width. When you are satisfied with the appearance of your data list, go on to creating a layout for your stacked pages as described in the next section.

## Creating Stacked Pages

Stacked pages are individual pages that correspond to the rows of data in a data list. When first created, there is only one stacked page, on which you create the design for all of the subsequent pages in the stack. Each subsequent stacked page starts with the same layout as the first stacked page. If you later rearrange and modify the layout on any stacked page, the new layout applies to all the stacked pages. Stacked pages also correspond to records in a database. When you store information internally in NetObjects Fusion, each stacked page lets you enter data into the fields of the data object. If you are drawing information from an external data file, each stacked page displays information from a single record.

The first stacked page determines the initial layout for all the stacked pages. When data fields and non-data elements (text, pictures, or other assets) are added to the layout of the first stacked page, they are repeated across all the stacked pages.

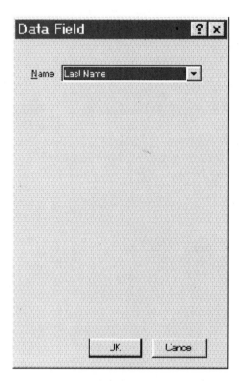

**Figure 15-12.** The Data Field dialog box.

To design stacked pages:

1. From the page containing the data list, navigate to the first stacked page. You can use the Down Page navigation button, or choose First Child from the Go To menu, or double-click the Stacked Page icon in the Site view. Unless you selected a stacked page option when you created your data list, NetObjects Fusion displays a blank page. You can add text and graphic elements to this page, just like any other page. The key items to be added, however, are the data fields you have defined in the data object and have included in the data list that has spawned this set of stacked pages.

2. Click the Data Field tool and draw an area in the body of the stacked page. NetObjects Fusion displays the Data Field dialog box (see figure 15-12), so that you can choose which field you want to display in the area you have drawn. The fields available are those in the data object you have used for the data list.

3. Select a field and then click OK. If you are using external data, NetObjects Fusion displays field data from the first record in the data file.

4. Add additional data fields, until you have placed as many as you want. Add text blocks to label your fields, lines and other graphics until you are satisfied with your layout.

5. If your stacked pages reference external data, you can use the Display Next and Display Previous Stacked Page buttons (left and right arrows) on the secondary control bar to scroll though all pages in the stack.

## Fusion in Action

You have begun work on a Web site for your employer, radio station KVYB "The Viiiiiiiiiiiiibe" 105.7 on your FM dial. The Vibe wants a strong presence on the Web to provide access to its schedule of events, play list, and on-air personalities. They also wish to obtain listener feedback and data.

Your Home page will provide access to the four major sections of your site: Events, Music, Us, and Listeners. You will start by creating the site's hierarchical structure, consisting of the Home page and the other four pages. These pages will contain banners and navigation bars created automatically by NetObjects Fusion. Figures 15-13 through 15-22 take you on a guided tour through Fusion in action.

To Construct a Site

1. Start NetObjects Fusion. Click on New Site.
2. Select Blank site, type "KVYB" in the Site Name field, and then click OK. The Site view appears, displaying an icon of the Home page. The Site view also displays the Tools palette and the Properties palette.
3. To create your site's structure, click the New Page button in the control bar four times. Four new pages are added to the site, each a child of the Home page.

**Figure 15-13.** Starting a new site.

Whenever you click the New Page button, NetObjects Fusion adds an Untitled child page to the selected page in the Site view. You can add as many pages as you want. You can now rename the pages.
4. Select the word Untitled in the page on the left. The entire word becomes highlighted.

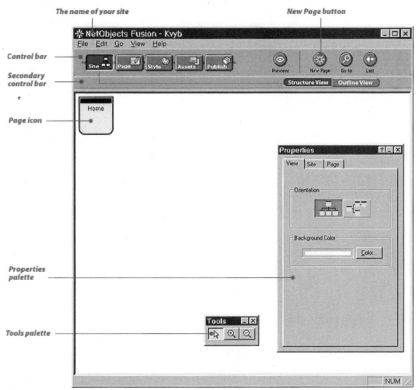

**Figure 15-14.** The Site view.

5. Type "Music" to rename the page. The name change is reflected in the Properties palette as well. The Page tab automatically comes to the front of the Properties palette.

6. Press the Tab key to select the next page name. Pressing the Tab key cycles you from name to name across a level of pages. You can either use the Tab key or click with your mouse.

7. Change the remaining page names to "Events," "Us," and ""Listeners." You can add pages at any time, rename them, and rearrange them whenever you like. As you'll see later, the pages are automatically linked, and the links are automatically updated whenever you rename the pages or rearrange them in the site.

## Designing a Page

Now that your site structure is started, you can begin to author the individual pages. Let's begin with the Music page. To open the Music page, click the Music page icon to select it, and then click the Page button. NetObjects Fusion displays the Page view for the Music page.

The Page view lets you design a page. You use the Page tools to add text,

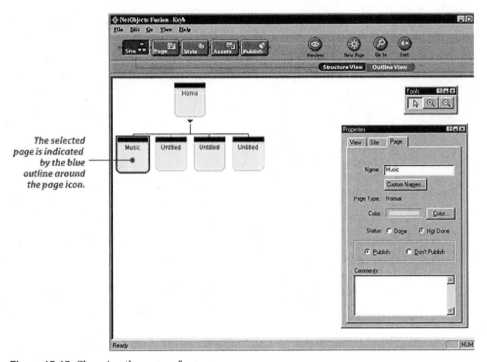

*The selected page is indicated by the blue outline around the page icon.*

**Figure 15-15.** Changing the name of a page.

graphics, and more. When you arrange them on the page, you are placing them exactly where they will appear in the browser, with pixel-level accuracy.

The page view displays the default MasterBorder in the areas outside the edges of your page layout. The MasterBorder lets you place elements which will appear on every page in your site such as banners, navigation bars, logos, or the Built with NetObjects Fusion icon. The horizontal banner already displays the name you gave to this page in the Site view, and the vertical navigation bars reflect the pages you have created.

If you add more pages on the first level in the Site view, their names will be added to the navigation bar automatically.

NetObjects Fusion automatically creates text navigation buttons which allow a site visitor to navigate quickly from the bottom of a page. Like the navigation bars on the left side of the page, these text buttons will automatically reflect changes in your site structure.

Let's add some text to get us started. Select the Text tool and drag the text bounding box anywhere in the layout area.

3. Now type the following, "Welcome to The Vibe. Our music is the hottest collection from a variety of genres." In the Properties palette, the Text tab has come to the front, automatically, ready for you to make any changes you want.

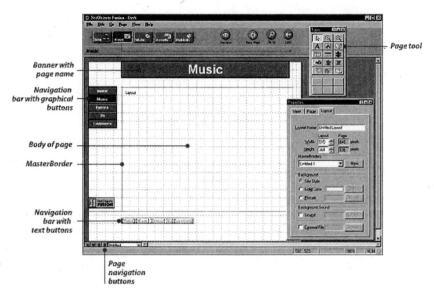

Banner with
page name

Navigation
bar with graphical
buttons

Body of page

MasterBorder

Navigation
bar with
text buttons

Page tool

Page
navigation
buttons

**Figure 15-16.** The Page view.

Notice it lets you change the alignment, font, size, and style of text. You can also set the text color and the background color.

4. Now, click the text block at its edge, and drag it so that it lines up with the first grid line from the left and the first grid line from the top. A text box can be moved when its handles are solid black and resized when its handles are hollow-white.

## Changing the Site Style

As you look at the Music page, you may not be completely satisfied with the appearance of your page. Let's examine the selection of SiteStyles available in NetObjects Fusion.

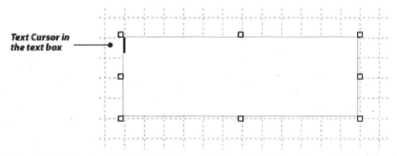

Text Cursor in
the text box

**Figure 15-17.** Using the text tool.

NetObjects Fusion SiteStyle elements include backgrounds, banners, buttons, icons, fonts, lines, and text colors. When you select and set a SiteStyle, you apply a consistent and well-designed look for all the pages in your site.

You can reapply a different SiteStyle quickly. You can customize any SiteStyle. And you can create your own original styles and incorporate them in the NetObjects Fusion Style view.

### Database Publishing

You have decided to put a directory listing of KVYB staff members on your Web site complete with telephone extension numbers.

1. In the Site view, select the "Us" page and click New Page.

2. Click once to select this new Untitled page and rename it Staff either on the page icon or in the Properties pallet.

3. Now click on Custom Names and give it a Banner name of "Staff Member Directory." Finally, open this new Staff page in Page view.

4. Select the Data List tool in the Tools palette and in the Tools subpalette select the New External Data Source tool. Now draw a long box across the width of the layout of the page.

5. A Data Source Type panel will be displayed. Scroll down to the type "Microsoft Excel 5-7 (*.xls)." Now click browse and locate the Vibe Employees Database. Select the Directory sheet from this Excel document and NetObjects Fusion will open the Data Publishing panel with additional options for you to select.

6. Now that we know which database to publish from, we need to select and sort the data we wish to take from the database. In the Data List section,

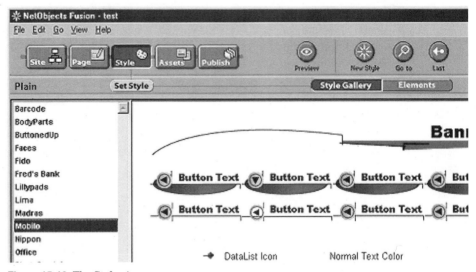

**Figure 15-18.** The Style view.

rename the Data List as "Employee Directory." Now click the fields you wish to bring in from each record. Don't worry about the order in which you select the fields; you will be able to reorder the list when you've decided what you want to bring in.

In our case, we want to click-select the following fields: First Name, Last Name, Title, Extension, Email. Now select the fields you don't want and use the Down Arrow icon to move those to the bottom of the list. Then select the First Name field and click the Up Arrow to promote to the top of the list. It will be the first field displayed. Also, select the Extension field and move it to display after Title and before Email.

7. Now click and drag-down on the dropdown menu next to Sort By so we can set the order in which the records come in. Select Last Name to sort the fields in alphabetical order by last name for our Staff Member Directory.

8. Now let's move to our Site view. A new icon has appeared under the Staff page. This is a set of stacked pages. Highlight the name of the stacked pages and rename it "Member." In fact, select Custom Names and give the pages a Banner name of "KVYB Staff Member."

9. Under the Style view button you will see a new yellow control that refers to the stack of pages which we are editing. Basically, stacked pages are a set of pages built from a data publishing query that all share the same page layout. The yellow box shows you left and right arrows for navigating among the individual pages in the stack and a reference to which page we are currently on among the total number in the stack. In this case, we are on page 1 of a stack of 5 pages. Let's set up the page to display the individual records.

10. Now select the Text tool and draw a box on the left side of the screen. Type in "Name, Title, Phone Extension, and Email", putting a carriage return

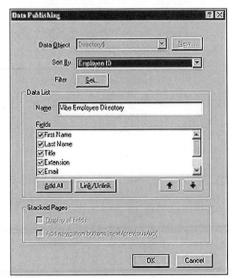

**Figure 15-19.** The Data Publishing dialog.

between each item. Then select the Data Field tool in the Tools palette and draw a small box just to the right of the word Name. As you let go of the box you have drawn, a panel will pop up asking you which field this Data Field should display; select First Name. Draw a second small Data Field box immediately next to the first one and select the Last Name field. Notice that Text boxes have a black border when deselected while Data Field boxes have a red border when deselected. This is to help you quickly differentiate between the two. Draw another Data Field box next to the text word Title and select the Title Field. Similarly add the appropriate Data Fields next to Phone Extension and Email. When you have finished placing all of the fields, click Preview to see what we've built.

### Staging and Publishing the Site

OK, let's say we have built our site and we are happy with our structure, our content, and our style and appearance. We think we might be ready to publish our site to the Internet.

NetObjects Fusion provides two functions for generating final HTML and setting up the final Web site Staging and Publishing. Before you make your site

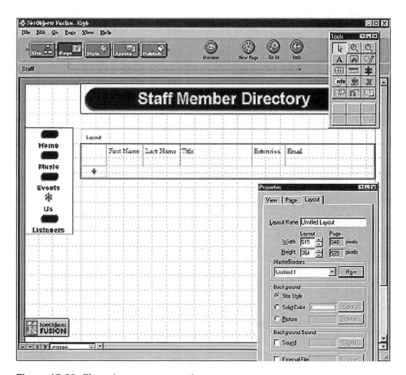

**Figure 15-20.** Changing page properties.

available to your audience, it's a good idea to test it on a test Web server. This is called Staging. Staging is exactly the same as Previewing, except that we have created two separate facilities for the process so you can maintain settings for your test server and your public Web server separately. Staging allows you to accurately test whether the HTML and associated files are correctly copied to the server. Since they are exactly the same in how they work, you can be assured that a test with Staging will reflect final Publishing.

When your design is complete and you've verified that everything in your site staged properly, you're ready to publish it. Publishing creates all of your HTML files and places them with their assets in the appropriate folder of your live Web server. Once published, your site is ready for browsing.

Click on the Settings button and look through the three tabs in the Configure Publish panel. The Stage tab lets you select the location where

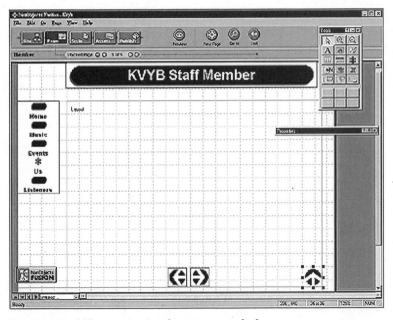

**Figure 15-21.** Adding navigational arrows to stacked pages.

NetObjects Fusion will create the ready-to-go folder with all the elements of your site in one place. You can stage locally or remotely. Several options are available for various naming conventions. If you are updating an existing Web site created by NetObjects Fusion from this .NOD file, you can also elect to Stage Only Changed Assets from the previously published version. This can save a lot of time.

The Publish tab lets you tell NetObjects Fusion where your Web server software resides. "Local" means the Web server software is running on the same computer on which you authored your NetObjects Fusion Web site. More likely, your site is Remote. Select Remote and click on the Configure button. In this

Remote panel, you can specify the host on which the Web server is running. You can specify this in the Remote Host field as the domain name or numeric IP address of the servers. You can also specify the exact directories where you want to place your HTML files & assets (base folder) and where you want your Common Gateway Interface Scripts (CGI folder). Finally, you can give your NetObjects Fusion site an account name and password so it has write-permission for the Web server. It can also remember your password so you need not reenter your password when you update your site.

The Modify tab has special settings you can use to make special additional versions to your Web site. If you want to supplement your original design with a low-bandwidth or greyscale or text only version, you can do so with no additional effort.

Click on OK to return to the Publish view then click Stage. NetObjects Fusion will begin generating your HTML pages and staging your assets into the specified folder on your hard drive. When finished, NetObjects Fusion will alert you with the message "Local Publish is Complete." You can now browse these HTML pages locally with any Web browser software that supports HTML version 3.2.

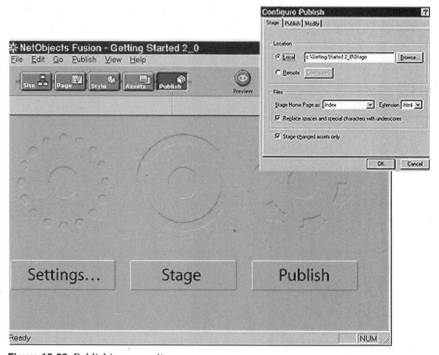

**Figure 15-22.** Publishing your site.

# 16

# Netscape's LDAP Protocol and Directory Service

## Introduction

A database is, after all, just an information resource. And like all information resources it needs to reside somewhere in such a way that is easily acessible to authorized users both inside the organization and outside the organization.

Much criticism has been leveled against the Internet regarding the difficulty in first locating and then accessing particular information resources. One solution is the implementation of a robust directory service that can handle files and people with equal aplomb. This chapter discusses in detail Netscape's (www.netscape.com) approach to this topic. Netscape provides a detailed manual online at

http://home.netscape.com/eng/server/directory/1.0/ag/contents.html.

In today's computing environment, the value of a corporate network is measured more and more by how well it exploits the global Internet. There are two facets to making effective use of the Intranet-Internet link:

Making the rich resources of the Internet readily available to corporate users, enabling them to gather information and to communicate with customers, partners, and suppliers. Employing open, scalable Internet technologies inside the corporation. Using the same protocols inside and outside of the corporate network leads to a seamless computing environment that scales to tens of millions of users and promotes competition among vendors.

Perhaps the most significant untapped resource on the Internet is the human one. Without a directory architecture that enables users to find each other easily, electronic communication cannot live up to its full potential. The virtues of a truly open directory architecture are also sorely missed inside corporations where user information is fragmented in pockets of proprietary technology. On the back end, MIS managers must struggle with maintaining employee information across a myriad of incompatible systems.

To address these problems, Netscape has developed an open strategy for enabling scalable, secure, multivendor, directory services for Intranets and the Internet.

The goals of Netscape's directory strategy are

- Logically centralized user management, that is, one place to add, move, change, or delete users
- Complete interoperability, including client-to-server communication and replication
- Internet scalability and interoperability
- No vendor lock-in, in other words, no proprietary ownership or control of the directory protocols. Free reference implementations of directory protocols should be available in order to maximize competition.

## Overview

| Application | Query Type |
|---|---|
| White Pages Server | attribute/value |
| Web Catalog Server | text search |
| Access Control Server | attribute/value |
| Certificate Server | attribute/value |
| Network Name Server | attribute/value |

| Application | Entries in Directory |
|---|---|
| White Pages Server | other people's email addresses |
| Web Catalog Server | relevant document URLs |
| Access Control Server | other people's access rights attributes |
| Certificate Server | other people's public keys |
| Network Name Server | network addresses for servers, printers, and other resources |

Figure 16-1. Types of directory applications.

In the broadest definition, a directory is the mechanism that clients use to locate entries and attributes about those entries. Clients are often people (for example, someone "querying the directory"), but they could also be programs (for instance, an application looking up an attribute about a user). Entries might include network resources such as printers or Web pages or people (a "white pages" directory). In addition to clients and entries, the type of query being used to access the information is important. The query structure defines the semantics of retrieving information from the directory. Different combinations of client type, entry type, and query type result in different kinds of directory applications as shown in figure 16-1.

Directories can be thought of as databases with the important characteristic that the number of database read operations generally exceeds the number of write operations by at least an order of magnitude.

You could imagine a single database technology that is highly optimized for read access but otherwise abstracts all possible combinations of clients, queries, and entries. However, as the generalization of the problem increases, the complexity increases and the potential to optimize performance and functionality for any specific application decreases. It is critical to choose the right level of abstraction to ensure timely, high-performance, commercially viable products.

One view is that the entry type and query type together determine the architecture of the directory. Therefore, applications that share similar entry types and similar query types are naturally combinable. In this view, the querying client is nearly irrelevant: people will query using human-readable interfaces (such as HTML) and applications will query via defined protocols (such as LDAP or WHOIS++).

If the applications above are grouped by query and entry type, it becomes apparent that there are two basic directory application groupings: those whose primary access is by attribute/value pairs (white pages, access control, certificate, network resource) and those whose primary access is by free text search (Web catalog).

Confusingly, both the directory applications of the attribute/value type and the text search type are colloquially known as directories. However, the white pages, network name, and access control applications have existed far longer and are far more prevalent then the more recent Web text search applications. Therefore, this document adopts the following nomenclature and core definitions:

> •A directory server is a repository of attribute/value pairs that clients can use to locate entries and attributes using structured queries.

> •A catalog server is a repository of textual citations that clients can use to locate documents using unstructured free text queries.

This chapter concerns itself primarily with the directory server and its architecture, implementation, and use by other products. The document also describes a mechanism for the interoperability of directory and catalog servers from Netscape or other vendors.

## Internet and Intranet Directories

Directories come in many different sizes and with many different potential transaction rates. One reasonable approximation of the transaction rates associated with different types of directories might be

| Directory | # Entries | # Reads/day | # Writes/day |
|-----------|-----------|-------------|--------------|
| Personal | 100-1000 | 10-100 | 1-10 |
| Departmental | 1000-10,000 | 100-1000 | 10-100 |
| Corporate | 10,000-100,000 | 100,000-1,000,000 | 100-1000 |
| Global | 10M-100M | 100M-1B | 10K-100K |

The Netscape directory strategy is based on an Internet standard client-server model. To satisfy this model, the client and server communicate via a predefined, open protocol. The choice of the directory protocol is arguably the most strategic decision that an IT organization will make.

By using an open, documented protocol, it becomes possible for other parties to develop servers to serve directory information to clients like Netscape Navigator. Historically strong LAN directory providers will support the open protocol, allowing Navigator users to query a LAN directory database. Service providers will support an open white pages service on the Net that Navigator can access.

Similarly, it will be possible for a customer to purchase a Netscape-supplied directory server and access it from non-Navigator clients. The Netscape Directory Server could serve names to and respond to administrative commands from a vertical application such as PeopleSoft. (For example, when a new employee is hired, the PeopleSoft application could even request the addition of the employee to the directory server.)

Netscape's own servers will be able to interact with the directory server. For example, an HTTP server might want to fetch a user's public key to authenticate her or his identity before accepting a form submittal.

In the future, all attribute/value information that multiple Netscape servers need will be migrated to a central Netscape Directory Server store.

Directory servers must also communicate with other directory servers. There are two cases in which this is important:

1. So that organizations can exchange directory information to create aggregated directories.

2. So that servers can replicate (mirror) themselves to other sites, thereby pro-

jecting directory information near to where it will be accessed and affecting load balancing.

From an implementation standpoint, it is convenient when the protocol used for directory server-server communication is the same as (or at least a subset or superset of) that used for client-server communication.

## The LDAP Protocol and Directory Service

The Lightweight Directory Access Protocol (LDAP) is Netscape's strategic directory protocol. (See RFC-1777, "Lightweight Directory Access Protocol.") It defines a reasonably simple mechanism for Internet clients to query and manage an arbitrary database of hierarchical attribute/value pairs over a TCP/IP connection (port 389). LDAP, a simplification of the X.500 directory access protocol (DAP), is also gaining significant Internet support, including the support of many significant companies. Importantly, major vendors, such as Novell, Sun, HP, IBM/Lotus, SGI, AT&T, and Banyan, intend to aggressively deploy Internet-wide white pages services that will ultimately support LDAP access.

The LDAP directory service model is based on entries. An entry is a collection of attributes that has a name, called a distinguished name (DN). The DN is used to refer to the entry unambiguously. Each of the entry's attributes has a type and one or more values. The types are typically mnemonic strings, like

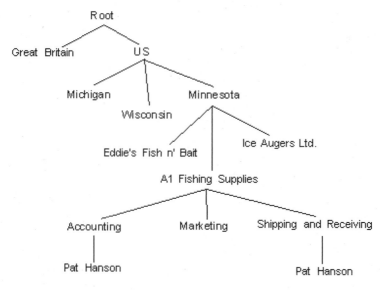

**Figure 16-2.** A LDAP directory tree.

"cn" for common name, or "mail" for email address. The values depend on the type of attribute. For example, a mail attribute might contain the value "babs@umich.edu." A jpegPhoto attribute would contain a photograph in binary JPEG/JFIF format. The syntax for the specification of attributes is given in RFC-1778, "The String Representation of Standard Attribute Syntaxes."

In LDAP, directory entries are arranged in a hierarchical treelike structure that reflects political, geographic, and/or organizational boundaries. Entries representing countries appear at the top of the tree. Below them are entries representing states or national organizations. Below them might be entries representing people, organizational units, printers, documents, or just about anything else you can think of. Figure 16-2 shows an example of an LDAP directory tree.

Note that the hierarchy in LDAP is a hierarchy of entries within a database, not a hierarchy of server connections or other network configuration information.

LDAP entries generally are typed by an object class attribute. For example, you could restrict searches of the directory to entries whose "objectclass=acl" to locate only entries that purport to be access control lists. LDAP allows you to control which attributes are required and allowed for a particular object class, thus determining the schema rules that the entry must obey.

The choice of attribute names and the hierarchical structure of LDAP are clearly derived from LDAP's X.500 roots. However, it is important to note that LDAP is not an X.500 directory. Rather, it is the protocol between parties transacting business relating to any hierarchical, attribute-based directory. In the degenerate case, the hierarchy can be a single level (for example, everything in a single Netscape tree), and the attributes could be arbitrarily proprietary (name=Marc Andreessen, smtp=marca@netscape.com). However, all else being equal, it is better to assume the de facto LDAP standards for organizing directory trees and naming entry object classes and attributes so that directory information can be practically exchanged with other LDAP clients and servers, including existing corporate X.500 servers.

An entry's distinguished name (DN) is constructed by taking the name of the entry itself (called the relative distinguished name, or RDN) and concatenating the names of its ancestor entries. For example, the entry for Barbara Jensen in the illustration above has an RDN of "cn=Barbara J Jensen" and a DN of "cn=Barbara J Jensen, o=U of M, c=US," The full DN format is described in RFC-1779, "A String Representation of Distinguished Names."

End users have not received these X.500-style distinguished names well. Many people attribute "the end-user challenges of adopting X.400" to the fact that people were expected to expose DN-like X.400 addresses on business cards and in other communications ("my X.400 address is C=us, O=Netscape, S=Hahn, G=Eric"). Ironically, users were forced to use this syntax because there wasn't a viable X.500 directory service available to resolve the common name ("Eric Hahn") to the DN. Using LDAP, people will be known by one or more common names that can be looked up to return the expected Simple Mail Transfer Protocol (SMTP) address without ever exposing a distinguished name to the user. In short, the Netscape directory strategy considers DNs and RDNs to be internal unique record identifiers and endeavors never to expose them to the user.

## Directory Operations

LDAP defines operations for interrogating and updating the directory. It provides operations for adding and deleting an entry from the directory, changing an existing entry, and changing the name of an entry. Most of the time, though, LDAP is used to search for information in the directory. The LDAP search operation allows some portion of the directory to be searched for entries that match some criteria specified by a search filter. A client can request information from each entry that matches the criteria.

For example, you might want to search the entire directory subtree below the University of Michigan for people with the name Barbara Jensen, retrieving the email address of each entry found. LDAP lets you do this easily. Or you might want to search the entries directly below the c=US entry for organizations that have the string "Acme" in their name and have a fax number. LDAP lets you do this too. RFC-1558, "A String Representation of LDAP Search Filters," specifies the syntax for the filters that define the search. Using this facility, client developers can easily provide powerful search capabilities.

Some directory services provide no protection, allowing anyone to see the information they contain. LDAP provides a method for a client to authenticate, or to prove its identity to, a directory server. This paves the way for rich access control to protect the information that the server contains. LDAP provides for multiple, extensible authentication protocols.

Beyond authentication, each LDAP server typically has robust access control lists (ACLs) that determine access rights to particular classes of information by particular classes of clients. Access levels include none, compare, search, read, write, and delete.

## Directory Topologies, Referral, and Replication

LDAP directory service is based on a client-server model. One or more LDAP servers contains the data making up the LDAP directory tree. An LDAP client connects to an LDAP server and asks it a question. The server responds with the answer. If a local answer is not available, the server attempts to connect to another server (typically, another LDAP server) that can fulfill the request. LDAP uses this referral capability to implement cooperating communities of disjoint LDAP servers and to force all database changes to be referred to certain master LDAP servers. (Referral corresponds roughly to query routing in the RDBMS world.)

When LDAP servers use the same naming convention, no matter which LDAP server a client connects to, it sees the same view of the directory; a name presented to one LDAP server references the same entry that it would at another LDAP server. This is an important feature of a global directory service like LDAP.

Netscape, like other implementers of the LDAP specification, will add extensions to support client referral. When a server cannot satisfy a request, it returns a specially coded result to the client, indicating the location of the server that it wishes to refer the client to. The client then makes a second (or nth) connection and continues with the operation, not unlike the link-following required to display a compound HTML page.

LDAP servers are also capable of retaining a transaction log chronicling recent adds, changes, and deletes of attribute/value pairs. An LDAP replication daemon is commonly used to propagate these changes (again using the LDAP protocol) to slave LDAP servers, who in turn apply the transaction locally. The replicas are commonly used to load-balance LDAP queries or to place copies of directory information local to the user community, thus reducing wide-area network bandwidth requirements.

## Topology Restrictions and Challenges

LDAP's distributed directory topology has the important limitation that, in any subtree, all attempts to add, change, or delete entries are referred to the subtree's master (root), where they are accepted and then replicated out to slave servers. That is, each entry must have a single master. For each entry, reads are distributed but writes are centralized. For Intranet use within a corporation, this does not appear to be particularly problematic: even a very large corporation with 100,000 employees should not expect more than a few hundred adds/changes/deletes per day (a volume that could reasonably be centralized). These writes may also be distributed across departmental masters in a decentralized organization (where each department is responsible for the master of its own subtree). The same company might well experience 100,000 to 1,000,000 directory reads each day, which is clearly beyond the capacity of any single server.

A potentially greater problem with current LDAP implementations is that when a server fails to find the requested entries, it can be instructed to refer the query to another LDAP server. The referral, however, is fixed, meaning that all failed searches refer to the same LDAP server(s). Thus, if a client issues a query across a forest of LDAP trees, the query is referred to a member of each tree in turn until the search is resolved.

For example, assume that you are looking for Barbara Jensen, but you don't know what company she works for or even what state she's in. All you know is that she is a U.S. resident. A search of the entire subtree may be what you want to do, but that's potentially very expensive because it involves contacting every server in the United States.

LDAP implementers are working on forward indexes to solve this problem. Servers construct reduced indexes of their contents and offer those indexes to other servers. When a search fails, the server doesn't have to refer the search to all other servers; it can instead consult these indexes and refer the query directly to an appropriate server that is likely to satisfy the search. In short, the current state of LDAP's replication and search topology limitations imply that

> •Organizations should connect all internal LDAP servers via replication with a master for each administrative division and all others as slaves. This eliminates the need for referral of any searches within the corporation.

> •The master server must be capable of servicing the subtree's directory writes (updates). Organizations that wish to replicate information to external LDAP servers must do so with more advanced techniques because a server cannot at once be an internal tree participant and a slave to the external LDAP server.

In practice, it is unlikely that any organization will wish to expose its unfiltered tree to the external server, so this isn't likely to be a problem. Instead, the organization would subset its local tree and transmit that subset to the governing body of the external LDAP server, which would inspect the proposed changes and apply the transactions locally. Note that this can all be accomplished with standard LDAP transaction logs.

The LDAP replication model, while not without its limitations, is sufficient for Intranet-scale directories. However, Netscape plans to support forward indexes and tools for publishing internal directories to external parties in the future.

## Directory API

Netscape will base its internal directory access on the C-binding for LDAP defined in RFC-1823, "The LDAP Application Programming Interface." The LDAP API is extremely simple and straightforward and supports both synchronous and asynchronous calls to the server. The use of an asynchronous search verb might well permit an address book user interface to support even the elusive "incremental search" capability. An example program using the LDAP API is included in the appendix to this chapter.

At the lowest level, any client needing access to directory information makes a connection to an LDAP server, sends LDAP commands over the TCP/IP connection, and interprets the results. In this case, a Domain Name System (DNS) name (or explicit Internet protocol address) for the server and a port number (well known as port 389) are all that are needed to begin an LDAP interaction.

Recent innovations suggest that an Internet URL definition for LDAP searches could be quite useful. (See ftp://ds.internic.net/internet-drafts/draft-ietf-asid-ldap-format-03.txt.) Not unlike the encodings used for Gopher, this URL representation not only identifies the protocol (LDAP) but also encodes the DNS host name. It includes an optional syntax for a search. The following examples illustrate the power of this syntax:

1. ldap://ldap.netscape.com: This URL identifies the use of the LDAP protocol and refers to a particular server (ldap.netscape.com).
2. ldap://ldap.netscape.com/o=Netscape,ou=Sales,c=US?one: The same URL, but it issues a base object search of the people working in the sales department in the United States at Netscape. All object classes and attributes of matching entries are returned.
3. ldap://ldap.netscape.com/o=Netscape,ou=Sales,c=US?postalAddress?one: The same query, but it retrieves only the postalAddress attribute of the resulting entries.

It is also possible to integrate LDAP and existing DNS servers easily. You could imagine adding a record to an existing DNS server that pointed LDAP URLs to an LDAP server within the domain. (The record could be a TEXT record; in the long term, a hypothetical DX record, like the MX record for email, could be created.) For example:

•A user at hp.com wants to know more about the author of an email message.
•Her client asks DNS to return DX records for netscape.com.
•DNS returns ldap://ldap.netscape.com.
•Her client queries the Netscape LDAP server for information about entries that have an email attribute of mail=maxxx@netscape.com.

The reverse is also possible: A corporation can add DNS entries to their internal LDAP server so that failing local searches can be referred over DNS to distant LDAP servers.

•A user at Boeing wants to locate the email address of David Hinson, administrator of the Federal Aviation Administration (FAA).

- His client issues the local LDAP query to: ldap://ldap.inhouse.boeing.com/cn=David%20Hinson,o=FAA.
- The Boeing LDAP server, having no knowledge of the FAA or David Hinson, returns a referral to DX://faa.gov.
- His client asks DNS for DX records at faa.gov.
- DNS returns ldap://ldap.faa.gov.
- His client queries the FAA LDAP server for cn=David Hinson.

Support for LDAP URLs and integration with DNS effectively couple LDAP with the rest of the Internet and are key to long-term success of any Internet-centric white pages strategy.

Netscape will support LDAP URLs and LDAP DX/TEXT entries in DNS, and will work with the IETF to standardize this important capability.

## External Representation and Interchange Formats

In addition to the APIs for querying (and possibly managing) an LDAP directory, Netscape will support standard formats for the interchange of directory information. Although LDAP replication tools will exchange directory entries between LDAP servers, the LDAP protocol is not particularly application-friendly and, in any case, lacks a standardized plain text encoding. The ideal external representation would be simple, self-describing, and significantly textual for platform and protocol independence.

Typical applications for an external representation include

- An "electronic business card" that could be transmitted between email users in lieu of the current signature file. The business card could carry cosmetic information and X.509 keys for private email.

- A standard "import/export format" in which LDAP and non-LDAP systems exchange directory information. The import/export format would facilitate transferring bulk directory information to or from a corporate database.

Netscape will adopt the MIME-based application/directory content-type representation defined in draft-ietf-asid-mime-direct-01.txt as its external representation for directory information and will provide API extensions to read and write this format.

Designed by the University of Michigan's LDAP team in conjunction with the IETF, the application/directory interchange format provides a simple attribute/value mechanism in MIME format. It also supports the notion of a profile to define the class of entry being transmitted, not unlike LDAP's own objectclass attribute.

The application/directory interchange format, while technically attractive, does not yet have wide industry support. Instead, the Versit PDI (formerly known as eCard) seems to have some momentum, despite its rather OpenDoc-centric technical character.

The Versit PDI specification is a joint effort among Apple, AT&T, IBM, Siemens Rolm, and Counterpoint Systems. The specification document defines an interchange format for an electronic business card object, or eCard. The format is intended to be useful for the exchange of such objects between diverse applications on heterogeneous computer platforms using many diverse transports. The specification effort is intended to provide the network computing industry with a common definition for a simple, interchange format for electronic business card objects.

Netscape will work with the Versit group to support a MIME-compliant representation for directory information while continuing its efforts to implement and support the IETF application/directory interchange format. Recently the Versit and application/directory interchange formats were synchronized to promote interoperability.

## Logins, Passwords, and Access Control

One of LDAP's strengths is its ability to represent arbitrary attribute/value pairs arranged as entries in the directory. One such attribute allows the recording of a user's public key (in X.509v3 format). An administrative utility to "create a user" would ask a certificate authority to issue a new key pair and to record the public key in that user's new directory entry as an attribute/value pair. Any party wishing to send private mail to that person could then easily look up the key from the directory service. However, this mechanism only provides a reasonable mechanism for advertising key information, not enforcing its use by other servers.

Future Access Control mechanisms such as SSL 4.0 will be configurable to authenticate users against keys stored in the Netscape Directory Server.

UNIX implementations of a stand-alone LDAP server (known as slapd) and an LDAP gateway to existing X.500 directories (known as ldapd) are available from the University of Michigan at no charge. A reference implementation, a replication daemon known as slurpd, is also available from the University.

The University of Michigan implementations have the interesting characteristic that they are abstracted by an internal API known as slapi, which allows the easy construction of LDAP directory providers. Two such back ends are implemented: one that passes control to arbitrary Unix shell programs and parses the results, and the other (more interestingly) that is a full database-based directory provider. The latter can be hosted on top of a variety of data-bases, including Berkeley btree, hash, GNU dbm, or Unix ndbm.

The University of Michigan team is working on an LDAP tool called cen-tipede that can extract and implant forward index information. The University of Michigan implementations are multithreaded and compile for a number of Unix systems but not for Windows NT.

This implementation is particularly attractive because the development team, lead by Tim Howes, has been operating a production version of much of this code base at the University of Michigan with the following characteristics:

> Number of entries in the directory
> 115,000
> Number of users of the directory
> 50,000
> Number of accesses per week
> 5,000,000
> Number of writes per week
> 100,000
> Number of groups/lists in directory
> 15,000
> Size of on-disk directory
> 300 Mbytes
> Number of replicated servers
> 5 (Sparc 20s)

Netscape has entered into a multiyear research agreement with the University of Michigan. Several members of the University's research team will join Netscape as part of this effort.

## Directories and Netscape Navigator

Netscape Navigator will use LDAP and the LDAP URL format for access to directory servers, whether supplied by Netscape or other parties.

The most obvious place to introduce the LDAP protocol is in the address book user interface and its related addressing fields during email composition. Using LDAP, the address book interface can browse or query entries in a departmental, corporate, or Internet-wide LDAP directory server. By support-ing multiple LDAP URLs in the user's preferences, it will be possible to search multiple directories without depending on well-coordinated server referrals.

Using the LDAP URL syntax further extends the power of the address book because it will be possible to use a URL containing search parameters to pro-duce automatically filtered subsets of large directories. For example, ldap://ldap.megacorp.com/ou=marketing, o=megacorp, c=us??one will auto-matically filter down to entries in the marketing department. The resulting address book display will include only the desired subset of the directory.

Netscape will use the LDAP API as Navigator's own directory abstraction layer, even for personal address book access. That way, a Navigator developer need only code to the LDAP API to get access to personal, corporate, or global directory information.

While it would be tempting to code all future Navigator address book and directory functions to the LDAP API and protocol, many vendors will not have viable LDAP-compliant directory servers for some time. Existing network white pages, such as Four11, do not currently support LDAP. Therefore, in addition to LDAP, Navigator will implement a minimal mechanism for access-ing email directory information stored in existing Web pages using HTML.

### Directory and Catalog Server Interoperability

Directory servers are repositories of entries consisting of attribute/value infor-mation accessed via structured queries. Catalog servers are repositories of doc-uments and document citations accessed via unstructured queries. Despite these differences in basic metaphor, you might reasonably wonder why a sin-gle query couldn't return matching information from both types of server. For example, you might search for "Bill Clinton" and expect to receive documents written by or about Bill Clinton, as well as Bill Clinton's email address.

The Netscape approach is a simple one: Allow catalog servers to catalog information in directory servers. Catalog servers are already adept at "crawl-ing" various information sources (nominally Web sites) and gleaning informa-tion to be indexed against some taxonomy. In this sense, entries in a directory server are just another data source.

This approach is easily implemented by having Netscape's Directory Server support the generation of resource description messages (RDMs). RDMs are high-level descriptions of information to be indexed by a catalog server. Derived from the Harvest project and the basis for the Catalog Server project within Netscape, the RDM syntax is being offered to the Internet community as a standard way for catalog servers to represent and exchange information to be indexed.

### Directories and Other Servers

Netscape will begin to migrate its common attribute/value access APIs to LDAP and will use LDAP servers to store and manage this information, even locally to one server. We will implement all attribute/value databases within the Netscape servers as an LDAP server that speaks the LDAP protocol to the local server using a local procedure call through. This approach has the follow-ing important advantages:

•The ACL information can be stored locally to the server needing it (for example, a Web server), dramatically improving performance.

•The ACL information will not require the presence of a Netscape Directory Server because the LDAP implementation will be self-sufficient. If a Netscape Directory Server is present, the ACL information can be replicated and managed centrally on that server.

As technologies and tools are developed to better manage directory information, all Netscape products will benefit immediately because they all share the same underlying LDAP implementation. Servers from other vendors can seamlessly plug into the Netscape SuiteSpot offering.

## Bibliography

T. Howes, "A String Representation of LDAP Search Filters," Internet RFC 1558, University of Michigan, December 1993.

W. Yeong, T. Howes, S. Kille, "Lightweight Directory Access Protocol," Internet RFC-1777, Performance Systems International, University of Michigan, ISODE Consortium, March 1995.

T. Howes, S. Kille, W. Yeong, "The String Representation of Standard Attribute Syntaxes," University of Michigan, ISODE Consortium, Performance Systems International, NeXor Ltd., Internet RFC 1778, March 1995.

S. Kille, "A String Representation of Distinguished Names," Internet RFC-1779, ISODE Consortium, March 1995.

K. Moore, "Multipurpose Internet Mail Extensions," Internet RFC-1522, University of Tennessee, September 1993.

T. Howes, M. Smith, "The LDAP Application Program Interface," Internet RFC-1823, University of Michigan, August 1995.

NAC Enterprise Directory Services Integration SIG: Requirements Paper, Network Applications Consortium, April 1995.

## Appendix A: LDAP Example

```c
#include

main()
{
        LDAP            *ld;
        LDAPMessage     *res, *e;
        int             i;
        char            *a, *dn;
        void            *ptr;
        char            **vals;

        /* open a connection */
        if ( (ld = ldap_open( "dotted.host.name", LDAP_PORT ))
                == NULL )
                exit( 1 );

        /* authenticate as nobody */
        if ( ldap_simple_bind_s( ld, NULL, NULL )
            != LDAP_SUC CESS ) {
                ldap_perror( ld, "ldap_simple_bind_s" );
                exit( 1 );
        }

        /* search for entries with cn of "Babs Jensen",
                return all attrs   */
        if ( ldap_search_s( ld, "o=University of Michigan,
          c=US",
            LDAP_SCOPE_SUBTREE, "(cn=Babs Jensen)", NULL, 0,
            &res )
            != LDAP_SUCCESS ) {
                ldap_perror( ld, "ldap_search_s" );
                exit( 1 );
        }

        /* step through each entry returned */
        for ( e = ldap_first_entry( ld, res ); e != NULL;
            e = ldap_next_entry( ld, e ) ) {
                /* print its name */
                dn = ldap_get_dn( ld, e );
                printf( "dn: %s0, dn );
                free( dn );

                /* print each attribute */
                for ( a = ldap_first_attribute( ld, e, &ptr );
```

```
                                a != NULL;
                   a = ldap_next_attribute( ld, e, ptr ) ) {
                        printf( "attribute: %s0, a );


                        /* print each value */


                        vals = ldap_get_values( ld, e, a );
                        for ( i = 0; vals[i] != NULL; i++ ) {
                                printf( "value: %s0, vals[i] );
                        }
                        ldap_value_free( vals );
                }
        }
        /* free the search results */
        ldap_msgfree( res );

        /* close and free connection resources */
        ldap_unbind( ld );
}
```

## Appendix B: LDAP MIME Record Example

The first example illustrates simple use of the application/directory Content-Type:

```
From: Whomever
To: Someone
Subject: whatever
MIME-Version: 1.0
Message-ID:
Content-Type: application/directory
Content-ID:

cn: Babs Jensen
cn: Barbara J Jensen
sn: Jensen
email: babs@umich.edu
phone: +1 313 747-4454
x-id: 1234567890
```

The next example illustrates the use of the Quoted-Printable encoding defined in RFC-1522, "Multipurpose Internet Mail Extensions," to include non-ASCII characters in some of the information returned and the use of the optional "name" and "source" parameters. Note the use of the "person" profile, as defined in MIME-WPP.

```
Content-Type: application/directory;
        charset="iso-8859-1";

source="ldap://cn=Bjorn%20Jensen,o=University%20of%20Michigan,
        c=US";
            name="cn=Bjorn Jensen, o=Universityr ofr Michigan,
            c=US";
            profile="person"
Content-ID:
Content-Transfer-Encoding: Quoted-Printable

cn: Bj=F8rn Jensen
sn: Jensen
email: bjorn@umich.edu
phone: +1 313 747-4454
```

The final example illustrates the use of the multipart/related Content-Type to include nontextual directory data:

```
Content-Type: multipart/related;
        boundary=woof;
        type="application/directory";
        start=""
Content-ID:

—woof
Content-Type: application/directory;
        charset="iso-8859-1";

source="ldap://cn=Bjorn%20Jensen,o=University%20of%20Michigan,c=US
"
Content-ID:
Content-Transfer-Encoding: Quoted-Printable

cn: Bj=F8rn Jensen
sn: Jensen
email: bjorn@umich.edu
image::
sound::
phone: +1 313 747-4454

—woof
Content-Type: image/jpeg
```

```
Content-ID:

<...image data...>
—woof
Content-Type: message/external-body;
        name="myvoice.au";
        site="myhost.com";
        access-type=ANON-FTP;
        directory="pub/myname";
        mode="image"
http://home.netscape.com/newsref/ref/ldap.html

Content-Type: audio/basic
Content-ID:

—woof—
```

# 17

# Oracle Designer/2000: Web-Enabling Your Applications

## Introduction

This chapter describes the process of reverse engineering, via Oracle's Designer/2000, an existing application deployed in Developer/2000. The application is then generated for the Web, using the Designer/2000 WebServer generator. The investment in producing the original application is not lost, as the reverse engineering process captures information about data accessed from the database and stores it in the repository, ready for generation into another deployment environment.

This also means that applications can be deployed over heterogeneous environments with no rework, e.g., deployed in Developer/2000, Visual Basic, Oracle Power Objects and the Web.

## Oracle WebServer Overview

We'll discuss the Oracle WebServer in more depth at the end of this chapter. In this section we'll present an overview of the product. The Oracle WebServer is integrated with the Oracle7 database. Business data stored on the Oracle7 database is dynamically formatted into Web (HTML) documents within the WebServer and then transmitted to Web Clients, on demand from the user as shown in figure 17-1.

Web users request information by entering an appropriate Uniform Resource Locator (URL). The URL specifies the target Oracle WebServer machine or site, the WebServer session (Oracle database logon information) and the PL/SQL routine which will run.

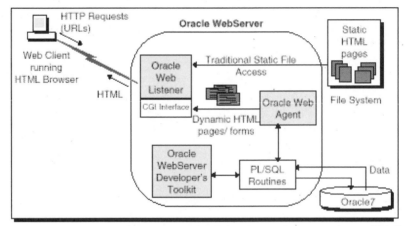

**Figure 17-1**. Oracle WebServer presents HTML pages and dynamic data to Web Browsers

## Designer/2000 WebServer Generator

The Oracle Designer/2000 WebServer Generator provides the benefits of modeling and team-working to sites who want to deploy applications on the Web. The WebServer Generator uses the same modeling techniques as the other Designer/2000 generators (i.e., Developer/2000 and Visual Basic). Thus it offers the ability to generate and deploy Web applications from definitions already built and deployed in Developer/2000 or Visual Basic.

Using Designer/2000 (figure 17-2) we can present not only static Web pages, but interactive query pages, where users can enter query parameters and use these to query a database. The query runs against a live, on-line database, resulting in a response which provides up-to-date data for the user. Consequently, we can present the user with an application which provides the same data as a traditional client-server application.

Designer/2000 uses a repository to store design information including data models, modules, module structure, module logic and preferences (style guide). From information in the repository, we can generate database definition language, which can be run to create tables, columns, constraints and other database objects. We can also generate program definitions into Web pages, as well as Developer/2000 and Visual Basic. Designer/2000 also has a reverse engineering utility, which will read definitions of Oracle7 objects including tables, views, constraints, indexes etc. in an existing database and write them to the repository. Reverse engineering of Developer/2000 Forms allows table and column usages for those forms to be stored in the repository. '

Using this information we can generate the same application (or a modified, re-engineered or new one) against the same database schema, giving users a new interface (e.g., the Web) to their data.

**Reverse
Engineering
and
Generation
for the Web**

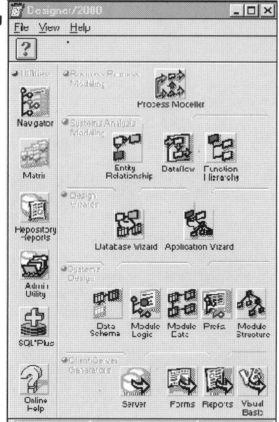

**Figure 17-2.** Oracle Designer/2000.

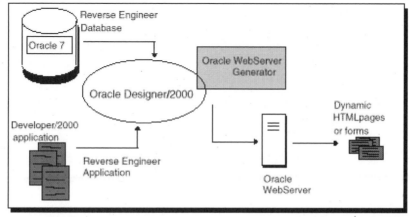

**Figure 17-3.** The process of repository-based engineering and generating.

This section describes the process of reverse engineering an Oracle application in Developer/2000 into the Designer/2000 repository, and generating the same application for the World Wide Web, shown in figure 17-3.

There are three main steps in the process:

1 Reverse engineering database tables
2 Reverse engineering your application
3 Generate for the Web

In the following example, we reverse engineer the module funds, which shows details of funds, fund sectors and fund holdings. The form is based on three tables called FUNDS, FUND_SECTORS and FUND_HOLDINGS. The Reverse Engineer Database utility recovers the data schema including these tables and updates the Designer/2000 repository.

An application has already been created using Developer/2000, and the module for funds relates the units together as master-detail-detail. The module definition is created in the repository by the "Reverse Engineer Forms" utility.

Finally, the WebServer generator is run to generate a Web application from the repository definition of the FUNDS module, using the preferences for appearance of Web applications also stored in the Repository, shown in figures 17-4 and 17-5.

1. Reverse engineering database tables: The Reverse Engineer Database utility puts the table definitions into the repository, along with definitions of any other Oracle7 database objects which exist, such as views, constraints, indexes, sequences etc. The server generator then creates the DDL for the objects, which you can execute against any Oracle 7 (or ANSI) database.

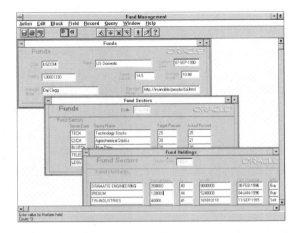

**Figure 17-4.** Funds application deployed in Developer/2000 Forms, with windows for funds, fund sectors and fund-holdings.

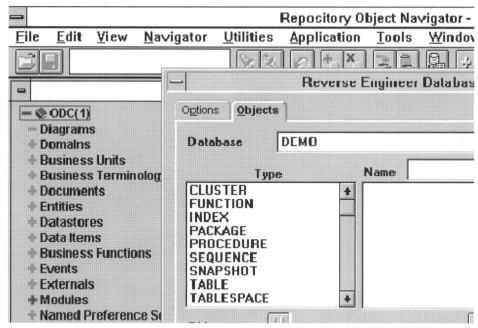

**Figure 17-5.** Reverse Engineering tables FUNDS, FUNDS_SECTORS and FUND_HOLDINGS.

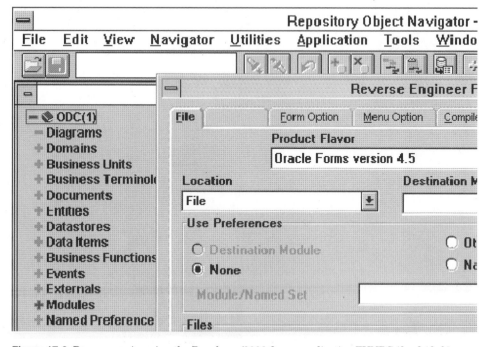

**Figure 17-6.** Reverse engineering the Developer/2000 forms application FUNDS (funds.fmb).

2. Reverse engineering your application: Designer/2000 will reverse engineer your Developer/2000 application into the repository. The Reverse Engineer Form utility will create a module definition and store table and column usages for that module in the repository, as shown in figure 17-6.

The utility produces a report to show which tables and column it has found used in the program. Using the Module Data Diagrammer (figure 17-7), one of the Designer/2000 toolset, we can visually represent the module definition which we now have in the repository. The diagram appears as below, with the table usages showing a master-detail-detail relationship.

At this stage it is necessary to add display prompts to the table and column definitions or to the module's detailed column usages, as they are not stored in the repository by the reverse engieer forms utility.

Reverse engineering a Developer/2000 report will also result in a module definition in the repository, which can be examined and modified if necessary, then generated into a Web-enabled application.

If you do not have Developer/2000 applications (Forms or Reports), then a module can be created in the repository, and a module data diagram created by

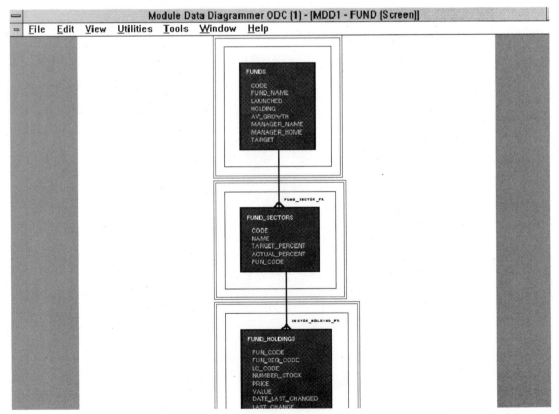

**Figure 17-7.** The Module Data Diagrammer visually represents the module definition of the FUNDS module.

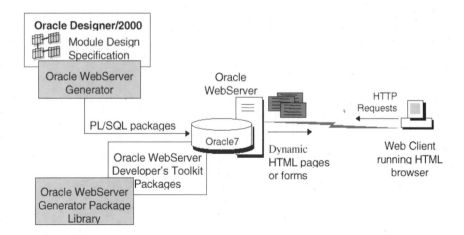

**Figure 17-8.** Oracle WebServer generator produces PL/SQL packages which are used to create dynamic Web pages.

dragging and dropping table definitions onto the drawing surface. The generation process from here is as described below.

3. Generate for the Web: The Designer/2000 Web generator generates a Web page (or set of pages ) for a module. During generation the Oracle WebServer Generator creates a set of PL/SQL packages, which are then installed into an Oracle WebServer database and is shown in figure 17-8.

Oracle PowerBrowser, or any other HTML Browser may be used to run generated applications. Preferences control the appearance of the generated output — for example; justification of number fields, layout of record lists and query pages.

## The Generated Web Application

Below (figures 17-9 to 17-16) is the set of Web pages generated from the Funds module after it was reverse engineered into the repository. The startup page has a query dialogue, in order to refine the data retrieved from the database. If the fields are left blank, all of the rows are retrieved. Subsequent links to detail records are automatically generated, so navigating through the master-detail-detail structure of the module is presented in exactly the same fashion as static Web pages, using HTTP links. Textual information on the page is generated from module help text stored in the repository. The query fields are based on those fields marked queryable in the repository.

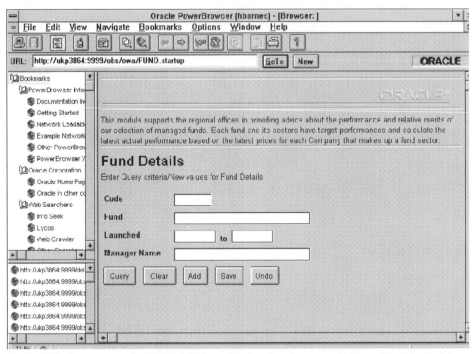

**Figure 17-9.** Startup page for FUNDS Web application showing query fields and text derived from module help.

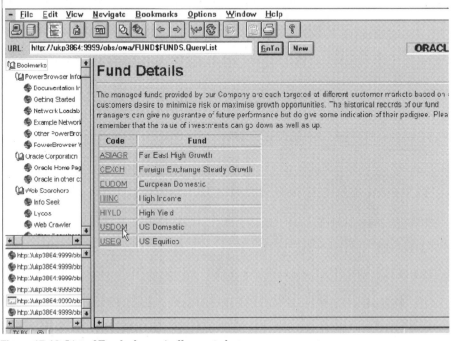

**Figure 17-10.** List of Funds dynamically created.

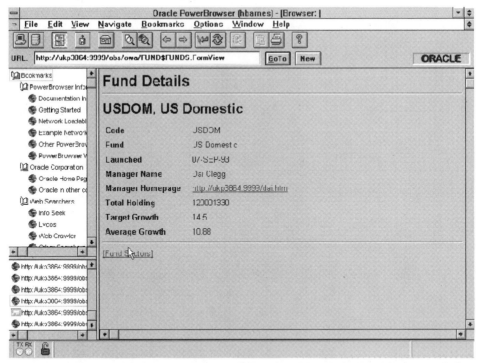

**Figure 17-11.** Generated Web page showing Fund Details and http links. Fund Sectors is a link to another generated page in this module.

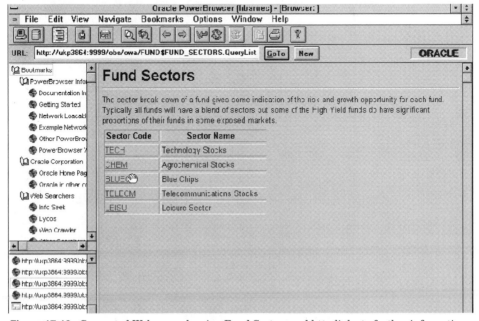

**Figure 17-12.** Generated Web page showing Fund Sectors and http links to further information .

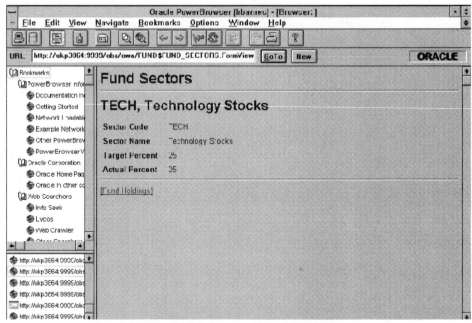

**Figure 17-13.** Fund Sector record details and link to Fund Holdings.

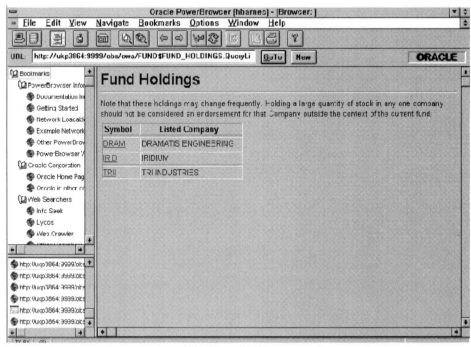

**Figure 17-14.** Fund holdings record list.

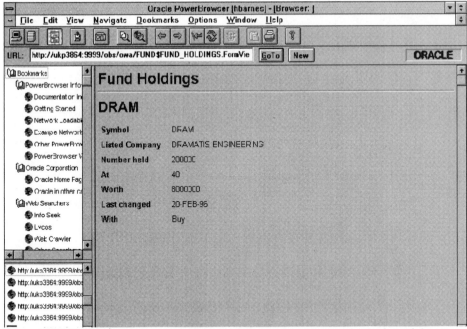

**Figure 17-15.** Fund Holdings record detail – the final generated page of the funds module.

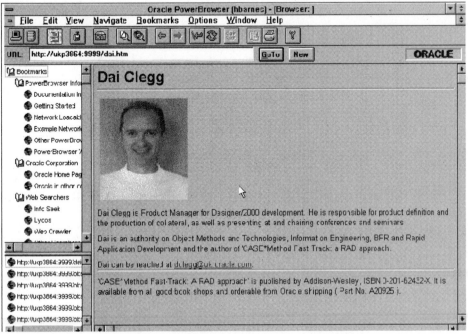

**Figure 17-16.** This static HTML page is linked from the URL in figure 17-10.

## The WebServer Generator

Designer/2000's WebServer generator produces Web applications very quickly and simply from module definitions in the repository. These module definitions may be created against table definitions, or reverse engineered from existing applications. Reverse engineering existing applications populates the repository with module definitions from which we can directly generate Web applications, obviating the need to create new module definitions. Consequently, the deployment of existing applications to the Web becomes a simple and quick process using the powerful Designer/2000 WebServer Generator.

The Oracle WebServer (figure 17-17) is an HTTP server tightly integrated with the Oracle7 database. Business data stored on the Oracle7 database is formatted into Web (HTML) documents within the WebServer and then transmitted to Web Clients, on request.

Web users request HTML information by entering an appropriate Uniform Resource Locator (URL). This URL specifies the target Oracle WebServer machine or site, the WebServer session (Oracle database logon information), and the PL/SQL routine to run on that database user. An example is shown in figure 17-18.

The PL/SQL routine specified within the URL fetches the data from the Oracle database and then makes use of other PL/SQL routines provided within the Oracle WebServer Developer's Toolkit to format the data within the required HTML syntax. The formatted data is then routed to the Web user originating the request, via the Web Agent.

The Oracle WebServer Generator creates fully functional applications that publish data retrieved from an Oracle database over the World Wide Web.

These generated applications are based on module and database design specifications recorded in the Designer/2000 Repository.

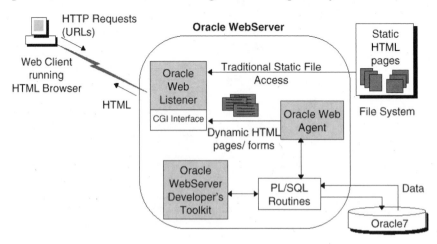

**Figure 17-17.** A tightly integrated HTTP/Database environment.

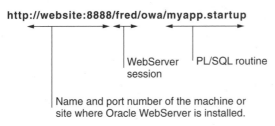

Figure 17-18. Requesting DB data via an URL.

The main input to the generation process is a module design specification recorded through the Module Data Diagrammer component of Designer/2000. This records the tables and columns used by the module, the links between them, and detailed information on how the module uses the data. Standard display details for the tables and columns defined within the Application System ( or Project ) provide default display details for generated applications, thus ensuring a consistent look and feel across applications generated by any number of developers.

Modules can be linked together using the Module Structure Diagrammer. In the generated application these module links allow navigation between the modules via hypertext links with full passing of current context via parameters. During generation the Oracle WebServer Generator creates a set of PL/SQL packages, which are then installed into an Oracle WebServer database. Preferences determine the general look and feel of the generated application and can be customized to suit particular requirements.

## How the Oracle WebServer Generator Works

### Module Design

To generate an Oracle WebServer application, you first specify the set of module definitions that make up the application and then define any links between them. The design of these modules provide the main input to the generation process as shown in figure 17-19.

### Generation Process

When you generate your application you choose which module you wish to generate and also whether or not to generate all the other modules called (directly or indirectly) by the chosen module. Oracle WebServer Generator examines the design specification of each module, detects any links between modules and determines the values of user preferences. During generation, the Generator creates a pair of PL/SQL files for each module:

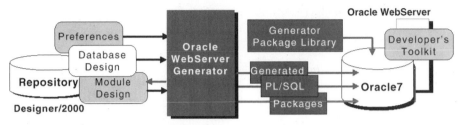

Figure 17-19. How Oracle WebServer works.

These files are
package specification file: PKS
package body file: PKB

   A PL/SQL package is created for each module component defined within a
module, plus one for the module itself . The Oracle WSG builds PL/SQL procedures inside these packages to provide the database querying and parameter
management functionality for the pages required. The generation process also
results in the creation of a single .SQL file which simply calls all the other generated files (.PKS and .PKB). After generation you are given the option to run
this file to install the generated Oracle WebServer application onto to an
Oracle database. After installation you may run the application using your chosen HTML Browser. In addition to generated packages, Oracle WebServer
Generator makes use of its own PL/SQL package library to provide generic
functionality within the application.

## Module Definitions and Data Usages

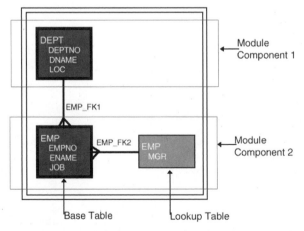

Figure 17-20. A module definition.

A generated Oracle WebServer application comprises one or more dynamic HTML Web pages. Each generated page contains one or more sections, displaying static HTML text and formatted data sourced from SQL queries. Module components form the basis of each SQL query and they are defined visually using the Module Data Diagrammer.

A single module definition may contain one or more module components, linked together via foreign keys. Module components are based on a specific table (the base table) but may also make use of other tables to provide lookup information (lookup tables).

The module definition illustrated in figure 17-20 has two module components, one based on a Departments table and the other on an Employee table.

For each module component you must define which columns are to be incorporated within the application and their display characteristics, e.g., caption, any special HTML formatting etc.

## Generated Application

Generating the example module shown previously produces an application listing the departments in a company and, when a department has been selected, listing the employees that work in that particular department showing the

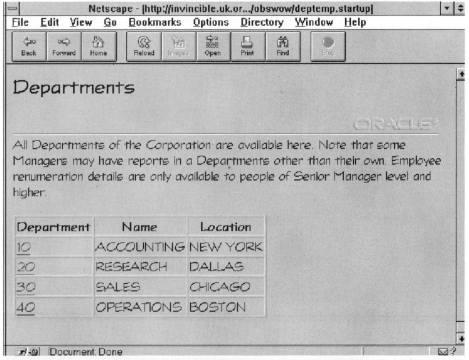

**Figure 17-21.** Screen dump of a generated application.

employee number, name and job title as well the name of their manager.

Figure 17-21 shows the startup page for this module containing the title, a boilerplate image, the module help text and an HTML table showing the list of departments in the Company. It is a screen dump of the generated application viewed through an Industry standard Browser.

## Generated Pages

From the module design specification, Oracle WebServer Generator generates a set of PL/SQL packages which at runtime dynamically build a series of linked Web pages. The Web pages created by the Oracle WSG break down into four types.

- Startup Page
- Query Form
- Record List
- View Form

A Startup Page is created for every module within the generated application. A Query Form allows the Web user to enter search criteria before executing the query. A Record List displays a set of queried records in an HTML table, or in an ordered or bulleted list. A View Form displays the full details for a chosen record. Figure 17-22 shows the relationship between the Query Form, Record List and View Form for an example module.

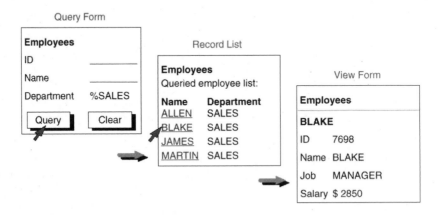

**Figure 17-22.** The relationship between the Query Form, Record List and View Form.

The appearance and sequence of pages depends on the module design specification and user preference values. For example, a Record List for a detail module component may be placed on the same page as its master's View Form, rather than on separate pages.

## Startup Page

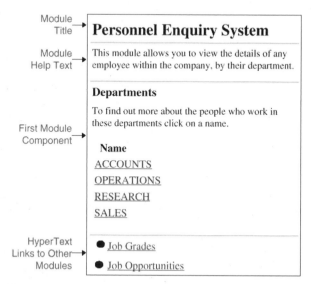

**Figure 17-23.** The structure of a generated Startup page.

A Startup Page (figure 17-23) is generated for every module within the Oracle WebServer application. If the module is the top level module for your Oracle WebServer application, this page will typically serve to introduce the entire application and provide a set of hypertext links to the rest of the modules within the application. For other modules, the Startup Page serves to introduce the module and may, if appropriate, display the query generated from the first module component.

The Help text may be added to describe the purpose of the module or give instructions. Such text is derived from the User Help Text recorded against the module definition. Module links allow you to navigate between the modules which make up the application and they are defined using the Module Structure Diagrammer. Calls to other modules may be organized into a hierarchical structure by the inclusion of MENU type modules in the overall module hierarchy. Within generated Oracle WebServer applications, calls to other modules appear as hypertext links.

## Query Form

The Query Form allows a Web user to enter search criteria to be incorporated when executing a query against a particular module component. The Query Form displays the set of column usages marked Select in the module design. In figure 17-24 four column usages had been marked as Select in the Module Definition; Name, ID, Job, and Salary.

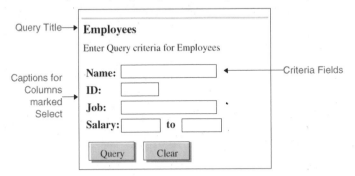

**Figure 17-24.** Illustrating the structure of a generated Query Form.

The buttons are

**Query**    Submits the query based on the given search criteria and then dynamically builds and displays the page containing the Record List.

**Clear**    Clears all the column values, ready for the Web user to enter new query conditions.

For column usages based on non-key DATE or NUMERIC columns, a pair of From/To column values is created to allow for range searching as illustrated in the example above.

A Query Form is only generated if one or more of the column usages are marked Select in the module design. If no such column usages are defined, then no Query Form is created and an unrestricted query is performed instead. This may be appropriate for a detail query that is automatically restricted by the chosen master record.

## Record List Page

The Record List Page displays a set of records for a particular module component (i.e., base table usage and its associated lookups). The list normally displays a subset of the table's columns, sufficient for the user to identify the records. A separate View Form is generated to display the full details of any record selected from the list.

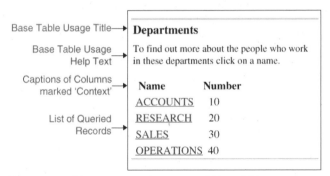

Figure 17-25. The structure of a generated Record List.

The Record List displays the set of column usages marked Context in the module design. In figure 17-25 two columns are marked Context; Name and Number.

## View Form

The View Form displays the details of any one record. It contains the full set of column usages defined against a particular module component (i.e., base table usage and its associated lookups).

When a Web user chooses a hypertext entry in the Record List the View Form is displayed on a new Web page as shown in figure 17-26.

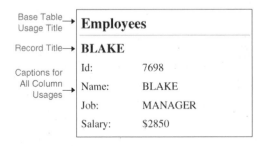

Figure 17-26. The structure of a generated View Form.

If the module design contains module components acting as details, the Record List (or Query Form) for the detail may be displayed on the same page as the master's View Form, as shown in figure 17-27.

The placement of master-detail components on the same, or separate Web pages is defined visually, using the Module Data Diagrammer.

Master Query's View Form

Detail Query's Record List

**Figure 17-27.** The structure of a generated View Form with detail records in a Record List on the same page.

## HTML Formatting

HTML formatting can be incorporated within the module design specification to enhance the appearance and add functionality to the generated application. HTML code can be recorded directly against column usages or embedded within help text. Some examples of HTML formatting:

### Image References

Through the use of image references embedded within the module design, image files stored on the Oracle WebServer file system may be used in various ways to enhance the appearance, or clarify the purpose of a generated application. Such images can provide a background to Web pages, be embedded within static text or referenced dynamically based on a column values. The most commonly supported image formats are GIF and JPEG.

### Character Text Styles

A range of standard HTML functions may be embedded within help text to highlight aspects of the text you define, for example bold or italic. The same functions may also be applied to column usages.

### Electronic Mail Addresses

Electronic mail addresses can be embedded within generated applications.

### Defining HTML Code Within Static Help Text

Static help text may be recorded against module definitions and individual module components. Within this static text you may reference any of the HTML functions provided by the HyperText Functions (HTF) package within the Oracle WebServer Developer's Toolkit. For example, the following static help text in the Designer/2000

```
Welcome to the htf.bold('ACME
Corporation') home page. Send any comments
on this page to
htf.MailTo('JBLOGGS@ACME.COM','Joe
Bloggs').
```

would be generated into HTML:

**Welcome to the ACME Corporation home page. Send any comments on this page to <u>Joe Bloggs.</u>**

### Defining HTML Code Against Column Usages

Oracle WebServer Generator supports a set of standard built-in formatting options that may be set against the column usage, such as BOLD, ITALIC, IMAGE and MAILTO. For more flexible formatting, calls to PL/SQL Toolkit functions may also be defined.

These formatting requirements are defined against the HTML Formatting property of the column usage.

# 18

# Microsoft's Advanced Data Connector

## Introduction

Microsoft Advanced Data Connector is a high-performance Web-based technology that brings plug-and-play database connectivity and corporate data publishing capabilities to Internet and Intranet applications. This chapter provides an overview into this product's capabilities. The product itself can be downloaded from http://www.microsoft.com/adc. You might also want to access a newgroup on the subject: microsoft.public.adc

With Microsoft Advanced Data Connector (ADC), you can build intelligent Web applications that let you access and update data from an ODBC-compliant Database Management System (DBMS). And because you implement ADC with familiar technology — off-the-shelf visual controls, HTML, and Microsoft Visual Basic Scripting Edition (VBScript) — ADC integrates seamlessly with existing Visual Basic applications, letting you transport them to the Web.

Microsoft Advanced Data Connector uses Open Database Connectivity (ODBC), the standardized architecture that supports building data-aware applications without targeting a specific DBMS. Using ODBC, you can easily modify ADC applications to suit different network and DBMS configurations.

In addition to ODBC, Advanced Data Connector is integrated with other Microsoft technologies, including Internet Information Server (IIS) 3.0, Microsoft Transaction Server, and OLE DB.

A key feature of Microsoft Advanced Data Connector is a client-side caching mechanism that minimizes connections to your DBMS. As a result, you get better performance than in traditional Web database access methods.

Architecturally, Microsoft Advanced Data Connector (ADC) is a logical development of component-based client/server applications as they migrate onto the Web. In addition to the traditional client and database-server spaces, ADC's model includes an application space that resides on a LAN, and consists of the logical or business components of an application. As shown in figure 18-1, the application server space can consist of one or more business objects.

Business objects are discrete pieces of code that implement the business functions, rules, and processes of an organization, such as password validation and order-entry objects. In ADC technology, business objects are typically created with Visual Basic or Visual C++. By using a model that partitions the application logic into groups of discrete components, ADC supports an efficient model for distributed Web applications. This model

> •Encapsulates business components, making them easier to change.
> •Focuses client-side programming on application front ends and simple validation routines.
> •Decreases the load from the database server.
> •Allows the building of generic, reusable business components that are independent of a particular front end.

The ADC architecture has the capability to connect to multiple DBMS's (with ODBC). Separating that component from the application frees application developers from having to code the DBMS connections, and makes it possible to build applications that use distributed data from multiple DBMS's.

In a typical Microsoft Advanced Data Connector (ADC) scenario, a user enters a request using a Visual Basic control on a Web page. (For example, a query to display all employees hired in the current year.) Figure 18-2 shows, at a high level, how ADC handles the request.

Business objects are discrete pieces of code that implement the business functions, rules, and processes of an organization, such as password validation and order-entry objects.

The main application component on the server side is a business object that contains information such as application logic, business rules, and the data access code from underlying databases. The client side components access these server-side business objects through business object proxies. Business objects can be any generic Automation objects created with Visual Basic or Visual C++, or server-side HTML pages with Active Server Page scripting code.

The actual communication with business objects is done by the ADISAPI component, which is responsible for creating instances of objects, invoking methods, and releasing them. Business objects use the ADO layer and the OLE DB layer to query and update the underlying databases. In Advanced Data

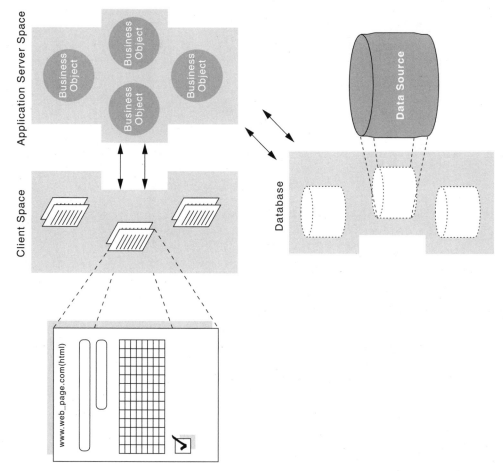

**Figure 18-1.** The application server space can consist of one or more business objects.

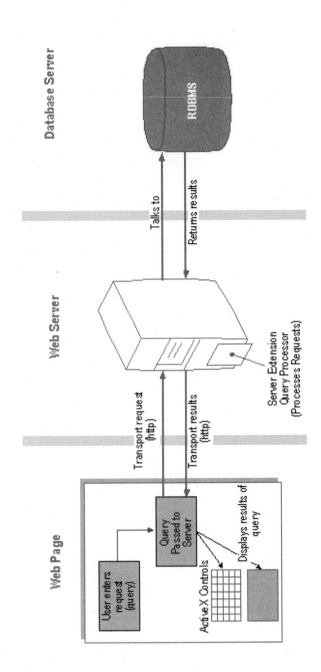

**Figure 18-2.** How ADC handles a Visual Basic request.

Connector, the lifespan of a business object is as long as the execution of a method call invoked by the client. Instances of the business objects are created with each method call, and no interim state is maintained.

Advanced Data Connector supplies a default business object, the AdvancedDataFactory object, that provides read and write access to data sources, but contains no business rules or application logic.

Once the user enters a request, the query is passed to a IIS Web server with the ADC server extensions installed (via HTTP) for processing. ADC handles all the preprocessing needed to respond to the request, and sends it to the DBMS, via a business object. The DBMS responds to the request, sending back the data (through the format of its ODBC driver). The ADC extensions on the Web server transform that data to Recordset objects. The recordset data is processed by the server extensions, parsed for transport to the client, and sent back across the network to the client computer. It is displayed in data-aware, ActiveX controls that are bound to the data by ADC.

The resulting recordset data is cached on the client computer, reducing the number of connections to the Web and making it easier for a user to manipulate the data (the only calls requiring a trip to the server are calls to the business object or updates to the data server).

## Detailed Component View

Figure 18-3 provides a more detailed view of the Advanced Data Connector architecture, showing the major components and their interconnections. Following is a description of the key components shown in the figure:

Client Components:
1. Client container: A Web browser that supports Microsoft Advanced Data Connector, such as Internet Explorer.
2. AdvancedDataControl object: An invisible control (as opposed to a visible control, such as a button) that allows you to publish back-end database data through embedded ActiveX controls (such as a text box, or grid) on Web browser HTML pages.
3. Client-side data cache: A cache on the client computer that maintains relational data, client updates, and record status information.
4. AdvancedDataFactory proxy: Because client-side components cannot directly access those on the server-side, business objects create client-side proxies each time they are instantiated. The AdvancedDataFactory proxy is the client side proxy object for the default AdvancedDataFactory business object. Its function is to pack and unpack parameters destined for the server-side AdvancedDataFactory object, translate them into HTTP requests, and ship the requests to the Internet Information Server (IIS).

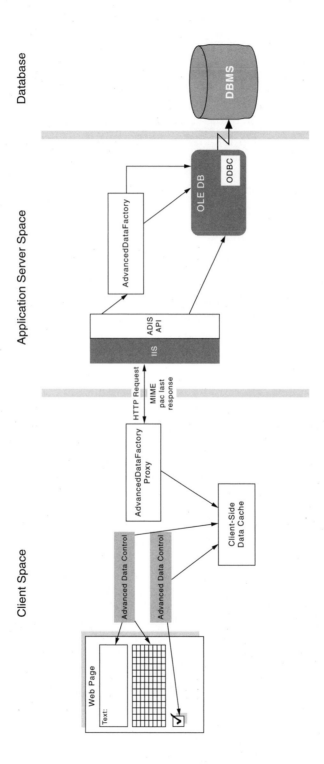

**Figure 18-3.** The ADV architecture.

Application-Tier Components:
1. AdvancedDataFactory object: A simple business object that sends SQL statements to a DBMS (through an ODBC driver), and passes the results back across the Internet or an intranet. This is provided as a default business object that allows ADC to provide live data to your Web page with little programming.
2. IIS (Internet Information Server): Microsoft's NT Server Web Server technology.
3. ADISAPI (Advanced Data Internet Server API): An extension language to IIS that is specific to handling Microsoft Advanced Data Connector code. ADISAPI processes information from the client-based components, allowing them to communicate with business objects (application-specific or database access code), by passing arguments and sending method calls over HTTP.
4. ODBC drivers: Allows Microsoft Advanced Data Connector applications to communicate with certain ODBC Level-2-enabled DBMSs.

## Detailed Control Flow

This section contains a control flow description of the programming events that occur when the Microsoft Advanced Data Connector (ADC) architecture processes a user event. This section is for advanced users, and is geared toward C++/Visual Basic programmers who want to build ADC client-based applications and business objects. Web page developers who intend only to implement Advanced Data Connector controls should skip this section.

Figure 18-4 shows the detailed control flow. The figure uses business objects from the Address Book sample application. The numbered labels correspond to processes in the control flow and are described as follows.

1. The user enters query text in a visual control that is linked to an AdvancedDataControl object. That query text will be sent to the Web server for processing.

2. When a user event occurs on the Web page (such as an On_Click event on a Search button), ADC creates a business object proxy on the client.

3. The business object proxy translates the call into an HTTP request. The parameters to the method are passed across the Internet via HTTP to a Web server (Internet Information Server, or IIS). IIS then passes the HTTP request to a server extension called the Advanced Data Internet Server API (ADISAPI).

4. ADISAPI examines the contents of the call. It determines which business object to create, and then creates the object.

5. The AdvancedDataFactory (default ADC business object) makes a call to the data source via OLE DB for the data.

6. OLE DB loads the Recordset into the server-side data cache, which goes to the AdvancedDataFactory.

7. ADISAPI packages the return value of the Recordset into MIME format by calling the Advanced Data VTM (Advanced Data Virtual Table Manager) to create a Tablegram stream.

8. ADISAPI marshals the data to the business object proxy on the client side.

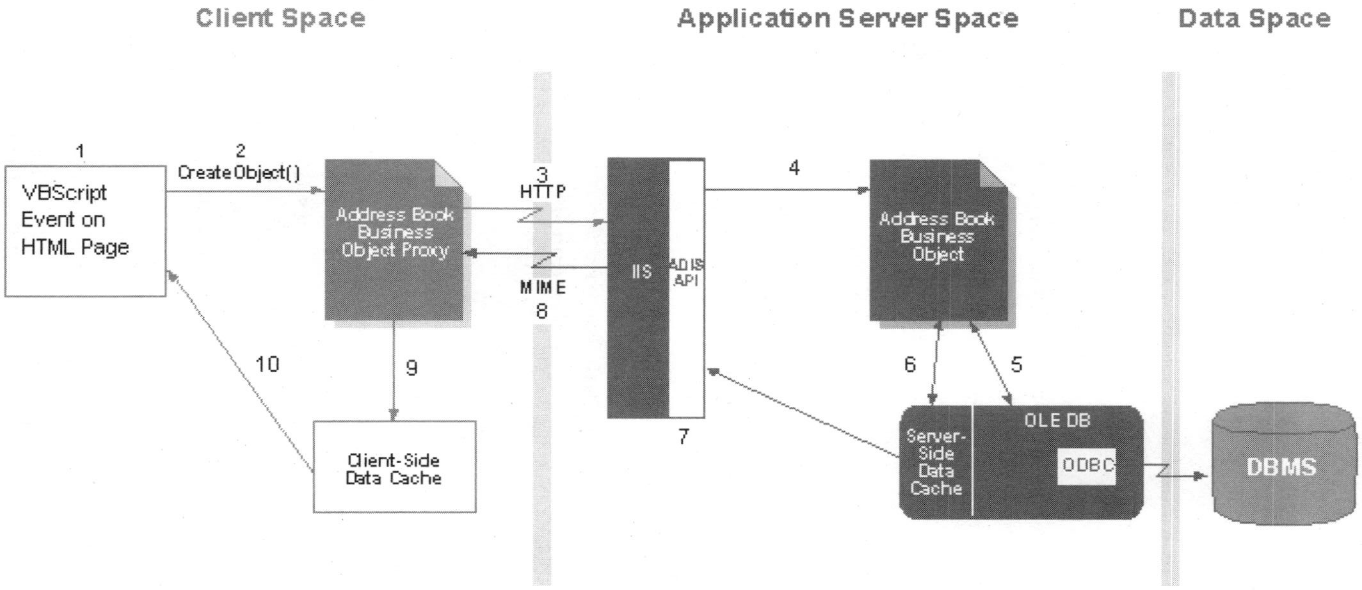

**Figure 18-4.** Detailed control flow.

9. The client-side business object proxy unpacks the results of the method call from HTTP format, and recreates the Recordset into the client-side Advanced Data VTM.

10. The AdvancedDataControl object binds the data in the Advanced Data VTM to the visual controls.

After the preceding steps have taken place, the user now has access to the Recordset object, representing the results of the query (displayed through the visual controls). He or she can perform tasks such as examining the record data, making changes, inserting new records, or deleting existing records.

When the user makes an update request, only the changed records are sent back via a process similar to that described above. When an attempt is made to save the updated data, either all the changes will be written back to the data source, or, if any individual change cannot be saved, none of the changes will be saved.

For a custom business object, the only difference to the steps outlined above is that an AdvancedDataSpace.CreateObject method is called on the client page to instantiate the business object proxy.

## Building ADC Applications

This section describes how to build a simple, data-aware Web application with Microsoft Advanced Data Connector (ADC) using an online corporate address book as the example. The example is useful for both beginning VBScript/ActiveX programmers who want to learn about data-aware ActiveX controls, and more experienced application developers who want to get a feel for building data-centric Web applications. The example assumes you understand basic HTML layout tags and the basics of programming with ActiveX controls.

### Connecting to the Database

You need to set up a system DSN on the Web server where the Microsoft Advanced Data Connector server components will be installed. To set up an ODBC Connection, you or your database administrator needs to follow the appropriate procedure.

This setup assumes that the Employee table is created in the AddrBookDB database on the local SQL Server running on the Web server.

If you are using Windows NT Workstation:

1. On the Web server, click Start, point to Settings, and then click Control Panel.
2. In Control Panel, double-click the ODBC icon.
3. In the System DSN tab, click Add.
4. In the System Data Sources box, select SQL Server and click Finish.
5. The ODBC SQL Server Setup dialog box appears. Click Options to expand the box. Fill in the information as shown in figure 18-5. Clear the Convert OEM

to ANSI characters and Generate Stored Procedure for Prepared Statement check boxes. (Clearing the latter check box provides best performance with high volume databases.)

6. When you are finished, click OK to return to the ODBC Data Source Administrator dialog box. Click Close to exit the ODBC setup.

If you are using Windows 95:

1. On the Web server, click Start, point to Settings, and then click Control Panel.

2. In Control Panel, double-click the ODBC icon.

3. Click System DSN.

4. In the System Data Sources box, click Add, select SQL Server, and click OK.

5. Follow steps 5 and 6 above.

Running the
SQL Script

**Figure 18-5.** ADC setup.

After setting up the ODBC connection, you or a database administrator needs to run an SQL script (either through the command line utility ISQL or the SQL Server Enterprise Manager) that

1. Creates a new Database, AddrBookDB, on the default device.
2. Connects to the correct database (AddrBookDB; if you rename your database, make sure to change this name) in preparation for creating the sample database table.
3. Creates an employee table.
4. Populates the table with sample data.
5. Runs a stored procedure to verify the creation of the table and its column metadata.
6. Runs a simple select statement to verify the population of the database table; it should return 5 rows of data.

To run the SQL script, you or your database administrator needs to enter the following command:

```
c:<path name>\isql -U <dba> -P <password> -S
<servername> -i <full path name>\sampleemp.sql
```

where
DBA: is a valid database administrator alias.

PASSWORD: is a valid password.

SERVERNAME: is the name of the server where the targeted SQL Server is installed. It can be left blank if you want to work on your local SQL Server. Full path name is the complete Windows path name identifying the subdirectory where you installed sampleemp.sql.

### Setting Up and Verifying the Database

Following is the code used to set up, populate, and verify the database for the Address Book example.

To run the SQL script, you or your database administrator needs to enter the following command at an MS-DOS prompt, where you have access to the SQL Server computer:

```
c:<path name>\isql -U <dba> -P <password> -S
<servername> -i <full path name>\sampleemp.sql

set quoted_identifier on
go

use master
```

```
go

if exists (select * from sysdatabases where name = 'AddrBookDB')
drop database AddrBookDB
go

create database AddrBookDb on default = 1
go

use AddrBookDB
go


/****** Object:User guest    Script Date: 10/25/96 3:32:34 PM ******/
if not exists (select * from sysusers where name = 'guest' and uid <
16382)
        EXEC sp_adduser 'guest'
GO

/****** Object:Table dbo.Employee Script Date: 10/25/96 3:32:35 PM**/
if exists (select * from sysobjects where id =
object_id('dbo.Employee') and sysstat & 0xf = 3)
        drop table "dbo"."Employee"
go

/****** Object:Table dbo.Employee Script Date: 10/25/96 3:32:35 PM**/
CREATE TABLE "dbo"."Employee" (
        "ID" "int" NOT NULL ,
        "FirstName" varchar (30) NOT NULL ,
        "LastName" varchar (30) NOT NULL ,
        "Name" varchar (60) NOT NULL ,
        "Title" varchar (20) NOT NULL ,
        "Type" varchar (20) NOT NULL ,
        "Email" varchar (20) NOT NULL ,
        "ManagerEmail" varchar (20) NOT NULL ,
        "Building" varchar (30) NOT NULL ,
        "Room" varchar (20) NOT NULL ,
        "Phone" varchar (20) NOT NULL ,
        CONSTRAINT "PK__Employee__id__02FC7413" PRIMARY
        KEY  CLUSTERED
        (
                "ID"
        )
)
go
```

```
GRANT REFERENCES , SELECT , INSERT , DELETE , UPDATE ON
"Employee" TO "public"
go
```

Now populate the table with sample data:

```
insert Employee values (1001, 'Amy', 'Anderson', 'Anderson, Amy',
'Purchase Manager', 'full-time', 'amya', 'jamesa', '6', '2001', '713-
2757')
go

insert Employee values (1020, 'Karen', 'Berge', 'Berge, Karen',
'Program Manager', 'full-time', 'karenb', 'jamesa', '4', '2002', '723-
2757')
go

insert Employee values (1300, 'Bill', 'Sornsin', 'Sornsin, Bill',
'Account Liason Officer', 'full-time', 'billso', 'darlener', '3',
'2003', '733-2757')
go

insert Employee values (1040, 'Jan', 'Trabandt', 'Trabandt, Jan',
'Program Manager', 'full-time', 'jantr', 'michaelc', '5', '2004', '743-
2757')
go

insert Employee values (1050, .'Viki', 'Parrott', 'Parrott, Viki',
'Sales Manager', 'full-time', 'vikip', 'amyan', '1', '2005', '753-
2757')
go
```

```
- (... Remainder of employee data ...)
```

Now run a stored procedure to verify the creation of the
table and metadata:

```
sp_help employee
go
```

Now do a simple select statement to verify the population of the database
table. It should return 20 rows of data:

```
select LastName, FirstName, Email from employee
go
```

Now grant read and write permissions to public for the

```
employee table (updates):

grant all on employee to public
go
```

## HTML Framework

The first step in building a Microsoft Advanced Data Connector (ADC) application is setting up the standard HTML Web page framework. Program code for the application objects you use, such as buttons, text boxes, and data-aware controls, lies within the confines of this HTML skeleton.

The following code portion shows the HTML skeleton for the address book application. This part includes the standard HTML heading and page structure tags, comments identifying the application, and Web page text, font, and color information.

```
<HTML>
<HEAD>
<TITLE>Corporate Address Book</TITLE>
</HEAD>

<!—
Purpose: To provide a company directory search service for Web users.
Written By: Microsoft Advanced Data Connector Team, Microsoft Corp.
Date: November, 1996
—>

<BODY BACKGROUND="Arcadia.gif" LANGUAGE="VBScript" onload="Load">
<tr>
        <td align="center" width="40%">
        <table border="2" cellpadding="7"
        cellspacing="7">
            <tr>
                <td width="100%"><font
                color="#160B5A"><font
                size="4"><strong>Arcadia Bay Corporate
                Phone Directory
                </strong></font></font></td>
            </tr>
        </table>
        </td>
</tr>

<hr>
<h2><font color = "#160B5A">Search Parameters</h2>
```

```
<h5><font color = "#160B5A">Please enter one or more search patterns
and press FIND to search.</h5>

<FONT COLOR = "#160B5A"><B>

<PRE>First Name
<!- CODE FOR "FIRST NAME" TEXT BOX GOES HERE ->
</PRE>
...
<!- CODE FOR REMAINING TEXT BOXES GOES HERE ->
..
<!- CODE FOR SEARCH BUTTONS GOES HERE GOES HERE->
...
<!- CODE FOR UPDATE PROFILE AND CANCEL BUTTONS GOES HERE ->
...
<hr>
<h2><font color = "#400040">Search Results</h2>
</B>
<br>
...
<!- CODE FOR DATA GRID GOES HERE ->
...
<!- CODE FOR NAVIGATION BUTTONS GOES HERE ->
...

<!- CODE FOR AdvancedDataControl OBJECT GOES HERE ->
...
</B>
</BODY>
      .

<SCRIPT Language="VBScript">>
<!- VBSCRIPT CODE FOR COMPOSING QUERIES, UPDATING PROFILES, AND
RETRIEVING SEARCH RESULTS GOES HERE ->
</SCRIPT>

<BR>
<font color = "#400040">This site powered by Microsoft Advanced Data
Connector. </font>
</BODY>
</HTML>
```

Most of the common HTML tags, and those that define the Web page background attributes, will not be defined here.

The SCRIPT tag indicates that the control is passed to a scripting language, which in this case is VBScript.

The Address Book application contains four text boxes for entering search phrases (for example, the First Name box). The code for the text box objects follows:

```
<PRE> First Name   <INPUT NAME=SFirst SIZE=30> </PRE>
<PRE> Last Name    <INPUT NAME=SLast  SIZE=30> </PRE>
<PRE> Title        <INPUT NAME=STitle SIZE=30> </PRE>
<PRE> E-mail Alias <INPUT NAME=SEmail SIZE=30> </PRE>
```

The INPUT box is built into HTML. The NAME parameter defines what it will be called in this example. For example, the VBScript code can check "SFirst.Value" for text. The SIZE parameter lets you adjust the length of the text box, in characters.

There are two search-related options available with the online Address Book:

1. Submit a query to the database.
2. Clear the text boxes of text before starting a new search.

Each of these options is associated with a user event, that is, clicking a button. Clicking Find submits the query, and clicking Clear removes all text the user entered in the text boxes. The HTML code for the two button definitions is as follows:

```
<INPUT TYPE=BUTTON NAME="Find"  VALUE="Find">
<INPUT TYPE=BUTTON NAME="Clear" VALUE="Clear">
```

The INPUT tag defines an element, such as a button, radio button, check box, or text. You use the TYPE parameter to specify the element, which in this case is a button. The NAME parameter is the application's internal name for the button. The VALUE parameter specifies the labels associated with the button (Find and Clear) that will show on the page.

VBScript processes the button information whenever an event is generated by a button click event.

When the user clicks Find, a Find_OnClick subroutine is activated. The subroutine checks the boxes for text, composes a dynamic SQL query based on what it finds, sends the query to the database, and displays the results.

When the user clicks Clear, a Clear_OnClick subroutine is activated. The subroutine clears the text boxes to reset them for a new search.

## Data-Binding Control

The Address Book application uses a special, invisible control, the AdvancedDataControl object. The AdvancedDataControl object binds data from the SQL Server database to a visual object (in this case, a grid display) in the application's client HTML page. The code for the AdvancedDataControl component follows.

```
<OBJECT CLASSID="clsid:9381D8F2-0288-11d0-9501-00AA00B911A5"
ID="SControl"
CODEBASE="HTTP://<%=Request.ServerVariables
("SERVER_NAME")%>/MSADC/msadc10.cab"
    WIDTH=1 HEIGHT=1>
    <PARAM NAME="BINDINGS" VALUE="Grid1;">
    <PARAM NAME="Connect" VALUE="DSN=ADCDEMO;UID=guest;PWD=guest;">
<PARAM NAME="Server" VALUE="http://<%=Request.ServerVariables("SERV-
ER_NAME")%>">
</OBJECT>
```

The OBJECT tag defines the AdvancedDataControl component in the program. The tag includes two types of parameters:

1. Those associated with the generic OBJECT tag
2. Those specific to the AdvancedDataControl object

where

CLASSID: identifies the object to the system. A unique, 128-bit number that identifies the type of embedded object to the system. This identifier is maintained in the local computer's system registry.

ID: defines a document-wide identifier for the embedded object. The event-based VBScript program logic uses the ID value of the AdvancedDataControl to target the destination of the queried data; identify update information to send to the database; manipulate the data displayed in the visual control (grid object).

CODEBASE: specifies the location of a source file of the object being called, if it is not on your local computer. In this case, CODEBASE specifies the location of the data-binding control. The program uses Active Server Page script (the code enclosed by the "<%" and "%>" signs) to request the server name part of the URL. (Active Server Pages are a feature of Internet Information Server (IIS) 3.0.)

WIDTH and HEIGHT: identifies the dimensions of the control, in pixels. Because this is an invisible control, the values of these parameters can be set to 1 for each.

Finally, the Results section of the Address Book application consists of objects that display the results of a query, initiate updates to the database, and manipulate the data display.

# 19

# Gluing Data to the Web with Sapphire/Web

**David Isaacson**

## Introduction

The Web and all of the technologies surrounding it are moving fast. Virtually overnight we've gone from static marketing type Web pages with a few images thrown in, to fully interactive mission critical applications being developed and deployed over corporate Intranets or the Internet. These applications are being built for consumers as well as inter-business commerce. Building and deploying these "higher order" types of applications requires a solution that provides flexibility, performance, and security. It requires a solution with features and functions that will scale to the enterprise, without locking organizations into proprietary technologies. It requires a solution that can meet the challenges of today, yet be flexibly enough to embrace tomorrow. Sapphire/Web from Bluestone Software (www.bluestone.com) is a development and deployment solution that takes advantage of the power of Java, and the scalability and flexibility of distributed object technology, to meet the challenges of creating enterprise scale Web applications.

## Web to Database Challenges

The Web has hit so hard and so fast and with so much visibility that the development community is having trouble reacting fast enough. What was traditionally the role of the company Information Technology (IT) department is now the purview of high level managers and even CEOs. Everybody in the company seems to have a stake and an interest in the company Web site and Web-related applications that are being planned, built, or upgraded. So, what do developers need? The general consensus, based on conversations with many developers and development groups, is the following:

Developers want to

•Leverage emerging technologies. That is, they want to be able to incorporate/utilize new technologies that enhance productivity as quickly as possible. They want to use these new technologies without having to rework/re-code existing applications.

•Maximize existing investments in tools, people, databases and applications. Developers want to build what they have, not start over. If they have existing databases or data files, they want to use them. If they have existing SQL or stored procedures, they want to use them. If they have existing code, they want to reuse it either in its entirety or possibly just individual functions. The same applies for the user interface. If developers have existing HTML, Java, or ActiveX components, they want to be able to incorporate them into new Web-based applications without having to re-type or re-code.

•Avoid technology lock-in. Developers do not want to become dependent on a proprietary (vendor controlled) technology. They understand that technology is progressing at an extremely rapid pace and that placing all bets on a specific technology or company is not prudent. They want to build for today, but anticipate tomorrow. That is, use the best technologies available now, but make sure that those technologies are open and will allow incorporation of technologies that may not have even been thought of yet.

•Use technologies that are affordable. Developers know when they are being gouged by vendors. They are willing to pay a fair price, but don't want to be locked in to high runtime fees.

•Use technologies that are easy to use. Many times a tool will indeed increase productivity once a developer learns how to use it. The problem is, sometimes learning how to use the tool takes more time and effort than the productivity gains achievable. Yes, maybe there would be productivity gains in the out years, but at the rate the Internet market is moving who knows what the industry will look like in a year? The point is, developers need tools that are easy to use and increase productivity rapidly.

•Use a tool that has been proven in the marketplace. They want a tool that companies have used successfully. They want a tool that is highly regarded in published media reviews, and a tool from a company that they feel is going to be around for the long haul.

## Various Approaches to Data/Web Integration

Web to database development tools use various approaches and development paradigms. Some tools are visual development environments, others are scripting based, and still others are wizard driven. Furthermore, different tools promote different types of Web architectures. Some promote dynamic database access and HTML generation with all of the processing and business logic handled by the Web server. Some tools generate applications that are heavily dependent on the processing power of the client machine (i.e., the machine of the person using the application.) Some development tools embed database access functionality and business logic into HTML pages, and in some cases introduce proprietary tags that require a proprietary module at the Web Server.

A Web based applications architecture that seems to optimize resources is one that is tiered. That is, the applications and the development paradigm itself is structured such that business logic is separate from database access logic and also from the graphical user interface. This type of architecture is outlined in figure 19-1.

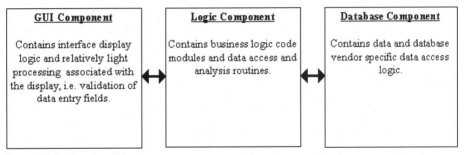

**Figure 19-1.** Tiered architecture.

There is nothing inherently wrong with any of the architectural approaches described above. As with any software development effort, the requirements of the project should drive design and architecture. What is important is that the tool being used to develop and deploy the application be flexible enough to accommodate all types of designs and requirements. If a design requirement calls for a two-tier architecture, the tool should be able to support it. If a requirement calls for the use of a scripting language, the tool should support that scripting language. A Web or Java to database solution should support and enhance development productivity and deployment manageability, not impose design, development, or deployment restrictions.

## Introduction to Sapphire/Web and Bluestone Software

Sapphire/Web is a Web and Java to Database development and deployment solution from Bluestone Software. It was introduced in October of 1995.

Considering the rapid emergence of the Web and the Web tools market, Sapphire/Web is a mature product that is packed with features and functionality that make it easy to create high performance Internet/Intranet applications. A 30 day trial of the software can be downloaded from the Bluestone website (www.bluestone.com).

## What is Sapphire/Web?

Sapphire/Web is a visual point-and-click/drag-and-drop Web applications development and deployment system. For development, it generates the underlying code that makes Web applications work. For deployment, it provides flip-of-a-switch options and easy to use interfaces that facilitate managing Web applications. Sapphire/Web has been described as "Super-glueware" because it allows developers to visually bind any Web front-end graphical user interface (GUI) with any back-end data source.

Sapphire/Web supports a "best of breed" approach to Web development. For example, Sapphire/Web provides a straightforward HTML editor. However, if developers want to use a different HTML editor they can. Also, developers need not only develop user interfaces with HTML. Sapphire/Web supports Java, JavaScript, ActiveX, VRML, and VBScript. So, for example, a Java interface developed in Visual J++ can be imported and used in a Sapphire/Web application. Sapphire/Web includes a Client-Objects Framework that automatically accommodates various interface technologies. The Client-Objects Framework will also automatically support new interface technologies as they become popular. Supporting this "best of breed" approach, Sapphire/Web provides direct access to Oracle, Sybase, Informix, MS SQL Server, and DB2 databases, or access to any database via ODBC (Open Data Base Connectivity). In addition to databases, Sapphire/Web allows developers to build Web applications that access flat files, stored procedures, functions, and legacy systems.

Sapphire/Web generates the code that makes Web applications work. A developer can, via flip-of-a-switch option settings, generate 100% pure JAVA, ANSI C, KR C, or C++ code. A developer can also specify how Sapphire/Web generated code is to interact with a Web Server and database, either as a project specific persistent process called an Application Server, as an Oracle Web Cartridge or as a CGI. Sapphire/Web works with any Web Server and any Web Server extension such as ISAPI, NSAPI, FastCGI, WRBAPI, and Active Server Pages. A developer is not locked in to any of the above configurations. By opening the application, setting option switches, and re-compiling, a developer can move between platforms (WindowsNT, Windows95 and UNIX) and configurations. Sapphire/Web provides several options for state management including a built in State Server. It also provides multiple mechanisms for security management, and provides tools for managing most any network deployment configuration.

## The Sapphire/Web Interface

The WindowsNT and Windows95 Sapphire/Web interface is shown in figure 19-2. Sapphire/Web generated applications are referred to as projects.

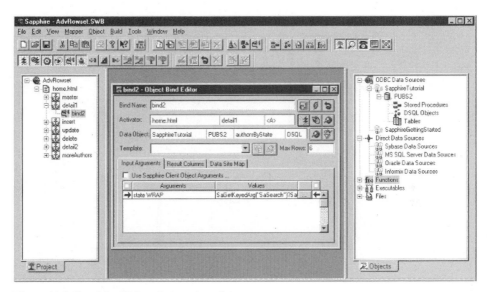

**Figure 19-2.** Sapphire/Web main user interface.

The Project Browser window is on the left hand side of the Sapphire/Web interface. It displays an entire project's interface hierarchy including HTML pages, anchors (HTML <A>HREF tags), forms, images Java script, and whatever other elements a developer defines for end user interaction.

The Data Object Browser on the right-hand side of the interface displays all of the data sources available to the developer. This may include Oracle, Informix, Sybase, MSSQL, and DB2, which are supported directly, and any other ODBC database such as MS Access, Excel, Foxpro, Dbase, etc. Also displayed in the Data Object Browser are alternate data sources such as flat files, functions, and executables. Essentially, any data source or code module that has recognizable input parameters and output parameters can be defined, accessed, and incorporated into a Sapphire/Web application.

In the center of the Sapphire/Web interface is the Bind Editor. The Bind Editor is the real heart of the Sapphire/Web development environment. It is where developers link the end-user interface elements in the Project Browser (left side of interface) to the back-end data source elements in the Object Browser (right side of interface).

## Sapphire/Web General Architecture Outline

The general architectural outline of Sapphire/Web is shown in figures 19-3a and 19-3b.

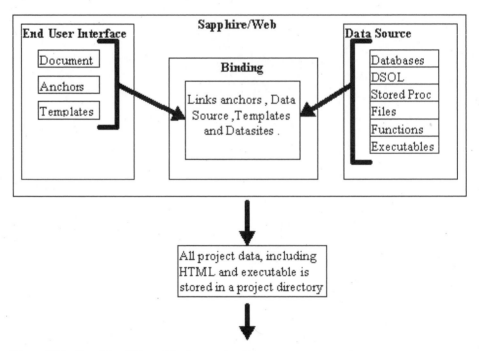

**Figure 19-3a.** Sapphire./Web architecture — top tier.

Building Web application with Sapphire/Web consists of developing or importing front end user interface elements and linking or "binding" those elements to back end data sources. This linking is all done visually. An application is then generated as Java, or compiled C or C++ code. For C or C++ code generation in the Windows 95 or NT environment, Sapphire/Web uses Microsoft Visual C++. In the UNIX environment, any C or C++ compiler will work. The Sapphire/Web generated executable can run, and access all databases or other data sources, anywhere on a network.

## Using Sapphire/Web

The following sections describe and explain how to create a sample Web application using Sapphire/Web. The application is simplistic, but should give you a basic idea of the Sapphire/Web development paradigm. The sample explained in the following sections is a two page HTML application that dynamically generates an HTML Table based on a database query.

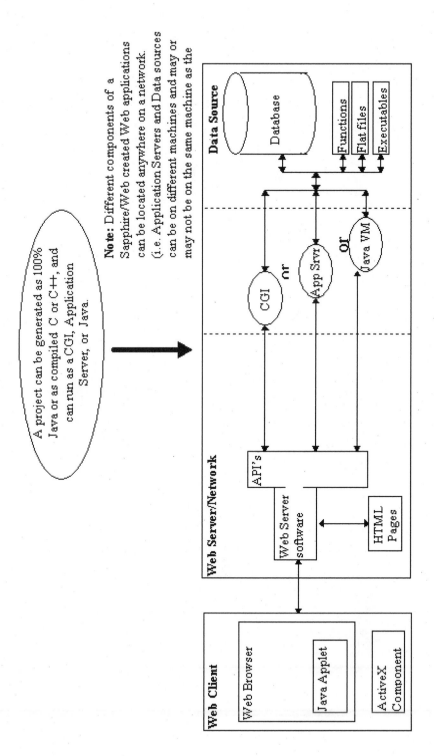

A project can be generated as 100% Java or as compiled C or C++, and can run as a CGI, Application Server, or Java.

**Note:** Different components of a Sapphire/Web created Web applications can be located anywhere on a network. (i.e. Application Servers and Data sources can be on different machines and may or may not be on the same machine as the

**Web Server/Network**

Web Server software

HTML Pages

API's

CGI

**or**

App Srvr

**or**

Java VM

**Data Source**

Database

Functions

Flat files

Executables

**Web Client**

Web Browser

Java Applet

ActiveX Component

**Figure 19-3b.** Sapphire/Web architecture — second tier.

419

The general steps to build this application are as follows:

1. Create a new project.
2. Create two HTML pages.
3. Create a database query.
4. Create a database bind.
5. Test and deploy the project.

Steps 2, 3,and 4 need not be done in sequence. It is up to the developer to decide whether to work from the front end to the back end (i.e., create the user interface, begin creation of the binding process, and then create the database query), work from the back end to the front end (i.e., create the database query, then create the user interface based on the query), or, as we have done for this sample application, create the user interface, then create the database query, then create the database bind.

Step 1: Create a new project

Creating a new project with Sapphire/Web is straightforward. A simple menu selection of File—> New and a panel appears for entering a project name and location as shown in figure 19-4.

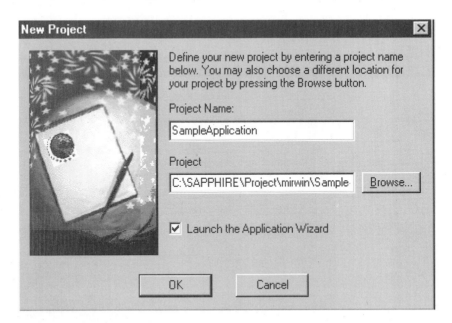

**Figure 19-4.** New Project Panel.

When a new project is created, an icon representing it shows up in the Project Browser. All projects have their own file folder where all files associated with that particular project are stored. Double clicking on the Project Icon brings up a project property sheet where a developer can set and modify project properties as shown in figure 19-5.

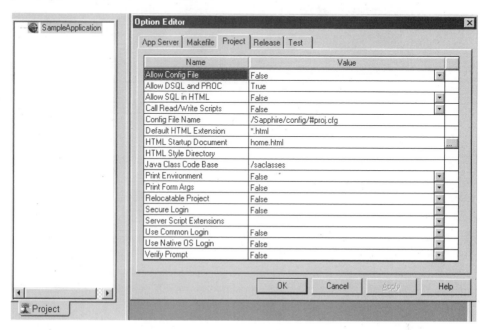

**Figure 19-5.** Project Icon and Property Sheet.

### Step 2: Creating HTML Pages

To create HTML pages a developer selects the "Create New Document" icon (figure 19-6) or uses menu options. This brings up the Create New Document Panel. HTML pages can also be imported into a project.

**Figure 19-6.** New document icon.

From the New Document Panel developers can select from a set of pre-defined HTML pages (figure 19-7). Sapphire/Web provides quite a few and developers can add their own. For this application we select the "anchor.html" template by highlighting and selecting OK or double clicking. This launches the Sapphire/Web HTML Tag Editor. If Sapphire/Web had been configured to use another HTML editor, the specified editor would launch instead.

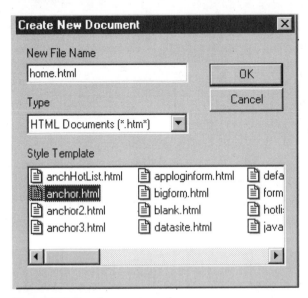

**Figure 19-7.** New document panel.

The anchor.html template (figure 19-8) chosen contains only HTML header text and a single <A HREF> anchor. All we do with this page is change the text of the anchor (In this case the word "Title" is changed to "Click here to generate a dynamic HTML table") as shown in figure 19-9.

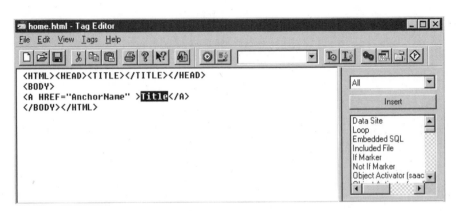

**Figure 19-8.** Tag Editor with Anchor tag highlighted.

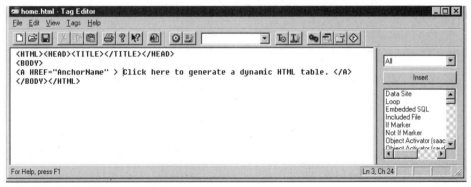

**Figure 19-9.** Anchor tag modification.

The procedure for creating the second HTML document of the application is the same, except this time we select the "datasite" template (figure 19-10).

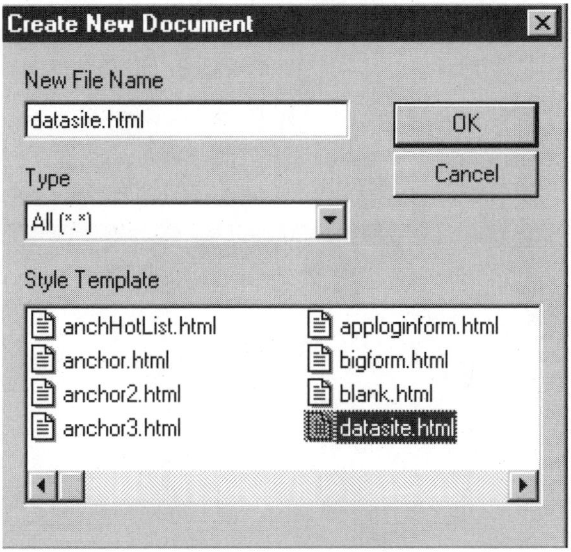

**Figure 19-10.** New document panel — Datasite.

The "datasite" template contains HTML and TITLE tags plus the character string "##Sa_data##" (figure 19-11). This string is the space holder for data that will be retrieved from the database. There are no restrictions on the number of datasites that can be put on a page or where datasites can be placed. They can be put in Headers, List boxes, Forms, Option lists, Tables, Scripts, etc.. Sapphire/Web recognizes the characters "##Sa_"; the remainder of the string can be anything a developer chooses as long as the string ends with the "##" characters. Usually a developer will name datasites to be consistent with the columns being returned from the database.

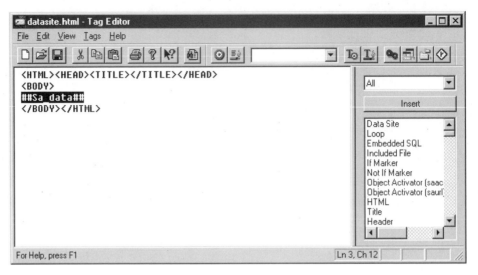

**Figure 19-11**. Datasite page HTML in tag editor.

Now the Sapphire/Web Project Window shows two documents (figure 19-12). Document 1 has a single HTML anchor represented by a small anchor icon. Document two has a single datasite represented by a small target icon.

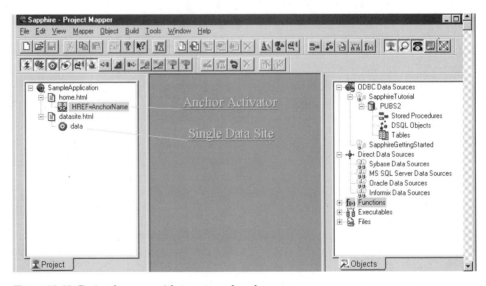

**Figure 19-12**. Project browser with targets and anchors.

Step 3: Create Database Query Using DSQL

Relational databases are accessed via Structured Query Language (SQL). Traditionally, SQL database access logic has been part of the database tier of client server applications. Dynamic SQL (DSQL) data objects extract the database access logic such that it resides separate from the database itself. This allows for things like placing variables in the SQL itself. Hence, the name Dynamic SQL. With Sapphire/Web, using the same paradigm as with datasites in HTML pages, you can place space holders (i.e., variables) in SQL statements such that SQL statements are built on-the-fly based on end user selections or input parameters.

You can generate DSQL objects in Sapphire using a DSQL wizard or directly using a DSQL editor (see figure 19-13). When you save the DSQL object it appears in the Object Browser.

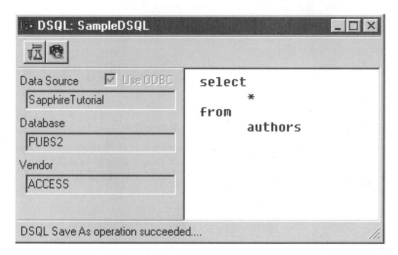

**Figure 19-13.** DSQL editor.

The example application we are currently building does not contain any dynamic input variables. Here we are only concerned with displaying all data from the Authors table of the Sapphire/Web tutorial, PUBS2 database. So, our DSQL statement is simply

```
SELECT *
FROM Authors.
```

Figure 19-14 shows the Data Object Browser. Displayed is the Sapphire/Web Tutorial PUBS2 Database. Notice that the Data Object Browser displays all Stored Procedures, DSQL objects, and Tables associated with the database. Note also that the Data Object Browser displays the real database and changes to the database are reflected immediately.

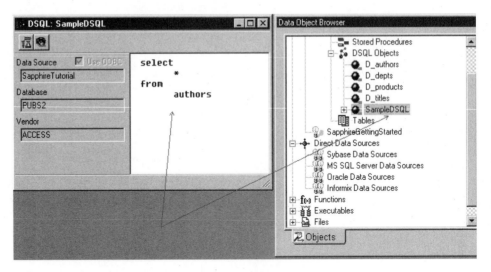

**Figure 19-14.** Data Object Browser with Authors Table.

Step 4: Binding Process

Now that the components for the sample application are in place, the next step is to link them. The first HTML page (home.html), and more specifically, the A HREF Anchor on the first HTML page, must be bound to the database access logic or DSQL object (sampleDSQL). Then, the resulting data from the DSQL statement must be bound to the datasite in the second HTML page (data-site.html). In Sapphire/Web this is referred to as a Bind. Binds are created with the Bind Editor. The Bind Editor allows you to visually map a user interface to a data source(s) and add formatting, behavior, and data field validation as needed. Figure 19-15 graphically depicts a Bind.

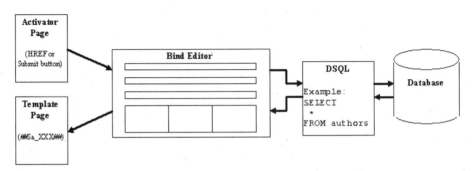

**Figure 19-15.** The Bind Editor.

To clarify some terms:

• An activator is any on-screen element that invokes an action based on end user input. Examples are <A HREF> HTML tags or HTML forms. However, developers can define their own activators.

• A data source can be a database, a file, a function, or a module of executable code. A data source can be accessed either directly, via DSQL (Dynamic Structured Query Language) or via a Stored procedure.

• A Template is the page or interface the end user will see after the data source interaction has occurred.

• A Target datasite(s)is the location within the Template that results coming from the data source will be placed and displayed to the end user (i.e., Anywhere a ##Sa_XXXXXX## is located in the user interface Template page (XXXXXX = any word a developer types in).

Defining a bind in Sapphire/Web related terms: A Bind links an activator to a data source, then links data from the data source to a Template that contains target datasite(s).

To create the bind for our sample application, the sequence of steps is:

1. Launch the Bind Editor
2. Bind to datasource
3. Bind to template
4. Specify target datasite
5. Specify data formatting

Double clicking on the activator in the Project Browser generates a panel that allows you to rename the Activator as shown in figure 19-16. Clicking "OK" launches the Bind Editor as shown in figure 19-17.

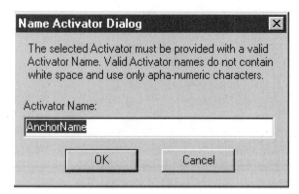

**Figure 19-16.** Anchor Name Confirmation Panel.

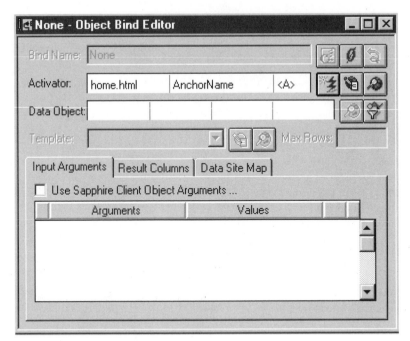

**Figure 19-17.** Bind Editor with Activator.

Drag and drop the DSQL object (sampleDSQL) from the Data Object Browser into the Bind Editor. There are three tabs in the Bind Editor as shown in figure 19-18: Input Arguments, Results, and Data Site Map. The Input arguments tab displays expected input arguments based on any variables in the DSQL statement. Since sampleDSQL doesn't contain any input variables the Input Arguments tab in the Bind Editor is empty. The Results tab displays all columns that will be returned from the database based on the DSQL statement (i.e., all columns from the Authors table). The Data Site Map tab is used to send individual columns of data to different pages. For this sample application, there are no data sites to be mapped. So, like the Input Arguments tab, it too is empty.

Select or drag and drop the Template page (datasite.html), where the data being returned from the database is to be displayed, into the Template field in the Bind Editor as shown in figure 19-19.

Specify a target datasite for each column displayed in the Results tab of the Bind Editor as shown in figure 19-20. In this sample application, datasite.html has only one target datasite. So, all columns are mapped to that same target datasite. This mapping can be done via drag and drop, pull down list, or text entry. If a Template page contains more than one datasite, different columns can be mapped to different target datasites.

Specify a data formatting template. Sapphire/Web provides approximately 30 templates. Developers with specific display requirements can create their

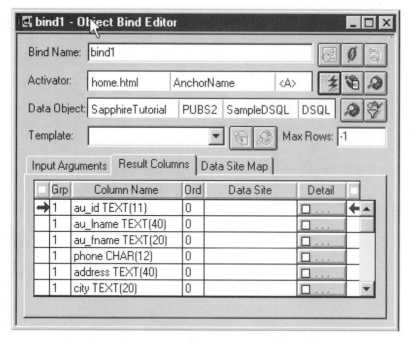

**Figure 19-18.** Bind Editor with DSQL.

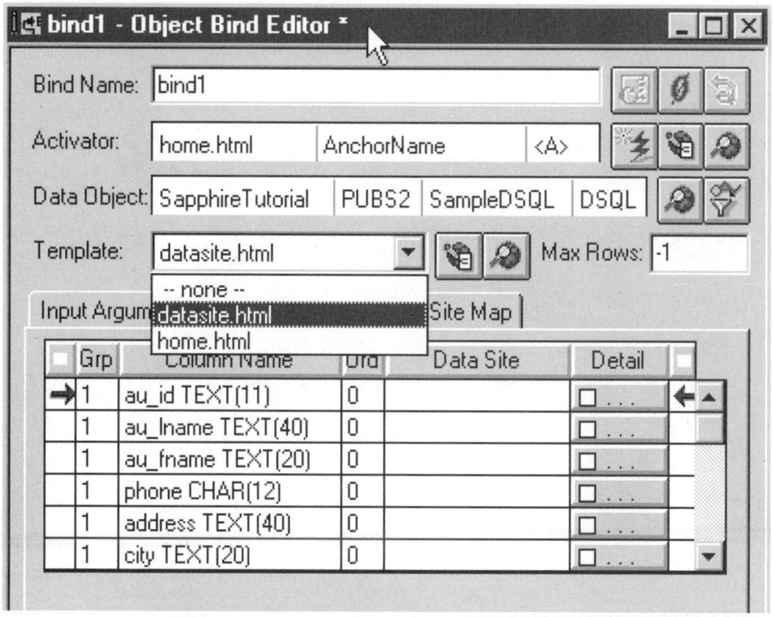

**Figure 19-19.** Bind Editor with Datasite.html.

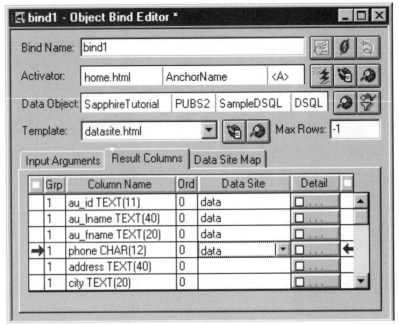

**Figure 19-20**. Bind Editor with Data Drop Sites.

own or modify those supplied. For this application the SaPopulateTable Population Callback is used as shown in figure 19-21.

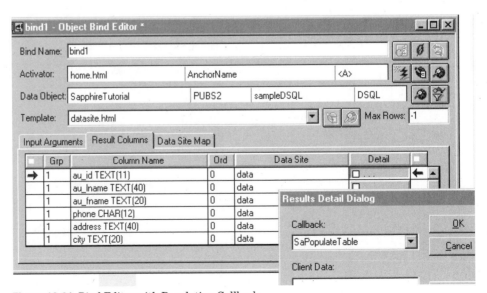

**Figure 19-21.** Bind Editor with Population Callback.

Step 5: Publish Completed Web Application

Once the binding has been completed and saved, all that is left to do is publish the project. You do this by pushing the Test icon as shown in figure 19-22. Figure 19-23 shows the first page of this sample application. Figure 19-24 shows the data that was dynamically generated and formatted into an HTML table as a result of a user clicking on the text in the first page.

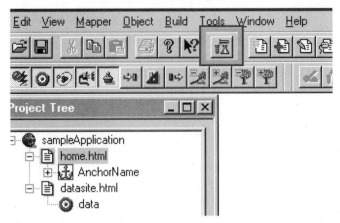

**Figure 19-22.** Test Icon.

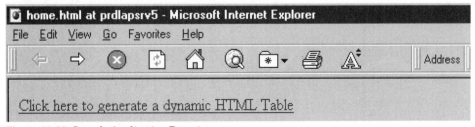

**Figure 19-23.** Sample Application Page 1.

## Runtime Application

At runtime (i.e., when the application is being used) Sapphire/Web replaces the Anchor string with the following:

```
<A HREF=
"http://PRDLAPSRV5:80/Scripts/att1/sampleApplication.exe?FNC=AnchorNam
e__Ahome_html" >click here to ccess database</A>
```

This string is the http path to the Web Server and the executable that

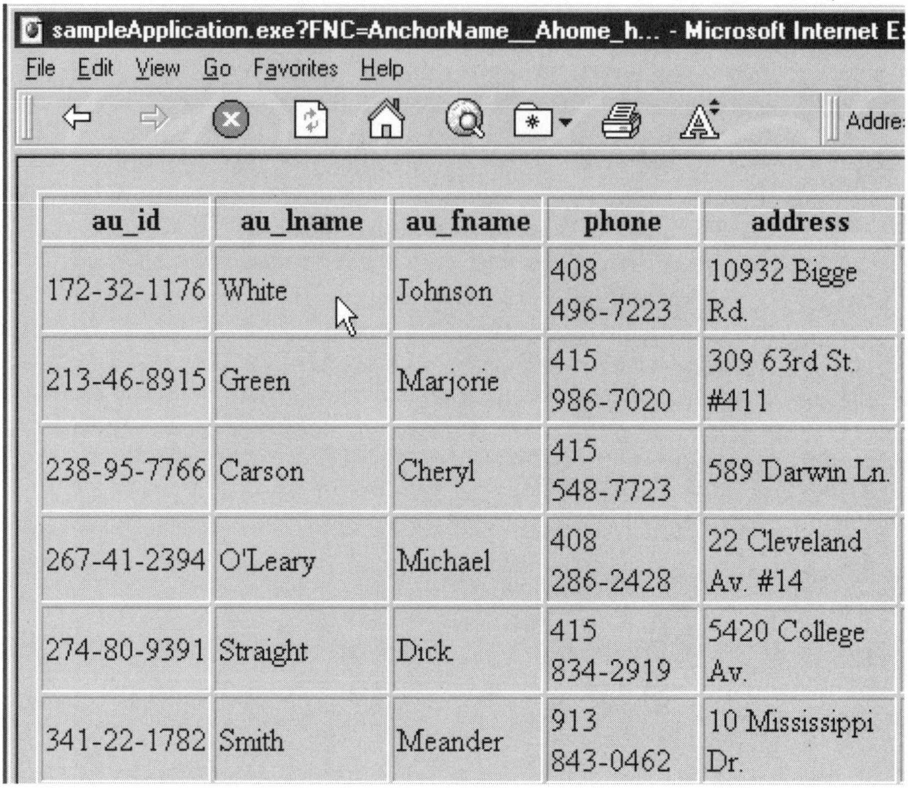

**Figure 19-24.** Sample Application Page 2.

Sapphire/Web created.

If you view the source of datasite.html while using the application you will see that the ##Sa_datasite## has been replaced with an HTML table containing the number of rows in the database. A sample is as follows:

```
<HTML><HEAD><TITLE></TITLE></HEAD>
<BODY>
<TABLE BORDER>
<CAPTION></CAPTION>
<TR>
<TH>au_id</TH>
<TH>au_lname</TH>
<TH>au_fname</TH>
<TH>phone</TH>
<TH>address</TH>
</TR>
<TR>
<TD>172-32-1176</TD>
```

```
<TD>White</TD>
<TD>Johnson</TD>
<TD>408 496-7223</TD>
<TD>10932 Bigge Rd.</TD>
</TR>
</BODY></HTML>
```

Note: The HTML table is generated dynamically each time the application is run.

## Sapphire/Web Features

Sapphire/Web has an abundance of features and functions. They can be broken down into features associated with building a Web applications user interface, features associated with database/datasource access, and features associated with the overall architecture of the Sapphire/Web solution.

The previous sections discussed Sapphire/Web's visual development and deployment environment. In addition to the point-and-click, drag-and-drop interface, Sapphire/Web also provides what is called a Project Mapper. This feature provides developers with a visual rendering of the structure and layout of an application. The Project Mapper is shown in figure 19-25.

As stated previously, Sapphire/Web comes with a basic HTML editor. However, since Sapphire/Web is an open solution, any HTML editor can be incorporated and launched from inside the development environment. Additionally, any user interface, whether designed and developed in Java, JavaScript, ActiveX, VBScript, or VRML, can be incorporated into a Sapphire/Web project. It doesn't matter what other tool is used to create the user interface. In fact, many off-the-shelf user interface objects such as Java or

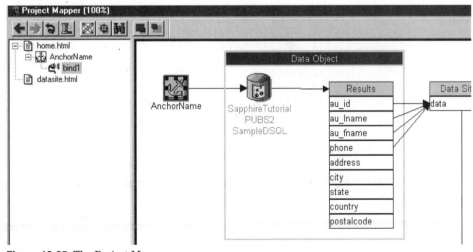

**Figure 19-25.** The Project Mapper.

ActiveX based charting and graphing packages can be imported and "data enabled" using Sapphire/Web.

With Sapphire/Web, all user interface code is maintained in its original form. This provides flexibility and ease of configuration management. Many scripting tools and other Web to Database development tools mandate that script and database access logic (SQL statements) be embedded into HTML code. This can make it difficult to track and maintain applications logic and database access code (i.e., if a database table name changes, you have to search through HTML documents for all references to that table).

Sapphire/Web provides wizards for creating binds, creating DSQL, developing drill-down applications, creating Java applications and other table based applications. Sapphire/Web, however, does not mandate the use of wizards. Some tools do, and that can be very restrictive from a developers perspective.

## Database Access Features

A key feature of Sapphire/Web is its ability to access virtually any data source. In addition to direct access to Oracle, Sybase, MS SQL Server, Informix and DB2, or and ODBC database, Sapphire/Web can also access flat files, functions, and executables. For Java applications database connectivity Sapphire/Web uses JDBC or ADO. Local or remote connections can also be established using RMI or IIOP.

The data access capabilities built into Sapphire/Web allows developers to use existing stored procedures and other data access logic. From a management perspective, this means that current investments in technology are not lost (i.e., the development team doesn't have to start from scratch).

From a productivity perspective, DSQL objects used in Sapphire/Web projects are stored independent of the project and independent of the document and database they are being used to access. In other words, a single DSQL

```
SELECT
        [SCOTT_EMP].[EMPNO],
        [SCOTT_EMP].[ENAME],
        [SCOTT_EMP].[JOB],
        [SCOTT_EMP].[MGR],
        [SCOTT_EMP].[HIREDATE],
        [SCOTT_EMP].[SAL],
        [SCOTT_EMP].[COMM],
        [SCOTT_EMP].[DEPTNO]
FROM
        [SCOTT_EMP]

WHERE [SCOTT_EMP].[DEPTNO] = #deptno.NO_WRAP#
```

**Figure 19-26.** Example DSQL object with Dynamic Where Clause.

object can be used anywhere, and any number of times in a project. The same DSQL object can be used in any number of different projects. DSQL objects can also be used to access different databases. (Note: Sometimes syntax will be specific to a particular database vendor and require modification.) As discussed previously, abstracting the database queries up a level into DSQL objects allows for the placement of variables inside SQL statements, thereby allowing dynamic generation of the SQL based on user input parameters. For example, the DSQL statement in figure 19-26 would select columns  from a database based on a department id number.

All a developer has to do is place a variable in the where clause of the SQL (i.e., where [SCOTT_EMP].[DEPTNO] = #deptno,NO_WRAP#).

Sapphire/Web also provides facilities for transaction processing including Begin, End, Rollback, Commit across multiple data sources and applications. It provides for routing multiple users to a single database login, holding open database connections, and accessing multiple databases in a single transaction.

## Architectural Features

Key architectural features of Sapphire/Web include:

•Ability to work with any Web Server, any Web browser, any Web Server Extension.
•Ability to Generate JAVA code, C code, or C++ code.
•Ability to Generate Application Servers, Oracle Web Cartridges, or CGI's. (Sapphire/Web can also generate other database vendor specific Web application code modules.)
•Ability to manage Web Application processes anywhere on a network.
•Ability to maintain state on the Web using a secure state server.
•Ability to add user defined code at the project level or before and after any database/data source binding.
•Ability to utilize operating system and/or database level security mechanisms.

In addition to the features listed above, Sapphire/Web has an open API that both developers and other software vendors can take advantage of.  Existing integration's with software vendors have produced modules for Mainframe data access, EDI applications, Web based storefronts, and high level security control. Figure 19-27 shows the Sapphire/Web overall architecture.

## Sapphire/Web Applications Servers

Application Servers provide a variety of technologically advanced features and services for Web applications performance, scalability, connectivity, security, and persistence.

An Application Server is a project specific module of executable code that

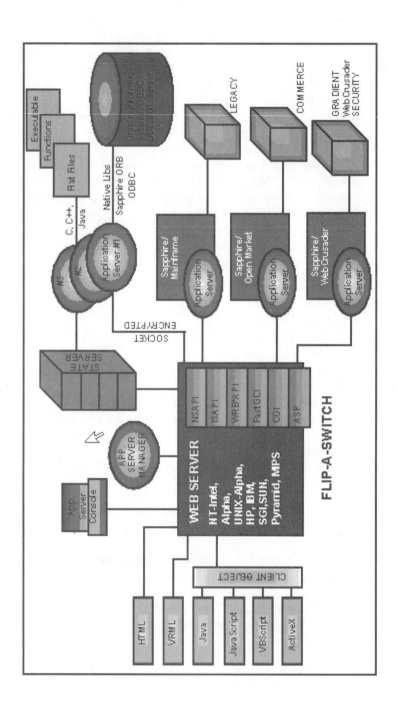

**Figure 19-27.** Sapphire/Web Overall Architecture.

performs some function(s) in response to user interaction on a page in a Web Browser. What distinguishes a Sapphire/Web Application Server is that it is a process that continues running after it services a user request. The performance and scalability advantages gained by this seemingly simple distinction are tremendous. Instead of a having to start a CGI with each user request, a running process on the Web Server handles incoming user requests, thereby saving time, memory space, and CPU cycles on the Web Server. What this means to the end user is an increase in performance (i.e., results are generated and displayed faster). What it means to a developer is less chance of overloading and possibly crashing a Web Server.

It is important to note that a Sapphire/Web Application Server is not a generic process that handles all Web application requests. Sapphire/Web Applications Servers are project specific processes. This means they deliver the advantages of having a persistent process without a lot of overhead or proprietary data handling code. Features of Sapphire/Web Application Servers include:

- Can be generated as 100% pure Java, C, or C++ code.
- Developer defined behavior specific to the particular application.
- No limit to number of Application Servers.
- Unlimited deployment flexibility.
- Automatic start/stop, time-out and load balancing.
- Real time scalability.
- Ability to run Application Servers securely behind a firewall.
- No Application Server runtime fees.

## Author Bio

David Isaacson is a Senior Systems/Sales Support Engineer for Bluestone Software. He is an evangelist for Sapphire/Web software and helps customers architect Web based business solutions. He has 20 years experience in design, development, and implementation of various technologies including mainframes, client/server, multimedia, and the Web. Mr. Isaacson also has extensive experience in development of computer based training (CBT) and Electronic Performance Support Systems (EPSS). Prior to joining Bluestone, Mr. Isaacson managed major multimedia projects for clients such as General Electric, Lockheed Martin, Computer Sciences Corporation, and Loral Data Systems. Mr. Isaacson has been a speaker at several multimedia conferences. He holds a Bachelor of Science degree in Mechanical Engineering Technology from Temple University and has completed many high level information management courses.

# 20

# Why Use COBOL for Web Database Applications?

Ron Langer

## Introduction

COBOL has been used for mission-critical business applications for well over thirty years. Many applications that were originally written in the 70s and 80s are still in use today. COBOL's English-like syntax makes it easy to create and maintain. Most COBOL programs bear a strong resemblance to each other. Thus it is relatively easy for COBOL programmers to understand and modify COBOL programs written by other programmers. Since existing COBOL applications are easy to understand they tend to get updated and enhanced rather than replaced. This approach makes sense in today's cost cutting business environment.

Many people who are involved in creating and maintaining Web systems do not have a background in COBOL. For this reason COBOL is not always considered a language that can be used with the Web. This is a mistake. As Web applications become more complex and more of the information stored in corporate databases needs to be accessed, COBOL and COBOL programmers can become a major asset to the Webmaster. Many Web applications have a relationship to existing in-house applications. Since many of these applications were written in COBOL much of the business logic for the applications already exists. Involving the traditional "glass house" COBOL programmer in the creation of Web applications will reap many benefits.

Accessing and manipulating corporate data is something that COBOL programs do every day. This chapter aims to show COBOL programmers how easy it is to create Web-based COBOL applications and to show webmasters why they should go talk to the COBOL programmers down the hall.

Most Web applications are intended to provide information, gather information or otherwise work with data. Working with databases is one of COBOL's primary strengths. All major SQL venders provide support for COBOL. In fact, SQL and COBOL were designed to work together in a natural and cooperative fashion. SQL is easily called by COBOL and the readability and maintainability of the COBOL code is preserved in an SQL COBOL program. Skilled SQL COBOL programming expertise is also readily available.

Complex Web-based applications are by nature dynamic. Web page contents are continuously updated with new information. With each release, new HTML constructs are added to the popular Web browsers. This allows for more complex Web page development which in turn spurs the need for even more new HTML constructs. Thus the cycle is in continual motion. The COBOL language is ideally suited to the notion of continuously evolving Web-based applications. As COBOL programs tend to be easy to understand and maintain, enhancements can be rapidly incorporated as the needs of the business drive the structure and content of Web-based applications.

A typical Web application is very similar to a typical display/accept COBOL application. In a Web application, information is displayed to the user based on the available actions for a particular page (for example, hypertext links, push buttons, user input fields). Depending upon the action selected, additional information is then displayed to the user. Display/accept COBOL programs have the same basic structure. The COBOL application displays the available actions. The user selects an action and the COBOL program then displays the requested information.

A simple Web-based application tends to be relatively static. The Web pages are largely predefined and usually do not change. However, using a COBOL program to create even simple Web pages allows you much more flexibility. The COBOL program can display different aspects of the information based on user input. This allows users to tailor the interaction to their particular interests or needs and Webmasters to target their pages toward specific users.

It is important to note that COBOL programmers are application programmers, not system programmers. In this regard, COBOL programmers tend to think at a higher (application) level than their C programming counterparts.

Many programming solutions for the Web require programmers to code at very low levels. This is not an ideal approach. Coding at a higher, application level allows programmers to focus on the business needs of the application, not the programming needs of the programming language. We feel the best approach is one that is analogous to a display/accept framework. This type of interface allows the program to display or send information to the browser and accept or read information from the browser. We recommend using a set of programming interfaces developed by England Technical Services. England Technical Services has Web development solutions that work with most COBOL vendors on most platforms. This allows you to develop and deploy your applications across multiple platforms. England Technical Services provides a set of routines called COBOLCGI.

COBOLCGI provides a CGIWRITE routine to display HTML information on a Web browser and a CGIREAD routine to obtain information from the Web browser. This is very similar to a typical display/accept COBOL application. The business logic is the same. The manner in which the information is displayed may change; however, the bulk of the application does not change. Replacing the display/accept logic with the CGIWRITE and CGIREAD routines is an easy way to think about Web programming with COBOLCGI.

For example, the COBOL statement to display the line of text shown in figure 20-1 would look like the following:

```
Display "This is a line of text."
```

The COBOL statement to display a line of text on a Web browser is very similar:

```
CALL "CGIWRITE" USING BY CON-
TENT "<P>This is a line of
text.</P>" & X"00".
```

Two things are made obvious by this example. Calling CGIWRITE requires more parameters and it is necessary to imbed HTML tags into the COBOL program. And while CGIWRITE makes it easy to send information to a Web browser, it does not format the information. This is left to the programmer. The benefit here is that any and all HTML tags are automatically supported in COBOL. When a new HTLM tag or option is created it can be immediately used. No waiting for a COBOL vendor to provide support!

Fujitsu COBOL, a robust COBOL development suite, enables you to easily create Web-based applications, from displaying simple, yet dynamic, bulleted lists to building complex tables in response to users' queries. The following is an example of a simple bulleted list that can be displayed on a Web page, and is shown in figure 20-2:

Adventure Travel Companies

- Urban Outfitters
- Wilderness Unlimited
- Safari Adventures
- Raft the Rivers of the World
- Kon-tiki Tours

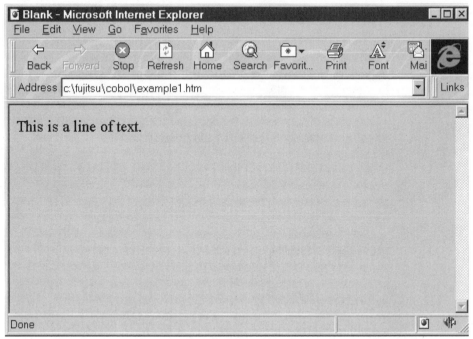

**Figure 20-1.** Displaying a line of text using COBOL.

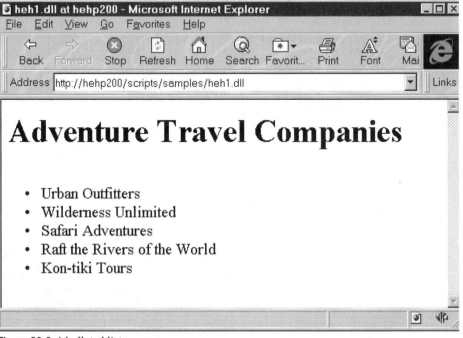

**Figure 20-2.** A bulleted list.

## The sample COBOL code for the  list is as follows:

```
IDENTIFICATION DIVISION.
PROGRAM-ID.  HEH1.
ENVIRONMENT DIVISION.
CONFIGURATION SECTION.
SPECIAL-NAMES.
   ARGUMENT-VALUE IS COMMAND-LINE.

DATA DIVISION.
WORKING-STORAGE SECTION.

01  FILE-NAME        PIC X(128).


*******************************************
* The following lines are HTML statements
* to be sent back to the Browser to
* create a results form (page). The CGI
* interface requires a blank line be sent
* back immediately following the first
* line (Content-type). A X"0A" will
* suffice for the blank line. All text
* strings going through the CGI interface
* must be null terminated and thus the
* X"00" appended to each line.
*******************************************




01 HTML-LINES.
   03 HTML-START PIC X(25) VALUE
"Content-type: text/html" & X"0A" & X"00".
   03 HTML-HEADER.
         05 FILLER PIC X(24) VALUE
"<BODY BGCOLOR=FFFFFF>".
         05 FILLER PIC X(40)VALUE
"<H1>Adventure Travel Companies</H1><BR>" & X"00".
   03 HTML-LINE PIC X(80).
   03 END-BODY PIC X(12) VALUE
'</P></BODY>' & X"00".
   03 END-HTML PIC X(08) VALUE
"</HTML>" & X"00".



PROCEDURE DIVISION.
```

```
MAIN-LOGIC.
* The first command line parameter must
* always be passed to CGISETUP before
* performing CGIREAD/CGIWRITE. The
*following ACCEPT statement will retrieve
* the name of the executable file for
* this program from the command line.
   ACCEPT FILE-NAME FROM COMMAND-LINE.

* Tell CGISETUP the name of this program.
   CALL "CGISETUP" USING FILE-NAME.

* The first line of code returned to the * browser indi-
cates which type of text
* (plain or HTML) is being returned. We
* will use HTML so that we can include
* ( HTML formatting tags. We now begin
* the new HTML form (screen).
   CALL "CGIWRITE" USING HTML-START.
   CALL "CGIWRITE" USING HTML-HEADER.

* Create the HTML Unordered List of items
   MOVE "<UL><LI>Urban Outfitters</LI>"        & X"00" TO
HTML-LINE.
   CALL "CGIWRITE" USING HTML-LINE.
   MOVE "<LI>Wilderness Unlimited</LI>"        & X"00" TO
HTML-LINE.
   CALL "CGIWRITE" USING HTML-LINE.

   MOVE "<LI>Safari Adventures</LI>" & X        "00" TO
HTML-LINE.
   CALL "CGIWRITE" USING HTML-LINE.

   MOVE "<LI>Raft the Rivers of the
World</LI>" & X"00" TO HTML-LINE.
   CALL "CGIWRITE" USING HTML-LINE.

   MOVE "<LI>Kon-tiki Tours</LI></UL>" &        X"00" TO
HTML-LINE.
   CALL "CGIWRITE" USING HTML-LINE.

* Now finish the HTML form (screen)
   CALL "CGIWRITE" USING END-BODY
   CALL "CGIWRITE" USING END-HTML.
   EXIT PROGRAM.
```

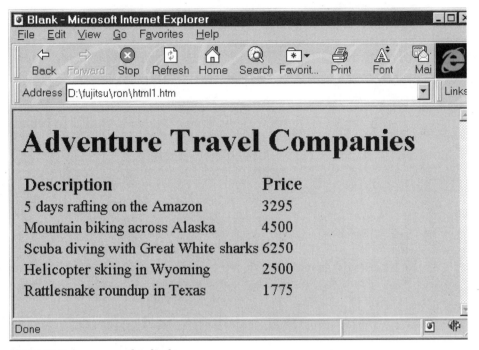

**Figure 20-3.** A more complex display.

Now let's look at more a complex situation. Suppose the previously mentioned adventure companies offer specialized tour packages whose prices fluctuated seasonally and are based on availability. Figure 20-3 shows a listing of the currently available tour package is given along with the most up-to-date prices for each package.

The available tour packages and price lists are stored in a corporate database. One of the biggest challenges for Webmasters is to keep the Web pages current and accurate. By using a COBOL program to access the data in an SQL database, you will always display the most current information and ensure that your Web page data is accurate.

## Accessing SQL Databases

Now that we have looked at creating simple Web-based applications with COBOL, let's examine the more complex tasks. We recommend using Fujitsu COBOL because of its support for multiple databases via ODBC. Refer to the end of this chapter for more information about Fujitsu COBOL and how to obtain a free Fujitsu COBOL compiler that includes the COBOLCGI Support for Web Development.

Fujitsu COBOL provides two ways to get at SQL data. The first is via traditional SQL preprocessors. COBOL programs that contain SQL statements are run through a program that converts the SQL statements into API calls to the database. The program is then compiled by the COBOL compiler. This is a good solution when the database is known and fixed. An example of this type of interface is PROCOBOL for Oracle.

The second access method is via ODBC. Microsoft created ODBC as a generic way to allow programs to access any database. Fujitsu COBOL provides an embedded SQL processor that converts SQL statements into ODBC calls. The ODBC calls are then routed to the intended database. The database vendor provides the ODBC driver. This approach allows the COBOL program to work with many databases without recompiling or relinking the application.

```
EXEC SQL SELECT PACKAGE_PRICE
INTO :CURRENT-PRICE
FROM PRICE_TABLE
WHERE PACKAGE_NAME =
'5 days rafting on the Amazon'
END-EXEC.
```

The above example shows how to query a database and then display the information to users. This works very well if there is a limited number of items to query. The SQL code is much more complex and is harder to maintain with a larger number of items. Sending pages of information to users would be very time consuming and possibly annoying. What is needed therefore is the ability for users to select only the information they are interested in and then to initiate a database query based solely upon their particular interests.

Most database vendors provide both static and dynamic SQL. Static SQL is very similar to a static Web page. The query is known and built at compile time. This approach provides fast access to SQL information. The SQL preprocessor can parse the SQL statements and transform them into efficient API calls to the database.

Dynamic SQL, on the other hand, is more flexible. SQL statements can be constructed while the application is running. This makes it possible to create complex queries that are not known at compile time. The down side is that these queries must be parsed at run-time. This slows down the query but adds a desired level of flexibility. Dynamic SQL also makes it easier to process more complex queries. For example, to query a table that contains 5 rows it is possible to have 5 factorial or (5*4*3*2*1=120) of queries. Pre-building all 120 queries is a very tedious and potentially error-prone process. By using dynamic SQL it's possible to create a simple COBOL program to build a complex query.

Let's look at an example (figure 20-4) where we obtain the user's input and then dynamically build an SQL query to access the desired information.

The COBOL program needs to determine what the user entered in the input field. This information will be stored as a CGI Variable. In the following example, the CGI Variable is ProductSelectionField. It is possible to access the CGI variable from the COBOL program. The following sample code will obtain the information from the ProductSelectionField and store it in the COBOL variable ProductName.

```
WORKING-STORAGE SECTION.
            .
            .
            .
01 F-PRODUCTCODE PIC X(22) VALUE "ProductSelectionField"
& X"00".
01 PRODUCTCODE   PIC X(9)  VALUE SPACES.
            .
            .
            .
PROCEDURE DIVISION.
            .
            .
            .
   CALL "CGIREAD"
   USING F-PRODUCTCODE PRODUCTCODE.
```

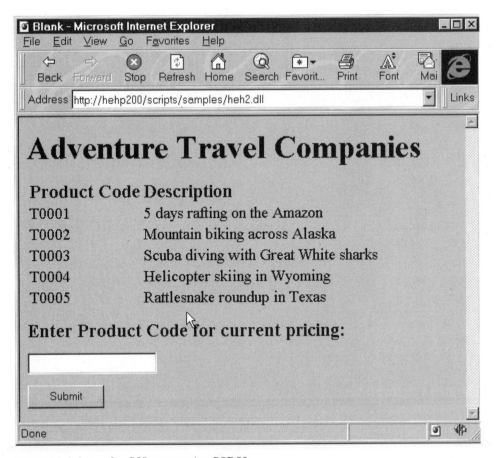

**Figure 20-4.** A complex SQL query using COBOL.

Now we need to build a dynamic SQL statement to query the database in order to get the product description and price information. The following dynamic SQL statements will return the product description and price information to the program and then display the information to the user.

```
IDENTIFICATION DIVISION.
PROGRAM-ID. HEH3.
DATA DIVISION.
WORKING-STORAGE SECTION.
* Declare SQL host variables
EXEC SQL BEGIN DECLARE SECTION END-EXEC.
01  DYNAMIC-SQL-STATEMENT   PIC X(128).
01  CURRENT-PRICE           PIC X(5).
01  SQLSTATE                PIC X(5).
EXEC SQL END DECLARE SECTION   END-EXEC.

01 F-PRODUCTCODE PIC X(22) VALUE "ProductSelectionField"
& X"00".

* Define static part of dynamic SQL
* SELECT statement. Note that
* SQL host variables above must all be 01
* level data items (no
* elementary data definitions allowed).
* We must define a second "work" SQL
* statement in order to take advantage of
* elementary data items to construct the * SQL statement.
01  SQL-STATEMENT.
   03  SQL-SELECT PIC X(56) VALUE
"SELECT PRICE INTO :CURRENT-PRICE FROM PRICE_TABLE WHERE
".
   03  SQL-WHERE-CLAUSE   PIC X(25) VALUE "Productcode =
' ".
   03  PRODUCTCODE        PIC X(5).
   03  FILLER                       PIC X     VALUE "'".

PROCEDURE DIVISION.

* Read Product Code entered on HTML form
* (screen) by user
   CALL "CGIREAD" USING F-PRODUCTCODE
                        PRODUCTCODE.

* Prepare (dynamic syntax check) dynamic
* SQL statement
```

```
    MOVE SQL-STATEMENT TO
           DYNAMIC-SQL-STATEMENT.
    EXEC SQL PREPARE STMIDT
           FROM :DYNAMIC-SQL-STATEMENT
    END-EXEC.


*   Execute the dynamic SQL statement
    EXEC SQL EXECUTE STMIDT END-EXEC.


*   Check results and act accordingly
    IF SQLSTATE = '00000'
*   Good result - post price on new Web
*   page using CGIWRITE routine. The data
*   item "CURRENT-PRICE" should now contain
*   the price that was retrieved from the
*   database.
    ELSE
*   Bad result (e.g. user entered invalid
*   product code) post error message on new
*   Web page using CGIWRITE routine.
    END-IF.


    EXIT PROGRAM.
```

The combination of COBOL and SQL is ideal for creating dynamic Web-based applications. The need for timely, accurate information on the Web is obvious. The ability to continuously update your business data via COBOL and SQL is the optimal solution for Web-based applications that are continuously evolving.

## Transforming Existing CICS Applications into Web-Based Applications

The business logic in a CICS transaction can also be reused to create Web-based applications. The structure and form of a CICS application remains the same; however, the EXEC CICS statements must be replaced. And, if the application already uses SQL to access data, it should be relatively easy to modify the application.

Many PC and UNIX COBOL applications use display/accept logic. On the mainframe most COBOL applications use CICS as a transaction management tool.

These CICS applications display requested information on the screen. The displayed information is called a BMS map. Transforming a CICS transaction into a Web-based solution is simple and straightforward. The CICS application displays a screen (BMS map) and receives information from the fields on the BMS map. The CICS commands to display a BMS map can be replaced by

CGIWRITE statements. The logic to obtain information from the available fields on the BMS map can be replaced by CGIREAD statements.

Figure 20-5 demonstrates this concept. The CICS code is written as follows:

```
EXEC CICS SEND MAP ('MAP1')
     MAPSET ('SET1')
     FROM (MAP1I)
     ERASE
     CURSOR
END-EXEC.
```

This code can easily be transformed to work on the Web. This will allow the Web application to be continuously updated with the most current and accurate information. Notice that a top down list has been added. Since the names of the tour packages are known, this information can be placed in a list. This makes the application logic much simpler.

Figure 20-6 shows how easy it is to modify the CICS application into a Web application. The application structure itself was not changed.

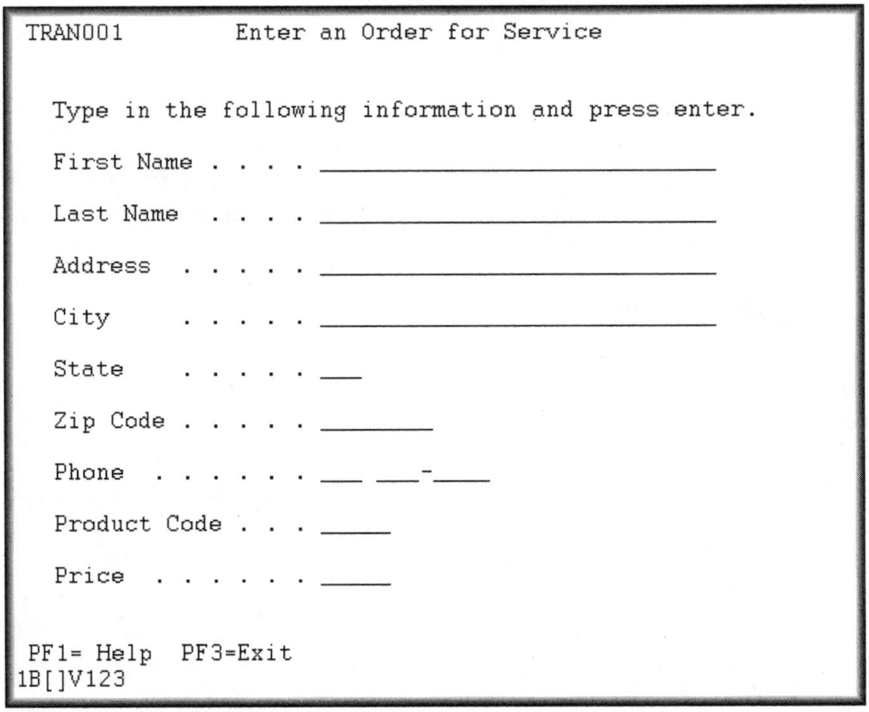

```
┌──────────────────────────────────────────────────────┐
│  TRAN001           Enter an Order for Service         │
│                                                        │
│   Type in the following information and press enter.   │
│                                                        │
│   First Name . . . . _____   │
│                                                        │
│   Last Name  . . . . _____   │
│                                                        │
│   Address  . . . . . _____   │
│                                                        │
│   City     . . . . . _____   │
│                                                        │
│   State    . . . . . ___                               │
│                                                        │
│   Zip Code . . . . . _____                          │
│                                                        │
│   Phone  . . . . . . ___ ___-____                      │
│                                                        │
│   Product Code . . . _____                            │
│                                                        │
│   Price  . . . . . . _____                            │
│                                                        │
│  PF1= Help  PF3=Exit                                   │
│  1B[]V123                                              │
└──────────────────────────────────────────────────────┘
```

**Figure 20-5.** A typical CICS screen.

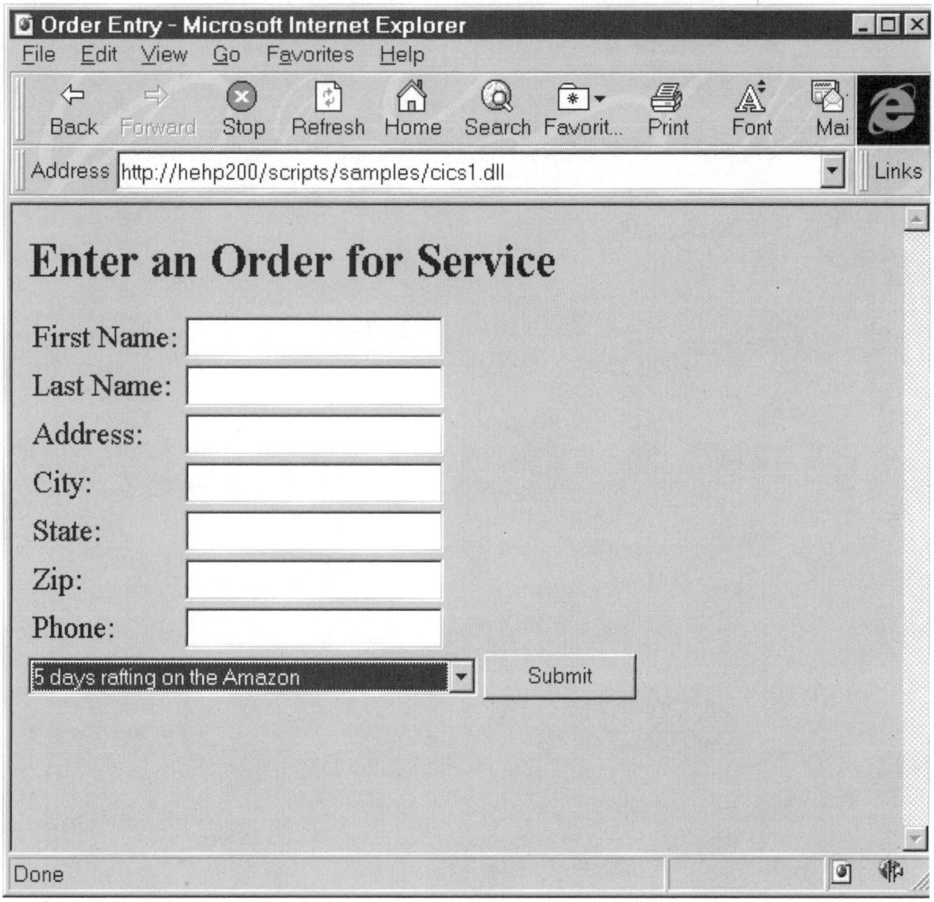

**Figure 20-6.** Turning a CICS transaction into a Web transaction.

```
IDENTIFICATION DIVISION.
PROGRAM-ID. HEH5.
ENVIRONMENT DIVISION.
CONFIGURATION SECTION.
SPECIAL-NAMES.
ARGUMENT-VALUE IS COMMAND-LINE.

DATA DIVISION.
WORKING-STORAGE SECTION.

01 FILE-NAME            PIC X(80).
01 HTML-LINE.
   03  HTML-TEXT  PIC X(128).
```

```
    03  HTML-END   PIC X VALUE X"00".

PROCEDURE DIVISION.
    ACCEPT FILE-NAME FROM COMMAND-LINE.
    CALL "CGISETUP" USING FILE-NAME.
* CREATE THE WEB FORM (SCREEN)
    MOVE
    '<HTML><HEAD><TITLE>
    Order Entry</TITLE></HEAD><BODY>'
          TO HTML-TEXT.
    CALL "CGIWRITE" USING HTML-LINE.
    MOVE '<H2>Enter an Order for Service</H2>
    <FORM ACTION='
          TO HTML-TEXT.
    CALL "CGIWRITE" USING HTML-LINE.
    MOVE '"..scripts/samples/heh4.dll" METHOD="POST">'
          TO HTML-TEXT.
    CALL "CGIWRITE" USING HTML-LINE.
    MOVE '<TABLE BORDER="0"><TR><TD>First Name:</TD>'
          TO HTML-TEXT.
    CALL "CGIWRITE" USING HTML-LINE.
    MOVE
    '<TD><INPUT TYPE="TEXT"
    NAME="FirstName"></TD></TR>'
          TO HTML-TEXT.
    CALL "CGIWRITE" USING HTML-LINE.
    MOVE '<TR><TD>Last Name:</TD>' TO HTML-TEXT.
    CALL "CGIWRITE" USING HTML-LINE.
    MOVE '<TD><INPUT TYPE="TEXT"
    NAME="LastName"></TD></TR>'
          TO HTML-TEXT.
    CALL "CGIWRITE" USING HTML-LINE.
    MOVE '<TR><TD>Address:</TD>' TO HTML-TEXT.
    CALL "CGIWRITE" USING HTML-LINE.
    MOVE '<TD><INPUT TYPE="TEXT"
    NAME="Address"></TD></TR>'
          TO HTML-TEXT.
    CALL "CGIWRITE" USING HTML-LINE.
    MOVE '<TR><TD>City:</TD>' To HTML-TEXT.
    CALL "CGIWRITE" USING HTML-LINE.
    MOVE '<TD><INPUT TYPE="TEXT"
    NAME="City"></TD></TR>'
          TO HTML-TEXT.
    CALL "CGIWRITE" USING HTML-LINE.
    MOVE '<TR><TD>State:</TD>' To HTML-TEXT.
```

```
CALL "CGIWRITE" USING HTML-LINE.
MOVE '<TD><INPUT TYPE="TEXT"
NAME="State"></TD></TR>'
        TO HTML-TEXT.
CALL "CGIWRITE" USING HTML-LINE.
MOVE '<TR><TD>Zip:</TD>' To HTML-TEXT.
CALL "CGIWRITE" USING HTML-LINE.
MOVE '<TD><INPUT TYPE="TEXT" NAME="Zip"></TD></TR>'
        TO HTML-TEXT.
CALL "CGIWRITE" USING HTML-LINE.
MOVE '<TR><TD>Phone:</TD>' To HTML-TEXT.
CALL "CGIWRITE" USING HTML-LINE.
MOVE '<TD><INPUT TYPE="TEXT"
NAME="Phone"></TD></TR>'
        TO HTML-TEXT.
CALL "CGIWRITE" USING HTML-LINE.
MOVE '</TABLE><SELECT NAME="SelectPrice">'
        TO HTML-TEXT.
CALL "CGIWRITE" USING HTML-LINE.
MOVE '<OPTION VALUE="$3295">
        5 days rafting on the Amazon
        TO HTML-TEXT.
CALL "CGIWRITE" USING HTML-LINE.
MOVE '</OPTION><OPTION VALUE="$4500">
        Mountain Biking across'
        TO HTML-TEXT.
CALL "CGIWRITE" USING HTML-LINE.
MOVE ' Alaska </OPTION><OPTION  VALUE="$6200">
        Scuba diving '
        TO HTML-TEXT.
CALL "CGIWRITE" USING HTML-LINE.
MOVE 'with Great White sharks </OPTION><OPTION '
        TO HTML-TEXT.
CALL "CGIWRITE" USING HTML-LINE.
MOVE 'VALUE="$2500">
        Helicopter Skiing in Wyoming </OPTION>'
        TO HTML-TEXT.
CALL "CGIWRITE" USING HTML-LINE.
MOVE '<OPTION VALUE="$1775">
        Rattlesnake roundup in Texas '
        TO HTML-TEXT.
CALL "CGIWRITE" USING HTML-LINE.
MOVE
'</OPTION></SELECT><INPUT TYPE="SUBMIT"
NAME="SUBMIT">'
```

```
        TO HTML-TEXT.

CALL "CGIWRITE" USING HTML-LINE.
MOVE '</FORM></BODY></HTML>' TO HTML-TEXT.
CALL "CGIWRITE" USING HTML-LINE.
EXIT PROGRAM.
```

Both display/accept COBOL applications and CICS applications are excellent candidates to migrate into Web-based applications. Using existing applications and existing business logic will speed the development of your Web applications and produce better applications that meet the needs of your users.

Fujitsu believes that COBOL programmers will love using COBOL to develop applications for the Web and is offering a free copy of the Fujitsu COBOL Compiler and the COBOLCGI routine developed by England Technical Services. Fujitsu COBOL includes the compiler, runtime libraries, and debug tool and supports industry extensions compatible with those from Micro Focus and IBM.

For more information on Fujitsu COBOL and to request a your free COBOL compiler, visit the Fujitsu COBOL Web site at http:\\adtools.com\datacasting. You will receive a CD containing the Fujitsu COBOL 32-bit compiler and the COBOLCGI routines. To contact Fujitsu COBOL please call 1-(800) 545-6774 or 1-(408)-428-0500.

## Author Bio

Ron Langer is the Senior Technical Sales and Support Manager for Fujitsu COBOL. He is a frequent speaker on COBOL and Client/Server Technologies at many industry conferences. Mr. Langer has been the technical focal point for integrating Fujitsu COBOL with technologies like Microsoft Transaction Server, C++, Visual Basic and COBOL/WEB Integration.

Prior to joining Fujitsu, Mr. Langer worked for IBM. He was responsible for COBOL Technical Marking and Trained the IBM's Sales force around the world on how to sell IBM's Object Oriented COBOL Compilers. Mr. Langer was an Architect for IBM's Strategic Cooperative Development Environment for MVS,AS/400 and OS/2. As well as a designer for IBM's distributed Debugger for debugging VM, MVS,CICS, IMS and AS/400 applications from the PC. He was a member of IBM's Institute of Technology which is a partnership between IBM development and IBM Research to speed products to the marketplace.

Mr. Langer obtained a Bachelors of Science in Mathematics and Computer Science from the University of California at Los Angeles (UCLA).

# 21

# WDB: A Shareware Interface between the Web and SQL Databases

## Introduction

This chapter describes a tool called WDB, developed by Bo Frese Rasmussen (bfrasmus@eso.org), which is a shareware interface between the World Wide Web and SQL-based relational databases.

WDB was written at the Space Telescope — European Coordinating Facility, to make the science data archive of observations made with the Hubble Space Telescope available to the European astronomers.

WDB allowed the ST—ECF to make a huge database, like the HST archive, available to a large number of users with relatively little effort, without having to worry about porting — or even writing — client software.

WDB has been available on the Internet as free software since September 1994, and is now being used by research institutes and commercial sites all over the world. The WDB mailing list counts more than 130 different sites, and it has been downloaded by a lot more. WDB has a World Wide Web homepage at http://archive.eso.org/wdb/html/wdb.html where the WDB script, all documentation, news and updates always are available.

## Overview

WDB lets you provide access to your databases without writing a single line of code. All you have to do is to install WDB as a CGI script on your HTTP server and write a set of Form Definition Files (FDF's) each describing a different view on your database. WDB will then, when activated by an URL request from a client, produce an HTML form which allows the user to enter a database query. When the user has entered a query it is sent back to your server, where WDB converts the user's input to a query in your database, converts the output according to your specifications in the FDF, and finally sends the result back to the user.

If the query results in more than one row, WDB will output the data in a tabular form containing a subset of the columns (the user can choose exactly which columns should be displayed ). A hyper-text link in each row will then allow the user to select a row and WDB will produce a nicely formatted page with all the data in this row.

To make the writing of the FDFs simple WDB comes with a small tool which, when given a name of a table and the unique key(s), extracts the information from the database and creates a working FDF.

The real power of WDB lies in the fact that you can specify actions, or computations to be made on any field in the FDF, either converting the user's input before it is used in the database query, or converting the data from the database before it is presented to the user. These actions or computations are specified as Perl expressions, and can be virtually anything — from simple computations on the data to complex functions which requests other network resources, includes images or sound, or constructs hypertext links to other data in your database or anywhere else on the net.

The ability to make hypertext links between the data in the database makes this interface different from other more traditional form based database interfaces. Without the hypertext capability you have to carefully think about what information the user might want to look at, and create forms that contain all the needed tables with the proper joins. With WDB you can simply make an FDF for each table and from each FDF make all the possible relations available as hyper-text links. This allows the users to enter anywhere in the database, and explore as much as they want, always being able to find any relevant data in the database

WDB was written in Perl, and used to provide access to a Sybase database (via the sybperl extension to Perl), but the database interface was written as a separate Perl package, and can easily be ported to other databases for which there exist a Perl interface (like Oracle, Informix, Ingres, etc.). An interface to Informix and the public domain database mSQL is included with the standard WDB distribution.

## How to Use WDB

To use WDB to access a specific form you start your WWW browser with a URL of the following form:

http:// server/cgi-bin/wdb/ database/ form-name/ mode/ keys

Where:

http:// server        is the base URL to the HTTP server where you have
                      installed WDB.

/cgi-bin/wdb/         is the path on the HTTP server to where you installed WDB.
                      This example assumes that you have a special directory
                      where you keep your CGI scripts called /cgi-bin. If your
                      server is configured to run scripts depending on a file
                      extension (e.g., cgi) then you'd have to rename the cgi script
                      (say to wdb.cgi) and change the above path accordingly.

database              is the name of the subdirectory where you have stored the
                      FDF files you are trying to access. Typically you would name
                      this directory after the database the FDF files are accessing.
                      This would be a subdirectory to the directory you defined in
                      $formdir in the configuration file. If you only have one data-
                      base and one or two FDF's this might seem ridiculous, but
                      wdb was designed to handle a large number of FDF's in
                      many different databases.

form-name             is the name of the FDF file you want to use. FDFs are dis-
                      cussed more thoroughly at the end of this chapter.

mode                  is the mode in which you want to start WDB. This can be one
                      of form, query or default.

keys                  is only used in the query mode.

## Form Mode

In form mode WDB reads the form definition file and creates an HTML form in
which the user can enter qualifiers. This is the normal use of WDB. For an
example you can try the ESO Telescope Schedule Report (figure 21-1) located
at http://arch-http.hq.eso.org/cgi-bin/wdb/eso/sched_rep/form

HTML for this report, which clearly demonstrates the usage of WDB, is
shown below:

```
<HTML><HEAD><TITLE>ESO Schedule Report</TITLE></HEAD>
<BODY bgcolor="#ffffff">
<H1><a href="http://archive.eso.org/eso/eso_schedule.html">
ESO Schedule Query Form</a></h1>
Enter qualifiers in the fields below if needed.
Press <strong>Search</strong> to query the database.<br>
<b>Please note</b> that the <a href="/eso/Sest_sched.html">SEST
Schedule</a>is available as a separate document. Service Observing
```

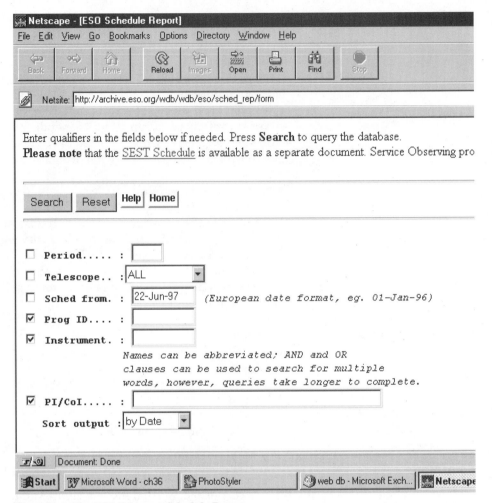

**Figure 21-1.** The ESO Telescope Schedule Report.

```
programmes are <b>not</b> included.<p>

<FORM ACTION="/wdb/wdb/eso/sched_rep/query"
METHOD="POST"><hr>
<INPUT TYPE="submit" VALUE="Search">
<INPUT TYPE="reset" VALUE="Reset">
<A HREF="/wdb/html/wdb_query_help.html">
<img border=0 align=bottom alt="[Help]"
src="/wdb/html/help_btn.gif"></A>
<a href="/"><img border=0 align=bottom alt="[Home]"
src="/wdb/html/home_btn.gif"></A><hr><p>
<pre><INPUT type=checkbox  name=tab_period>
<b>Period..... :</b>
```

```
<INPUT name="period" size=4 value="" >
<INPUT type=checkbox  name=tab_tel> <b>Telescope.. :</b>
<SELECT name="tel"><OPTION value="%"> ALL
     <OPTION value="3.6"> 3.6m
     <OPTION value="NTT%"> 3.5m NTT
     <OPTION value="2.2"> 2.2m
     <OPTION value="1.5D"> 1.5 Danish
     <OPTION value="1.5"> ESO 1.5m
     <OPTION value="CAT"> 1.4m CAT
     <OPTION value="1"> 1m
     <OPTION value="0.9D"> 0.9m Dutch
     <OPTION value="0.5D"> 0.5m Danish
     <OPTION value="0.5"> ESO 0.5m
</SELECT>
<INPUT type=checkbox  name=tab_start> <b>Sched from. :</b>
<INPUT name="start" size=10 value="22-Jun-97" > <i>(European date for-
mat, eg. 01-Jan-96)</i>
<INPUT type=checkbox checked name=tab_progid> <b>Prog ID.... :</b>
<INPUT name="progid" size=10 value="" >
<INPUT type=checkbox checked name=tab_instrument> <b>Instrument.:</b>
<INPUT name="instrument" size=10 value="" >
<p><i>Names can be abbreviated; AND and OR<br>clauses can be used to
search for multiple<br>words, however, queries take longer to com-
plete.</i><p>
<INPUT type=checkbox checked name=tab_pi_coi> <b>PI/CoI:</b>
<INPUT name="pi_coi" size=44 value="" >
   <b>Sort output :</b>
<SELECT name="order">
     <OPTION value="from_date"> by Date
     <OPTION value="progid"> by Progid
</SELECT></pre>      <hr>
<INPUT type=checkbox name=full_screen_mode>
Use full-screen output even if more than one row is returned.<br>
Return max <INPUT VALUE=100 SIZE=3 NAME=max_rows_returned>rows.
<hr>
<INPUT TYPE="submit" VALUE="Search">
<INPUT TYPE="reset" VALUE="Reset">
<A HREF="/wdb/html/wdb_query_help.html"><img border=0 align=bottom
alt="[Help]" src="/wdb/html/help_btn.gif"></A>
<a href="/"><img border=0 align=bottom alt="[Home]"
src="/wdb/html/home_btn.gif"></A>
<hr><p></FORM><hr>
<a href="/wdb/wdb.html">
     wdb 1.4</a>
     - 10-Aug-1995 ......
<a href="/comments/Elisabeth.Hoppe@eso.org/wdb_form:sched_rep">
```

```
Send comments</a> to <i>Elisabeth.Hoppe@eso.org</i>
</BODY></HTML>
```

## Query Mode

This mode is used by WDB internally as the action script to activate when the user presses Search in the query form. However, you can also use this mode to ask WDB to search for something in the database and present it according to the FDF specified. If one row is returned it will be displayed in full-screen output mode; otherwise the tabular output mode is used.

There are two methods you can use to specify what to search for. The first and most used is to specify the key(s) for the table(s) in the FDF. Which fields in the FDF that are the keys is specified with the field attribute " key" on one or more fields.

To access a specific row via these keys you have to add the key values to the URL. If there are more than one key you have to specify the values in the same order as the key fields in the FDF, separated with a double colon ( :: ). Please note that this is the raw database values (i.e., the to_db function is not used ).

The normal use of this is from an FDF file to provide hypertext links from one database row to another using the "URL" attribute. In fact you will need to use this in every FDF you write to provide access from the tabular output to the full-screen output. For example:

```
FIELD  = more
  label  = More
  type   = char
  length = 4
  from_db= "MORE"
  URL    = "$WDB/mydb/$form{'NAME'}/query/$val{'key1'}::$val{'key2'}"
  computed
  forcetab
  no_query
  no_full
```

This will create a hypertext link labeled "MORE" in the tabular output which when activated will start WDB again using the same form, but this time searching on the two columns key1 and key2. Assuming these two columns together form the unique key on this form, this will lead to the full-screen output of the current row in the tabular output.

mkfdf will automatically add a field like the one above to your FDF files but you might want to modify it, or add URL tags to other fields to create links from one form to another.

You can also create URL's to search on something different than the key values. To do this you have to use the HTTP GET method. The general syntax is

http:// server /cgi-bin/wdb/ database / form-name/ query? fieldname = query &

fieldname = query ...

Where fieldname is the name of a field in the form, and query is a query on that field as if the user had typed it in. This means you can use operators (like > and < ) and the values will be passed through the functions in the to_db attributes.

## Default Mode

The default mode can be used to execute a default query. This is normally used in conjunction with the default field attribute in the FDF. The values in the 'default' field attributes are used as query constraints and the result shown in tabular output format. This is especially useful when the default attributes are expression that depends on the current time, or other external factors.

For example, let's say you have a table with schedule information. The table has a field called start_time with a default attribute like this:

```
default = ">= `date +'%Y.%m.%d'`"
```

Now you can create a link like "click here to see schedule starting from today" using the default method. For example to see the ESO telescope allocation schedule, starting from today, you can use

http://arch-http.hq.eso.org/cgi-bin/wdb/eso/sched_rep/default

## Porting WDB to Other Database Systems

With WDB 1.2 the Sybase specific code has been isolated into a separate Database interface package (DBI). This should make it relatively easy to port WDB to other databases like Oracle, Informix, Ingres, etc. (any database which supports standard SQL and has a Perl interface.)

Currently there are interfaces to Sybase, Informix and mSQL (a public domain database). A port to Oracle is on its way. If you want to use WDB with another database system the first thing you have to do is to get a Perl interface to it. Several of these are available on the Internet. A collection of pointers to Perl reference material in general are available at

http://www.eecs.nwu.edu/perl/perl.html

Another important factor when porting WDB to another database is the SQL used. Each database system seems to implement it's own flavor of SQL, but fortunately the only SQL command that WDB sends directly to the DBI is a select statement. The select statement used by wdb has the following format:

```
select column field, column field, ...
```

```
from table where where-list and constraints and join
order by order
```

where:

column:   is the value of the column attribute in the FDF. It is inserted in the
          select statement without any parsing in WDB, all computations,
          etc., supported by the database can be used in the FDF.

field:    is the value of the FIELD attribute in the FDF. This is used as the
          label in the select, as the dbi_nextrow function should return the
          rows as an associative array keyed on this value.

table:    is this is the value of the TABLE attribute in the FDF. It can contain
          one or more table names separated by commas.

where-list:
          is a list of search conditions composed by WDB from the input fields
          in the query form. The conditions of each field is and'ed together, and
          the standard operators <=, >=, !=, <, >, = and like are used.

constraints:
          is the value of the CONSTRAINTS attribute in the FDF.

join:     is the value of the JOIN attribute in the FDF.

order:    is the value of the ORDER attribute in the FDF.

If your database does not support the column field notation described above,
an alternative notation is supported. Rather than specifying the field names as
column labels in the select list they can be send separately to the DBI via a
function called dbi_fieldnames. WDB automatically detects if such a function
is defined in the DBI and uses this second notation.

Frese Rasmussen's Sybase DBI file appears below. As you can see it is simply an encapsulation of the sybperl functions.

```
#+++++++++++++++++++++++++++++++++++++++++++++
#.IDENTIFICATION  syb_dbi.pl
#.LANGUAGE        SybPerl script
#
#.PURPOSE         Database Interface to Sybase.
#
#                 &dbi_connect( $user, $pswd,
#................$server, $database );
#                 &dbi_dosql( "... SQL commands
#                 %row = &dbi_nextrow;
```

```
#                       &dbi_disconnect;
#                       &dbi_rowcount( $rows );
#                       &dbi_dateformat( $format );
#
#.AUTHOR          Bo Frese Rasmussen [ST-ECF]
# <bfrasmus@eso.org>
#
#.VERSION         1.0     22/12-1994        Creation
#————————————————————————————————————
package WDB_DatabaseInterface;
require "sybperl.pl";


#++++++++++++++++++++++++++++++++++++++++++++++++++++++
#.PURPOSE        Connects to a database.
#
#.REMARKS        This function must be called before
#                any of the other functions
#                in this package.
#                It logs in to the given database
#                server and connects to a
#                database.
#
#.RETURNS        Dies on error !
#————————————————————————————————————
sub main'dbi_connect
{
    local( $user, $pswd, $server, $database ) = @_;
    $dbproc = &main'dblogin( $user, $pswd, $server
);
    $dbproc != -1 || die
    "Can't connect to server $server ...\n";
    &main'dbuse( $database ) || die
    "Can't connect to database $database ...\n";
}
#++++++++++++++++++++++++++++++++++++++++++++++++++++++
#.PURPOSE        Prepares and executes an SQL state-
#                ment, with error check etc.
#
#.REMARKS        Dies on error !
#
#.RETURNS        Return value of &dbresults (not used
#                in WDB)
#————————————————————————————————————



sub main'dbi_dosql
```

```
{
    local($sql) = @_;

    &main'dbcmd( $sql ) || die "Error in dbcmd.\n" ;
    &main'dbsqlexec || die "Error in dbsqlexec.\n" ;
    &main'dbresults;
}
#+++++++++++++++++++++++++++++++++++++++++++++++++++++
#.PURPOSE        Gets the next row from a previous
#                select (dbi_dosql).
#
#.REMARKS        After a dbi_dosql("select ... ")
#                call, this function can be
#                called repeatedly to retrieve all
#                rows of the query.
#
#                Example :
#                &dbi_dosql("select * from mytab");
#                while( %row = &dbi_nextrow  ) {
#                print $row{'columnname'};
#                        ...
#                        }
#
#.RETURNS        An associative array (keyed on the
#                column label) of formatted
#                data, based on the datatype of the
#                corresponding columns.
#————————————————————————————————————————————
sub main'dbi_nextrow
{
    %row = &main'dbnextrow($dbproc, 1);
    return %row;
}


#+++++++++++++++++++++++++++++++++++++++++++++++++++++
#.PURPOSE        Disconnects the current database
#                connection
#
#.REMARKS        After this function is called there
#                are no current database
#                connection => no other function from
#                this package can be
#                called before a new dbi_connect
#                call.
#
```

```
#.RETURNS        nothing.
#——————————————————————————————————————————————
sub main'dbi_disconnect
{
    &main'dbclose($dbproc);
}


#+++++++++++++++++++++++++++++++++++++++++++++++++++++
#.PURPOSE      Sets the maximum number of rows
#              returned from a query.
#
#.REMARKS      Causes SQL server to stop process
#              ing the query ( select,
#              insert update, delete) after the
#              specified number of rows
#              are affected.
#
#              PORTING NOTE: This function is
#              added for efficiency only.
#              When used with WDB it can safely be
#              ignored ( leave an
#              empty function body : {} )
#
#.RETURNS      nothing.
#——————————————————————————————————————————————
sub main'dbi_rowcount
{
    local ($rowcount) = @_;
    &main'dbi_dosql( "set rowcount $rowcount");
}


#+++++++++++++++++++++++++++++++++++++++++++++++++++++
#.PURPOSE      Sets the default output format for
#              dates.
#
#.REMARKS      Sets the order of the date parts
#              month/day/year for entering
#              datetime data. Valid arguments are
#              mdy, dmy, ymd, ydm, myd, dym.
#
#.RETURNS      nothing.
#——————————————————————————————————————————————
sub main'dbi_dateformat
{
    local ($dateformat) = @_;
    &main'dbi_dosql( "set dateformat $dateformat");
```

}

## Installation

To install WDB is quite easy, but you need a few other products like an HTTP server, a database system, and an interface between Perl an your database system. (Installing these are actually the hard part.)

To make things a little bit more complicated, WDB supports several different database systems and the exact installation procedures varies slightly depending on which database system you are going to use. The following are therefore generic instructions that are common for all database systems. Support of the different databases is implemented through a separate database interface module (DBI) for each database system. Specific details and exceptions are documented in the notes for the individual WDB DBI's.

At the time of this writing, WDB supports three database systems: Sybase, Informix and mSQL.

WDB is written in Perl, but we need to add some commands to your Perl interpreter to enable it to talk to your database. Fortunately packages with these commands are already available on the Internet. There are sybperl for Sybase, oraperl for Oracle, isqlperl for Informix, etc.

WDB uses a separate database interface module for each database system, which is simply an encapsulation of the real database commands. All you have to do is to install Perl — with the commands for your database — and tell WDB which interface to use.

To be able to interface to the World Wide Web you need a server that understands Hyper Text Transfer Protocol (HTTP). CGI is the Common Gateway Interface standard for how HTTP servers communicate with programs on the server. As these programs are started on request from the clients by simply referencing them in a URL like any other HTTP request, the server has to have some way of knowing when to send a file back to the client, and when to execute it and send the result back instead. This is normally done by configuring the server to treat all files in a specified directory as CGI programs. There are a few other methods, but in the following I will assume that you have configured your HTTP server to use the /cgi-bin directory for this.

Online hypertext documentation including installation instructions, feature list, demonstration, etc., for the NCSA http server is available from

http://hoohoo.ncsa.uiuc.edu/

## Writing Form Definition Files

Once you have installed WDB you have to define which parts of your database you want to make available, and how it should look. This is done by creating a set of Form Definition Files (FDFs).

An FDF is like a view on the database specifying which table(s) and fields should be accessible through each WDB Query Form.

As your first FDF try to make a simple one — only involving one table, with a unique index on one field. Let's say the table is called sample and is located in a database called mydb. The table looks like this (the unique key is the "userid" column):

```
create table sample
        (userid          char(10)         not null,
         name            varchar(50)      not null,
         office          smallint         null,
         phone           char(4)          null)
```

Now create a subdirectory in your FDF directory and call it mydb:

```
mkdir   mydb
```

Now change to this new directory and run mkfdf:

```
cd mydb
mkfdf -d mydb -t sample -k userid
```

That's it ! Now you have a file called sample.fdf, which can be used via the URL http://your.server/cgi-bin/wdb/mydb/sample/form.

Please note how the URL is composed: http://your.server/cgi-bin/wdb is the normal path to the wdb script you just installed. mydb is the name of the directory you created above and sample is the name of the FDF without the .fdf extension. The keyword form tells WDB to create a query form for the specified FDF file.

The sample.fdf file will look like this :

```
NAME            = sample
TABLE           = sample
DATABASE        = mydb
TITLE           = sample
Q_HEADER        = sample Query Form
R_HEADER        = sample Query Result
#DOCURL         = # URL to documentation.
#JOIN           = # Join condition goes here ..
#CONSTRAINTS    = # Extra query constraints goes here ....
#ORDER          = # ORDER BY columns goes here ...
#RECTOP         = # Record title goes here ....
#PERL           = # Extra perl commands goes here ....
#————————————————————

FIELD   = more
label   = More
```

```
type    = char
length = 4
from_db= "MORE"
URL     = "$WDB/mydb/$form{'NAME'}/query/$val{'userid'}"
computed
forcetab
no_query
no_full

FIELD   = userid
label   = Userid
column = userid
type    = char                        # char
length = 10
key

FIELD   = name
label   = Name
column = name
type    = char                        # varchar
length = 50

FIELD   = office
label   = Office
column = office
type    = int                         # smallint
length = 2

FIELD   = phone
label   = Phone
column = phone
type    = char                        # char
length = 4
```

The real power of WDB lies in the fact that some of the fields are evaluated as Perl expressions. In the above example the table stored only the local extension number in the 'phone' field. Now say that you would like to prefix this with the number of the your company then a ' +' sign and then the local number from the database, so outside users could use the telephone numbers as well. All you have to do is to add the following line in the definition of the phone field (and change the length attribute to the new length):

```
from_db = "(089) 320 06 + " . $val{'phone'}
length = 19
```

## Form Definition File Syntax

Form definition files (.fdf's) are basically just a set of attribute definitions. First a set of attributes for the form as a whole are defined, then a set of attributes for each field in the form. All attribute definitions are of the form

Attribute = value

Blank lines and all characters after a ' #' are ignored. It is important that there are no white spaces before the attribute name. Lines beginning with white space are considered continuation lines of the previous attribute definition. Leading and trailing white space are removed from the attribute values.

All form attributes are always before any field definitions in the file, and always in CAPITAL letters.

In the following an (R) means that the attribute is required, and an (E) means that the attribute values is evaluated by a Perl eval command. Remember to quote strings in attribute values that are evaluated.

NAME:     Name of this form. Typically the same as the filename without the fdf extension. This field is optional but should be included for documentation purposes. It could also be used for reference in URL attributes.

TABLE (R):
        List of tables to query. Use commas as separator if more than one table is needed. ( Used directly in a SQL from clause. )

DATABASE (R):
        Name of the database to use.

TITLE (R) :
        Text for the <TITLE> tag in the query form and the result page.

Q_HEADER:
        Text for the first <H1> tag in the query form.

R_HEADER:
        Text for the first <H1> tag in the result page.

D_HEADER:
        Text for the first <H1> tag in the result of a default query page.

DOCURL: An URL pointing to the documentation for the current form. This URL is automatically added as a hypertext link to the Q_HEADER and the R_HEADER texts.

Q_HTML: Extra HTML text to add to the query form just below the header.

R_HTML: Extra HTML text to add to the result page just below the header.

D_HTML: Extra HTML text to add to the result page of a default query just below the header.

RECTOP (E):

<H2> tag to add as a header to a record in full-screen output mode. Typically the title of the row. For example in a FDF that queries per sons you might want a RECTOP like this :

```
RECTOP = "$val{'last_name'}, $val{'first_name'}";
```

CONSTRAINTS:

Extra query constraints added to the where clause in the SQL select statement.

JOIN:    If more than one table is specified, join conditions must be specified here. (Use the column names given in the field definitions.)

ORDER:   Column(s) to order by. If more than one column is given, separate by commas. (Used directly in a SQL select order by clause.)

PERL (E): Extra perl statements that should be interpreted when the form is read. This is typically used to define functions, etc. , used later in some of the attributes like from_db and to_db.

COMMENTS_TO:

E-mail address of the person to send comments to regarding this form. This will show up at the end of each page, with a link to a page from which the user can send comments via e-mail to the person mentioned. ( See also the html_tail definition in the wdb.conf file. )

Field attributes always appears after all form attributes in the file. The 'FIELD' attribute should always be the first attribute for a field. All attributes defined after this will belong to that field, until the next 'FIELD' attribute is met.

In the following an (R) means that the attribute is required, and an (E) means that the attribute value is evaluated by a Perl eval command. Remember to quote strings in attribute values that are evaluated !

FIELD (R):

Field identifier. Used internally to uniquely identify a field.

Label:   Label/title in forms, etc., Defaults to the value of FIELD
Depending on your database, column values can include computed
fields, and table-names, etc.

type (R):   Database type of field [ int | char | datetime ]. This is currently only
used in the construction of the query to decide whether or not to put
quotes around the values, and whether or not the LIKE operator can
be used.

Unitlabel: Unit label to add at the end of the query fields / result values.

help (E):   A URL to some help about the content of the current field. If this
field starts with a # sign, the value of DOCURL will be prefixed to
the URL. This is added as a hypertext link to the field label in the
query form.

length (R):
Length of field including formatting, etc.

key:   If set, this is a key field. Key fields are needed to make direct references to a specific row in the database via a URL. More than one key
field can be specified. If this is the case the keys listed in the URL
attribute should be given in the same order as they appear in the
FDF file. ( No value is needed for this attribute. )

URL (E):   URL link to add to field when displaying results. Embedded perl
expressions are evaluated before the URL are added to the field. A
typical example is adding a URL to the key field pointing to itself;
in this way the user can click on a row in tabular output and see the
full screen representation of the row. Here is an example with two
keys ( when more than one key is specified they should be separated by double colon ' ::' ) :

```
url=$WDB/$form{'NAME'}/query/
$val{'keyfield1'}::$val{'keyfield2'}
```

Please note the use of the $WDB variable instead of the name of the
script (http://.../cgi-bin/wdb/). This makes it easier to use more than
one version of the wdb script ( for example, a development version
and an installed version ).

from_db (E):
Formatting function used when converting data from database format to the format that should be presented to the user. A typical
example could be formatting a number with proper precision:

```
from_db = sprintf("%8.2f", $val{'salary'} );
```

to_db (E): Formatting function to use when converting what the user typed to the format understood by the database.

default (E):

Default value to insert in the query forms input field before presenting it to the user. The users are free to change or remove this value.

Enum:    Enumerate type. The value of this attribute is a list of the form : " dbval= userval, dbval= userval,..." where dbval is the value in the database and userval is the value as presented to the user. The first value set listed will be the default when the form are displayed to the user. A special dbval of % is interpreted as a match-all value and is not included in the SQL query. An example:

```
enum = %=ALL,SOFT=Software,
DATA=Data,DOC=Documentation
```

no_query:

If set, it will not be possible to query on this field.

no_tab:    If set, the field will not appear in tabular output. ( The user can override this for query fields, i.e., those without no_query.)

no_full:    If set, the field will not appear in the full-screen output. This is typically used when a table has a 'title' field that should appear at the top of the full-screen output as a real title (using the RECTOP form attribute), then the no_full attribute should be used for the field to prevent it from being repeated twice on the screen.

Tablen:    The field can appear in the tabular output, but will be truncated to the length specified as the value of this attribute.

Forcetab: The field will always appear in the tabular output. This is typically used on the key field with the URL leading to the current record (to allow the user to click on a row in the tabular output and get the full-screen version of the row).

Hidden:    The field is not displayed. The value can be referenced with the $val{'fieldname'} variable from other fields (computed fields, input converters, URL specifications etc.)

computed: This is not a database field, but is computed at runtime. The value of the field must be computed in the from_db attribute. The value of other fields can be accessed with the $val{' fieldname'} variable. Normally the no_query   attribute should be set for computed fields. However, it is possible to allow the user to query on a computed field, and then use the entered value to affect the queries on other, possibly hidden, fields. If you want to do that you have to write a function to parse the users typed in value, and insert it in the to_db attribute of the computed field. To modify the query on another field, set the $in{' field-name'} variable.

Sameline: If set the field will appear on the same line as the previous field in the query form and the full-screen output.

Html:    The value of this attribute is inserted as HTML text on the line before the current field in the query form and the full-screen output.

## Internal variables

There are some internal Perl variables that can be referenced in the attribute definitions above:

$val{' fieldname '}:
    Value returned from the database after the query has been performed. This is typically used in from_db and URL.

$val:    Value of the users input in the current field after special characters ( <, >, =) has been removed. This is typically used in to_db.

$form{' form-attribute '}:
    The value of a form attribute. This is not really needed, unless in order to avoid duplicating things. For example, $form{'NAME'} could be used in the URL attribute, so if the name of the form is changed only the NAME attribute needs to be changed.

$field{' field-name ',' attribute-name '}:
    The value of a field attribute. Not really needed by the form writer.

$WDB:    The name of the script used to access this form. This is set by wdb on each invocation. If used in URL references it is a lot easier to test different versions of wdb on the same FDF files. This variable should not be changed!

$MAIN_MENU:
    An URL to the main menu of forms or the homepage. This URL is used for the 'Home' button.

$QUERY_HELP:

> A URL to the query help. This URL is used for the 'Help' button.

$NULL_VALUE:

> The value to display as the NULL value. (The default is an empty string "".)

$MAXROWCOUNT:

> The Maximum allowed value for the 'Return max .... rows' field.

$rowcount:

> The default value for the above field. This controls the maximum number of rows that can be returned from a query.

## Functions

These are functions built into WDB. However, you can always add your own functions as well and include them either directly in the FDF file (under the PERL form attribute) or include them in your own Perl package and install it in your Perl library directory, then include them with the Perl "require" statement in the PERL attribute or in the wdb.conf file to make them available in all your FDF files.

&add_menu( $text, $href, $img ):

> This function can be used in the PERL form attribute to add extra menu options next to the Submit, Reset, Help, etc., buttons. Either a text or a GIF button can be used.

$text — is the text label to use, either directly or as the ALT attribute if a GIF button is supplied.

$href — is the URL to execute when the button is pressed.

$img — is the URL to the GIF file to use as button. If this argument is left out a normal text link is created instead.

&cgi_encode( $str ):

> Encodes a string so it doesn't cause problems in a URL. If you have a keyvalue that could contain special characters like spaces, % signs, etc., you can't just include it in a normal URL like

```
URL =
"$WDB/$form{'DATABASE'}/$form{'NAME'}/quer
y/$val{'keyfield'}"
```

In this case you would have to encode the key value using cgi_encode like this :

```
URL=
"$WDB/$form{'DATABASE'}/$form{'NAME'}/
query/" . &cgi_encode($val{'keyfield'})
```

Note: Parts of this chapter are protected by the following:
Copyright (c) 1994, Bo Frese Rasmussen — All Rights Reserved
Copyright (c) 1994, European Southern Observatory — All Rights Reserved
Copyright (c) 1994, Space Telescope — European Coordinating Facility — All
Rights Reserved.

# 22

# 001 for Better, Faster, Cheaper Internet-Based Applications

**Margaret Hamilton**

## Introduction

The software industry is yet again undergoing a rapid and rocky transition to another set of technologies. This time, it's the distributed client server technologies as typified by the Internet. Even as the "first generation" of Internet technologies are being deployed, a second wave which transforms static Internet/Intranet systems into dynamic reflections of a corporation through live links to commercial database products is destined to follow. This is a necessary transition and one which must be managed properly.

In fact, the database market itself has, for a number of years, been undergoing a quiet, yet nonetheless, as far reaching a transition as that evident with Internet technologies. As we move from relational to hybrid relational/object oriented database structures, or realize the need to "connect" the database silos that litter our corporate world, or want to connect these databases to the new Internet/Intranet systems that we are starting to deploy, it becomes evident that what is really needed is a way to create durable systems. Durable because they incorporate a structure and process for the continuous evolution of any or all parts of a system. Durable because they provide a way to productively, instead of destructively, manage change to a system — change in the businesses they support and change in the technologies used to implement them.

Once we build durable systems, we are free to safely make the key decision of when and how we transition what we have today to what we need tomorrow. Within such an environment we can either keep the relational databases we have or incorporate the newest object database technologies as economics dictates.

So, in reality, these transitions present a major opportunity — an opportunity to take a step back and examine the underlying process used to design, build and deploy software and examine where Internet or commercial database products truly fit within the systems development framework. For despite the continuing pronouncements of Internet software and database vendors, two things remain constant. One is that systems and software fail more often than necessary; the other is that change is inevitable.

Software fails when either the application being developed or the process of building (where building can include its evolution) it fails. The application fails when it doesn't work as intended. The process of building that application fails if it takes too long or costs too much to build that application.

Change in the software industry needs no introduction. But it is this facet of our industry which has provided at best a foundation of quicksand for the systems that we have deployed to date.

The good news is that many continue to strive for ways to make software that is both reliable and affordable, resulting in better, faster, cheaper software. This means the degree of failure of both the software and the process that develops that software is minimized. Encouraging are the attempts to revamp entire enterprises by bringing in truly modern technologies, ones with paradigms that will change significantly business as is. The case studies that follow this chapter are illustrations of this transformation. Another case in point is NASA and its "faster, better, cheaper" initiative (note the variation on this phrase [1]).

In this chapter we explain the properties of better, faster, cheaper software and how to develop it in terms of the development before the fact (DBTF) preventative approach [2,3,4,5] and its automation, the 001 (pronounced "double-oh-one") Tool Suite [6]. Using this approach over a traditional one consistently shows dramatic improvement [7,8,9,10].

This chapter serves as an introduction to help understand how the DBTF approach was used for 001-developed applications deployed using Internet and commercial database technologies. Three of these applications are described in subsequent chapters.

As we gain an understanding of DBTF, we will develop a view of where Internet and commercial database technologies fit within the framework of a 001 developed system. It will become clear in a 001 world that databases are relegated to the lower layers of a system since 001 automation allows us to deal with much more abstract objects each of which (or a set of which) is a system oriented object (SOO). In essence, the persistence mechanism of a database becomes a supercharged transparent file system (interestingly enough it is likely that all the major PC, workstation and server operating systems will move to this model of a file system within the next few years) for storing and retrieving persistent SOOs within a 001 system.

## Why Software Fails

The reason that software fails is not so much that the technology is new, as some would argue, or old, as others would argue. Rather, it's related to the very reason that so much else in the world seems to fail: we do not take advantage of what we have learned in the past. In software development environments as in life, knowledge is not gathered intelligently, not analyzed appropriately, nor put to intelligent reuse. In short, wisdom is lacking.

That intelligence-gathering deficiency is part and parcel of conventional development techniques — even today, an era of great advances in computer technology and computer science. Under the conventional development scenario the probability approaches zero that a software-based system will be reliable, let alone durable, and that it will be developed within a reasonable time and within budget.

The broader in scope and more complex the system, the less likely it is that it will be reliable. It doesn't seem to matter that developers expend enormous resources on prototyping, design, performance analysis, and testing.

### Failure Compounded by the New

Unfortunately, things have not really changed with newer types of applications, whether they be client server, Internet based or object oriented using whatever mix of approaches and tools. And to add to the confusion, with each new generation of developers and users, new popularized terms and disjunct tools to deal with these terms camouflage "old" ideas, both good and bad, and old solutions — whether good and bad. A new set of "experts," often with lack of real systems expertise is born around these terms and tools. "New," less proven ways of doing things often based on misguided rationales surface.

How often have you heard: "We have to go in that direction because everyone else is doing it"; " if everyone else is using it, it must be good"; "it is inferior if we build it this way but we'll get there faster and make more money";  or: "let's use that software we got for free?"  The latest buzz words take the masses off to the latest set of tools to respond to the latest fads.  Again, a new generation of designers and developers reinvents the wheel, often throwing out the baby with the imperfect bath water.  Is it any wonder that familiar problems, already solved, arise again?

Meanwhile "old experts," having become "hard wired" to one way of doing things, take the path of least resistance by always using the same tools and techniques even if they don't work as well as some newer approaches for the project in question because that is what they learned in school or on their first assignment and it is too late to teach an "old" programmer new tricks. "All the other applications in the organization use this technology, therefore every new application in the organization should use it."

Conversely an organization's response to a nontraditional technology that does show real promise includes things like; "we just don't have time," "we don't have the budget" or "we tried such things as structured approaches, CASE tools, object oriented techniques and they do not meet promised expectations." "First we had to learn C++, now this is being replaced by Java. Why bother learning anything new at all?"

Just as there is a need to have openness within the software to be successful, there is a need for its developers, both old and new, to have openness when dealing with the complexities of developing software.

And to compound things is the everlasting software development culture with which to contend. Consider some typical scenarios.

On one project, everything that could go wrong did go wrong. The prime contractor was unable to deliver a working system and everyone agreed that the root problem was the prime contractor. Yet, when it came time to try again the same prime won the bid to build the new system. According to the customer it was because the prime contractor was more experienced than the other bidders with building this kind of system! This is the norm, not the exception.

When things go wrong a typical solution is to throw more people on the project and more managers on the project to manage the people. The new managers still cannot deliver and more managers are added to manage the new managers. The end user is forced to play the "telephone" game. His set of requirements are given to one of the higher tiers of management who pass it down to the next tier(s) of management until it reaches the lowest level tier for development. The user's requirements become implemented as a system which is "exactly what he did not want."

Now is the time for Quality Assurance (QA) to come in and attempt to understand what went wrong "in the software." More time, energy and dollars are wasted. Once again management takes the "safe" path by throwing more people and "experts" on the job. Hence the failure of software whether it be for the Internet or anything else.

Of course, some systems "work "— but usually at the cost of compromised functionality, wasted dollars, lost time, and missed deadlines. For businesses, this often translates into lost opportunities and a competitive disadvantage.

The problems we've described don't arise only because of the people involved. It's more complicated than simply blaming systems developers for their lack of foresight in the way they do things. After all, most are forced to think and design in ways that are governed by the limitations of the methodologies available to them.

## "Fixing Wrong Things Up"

Over the last decade and even longer, a "quality" movement has swept industry. It's mantra: *do things right the first time*. But this movement has largely bypassed systems engineering and software development. In those environments, the norm is one of "fixing wrong things up." What do we mean by this?

The problems start with the definition of requirements. Developers rely on many different types of mismatched methods to capture aspects of even a single definition. Typically, data flow is defined using one method, state transitions another, dynamics another, data types yet another, and structures using still another method. The result is a disaster waiting to happen, because once these aspects of requirements are defined there is no way to integrate them.

Unfortunately, requirements definition is only the beginning of the problems. Integration of object to object, module to module, phase to phase, or type of application to type of application becomes even more of a challenge than solving the business problem at hand. And this is compounded by a mismatch of products used for design and development. Integration is left to the devices of myriad developers well into the development process. The resulting systems are hard to understand, and objects cannot be traced. At best, the system corresponds only a bit to the real world.

Often, developers are forced to codify requirements or design in terms of specific implementation technologies such as those that describe a database schema or are used to build a graphical user interface (GUI). More often than not, a system's key requirements and design information are buried or lost deep in a tangled web of thousands of lines of manually constructed program code — or worse yet, left trapped in the mind of the original developer and never successfully transferred to those left to maintain or evolve the system.

We would go so far as to argue that these traditional methods actually encourage the ambiguous and ultimately incorrect definition of systems, which leads to incompatible interfaces and the propagation of errors throughout the development process. Again, to be fair, the developers inherit the problem.

## Systems and Development Are Out of Control

To their credit, most systems developers do define requirements that concentrate on the application needs of users. But users change their minds. Computing environments change. What about taking these into account?

Under the traditional development scenario, flexibility for change and handling the unpredictable are simply not dealt with up front. Requirements definitions take little note of the potential for the user's needs or environment to change. Unfortunately, porting to a new environment becomes a new development; for each new architecture, operating system, database, graphics environment, language, or language configuration. Critical functionality is avoided out of fear of the unknown. Maintenance — because it is risky and the most expensive part of a system's life cycle — is left unaccounted for during the development phase. And when a system is targeted for a distributed environment, it is often defined and developed for a single processor environment and then redeveloped for a distributed environment.

From there, insufficient information about a system's run-time performance — including the information about decisions to be made between algorithms or architectures — is incorporated into a system definition. This results in design decisions that depend on analysis of outputs from exercising ad hoc implementations and associated testing scenarios. A system is defined without considering how to separate it from its target environment.

With this typical approach, developers have no way of knowing whether their design is a good one until the system is implemented and either fails or works. Any focus on reuse is late into development, during the coding phase. Compounding the problem, requirements definitions lack properties to help find, create, and make use of commonalty. Modelers are forced to use informal and manual methods in their effort to find ways to divide a system into components natural for reuse.

This makes redundancy a way of life, and provides little incentive for reuse. Errors proliferate.

Add to all this the problem of automation, or lack thereof. The typical development process is needlessly manual. Today's systems are defined with insufficient intelligence for automated tools to use them as input.

In fact, most automated tools concentrate on supporting the manual process instead of doing the real work. Developers manually convert definitions into code. A process that could have been mechanized once for reuse is performed manually over and over. And even when automation attempts to do the real work, it is often incomplete across application domains or even within a domain, resulting in incomplete code (such as shell code). The generated code is often inefficient or hard-wired to an architecture, a language, or even a version of a language. In many cases, partial automations need to be integrated with incompatible partial automations or manual processes. Manual processes are then needed to complete what was left unfinished.

## How Things Got to Where They Are

While developers may think they can overcome any problem through sheer skill, managers need to know that development tools and practices themselves have a tremendous impact on the quality of software, and the expense of creating that software. Most of today's design and programming environments contain only a fragment of what is really needed to develop a complete system; sometimes they even make things worse.

For a good example of this phenomenon, take the traditional computer-aided software engineering tools — what were earlier designated as traditional CASE and many of these more recently recast and renamed in different forms. These tools were developed to help manage the development of large software applications. Focused on supporting the traditional paradigm with an evolving sophistication of user friendliness features (such as going from text to pictures), these tools added more enhancements as hardware and software advanced. But they didn't solve the root development problems.

There are tools available that handle analysis and design and tools used for generating some code. But there are few integrated tools available that handle the spectrum of "upper," "middle" and "lower" system functionality. Even fewer can be integrated with other support tools such as simulations, debuggers, and database managers. A seamless integration of the components of these tools is an even rarer phenomenon. And any choice of keeping up with new components as they enter the marketplace is all but nonexistent

In many respects, things got worse with the move to GUIs. With the movement of systems from a host-based environment to the workstation and/or PC, we saw the introduction of a plethora of GUI development programs in the marketplace. The vast majority of these do not support the development of the entire system. Largely ignoring the core processing requirements of a system, they focus solely on the front end. This has created a new generation of systems, more sophisticated but ultimately just as fragmented and error-prone as those of the past.

Many of these earlier tools have had incorporated into themselves object-oriented features, "after the fact." While it may prove that to master object-orientation is to provide increases in productivity, there is a significant downside risk. Done inappropriately, object-oriented development can cause problems more profound than those that flow from other development techniques. Object-oriented development carries high stakes. Object-oriented environments are more complex than any other, and the business problems developers seek to solve by using object-oriented techniques are far more complex than other types of problems. While languages such as C++ and Smalltalk can create hierarchies of many neat little packages called objects, the code used to define the interaction between the objects can easily resemble spaghetti (reminiscent of the "old" days), thus jeopardizing reliable reuse.

Today's migration to distributed technologies such as client/server (where the organization's data can be spread across one or more geographically distributed servers while the end-user uses his or her GUI of choice to perform local processing) disables most of the utility of earlier and traditional methodologies.

Client server, including those that are Internet based, are characterized by their diversity. In these models, a client initiates a distributed activity and a server(s) carries out that activity. One organization may store its data on multiple databases, program in several programming languages and use more than one operating system — hence different GUIs.

Since the complexity of software development is increased a hundred-fold in this new environment, the need for a better methodology is heightened. Today's object-oriented techniques help solve some of the problem. Given the complexity of such things as client/server though, code trapped in programs is not flexible enough to meet the needs of this type of environment.

Unfortunately, there are no conventional object-oriented methodologies and associated tools to help developers develop systems that hit the better, faster, cheaper mark. As a result, most of today's systems still require more resources allocated to maintenance than to the original development effort.

It is to their credit that many of the people in the software engineering field are attempting to rectify the causes of declining productivity and quality that accompany the conventional systems development approach. But their efforts continue to fall short because the core paradigm on which their work is based treats symptoms rather than the root problem. Current software engineering approaches fail to see the software development process from the larger perspective that is so critical. They continue to travel the traditional path.

## A Radically Different Approach

We think solutions to these problems will be found only along nontraditional paths, through innovation — which means creating new methods or new environments for using new methods. In fact, the road to success may well exist within past mistakes.

The first step to a new approach is to recognize the problems that are truly at the root, and categorize those problems in terms of how they might be prevented in the future. Deriving practical solutions comes next, and the process can be repeated again and again, as we look to solve new problems with the benefit of what we know from our new solution environment.

What if that kind of thinking governed systems development? What if there were a different way to build systems, one that concentrated on preventing all the problems we discussed above rather than fixing them after they've surfaced at the most inopportune and expensive point in time? How might it work? Wouldn't it require a radical revision of the way we do software?

Radical, indeed, because it would have to provide a formal framework for doing things right the first time. And that is precisely what we have with Development Before the Fact (DBTF).

The DBTF paradigm is about beginnings. It was derived from the combination of steps taken to solve the problems of traditional systems engineering and software development. What makes DBTF radically different is that it is preventative (before) rather than curative (after).

We can make an analogy to a human system to explain the difference. John goes to the dentist because he has a cavity in his tooth, and the dentist determines that a root canal is needed. Had John gone sooner, the dentist might have been able simply to fill the cavity, which would have been curative with respect to the cavity and preventative with respect to the root canal. Had John eaten properly and brushed regularly, he might have prevented not only the root canal, but the cavity as well.

If we add in the cost of dental care, this analogy becomes particularly instructive with respect to systems development. To treat a cavity with a root canal — that is, after the fact — is expensive. To fill a cavity on time is far less expensive. And to prevent the cavity in the first place — that is, before the fact — is far less expensive again.

Another illustration comes from our own experience developing systems. A few years ago, one of the students in training in our group was in awe of one of the developers because he could "program so fast." But this developer's stuff was full of bugs and impossible to understand. In fact, we spent a lot of time redeveloping his application to make it work, because it wasn't done right in the first place.

There was another developer in the group who was not nearly as fast, but almost everything he did worked and was easy to understand. The time we spent redeveloping the "fast" developer's work exceeded the time this "slower" developer spent on his stuff.

A third developer in the group got little attention from this student. He was always deep in thought, looking for ways to abstract, looking for ways to build more generic software. He often took even longer to program than the "slower" developer above. On more than one occasion, he found out that it was not necessary at all to develop the program in question because he had already created reusables.

In the end, the third developer was really the "fastest," because his approach was more "before the fact" than the others.

The first developer — the one with whom our student was in awe — might learn to develop modules for the rest of us to reuse. But what would be missing without the benefit of the right experience, or reusable knowledge, is that deep thought the third developer put into his work.

## The DBTF Philosophy

Reliability is at the heart of Development Before the Fact. The philosophy behind DBTF is that its objects are recursively reusable and reliable. Reliable systems are defined in terms of reliable systems: only reliable systems are used as building blocks, and only reliable systems are used as mechanisms to integrate these building blocks to form a new system. The new system becomes reusable for building other systems. All layers of a system have to be reliable for a system to be reliable.

DBTF is based on a set of axioms and on the assumption of a universal set of objects. Each DBTF system is defined with properties that control its own design and development throughout its life cycle(s), where the life cycle itself is an evolving system that could be defined and developed as a target system using this approach. The emphasis on defining things with the right methods the first time prevents problems before they happen. Both function and object-oriented, DBTF is based on a unique concept of control of a system's objects (e.g., control of organization of objects, timing, priority, resources, data flow and data), lacking in other software engineering paradigms.

From the very beginning, a DBTF system inherently integrates all of its own objects (and all aspects, relationships, and viewpoints of these objects) and the combinations of functionality using these objects. A DBTF system maximizes its own reliability and flexibility to change (including reconfiguration in real time and the change of target requirements, static and dynamic architectures, and processes). A DBTF system capitalizes on its own parallelism; supports its own run-time performance analysis; and maximizes the potential for its own reuse and automation. It is defined with built-in quality, built-in productivity, and built-in control.

Our concept of automation is central to this whole discussion. When you think about it, automation itself is an inherently reusable process. If a system cannot be reused, it certainly cannot be automated. Consider for example, the process of software development used within a particular organization. Were that process (or subprocess) mechanized it could be reused again and again. That in itself implies the process could be automated.

Again, a DBTF system achieves its high level of quality through a preventative rather than curative approach. Whereas the curative approach requires continuously testing the system until the errors are eliminated, the preventative approach of DBTF means not allowing those errors to appear in the first place. Whereas accelerating a particular design and development process under the curative scenario means adding resources, be they people or processors, the preventative approach finds a more efficient way, capitalizing more on reuse or eliminating parts of the process altogether.

DBTF is centered on doing things right in the first place by using a unique yet straightforward way of definition. The starting point is concept formulation and requirements definition, done in a way that eliminates many of the common problems of traditional software development.

This method concentrates on how one can define a system model that captures — to the greatest extent practical — goals such as reuse, portability, and interoperability. Engineering judgment is useful in determining when to use which type of modeling, and how these sides of a system should play together depending on the requirements of the target system. Under this scenario, "design" and "programming" become relative terms. Higher-level "programming" becomes design to lower layers. We focus on a systems viewpoint, keeping in mind that even lower levels of a program can be defined as a set of models.

With DBTF, we model objects from the real world with a formal but friendly graphical language and then use that model to build an implementation-independent design around those objects. We describe a set of system-oriented concepts and a modeling technique that can be used to analyze problem requirements, design a solution to the problem, and then automatically implement that solution in terms of an architecture of choice (e.g., operating system, programming language, graphical user interface, communications protocol, database, or legacy code).

We see effective reuse itself as an inherently preventative concept. Reusing something that has no errors, to obtain a desired functionality, avoids the errors of a newly developed system; time and money will not be wasted in developing that new system. Reuse can be successful only if the system is worth reusing. The functionality requirements of each have to be equivalent to the system being reused. This means starting from the beginning of a life cycle, not end — as is typically the case with traditional methods. From there, a system can be reused for each new phase of development. No matter what kind, every ten reuses saves ten unnecessary developments.

Because DBTF systems can be developed with properties that control their very own design and development, the methodology results in the creation of reusable systems that promote automation. Each system definition models both its application and its lifecycle.

It has been our experience that the requirements definition for a software-based system determines to a great extent the degree to which the development of that system is a success. Not only should the requirements be defined to state the user's explicit intent, but they should also support the process of defining themselves and the systems implemented from them. These are underlying concepts of DBTF.

001, the first automation of DBTF, automates DBTF's life cycle. The same concepts and same notation can be used throughout the entire systems design and software development process. There's no need for the software engineer to translate into a new notation at each development stage, as is required by many other methodologies.

The DBTF approach includes a language, an approach, and a process (the methodology), all of which are based on a formal theory.

## Formal, but Friendly Language

Once understood, the characteristics of good design can be reused by incorporating them into a language for defining systems. The DBTF language — meta-language, really — is the key to DBTF. It can define any aspect of any system and integrate it with any other aspect, whether it is used to define highway, banking, library, missile or enterprise systems; Internet based, real-time, client server or database environments; across industries, academia or government. The same language can be used to define system requirements, specifications, design, and detailed design for functional, resource, and resource allocation architectures throughout all levels and layers of seamless definition, including hardware, software, and peopleware.

Overarching this is that all of these aspects are directly related to the real world and that the language inherently captures this.

DBTF's language is used to define system oriented objects. A SOO is a system that is both object oriented and function oriented. Its function oriented definitions are inherently integrated with its object oriented definitions. Figure 22-1 summarizes some properties of objects within DBTF systems.

Unlike traditional approaches, DBTF concentrates on delivering formal and reliable systems as its main focus. Whereas traditional tools support a user in managing the process of developing software, DBTF's automation develops the software. In fact it developed itself.

DBTF is used throughout a life cycle, starting with the formulation of concepts and interviewing the user and continuing with the definition of requirements, analysis, simulation, specification, design, system architecture design, algorithm development, implementation, configuration management, testing, maintenance, and reverse engineering. Its users include end users, managers, system engineers, software engineers, and test engineers.

System Oriented Object Properties of Development Before the Fact

*Quality (better, faster,cheaper)*
~Reliable
~Affordable

*Reliable (better)*
~In control and under control
~Based on a set of axioms
  --domain identification (intended, unintended)
  --ordering (priority and timing)
  --access rights:incoming object (or relation), outgoing
    object (or relation)
  --replacement
~Formal
  --consistent, logically complete
  --necessary and sufficient
  --common semantic base
  --unique state identification
~Error free (based on formal definition of "error")
  --always gets the right answer at the right time and in
    the right place
  --satisfies users and developers intent
~Handles the unpredictable
~Predictable

*Affordable (faster,cheaper)*
~Reusable
~Optimizes resources in operation and development
  --in minimum time and space
  --with best fit of objects to resources

*Reusable*
~Understandable, integratable and maintainable
~Flexible
~Follows standards
~Automation
~Common definitions
  --natural modularity
    -natural separation (e.g., functional architecture from
     its resource architectures);
    -dumb modules
    -an object is integrated with respect to structure,
     behavior and properties of control
  --integration in terms of structure and behavior
  --type of mechanisms
    -function maps (relate an object's function to other
     functions)
    -object type maps (relate objects to objects)
    -structures of functions and types
  --category
    -relativity
      instantiation
      polymorphism
      parent/child
      being/doing
      having/not having
    -abstraction
      encapsulation
      replacement
      relation including function
      typing including classification
      form including both structure and
      behavior (for object types and functions)
    -derivation
      deduction
      inference
      inheritance

* all underlined words point to a reusable
** Taken from Hamilton, Margaret, Software Design and Development,
Chap. 122, The Electronics Handbook,, CRC Press, IEEE Press, 1996

*Handles the unpredictable*
~throughout development and operation
~Without affecting unintended areas
~Error detect and recover from the unexpected
~Interface with, change and reconfigure in asynchronous,
  distributed, real time environment

*Flexible*
~Changeable without side effects
~Evolvable
~Durable
~Reliable
~Extensible
~Ability to break up and put together
  --one object to many: modularity, decomposition,
    instantiation
  --many objects to one: composition, applicative
    operators, integration, abstraction
~Portable
  --secure
  --diverse and changing layered developments
  --open architecture (implementation, resource allocation,
    and execution independence)
  --plug-in (or be plugged into) or reconfiguration of
    different modules
  --adaptable for different organizations, applications,
    functionality, people, products

*Automation*
~the ultimate form of reusable
~formalize, mechanize, then automate
  --it
  --its development
  --that which automates its development

*Understandable, integratable and maintainable*
~Reliable
~A measurable history
~Natural correspondence to real world
  --persistence, create and delete
  --appear and disappear
  --accessibility
  --reference
  --assumes existence of objects
  --real time and space constraints
  --representation
  --relativity, abstraction, derivation
~Provides user friendly definitions
  --recognizes that one user's friendliness is another user's
    nightmare
  --hides unnecessary detail (abstraction)
  --variable, user selected syntax
  --self teaching
  --derived from a common semantic base
  --common definition mechanisms
~Communicates with common semantics to all entities
~Defined to be simple as possible but not simpler
~Defined with integration of all of its objects (and all
  aspects of these objects)
~Traceability of behavior and structure and their changes
  (maintenance) throughout its birth, life and death
~Knows and able to reach the state of completion
  --definition
  --development of itself and that which develops it
    -analysis
    -design
    -implementation
    -instantiation
    -testing
    -maintenance

**Figure 22-1**. System Oriented Object properties of Development Before the Fact.

## Modeling a System Oriented Object (SOO)

Every SOO model is defined in terms of functional hierarchies (FMaps) to capture time characteristics and type hierarchies (TMaps) to capture space characteristics (figure 22-2). A map is both a control hierarchy and a network of interacting objects. FMaps and TMaps guide the designer in thinking through his concepts at all levels of system design. With these hierarchies, everything you need to know (no more, no less) is available. All model viewpoints can be obtained from FMaps and TMaps, including data flow, control flow, state transitions, data structure and dynamics. Maps of functions are integrated with maps of types.

# Building Blocks

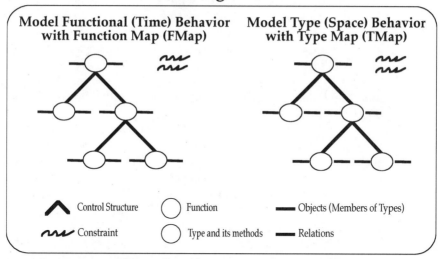

**All model viewpoints can be obtained from FMaps and TMaps.  Maps of functions are integrated with maps of types** *

**A system is defined from the very beginning to inherently *integrate* and *make understandable* its own real world definition**

\* A map is both a control hierarchy and a network of interacting objects

**Figure 22-2.** Building blocks.

On an FMap there is a function at each node, which is defined in terms of and controls its children functions. For example, the function—build the table—could be decomposed into and control its children functions—make parts and assemble. On a TMap there is a type at each node that is defined in terms of and controls its children types. For example, a type, table could be decomposed into and control its children types, legs and top.

Every type on a TMap owns a set of inherited primitive operations. Each function on an FMap has one or more objects as its input and one or more objects as its output. Each object (a member of a type from a TMap) is an instantiation of a TMap type and resides in an object hierarchy (OMap). FMaps are inherently integrated with TMaps by using these objects and their primitive operations. FMaps are used to define, integrate, and control the transformations of objects from one state to another state (for example, a table with a broken leg to a table with a fixed leg). Primitive functions corresponding to primitive operations on types defined in the TMap reside at the bottom nodes of an FMap. Primitive types reside at the bottom nodes of a TMap.

In this context, primitive does not imply low level; rather it is a term that describes the encapsulation of behavior and data behind a well defined interface, raising the level of abstraction of a system. New primitive types are defined using 001 and recursively reused in new 001 systems. Primitive types are also used to define boundaries between a 001 system and other existing systems (such as database managers or existing legacy systems).

When a system has its input object states instantiated with values plugged in for a particular performance pass, it exists in the form of an execution hierarchy (EMap).

Typically, a team of designers will begin to design a system at any level (this system could be hardware, software, peopleware or some combination) by sketching a TMap of their application. This is where they decide on the types of objects (and the relationships between these objects) that they will have in their system. Often a Road Map (RMap), which organizes all system objects (including FMaps, TMaps and other RMaps), will be sketched in parallel with the TMap.

Once a TMap has been agreed upon, the FMaps begin almost to fall into place for the designers because of the natural partitioning of functionality (or groups of functionality) provided to the designers by the TMap system. The structure of a TMap by its very nature defines several universal mechanisms that support its life cycle. For example, a TMap has an inherent way to be instantiated, to be populated using a GUI, to be stored persistently, etc. The TMap provides the structural criteria from which to evaluate the functional partitioning of the system (for example, the shape of the structural partitioning of the FMaps is balanced against the structural organization of the shape of the objects as defined by the TMap). With FMaps and TMaps a system (and its viewpoints) is divided into functionally natural components and groups of functional components which naturally work together; a system is defined from the very beginning to inherently integrate and make understandable its own real world definition.

All FMaps and TMaps are ultimately defined in terms of three primitive control structures: a parent controls its children to have a dependent relationship, an independent relationship, or a decision making relationship. We say "ultimately" because, as we'll see below, more abstract structures can be defined in terms of the primitive ones. A formal set of rules is associated with each primitive structure. If these rules are followed, interface errors — which account for up to 90% of all system errors — are "removed" before the fact (that is, during the definition phase) by preventing them in the first place. In traditional development these errors would not even be discovered until testing. Using the primitive structures and their derivatives supports a system to be defined from the very beginning to inherently maximize its own elimination of errors.

The TMap provides universal primitive operations of type Any, which are used for controlling objects and their object states which are inherited by all types. They create, destroy, copy, reference, move, access a value, detect and recover from errors and access the type of an object. They provide an easy way to manipulate and think about different types of objects.

With the universal primitive operations, building systems can be accomplished in a more uniform manner. TMap and OMap are also available as types to facilitate the ability of a system to understand itself better and manipulate all objects the same way when it is beneficial to do so.

TMap properties ensure the proper use of objects in an FMap. A TMap has a corresponding set of control properties for controlling spatial relationships between objects.

Any system can be defined completely using only the primitive structures, but less primitive structures can be derived from the primitive ones and accelerate the process of defining and understanding a system. Non-primitive structures can be defined for both FMaps and TMaps. They can be created for asynchronous, synchronous, and interrupt scenarios used in real-time, distributed systems such as those found in Internet applications. Similarly, retrieval and query structures can be defined for database management systems within a client server environment. Non-primitive structures can also be created for more vertical market driven reusables, for example for a cash management or accident reporting system.

## Development Process

The first step in Building a Before the Fact system is to define a model with its SOO language called 001 AXES (figure 22-3). This process could be in any phase of the lifecycle, including problem analysis, operational scenarios, and design. Once defined, the model is automatically analyzed by the 001 Analyzer to ensure that it was defined properly. This includes static analysis for preventative properties and dynamic analysis for user intent properties. Next, the generic source code generator (the RAT which stands for resource allocation tool) automatically generates a fully production-ready and fully integrated

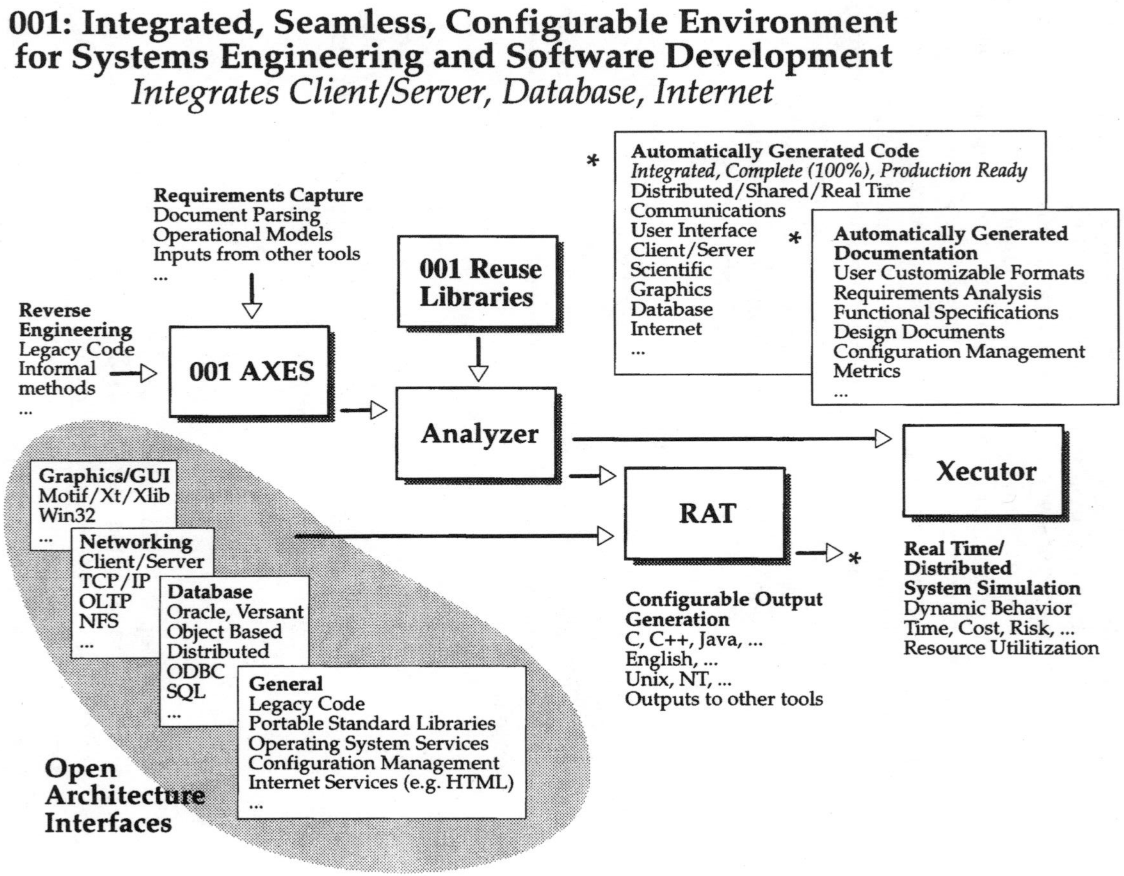

# 001: Integrated, Seamless, Configurable Environment for Systems Engineering and Software Development

*Integrates Client/Server, Database, Internet*

**Reverse Engineering**
Legacy Code
Informal methods
...

**Requirements Capture**
Document Parsing
Operational Models
Inputs from other tools
...

**001 AXES**

**001 Reuse Libraries**

**Analyzer**

**RAT**

**Xecutor**

*

**Automatically Generated Code**
*Integrated, Complete (100%), Production Ready*
*Distributed/Shared/Real Time*
Communications
User Interface
Client/Server
Scientific
Graphics
Database
Internet
...

*

**Automatically Generated Documentation**
User Customizable Formats
Requirements Analysis
Functional Specifications
Design Documents
Configuration Management
Metrics
...

**Configurable Output Generation**
C, C++, Java, ...
English, ...
Unix, NT, ...
Outputs to other tools

*

**Real Time/ Distributed System Simulation**
Dynamic Behavior
Time, Cost, Risk, ...
Resource Utilitization

**Graphics/GUI**
Motif/Xt/Xlib
Win32
...

**Networking**
Client/Server
TCP/IP
OLTP
NFS
...

**Database**
Oracle, Versant
Object Based
Distributed
ODBC
SQL
...

**General**
Legacy Code
Portable Standard Libraries
Operating System Services
Configuration Management
Internet Services (e.g. HTML)
...

**Open Architecture Interfaces**

**Figure 22-3.** 001: integrated, seamless, configurable environment for systems engineering and software development.

software implementation for any kind of application, consistent with the model, for a selected target environment in the language and architecture of choice. If the selected environment has already been configured, the generator selects that environment directly; otherwise, the generator is first configured for a new language and architecture.

It then becomes possible to execute the resulting system. If it is software, the system can undergo testing for further user intent errors. It becomes operational after testing. Changes are made to the requirements definition, not to the code. Target architecture changes are made to the configuration of the generator environment, not to the code. If the real system is hardware or peopleware, the software system serves as a simulation upon which the real system can be based. Once a system has been developed, the system and the process used to develop it are analyzed with tools such as simulation together with metrics to understand how to improve the next round of system development.

The design and development environment for DBTF along with its automation, 001, is integrated and seamless. Inherently reusable, 001's systems (SOOs) can be object oriented, function oriented or an integration of both. Systems are defined to handle changes both during development and operation. All interface errors are automatically found, starting with the definition of a system. Objects are under control and traceable.

A DBTF definition has information in it for the 001 simulator (the Xecutor) to understand its behavior and dynamically analyze it for things such as risk, timing and cost; and a higher layer operating system to execute it. That same definition if it is for software can be used as input to 001's automatic code generator. The result is a rapid prototype for a system designer or a production ready system for a software developer. That which is simulated can be integrated to that which is automatically generated using dynamically bound objects to a very fine or loosely grained level.

A definition can have additional information about it and its relationships provided by the user. This information, together with its formal definition, is used for gathering metrics (such as who is responsible for the object in question, constraints, TBD's, requirements from the user, etc.) about the system and its development, providing a mechanism to trace from requirements to code and back again, ensuring that the implemented system meets the requirements. The 001 generator can use this information to generate metrics and reports on the progress or state of the development of the current target system and its relation to the original requirements.

Complete (100%), integrated, fully production ready code for any kind of system is automatically generated by 001 whether it be for GUI, database, communications, real time, distributed (including client server, Internet and Intranet based), multi-user or mathematical algorithms. There is no manual work to be done to finish the coding task.

The user configurable generator of 001 has been configured for several languages including C, Ada, FORTRAN, COBOL and English. It could as well be configured for Java or HTML or some language we have still not yet heard of.

This generator can be used to provide output information that can be used as input by other tools or as output for testing (such as showing all of the decision points in the system). This feature can also be used as another means of rapid prototyping for systems design studies. Once the code is automatically generated, it is automatically compiled and linked and executed.

001 supports an open architecture in that it allows a user to put wrappers around the capabilities provided by databases (e.g., Oracle, Versant), operating systems (e.g., UNIX, NT), user interface (e.g., Motif, Windows), communication protocols (e.g., TCP/IP, SNMP, SNA) and Web packages such as Front Page and legacy code of choice (all of which are user configurable). There is no need to lose time to market and spend unnecessary money to port to a new environment. A choice of code generation can be made using a single solution specification (also user configurable). Once the generator is configured for a new environment, a system can be automatically regenerated to reside on that environment.

As we mentioned earlier, with traditional environments, after the shell code or partial code has been generated, it is necessary for programmers to add more code manually; as more code is written, it becomes less possible to regenerate the shell or partial code from changes in the requirements, because the manual code would be destroyed or made obsolete. The maintenance process becomes increasingly manual as the software evolves. This wastes needless time and money. With 001, the user doesn't ever need to change the code, only the specification, and then regenerates (automatically) only that part of the system that has changed. Once again the system is automatically compiled, linked and executed without manual intervention.

001's GUI environment is tightly integrated with the development of an application. GUI (e.g., Motif) support is provided while preserving traceability, interface integrity and control. Its automatic data driven interface generator supports rapid program evolution. Run time constraint tests that validate correct object manipulation and construction as well as unit test harnesses for testing each object and its relationships are automatically generated. An automatic user interface is provided with an object editor for populating and manipulating complex objects, including storage and retrieval for persistent objects. This provides the ability to test the target system at any input/output interface with predefined object test data sets.

With DBTF, all aspects of system design and development are integrated with one systems language and its associated automation. Reuse naturally takes place throughout the life cycle. Objects, no matter how complex, can be reused and integrated. Environment configurations for different kinds of architectures can be reused. A newly developed system can be safely reused to increase even further the productivity of the systems developed with it.

### No Longer Needed

The shift to a new paradigm, or generation of development, occurs once a developer realizes the multitude of processes, methods and tools that are no longer needed. With one formal semantic language to define and integrate all aspects of a system, diverse modeling languages (and methodologies for using them), each of which defines only part of a system, are no longer necessary. No longer is there a need to reconcile multiple techniques with semantics that interfere with each other. Why, for example, learn C, followed by a replacement of C with a more modern C++ followed by a replacement of C++ with Java? Each is a major step which requires significant training and reverse engineering. One could instead use — and continue to use — a single definition language and automatically generate the latest implementation environment.

Techniques and tools for transitioning from one phase of the life cycle to another become obsolete. Techniques for maintaining source code as a separate process are no longer needed, since the source is automatically generated from the system specification. Verification too becomes obsolete. Techniques for managing paper documents give way to entering requirements and their changes directly into the requirements specification database. Testing procedures and tools for finding most errors are no longer needed because those errors no longer exist. Tools developed to support programming as a manual process are no longer needed.

Not only is an increase in productivity significant with the use of 001 but as more reuse is employed, productivity continues to increase. Measuring productivity becomes a process of relativity, relative to the last system that was developed. Older methods for measuring productivity are no longer applicable.

No longer needed are tools that focus on the measurement of complexity. Complexity does not increase with the size of the system since all objects are under control, integrated and traceable. Unlike with traditional systems, it has been shown with 001 developed systems that productivity is even higher with larger systems including those that have been around for a while. This is thought to be the case since the larger the system and the longer the time it has been around, the more reusables that are used.

And, what happens to the QA function? Perhaps QA's main function is to ensure the proper use of a right technology and its automation.

Most important, it is no longer necessary to do something over and over again when there is a way to do it right the first time.

### 001 Applications Developed for the Internet:
### Three Case Studies

In the following three chapters are case studies of three applications (each of which integrates the Internet, client server and data base) developed using 001. These systems all use 001's client server reusables, developed in terms of a unified systems model based on the DBTF Escher and VSphere foundations [11]. Each application was defined in terms of SOOs. Each was automatically generated and automatically integrated by 001.

## Conclusion

Whether or not software is Internet and/or database related, it fails in large part because we do not take advantage of what we learn from history. A substantial part of the problem stems from the manner in which organizations are building their automated systems.

Reuse clearly will help, but it needs to be an intelligent and formal process of reuse, under control. Such is the case with SOOs. Reuse with SOOs recursively raises objects to a new and higher level, inherently integrating the database side of a system with all of its other parts. This culminates in the ultimate reuse which is automation itself. With this approach the answer is in the results; automated development is where the systems of tomorrow will inherit the best of the systems of today.

Software is so ingrained in our society that its success or failure will dramatically influence both the operation and the success of the business. For that reason, today's decisions about systems engineering and software development techniques and tools will have far-reaching effects.

While hardware capabilities have increased dramatically, organizations are still mired in the same old methodologies that saw the rise of the behemoth mainframes. This is why the "new" technologies they tried did not deliver as promised — they were not really new since they were still based on the old paradigm. Old methodologies simply are not upwards compatible with building the new systems of today. Once organizations begin to understand what can be done with a technology such as DBTF, comments like "we just don't have time" or "we don't have the budget" will change to comments like "we don't have the time not to" or "we don't have the budget not to."

The right combination of the methodology and the technology that executes it  forms the foundation of better, faster, cheaper software. Collective experience strongly confirms that quality and productivity increase with the increased use of DBTF's properties and its automation. Its preventative philosophy, to solve a given problem as early as possible, means finding a problem statically is better than finding it dynamically. Preventing it by the way a system is defined is even better. Better, faster, cheaper, yet, is not having to define (and build) it at all.

Within the commercial enterprise users demand much more functionality and flexibility, which includes durabilty, in their systems than before. Models are distributed, including  the client server model (two-tier), and the Internet and Intranet models (n-tier) which are the most popular forms of distribution in use today. And given the nature of many of the problems to be solved, their systems must also be error-free as well. These environments and object oriented projects begin to sound like the earlier days of real time, distributed environments where complexity gave rise to new kinds of problems, including those having to do with interface and integration issues.

The three systems described as case studies in the following chapters were developed with DBTF and 001. All of these systems are examples of Internet based and data base related systems that demand the type of functionality and flexibility typical of this environment. Common themes were shared among these systems as well as with the other systems developed with the DBTF paradigm. For example, not only did these systems work, but a significant amount of time and money was saved when comparing for each system its DBTF development experience with what would have been a traditional development experience. This is in large part due to the fact that many of the processes, methods and tools considered necessary within the traditional life style are no longer necessary with DBTF.

Not only is this a savings in time and money, but it also means that there is no longer a dependency on those processes, methods and tools that are no longer needed. More importantly there is no longer a dependency on the armies of people that are needed to support obsolescence. And isn't freedom the most valuable commodity of them all?

## Author Bio

Margaret Hamilton (mhh@htius.com) is the founder and CEO of Hamilton Technologies, Inc. (HTI), based in Cambridge, MA (17 Inman Street, Cambridge, MA 02139, 617-492-0058), a pioneer in the systems engineering and software development industry. Hamilton's mission has been to bring to market a completely integrated and robust tool suite that is based on the unique systems theory paradigm, which she created, called Development Before the Fact (DBTF). In bringing her product to market, her company leveraged the power of reusability and the reliability of seamless integration to provide a tool that sharply decreases errors while simultaneously increasing productivity. The result is an ultrareliable system at a fraction of the cost of conventional systems. Hamilton's goal was to embed this formal and completely systems oriented object (SOO) framework into a highly efficient, high performance, completely graphical, portable workbench of "smart" tools which the systems engineer and software developer could use throughout the entire design and development life cycle. Today this ideal has been surpassed with 001.

Earlier in her career, as the leader of the Software Engineering Division at MIT's Charles Stark Draper Laboratory, Hamilton was the director of the Apollo on-board flight software project and created Higher Order Software (HOS), a formal systems design theory.

After this, Hamilton founded and was CEO of Higher Order Software where she was responsible for the development of the first comprehensive CASE tool in the industry. This tool, called USE.IT, was based on her formal design theory, HOS.

## References

1) R. Shaller Hornstein, "A Cross-Cutting Agenda for Achieving a Faster, Better, Cheaper Space Operations Infrastructure," AIAA Workshop on Reducing the Costs of Space Operations, Arlington, VA, 1995.

2) M. Hamilton, "Zero-Defect Software: The Elusive Goal," IEEE Spectrum, Vol. 23, No. 3, pp. 48–53, March 1986.

3) M. Hamilton and R. Hackler, "001: A Rapid Development Approach for Rapid Prototyping Based on a System that Supports its Own Life Cycle," IEEE Proceedings, First International Workshop on Rapid System Prototyping, Research Triangle Park, NC, June 4, 1990.

4) Hamilton, M., "Inside Development Before the Fact," Electronic Design, April 4, 1994, ES.

5) Hamilton, M., " Development Before the Fact in Action", Electronic Design, June 13, 1994, ES.

6) The 001 Tool Suite Reference Manual, Version 3. Cambridge, MA: Hamilton Technologies, Inc., January 1993.

7) Krut, Jr., B. "Integrating 001 Tool Support in the Feature-Oriented Domain Analysis Methodology" (CMU/SEI-93-TR-11, ESC-TR-93-188), Pittsburgh, PA: Software Engineering Institute, Carnegie-Mellon University, 1993.

8) McCauley, B. "Software Development Tools in the 1990s," AIS Security Technology for Space Operations Conference, July 1993, Houston, Texas.

9) Software Engineering Tools Experiment-Final Report, Vol. 1, Experiment Summary, Table 1, Page 9, Department of Defense, Strategic Defense Initiative, Washington, D. C., 20301-7100.

10) Ouyang, M., Golay, M.W., "An Integrated Formal Approach for Developing High Quality Software of Safety-Critical Systems", Massachusetts Institute of Technology, Cambridge, MA, Report No. MIT-ANP-TR-035.

11) Hamilton Technologies, Inc. (HTI), "Final Report: AIOS Xecutor Demonstration", Prepared for Los Alamos National Laboratory, Los Alamos, NM, Order No. 9-XG1-K9937-1, November 1991.

[Trademarks are for 001, 001 Tool Suite, Function Map, Type Map, Object Map, Execution Map, Road Map, FMap, TMap, Escher, EMap, RMap, VSphere, RAT, Xecutor, OMap Editor, 001 Analyzer, SOO, System Oriented Object, Resource Allocation Tool, AntiRAT, Object Editor, Primitive Control Structures, Development Before the Fact, DBTF, RT(x), 001 AXES, AIOS, Agent 001DB are all trademarks of Hamilton Technologies, Inc.]

# 23

# Accident Record System for State Highway Department Traffic Operations

Margaret Hamilton
Ron Hackler

## Introduction

The Accident Record System (ARS) was developed for State Highway Departments (SHD) within the United States. It supports Traffic Operations to comply with the Intermodal Surface Transportation Efficiency Act (ISTEA) of the Federal Highway Association (FWHA) federal mandates, to provide standard accident record systems in all states across the U.S. The ARS is designed so that it can be tailored for each individual state's particular needs. 001 was used to develop and tailor this Internet based product for versions that are currently operational within SHD Traffic Operations.

ARS was developed to address the many problems existing within state accident record systems: the process of an accident record system has several inter-operational systems that are not interfaced to work together cooperatively; approximately one half of the annual accidents reported statewide are not within a government agency's control since they are from operators providing incomplete information; most notably, poor location information hinders SHD's ability to analyze accident volumes and recommend mitigation action; many local jurisdictions have more current, computerized accident information than state agencies, leaving the SHD in a vulnerable, reactive stance to local construction requests; and systems do not include a specific interface to traffic records volume data directly, leaving the accident rate computation (accidents/traffic) as an unintegrated, manual function.

The overall result is that statewide traffic records users' needs are not met, and the Highway Safety Improvement Program is not based on accident/crash data as is federally mandated, threatening acquisition of Federal highway funds by the individual states.

The ARS can be understood from within a road system, a complex organization of interacting systems. These include systems for a network of roads, management and planning, accident report collection, accident analysis and reporting, traffic monitoring systems and road maintenance. The primary focus of the ARS is to support the Traffic Operations concentrating on traffic safety engineering requirements.

The objectives of Road Safety Engineering are to identify hazardous road locations, diagnose crash problems, select appropriate countermeasures, rank design plans in terms of treatment and preparation, program and implement countermeasures and evaluate countermeasures. The ARS provides access to accident reports, the road network topology, physical road characteristics, and traffic monitoring information. In addition it supports analysis of traffic engineering problems and generation of analysis reports.

ARS supports an evolutionary approach to accident investigation and road

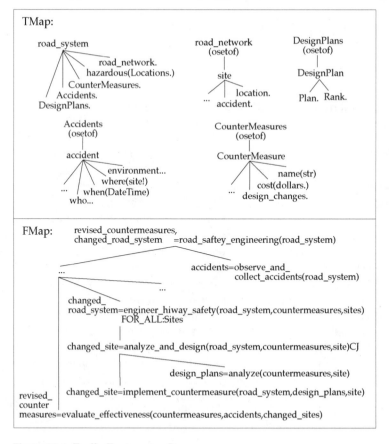

**Figure 23-1**. Traffic Engineering Process.

system analysis as part of the road safety engineering process. It provides for the exploration of accident data to hone in on road system sites which "have a demonstrated priority for treatment." Based on 001's graphical and formal modeling language, Function Map (FMap) and Type Map (TMap) models were used to provide a formal statement of the road safety engineering process as described in "Safer Roads" by K. W. Ogden.

The TMap defines the relationships established between an accident and the other objects which characterize an accident and which can be used for future analysis by ARS users. A road_system object (in the TMap of figure 23-1) contains a road_network object and a set of CounterMeasures. The FMap is used to describe the functionality of what is being done by the objects and how they are interacting with each other. For example, the countermeasures object is interacting with the road_system object when they are input to the function "engineer_hiway_safety."

This ARS requirements model drives the decisions made in the ARS architecture. 001 can be used to evaluate system requirements as well as provide formal specifications that can be used to automatically develop the target system to be developed (in this case the ARS itself).

## Road Safety Engineering Process

The central object in the road safety engineering process is an accident. When an accident happens, it is recorded in an accident record. It is necessary that the accident data used for road safety engineering purposes be as accurate, consistent and complete as possible to ensure effective future traffic engineering analysis. Standard information such as time (when), location (where), contributing factors (why and how) and results of an accident (what) are captured about the accident from several key perspectives so that correct accident analysis can be performed.

A traffic engineer is provided with the accident site (e.g., location and cause information), road network information, and road characteristics (e.g., physical road features, traffic monitoring data). This can then be used to determine if changes need to be made in the road and/or road network within the road system. Traffic engineering analysis implies the ability to examine the road system objects at different levels of detail. This provides a basic framework within which accidents can be located: at an intersection, or on a section of a road (between an intersection and another intersection or a road endpoint, see figure 23-2). From a traffic engineering point of view, this provides information that can be used to answer basic questions about where an accident occurred. The location of an accident is at an intersection or on a road section.

Given this abstract view of the road network, road characteristics need to be accessible in order to perform an analysis of an accident. The road system topology evolves over time. As the road system changes, as new roads are added to the road system or older roads are being repaired, time must be recorded. A segment needs to have a time associated with it because an analysis may be

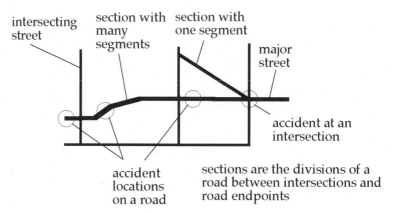

**Figure 23-2.** Traffic engineering view of road network.

performed on accidents that happened at different times during the evolution of the road system. In the road system, an inventory of each segment is maintained to keep track of the changes to a piece of road.

The road maintenance and monitoring sub-systems store physical road characteristics as well as road monitoring information in the road inventory and associate it with a segment. For example, the average daily traffic is a traffic monitoring attribute that is associated with a segment.

The official street name of a road may change. A history of official street name changes are maintained as a list of aliases so that accident reports that use any of the names may be correctly correlated with the official name. In addition, two physically different streets may have the same name. Because of these facts, a street name is not used to uniquely identify the road within the road system. A road is uniquely identified within the road system by a road inventory record that corresponds to the real physical road object.

The accident record has data that indicates the location of the accident site. This data captures the location with numerous methods of location including major and intersecting street names, landmarks and linear referencing methods (e.g., mile markers, street addresses). Any of this information may be partial, missing, or incorrect. The ARS supports the resolution of imprecise location data provided by the accident recording function. There are two basic methods that can be used to identify an accident site given the type of location information in the accident records: street name pattern matching methods or geographic analysis using coordinate systems, including linear referencing. One challenge for the ARS was to raise the percentage of locatable accidents based on accident record data, given these basic methods location resolution.

A global positioning system (GPS) can be used to resolve the accurate accident location issue, given that the accident observer/recorder has a GPS device. Even when GPS becomes the norm there is still the need to analyze imprecise information for all of the other characteristics that are not being captured accurately. The human observer will always relay information in an imprecise way and there will always be a need to resolve information based on the mix of the recording instruments of the observer/recorder of the accident as a road event.

Given an accurate road location, a traffic engineer can then obtain the road characteristics to perform accident/traffic analysis. In order to perform this analysis both physical road assets and geographical information come into play. In order to support the traffic engineer in these two areas, the ARS locates all accidents within some geographical area and is able to gather road characteristics from the road inventory that correspond to the identified set of accidents.

Accident analysis is the key process which is used to obtain information about accidents and their relationships to the road system and other systems (directly or indirectly related). For example, driving a car has a direct relation to the road system, but consumption of alcoholic beverages are indirectly related to the road system. Safety analysis implies the need to qualify the road characteristics based on the type of analysis being performed. An analysis might need to examine the rate of traffic at all intersections of a particular road for a city. For example, "examine the rate of traffic at all intersections of Alameda Ave. in Denver."

For safety engineering to occur at all, it is mandatory to maintain a historical record of countermeasures applied to hazardous accident sites as road design changes. Given this history, then countermeasures can be evaluated in order to understand the impact of the countermeasure in terms of a road system design strategy. A road safety countermeasure might be to reduce vehicle speeds on a road by stationing a police car with a radar gun at peak traffic volume times on the most highly traveled roads with the most speeding accidents. In order to determine where to place the police cars, the ARS needs to maximize the multiple objectives of speed caused accidents against traffic rates and minimize the number of police cars.

## The ARS System

The functional architecture of the ARS (e.g., what is to be done) is defined with FMaps and TMaps independent of how it is implemented (e.g., which database or what machines are used). It takes into account those systems with which it must inter-operate by identifying their interfaces and functionality.

These interfaces as well as its own functionality in response to these interfaces help to define the constraints to be placed on a design. For example, the ARS resides within the safety engineering system and thus must respond to inaccurate accident location information as a result of the way accident records have been documented.

Therefore, one of the major functions of the ARS is to resolve the inaccurate locations to be as accurate as possible. This accident location then allows the ARS to correlate the rest of the accident information (e.g., weather) with road characteristics maintained in the road inventory database (e.g., type of pavement) to support road safety engineering analysis.

Also, the ARS supports requests for accident analysis by external agencies involved in the road system. The services provided to these agencies range from legal services, to road construction engineering support, to the physical maintenance of the road system itself.

The ARS system architecture is divided into two levels of inter/intra-systems. An inter-system is one in which two systems participate. An intra-system is one in which a set of components or individuals within a group equally and locally participate. The first inter/intra-system boundary is between state external systems and the SHD as a system. For example, the FHWA or another state agency having interfaces with the SHD would be considered to be part of the inter-system boundary. The next level of detail in the SHD intra-system is used to distinguish the interface boundaries between the ARS intra-system participants (e.g., Traffic Operations, Information Technologies, IT, and Transportation Planning Development, TP&D).

The ARS system functional architecture (operational) model includes the following functional areas:

> • the import of accident record data from a Registry of Motor Vehicles (RMV) or from an existing legacy system
> • accident site location resolution using data cleaning strategies to validate accident record information (e.g., text cleanup of street names based on valid street names)
> • update of the ARS database as new accident records are imported (connecting accident records to other databases, e.g., TP&D's road network information)
> • access to information in the ARS database as well as related information that may be accessible via other databases
> • user interface query and reporting facilities on the ARS database
> • ARS maintenance and building of tailored query/report templates

Input to the ARS can come from an RMV, a legacy system, or interactively from an authorized ARS user. The accident information is validated and cleaned if necessary and possible. Accident location resolution is focused on correct data, since any analysis is valid only if the data is accurate. The ARS database is then updated with this accident information and any interconnections to other database information is updated. Once authorized by Traffic Operations, the official external view of the ARS data is available by the connected intra- and inter-systems. At this time, ARS users have access to validated accident information to perform accident analysis using the set of pre-defined query/reports and an all purpose ad-hoc query/report. On an ongoing basis and as needed, the

ARS system administrator configures new query/report templates and imports new accident record information into the system.

Each of the above functional areas indicated will be associated with an ARS system component that has the capability to support one or more of these areas.

## Design for Change/Evolution/Maintenance

The key design objectives of the ARS are that it is easy to maintain, incorporates the use of cross-platform standards for a high degree of platform independence, provides an open architecture to allow integration of future implementation technologies, improves on the imported data's value (e.g., the resolution of accident locations for imported accident records), allows for large

| MAINTENANCE AREA | MAINTAINABILITY GOAL |
| --- | --- |
| report output formatting options (both detail and summary reporting requirements). | Provide the ability to create or change report output formats and to target alternative output rendering choices (allowing for example the ability to generte straight text vs. HTML vs. Postscript vs. RTF) with no programming changes to ARS. |
| data summarization options. | Give the user the ability to summarize any valid combination of accident data to any number of levels with a single pass through the accident data. Provide parallel processing options to allow the summary process to scale easily as additional CPUs are available. |
| allow additional data from outside sources to be integrated into ARS so that it can be included in ARS reports. | Allow data stored in an external database (e.g., Oracle) to be included in ARS reports at both a summary and detailed level. |
| ability to move ARS reporting data to other application environments. | Provide the ability to export ARS report data to alternative application environments (such as spreadsheets, word processors, statistical analysis packages, etc.) |
| definition of query criteria screens. | Be able to define input query screens based on the requirements of a newly defined ARS report. |
| input and validation of query data. | Input choices are defined by the data available within ARS and external tool and database linkages. Validation of this data is defined by the TMap model of the ARS and its associated data. This will be a very stable approach provided the TMap always models a real world view of the ARS data. The objective is to allow query of data to be dynamically defined based on the ARS TMap model and to be validated to prevent invalid queries from being processed. |
| selection and display of detail data. | Provide basic search and data display/entry capability for detailed accident data which is dynamic based on the ARS TMap. |

**Figure 23-3.** Maintainability goals.

volumes of accident record data and is reliable.

The effort needed to maintain any system is measured by the ease, speed and level of difficulty needed to respond to changes in ways of doing business and their supporting technologies. While it is difficult to forecast future changes that can impact a system, it is necessary to try to anticipate the affected areas during the design phases of a system development. Maintainability is clearly one of the areas a design must consider (see figure 23-3).

Maintainability is a continuum between maintenance requiring design modifications at the FMap/TMap level and maintenance requiring configuration of a component by a user of the system. The goal was to design and implement the ARS so that it is positioned close to the user maintenance end of this continuum.

In addition to maintainability, choices of targeted implementation technologies are based on other design constraints such as legacy systems, level of user acceptance, and political objectives.

These design objectives were met by using the strengths of the 001 Tool Suite as a development environment and it's ability to adjust to a supporting cast of current business technologies (e.g., Internet, client/server) as an integrator of technology foundations upon which to develop the ARS system.

## The Spiral Development Process with FMaps and TMaps

Unlike a traditional waterfall development approach which saves the implementation (build) functions to the end of the project, we used a spiral development technique. This means that analysis, design, build and testing tasks take place in parallel throughout the ARS development life cycle. Each spiral in development results in an operational system with increasing functionality as the system evolves.

The requirements analysis, specification and design models of the ARS have been defined and refined throughout several iterations using the same modeling language. These evolving models will continue to serve as the master from which satisfaction of objectives are gauged. The models of the ARS are defined with evolving FMaps and TMaps. The prototype ARS FMaps and TMaps served as a starting point.

FMap and TMap models are automatically analyzed by 001's analyzer to check for errors, including ambiguities, inconsistencies, and redundancies. Evolving, working, executable developer versions/releases of the ARS were automatically generated from the FMaps and TMaps by 001 during the analysis and design phase.

Having completed an evolution of the FMaps and TMaps means that an important milestone has been reached. Since 001 can automatically generate complete running code from FMaps and TMaps, it means that the user can be shown a running system at an early stage of spiral development. The FMaps and TMaps created during analysis and design are used to automatically create what is required in the build phase of development.

This process is possible because 001 can automatically generate and regenerate a complete system (or selectively generate only those portions of the system that are impacted by a change), including Graphical User Interface (GUI), database, communications and mathematical algorithms, as the system continues to evolve.

All of the automatically generated code is production ready, including the code for GUI, database (e.g., Oracle) and the mathematical algorithms. For testing, 001 automatically generates runtime constraint test cases to validate correct object construction and unit test harnesses for any user function, providing an automatic user interface for the testing data sets with an object editor for any of the objects in the systems to be tested. All of the changes to the system (both for this project and for the future) will be made to the specification instead of the code. That part of the system which is changed can then be regenerated automatically by 001. All parts of the system that are affected by that change are traceable with the 001 tool suite. What this means is that maintenance of the system becomes a very straightforward, reliable and efficient process both for the ARS project and for SHD systems in the future as they evolve. This will reduce the cost of maintenance significantly for the ARS once the basic components are in place.

In order to support an SHD, interfaces consistent with 001's open architecture approach were reused from 001's reuse library. More sophisticated types or interfaces to pre-existing services can be constructed using 001 primitive types. Each primitive data type has a set of primitive operations. A primitive operation (with some number of inputs and some number of outputs) behaves like an object oriented method or action that can be performed on an object of its type. Each primitive type has an associated implementation that contains the interfaces relevant to each of the primitive operations of the primitive type. The implementation can be C code that either calls an API or calls code that was generated by 001 from an FMap. Examples of primitive types that were reused are

- 001's basic core types
- Database types such as SQL and Oracle Call Interface (OCI) types
- Geographic Information System (GIS) types
- Client/Server types for distributed processing
- Internet functionality with types to support Common Gateway Interface (CGI) processing
- GUI types

The above set of data types allows the 001 Tool Suite to have access to the technologies needed to support the smooth evolution and extension of the ARS as needed. With the use of HTI's 001 along with HTI's spiral development process, the ARS system is inherently flexible to changing requirements, ensuring that changes in the future are straightforward.

Because 001 is used for development, testing is minimized. The reasons for this are many. Correct use of the 001 language eliminates approximately 75% of the errors right up front that would have been still around after implementation with a traditional approach. The 001 analyzer ensures that the language is used correctly and therefore eliminates all interface errors. The 001 code generator automatically generates a set of runtime constraint test cases with the code. Then, when the code is executed these tests find an additional set of errors automatically. Test harnesses for functions are also automatically generated by 001 for unit testing of the different objects in the system. Other tests are developed as systems, themselves, using 001 in the same way as 001 is used for developing the ARS system.

Testing is performed by the developer and the end user. Whereas the focus of testing for the developer is "inside out" testing, the focus of testing for the end user is "outside in" testing. For testing, the end user supplies test data, the developer enters the test data and tests the system, and the end user reviews the results for technical content.

The ARS was developed with 001 on Unix workstations and automatically generated for Unix and/or the PC depending on the requirements of the particular SHD environment.

## System Architecture

A system architecture is the integration of a functional architecture (what is to be done) that has been allocated to a resource architecture (how it is to be done) using an allocation architecture. The allocation architecture is the result of a design process during development which makes a set of resource component implementation choices based on the options of both the developer and those of the target system (here, the ARS) deployment environment of the user.

A resource component is considered to be a composite of the software and hardware needed to support a particular capability. A component will typically raise the level and simplify the domain technology upon which it is layered. For example, the 001 client/server reusables are layered onto TCP/IP which is provided as a standard for inter-networking of systems.

The ARS system resource architecture is designed to maximize flexibility and scalability and to minimize maintenance costs through an open and extendible architecture in order to easily adapt to the changing needs of the ARS as it evolves.

The design goals and constraints provide the criteria for the selection of appropriate technologies. For example, flexibility and scalability are goals that can be used as selection criteria to decide upon the use of an n-tiered parallel and distributed client/server processing implementation architecture as opposed to using a simplified two-tier architecture.

Each component was designed with alternative implementation choices (and their relationship to future trends) in the industry in mind, such as Internet

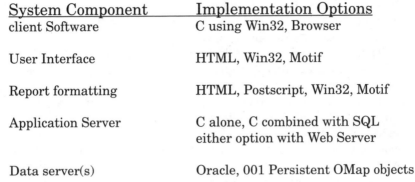

| System Component | Implementation Options |
| --- | --- |
| client Software | C using Win32, Browser |
| User Interface | HTML, Win32, Motif |
| Report formatting | HTML, Postscript, Win32, Motif |
| Application Server | C alone, C combined with SQL either option with Web Server |
| Data server(s) | Oracle, 001 Persistent OMap objects |

**Figure 23-4.** Component implementation options.

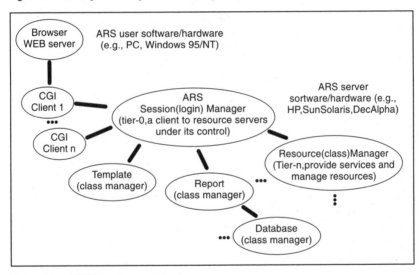

**Figure 23-5.** ARS Resource architecture.

browsers and n-tier client/server architectures (see figure 23-4 for some of the allocation choices considered).

Given a set of resource implementation options, 001 is used as the integrator by providing the technology to interface to those technologies.

ARS configurations use the implementation options of Oracle/001 persistent objects, Hypertext Markup Language (HTML), C with SQL and client HTML browsers. The ARS resource architecture (see figure 23-5) was chosen because of a key ARS requirement for a relatively easily supported and open environment. All of the components of this architecture have been designed to work with 001 using the open standards: HTML, POSIX, CGI, SQL, Classic C language. Using these standards provides a high degree of flexibility for implementing ARS under a number of different runtime environments.

All parts of the ARS system between the CGI interface boundary and the

OCI interface were developed using 001 FMaps and TMaps and generated as high performance "C" code to run on the Unix host. The standard "C" and POSIX compliant runtime libraries are used to provide Unix host platform independence.

The ARS user interface allows users to use PC based machines for their interface while using ARS services that are provided on Unix hosts. 001's integration to the Internet technology was used to accomplish this. User presentation and interaction is provided by a browser using HTML and a WEB/CGI server (both of which are accessed through 001 primitive types) to provide network connectivity to the Unix host with C programming capability to access ARS services (via 001's code generation capability). Database technologies were used to provide storage and backup facilities (via 001's OCI primitive type reusables) and available SHD GIS support tool capabilities were used to provide support for the processing and display of geographic information. The ARS Session Manager is used to coordinate and validate ARS user connections. The Template Manager defines the data display and user interaction characteristics.

## User Interface

The ARS uses templates to drive the user interface screen presentation engine. This architecture allows report templates to be designed and built which are independent of the presentation engine, e.g., HTML (browsers or Postscript based printers). These templates provide ARS users with the ability to flexibly create and modify report presentation formats as business needs dictate without additional ARS FMap and TMap modifications.

For Internet technology, this consists of HTML (to define the presentation) with embedded 001 query statements (to define the content). The embedded query statements select the content using control statements (e.g., to select a set of elements to be gathered) and object selection paths (OSP) to identify some location in an Object Map (OMap), which is a tree of objects instantiated from a TMap. The OSP is a unique path down the tree (based on the node names of the TMap) to some descendent child object node. These query statements in essence target the information content to be retrieved from the ARS database. The ARS generates dynamic HTML based on these embedded OMap query statements and associated OSPs to be used for query and report presentation by a browser.

These templates are maintained by the ARS template server. They are then used by the ARS output processing to mix-in the HTML screen presentation with the specific report information gathered as a result of the ARS user's request for accident information. This is done by indicating which accident criteria they are interested in (see figure 23-6). The HTML screens are tightly coupled with the ARS query system TMaps (see figure 23-7). For example, the HTML screen contains a field having "[majorStreet]." This is an OSP indicating that when the user enters data in this field it will be interpreted as the name of the major street and will be put into an OMap that mimics the users

**Report Criteria for "Collision Conditions Report"**

Time Period(s): [dateSelected]          (dd/mm/yyyy or dd/mm or yyyy)

○ Entire State of Colorado

| ○ District(s): | ○ RPA(s): | ○ Counties: | ⊙ City(s): |
|---|---|---|---|
| District 1 | CCC | Adams | Adams |
| District 2 | SRPEDD | Alamosa | Agate |
| District 3 | PVPC | Arapahoe | Aguilar |
| District 5 | OCPC | Archuleta | Akron |
| District 5 | NPEDC | Baca | Alamosa |

○ City/Neighborhood: [Denver ▼]    Neighborhood: [Washington ▼]

**Intersection/Street/Route Criteria:** [More Street Criteria] [More RMV Criteria] [Less]

1. A ( ⊙ Street  ○ Route) named [majorStreet]
   ○ all  ⊙ intersecting: [minorStreet]                ○ segment: [start]

2. **Search RMV Data:** Major street [intersecting_street]    Intersecting street [major_street]
   Nearest mile marker: [nearest_mile_marker]    Ramp [ramp]              Ramp route n
   will be ignored. All fields support regular expression matches.)

[Submit Query] **Demo Report**

**Figure 23-6.** Accident selection criteria.

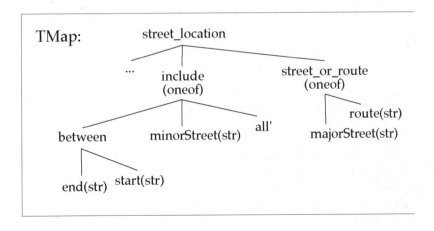

**Figure 23-7.** TMap for street_location criteria.

screen at the leaf node in the TMap "MajorStreet(str)." The "(str)" indicates that the entry is string data.

The specification of these templates is accomplished using an HTML editor. We chose to use Microsoft's FrontPage HTML editor which is tightly integrated with most http servers and provides a WYSIWYG (What You See Is What You Get, as seen in figure 23-6) interface for HTML editing. The following were also reviewed in making this choice: Netscape Navigator GOLD, HotMetal Pro and several shareware products. Note that this choice was an ergonomic one, since one could just as well write HTML statements by hand in a normal text editor.

The ARS Internet user interface is supported by a standard HTML browser (e.g., one from Netscape or Microsoft ). The advantage of the Microsoft Browser is its support for OLE (Object Linking and Embedding). This means that the ARS can make use of embedded documents (such as Excel for charting) or ActiveX components to integrate new tools and capabilities into its environment.

## Example Queries/Reports

There are two basic information gathering strategies in the ARS: summary and detailed for queries/reports. Detailed reports display attributes from individual accidents and summary reports which provide multilevel summaries of accident data. See figure 23-8, which illustrates an ARS summary report as displayed on a browser. Again, this report output can be seen to closely correlate to a TMap. The TMap in figure 23-9 shows excerpts of some of the information that is associated with an accident.

Queries/reports are qualified by filtering, or limiting, the information to be gathered through selection criteria at the user interface. For example, the user is able to specify a range of dates, a town, or a specific highway segment or intersection, and the resulting report would include only the information that meets the stated criteria. A user is also able to specify ad-hoc reports, including the creation of calculated columns using ARS toolkit functions. As examples, the following are typical reports that provide statistics for a specified reporting period:

All Road Traffic Accident Report: for a specified city or town, and specified street or intersection, the details related to each accident, including the date, hour, number of vehicles, number of injured, number of fatalities, collision types, collision objects, vehicle actions, traffic controls, and environmental conditions.

Top (n) Accident Sites: for a state or city, the intersections, sections, or locations having the highest number of accidents (based on a weighted average of injures and fatalities).

Type of Accident by Intersection, Section, or Location: a summary of the type of

Accident Reporting System (ARS)

Report Date: 09/21/1996

Page 1

**Highway Department**
**Traffic Operations Section**

COLLISION CONDITIONS REPORT
City--DENVER;Period--01/01/1995-01/31/1995

| Road Surface Conditions | Accident Type | | | | | | | |
|---|---|---|---|---|---|---|---|---|
| | All | | Fatal | | Injury | | Property Damage | |
| | Count | % | Count | % | Count | % | Count | % |
| No Defects | 13 | | 2 | | 5 | | 6 | |
| Holes Ruts Bumps | 4 | | 0 | | 3 | | 1 | |
| Foreign Matter on Surface | 5 | | 2 | | 2 | | 1 | |
| Defective Shoulder | | | | | | | | |
| Road Under Construction | | | | | | | | |
| Other | | | | | | | | |
| Unknown | | | | | | | | |

©1996 by Hamilton Technologies Inc.

**Figure 23-8.** Collision Conditions Report Output.

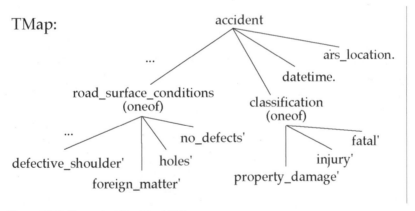

**Figure 23-9.** Excerpts of Accident TMap.

accidents, weather, road conditions, and collision factors.

Contributing Factors Report: a summary of the number of accidents in which weather, light, pavement condition, or time of day played a contributing role.

Accident Rate Report: the number of accidents, injured, fatalities, and a weighted average, for the intersections, segments, or locations with the highest accident rate.

## 001 Client/Server Support Layer

The ARS was layered on top of 001's general purpose client/server layer that uses TCP/IP. This layer provides an n-tiered networked client/server model which can be thought of as a management hierarchy of controllers with a parent being a client to its child as a server (see figure 23-5). Parent and children can communicate up and down the hierarchy and a parent can interrupt its children. Controllers can also communicate to other controllers in a networked fashion outside of the standard lines of control as long as they have been authorized to do so by their parent controllers. Each controller can perform local functionality as well as delegate functions to be performed by their children controllers. Each node is also thought of as an active class dispatcher where the controller is the agent that performers the methods of that class.

In the ARS Internet version, a CGI client initiates or attaches to the Session Manager as a server. Multiple CGI clients are managed by the Session Manager. The Session Manager controls access to the ARS system resource class services (via a child controller). If the CGI client is recognized, then the Session Manager as a client initiates or attaches to one of its children controllers as a server to service the request. The child controller could in turn activate or connect to other controllers under it's control.

This architecture provides for a very high degree of scalability since any number of ARS servers can be targeted to run on any number of networked Unix hosts or CPUs.

Excerpts from the client/server layer of the ARS show how the generic client/server model described in figure 23-5 is instantiated. The first FMap in figure 23-10 shows the SessionManager making a connection to one of the resource managers that it controls. The sub-function "connect_to_report_manager" starts (or attaches to) the "arsreports" server. When this completes, the send and receive function performs generically to provide communication between a client and its server. Any OMap object constructed from a TMap can be passed between the client and server via automatic marshaling of data. For example, the action parameter to the communications functions indicates the TMap type of the OMap to be communicated.

The second FMap is the arsreports_manager that is the server being connected to. It uses a RUN_SERVER structure that does all of the client server protocol and database management functions. The "do_work" function is the function that it applies to all of the report requests that it handles for the SessionManager or other clients that may call it. Note that this server may be on a different networked machine than the one that the SessionManager is on. The "arsreportsdb_server" FMap implementation is automatically generated by 001 as a C function. Excerpts of the code generated by 001 can be seen below. Note that the system is designed to append "db_server" to the name of the server "arsreports" internal to the function "runstart_server." The third FMap "ars_reports_class" is called from the leaf function of the second FMap and dispatches the specific types of requests as primitive operations (or methods) on the action class for the different report requests.

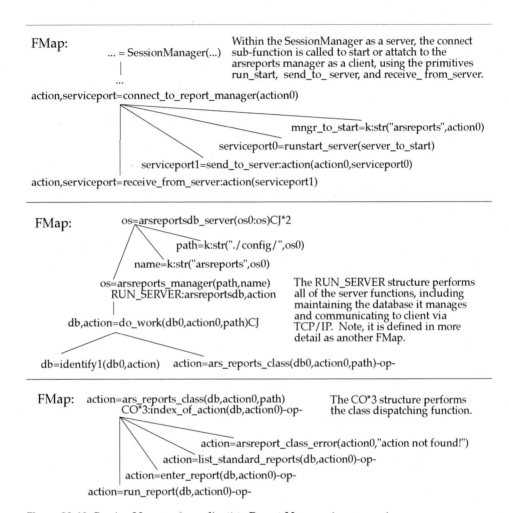

FMap:

... = SessionManager(...)

Within the SessionManager as a server, the connect sub-function is called to start or attatch to the arsreports manager as a client, using the primitives run_start, send_to_ server, and receive_ from_server.

action,serviceport=connect_to_report_manager(action0)

mngr_to_start=k:str("arsreports",action0)

serviceport0=runstart_server(server_to_start)

serviceport1=send_to_server:action(action0,serviceport0)

action,serviceport=receive_from_server:action(serviceport1)

FMap:

os=arsreportsdb_server(os0:os)CJ*2

path=k:str("./config/",os0)

name=k:str("arsreports",os0)

os=arsreports_manager(path,name)
RUN_SERVER:arsreportsdb,action

The RUN_SERVER structure performs all of the server functions, including maintaining the database it manages and communicating to client via TCP/IP. Note, it is defined in more detail as another FMap.

db,action=do_work(db0,action0,path)CJ

db=identify1(db0,action)    action=ars_reports_class(db0,action0,path)-op-

FMap:    action=ars_reports_class(db,action0,path)
CO*3:index_of_action(db,action0)-op-

The CO*3 structure performs the class dispatching function.

action=arsreport_class_error(action0,"action not found!")

action=list_standard_reports(db,action0)-op-

action=enter_report(db,action0)-op-

action=run_report(db,action0)-op-

**Figure 23-10.** Session Manager (as a client) to Report Manager (as a server).

```
/*001-Generated C code for functional specification 'ARSREPORTSDB_SERVER'
     VERSION: 3.2.3.9 C-RAT
     AUTHOR: Hamilton Technologies Inc. Copyright 1991.
     OPERATION: ARSREPORTSDB_SERVER
     GENERATED: Sat Jun  7 19:41:11 1997
  SCCSID: @(#) %M% %I% of %G%.
*/
#include "ACTION.h"
#include "OMAP.h"
#include "SERVICEPORT.h"
#include "CPORT.h"
#include "PORTADDR.h"
```

```
...
#include <stdio.h>
...
fARSREPORTSDB_SERVER(V0OS0,
              V0OS)
IDECLARE_OS(V0OS0)
ODECLARE_OS(V0OS)
{
         /* __LOCAL_VARIABLE_DECLARATIONS__ */
DECLARE_ACTION(V0A1)
DECLARE_STR(V0FNM)
...
         /* __ITERATION_VARIABLE_DECLARATIONS__ */
int rec1_RUN;
DECLARE_OS(R121_OS0)
DECLARE_OMAP(R121_SVOM1)
DECLARE_STR(R120PATH)
         /* __CONSTANT_DECLARATIONS_AND_ASSIGNMENTS__ */
NEWSTACK_TRACE_IDSC("ARSREPORTSDB_SERVER");
...
DOT_K_STR(".omap",C44)
         /* __FUNCTION_SOURCE_CODE_BEGINNING__ */
...
   fDEBUG_SERVER(V0PATH,V0NAME,V1_OS00,&V1_B);
   CLONE_OS(V1_OS00,V1_OS0)
   fLOADOMAP_SERVER(V0PATH,V0NAME,&V1_SVOM0);
   ISREJECT_OMAP(V1_SVOM0,D1_D6)
     if(D1_D6<1)
 {if(D1_D6 == REJECT_BOOLEAN) {REJECT_TEST_BOOLEAN()}
   fSTARTUP_SERVER(V1_OS0,V0PATH,V1_SVOM0,&V1_SVOM1);
R121_OS0=V1_OS0;
R121_SVOM1=V1_SVOM1;
R120PATH=V0PATH;
rec1_RUN=1;
while(rec1_RUN--){
   fTRY_CONNECTING_TO_CLIENT(V1_SVOM1,&V1_CPA0,&V1_CLIENT0,&V1_SVOM3);
   ISREJECT_CPORT(V1_CLIENT0,D1_D11)
     if(D1_D11<1)
 {if(D1_D11 == REJECT_BOOLEAN) {REJECT_TEST_BOOLEAN()}
   READTMAP_ACTION(V1_CLIENT0,V1_TM)
   fRECEIVE_FROM_CLIENT(V1_TM,V1_SVOM3,V1_CPA0,V1_CLIENT0,
                        &V1_CLIENT,&V1_CSP,&V1_RQOM0,&V1_SVOM4);
   fGET_DATA_SERVER(V1_SVOM4,&V1_DBOM0,&V1_SVOM5);
   CONVERT_ACTION_OMAP(V1_RQOM0,V0A0)
   CONVERT_ARSREPORTSDB_OMAP(V1_DBOM0,V0DB0)
```

```
      K_STR(C3,V0A0,V0FNM)
      K_OS(V0FNM,V2_OS)
      READTMAP_ACTION(V2_OS,V2_TM)
      NODENAME_TMAP(V2_TM,V2_TYPENM)
      K_STR(C44,V2_TYPENM,V2_OMF0)
      MERGE_STR(C42,V2_TYPENM,V2_OMF0,V2_OMFNM0)
      MERGE_STR(C40,V0FNM,V2_OMFNM0,V2_OMFNM1)
      CASE_STR(C38,C37,V2_OMFNM1,V2_OMFNM2)
      STORE_ACTION(V2_OMFNM2,V0A0,V2_B)
      CLONE_ACTION(V0A0,V0A1)
      fARS_REPORTS_CLASS(V0DB0,V0A1,V0PATH,&V0A);
      CLONE_ARSREPORTSDB(V0DB0,V0DB)
      CONVERT_OMAP_ACTION(V0A,V1_RQOM)
      CONVERT_OMAP_ARSREPORTSDB(V0DB,V1_DBOM)
      fPUT_DATA_SERVER(V1_DBOM,V1_SVOM5,&V1_SVOM6);
      fSEND_TO_CLIENT(V1_SVOM6,V1_CLIENT,V1_CSP,V1_RQOM,&V1_SVOMN);
         rec1_RUN=1;
         V1_OS0=V1_OS0;
         V1_SVOM1=V1_SVOMN;
         V0PATH=V0PATH;
}/*FALSE*/
else{/*TIMEOUT_EXIT_SERVER*/
      fTIMEOUT_EXIT_SERVER(V1_OS0,V1_SVOM3,V0OS);
}/*TRUE*/
}
V1_OS0=R121_OS0;
V1_SVOM1=R121_SVOM1;
V0PATH=R120PATH;
}/*FALSE*/
else{/*CLONE1_OS*/
      CLONE_OS(V1_OS0,*V0OS)
}/*TRUE*/
ENDSTACK_IDSC(); /* STR Garbage Collector */
return;
}
/*  ———— end of source ————*/
```

Any number of different WEB servers can be used to support the ARS internetworking needs. Possible choices can be either the standard NCSA or CERN httpd servers or commercially available servers. The only constraint imposed is that it must support CGI.

## Database Design

The TMap design takes into consideration the tradeoffs between a real-world view of an accident and the following:

1. the need to incorporate information via interfaces from interacting systems (e.g., provided by the RMV, TP&D),

2. the need to access or provide access to this information via a common storage technology (e.g., Oracle), and

3. the immediate query and reporting needs of ARS users.

In addition, when the TMap was defined, care was taken to use type names that closely resemble objects that would be recognizable to a traffic engineer. Because of this, user queries are able to be validated and specified by the user directly from the TMap. This also makes the job of training end users easier.

The ARS TMap provides more than enough information for the Oracle table design implemented as Oracle schemas to allow SHD access to ARS information. In some cases, we had to limit the use of 001 TMap constructs, since Oracle was not able to handle these more complex structural mechanisms.

The first installation used only 001 persistent OMap objects. Later versions use both Oracle and 001 persistent objects. Oracle was introduced to provide access to existing Oracle database information (e.g., TP&D GIS roadway information) and to support external inter-system connectivity (e.g., to insurance company databases).

Access to Oracle was provided by 001's reuse library interface to Oracle's OCI interface, which is a cross-platform, high performance API for accessing Oracle data using standard SQL. 001 takes advantage of the OCI array processing to maximize throughput when performing queries against Oracle.

001 supports application maintenance by the automatic demotion of the status of an FMap if the TMap has been changed and that change could affect that FMap. Information structures may be added to the end of tuple grouped information (similar to a record structure) and new abstract types may be added to the TMap without affecting any of the FMaps in the ARS application. The ARS developer also has the ability to use 001 to define transformation functions to convert one information structure to another when the organization of the information changes significantly.

In some configurations of the ARS, typical database administration functions are performed using the Oracle database administration tools provided with the Oracle software together with the 001 environment whereas other versions use only the 001 tool suite environment.

## Conclusion

Following are some observations and conclusions that were made as a result of designing and developing the ARS with 001.

Since 001 FMaps and TMaps are used as a model and not directly as a programming language, they were able to be used at all stages of the life cycle process. For example, they were used to define the engineering processes and they were also used to model the ARS tool. The ARS code was then automatically generated from the model by 001. Providing a model allows one to select alternative implementations while maintaining an accurate description of the system at a higher level of abstraction that is more consistent with the actual physical components of the real world aspects of the system.

001's methodology of "Development Before the Fact" embedded within its 001 language and Tool Suite development environment led to a reliable construction process for building the ARS. 001 provided both strong analysis support for the language. This ranged from sketching FMaps and TMaps early in the requirements and user interviewing process to later in the life cycle when a concrete solution had to be completely modeled in terms of FMaps and TMaps. The thinking process and the reliability of the solutions generated were significantly enhanced by the abstraction capabilities of 001 as a language. For example, the ability for a user to define reusable structures and generic universal functionalities allowed developers to hide unnecessary details, thus enhancing reliability. The 001 Tool Suite provided much needed coordination among members of the developer team.

001's object orientation and its support for persistent objects significantly simplified many of the modeling areas. For example, patterns of objects could be stored as a persistent OMap object to be used later in many different ways (e.g., to verify against another object or to use as a default starting pattern). The ability to use the range of strong typing (e.g., an object as type accident) to weak typing (e.g., the accident object as type OMap) allowed for generic FMaps that would work with accident objects as well as vehicle objects. This generic capability along with the ability to switch between these two different ways of treating the same object made it possible to use the strong points of each view when appropriate.

Our use of 001's library of reusables simplified the design of the ARS system. Having the reusables available also significantly shortened the time to complete the first prototype and successive evolutions of the ARS. Following are some of the contributing reusables that made the difference:

-

- •the generic client/server reusables which provided for automatic marshaling of OMap objects between machines
- •seamless integration of external database facilities via 001's OCI primitive type reusables
- •CGI primitive types and other Internet related reusables

Putting all this together — coupled with the understanding of the objectives of the system and the ease with which changes were able to be made — allowed the team to develop functionality well beyond what was orginally thought to be reasonable. In essence, 001 made the difference.

## Author Bios

Margaret Hamilton (mhh@htius.com) is the founder and CEO of Hamilton Technologies, Inc. (HTI), based in Cambridge, MA (17 Inman Street, Cambridge, MA 02139, 617-492-0058) a pioneer in the systems engineering and software development industry. Hamilton's mission has been to bring to market a completely integrated and robust tool suite that is based on the unique systems theory paradigm, which she created, called Development Before the Fact (DBTF). In bringing her product to market, her company leveraged the power of reusability and the reliability of seamless integration to provide a tool that sharply decreases errors while simultaneously increasing productivity. The result is an ultrareliable system at a fraction of the cost of conventional systems. Hamilton's goal was to embed this formal and completely systems oriented object (SOO) framework into a highly efficient, high performance, completely graphical, portable workbench of "smart" tools which the systems engineer and software developer could use throughout the entire design and development life cycle. Today this ideal has been surpassed with 001.

Earlier in her career, as the leader of the Software Engineering Division at MIT's Charles Stark Draper Laboratory, Hamilton was the director of the Apollo on-board flight software project and created Higher Order Software (HOS), a formal systems design theory.

After this, Hamilton founded and was CEO of Higher Order Software where she was responsible for the development of the first comprehensive CASE tool in the industry. This tool, called USE.IT, was based on her formal design theory, HOS.

Ron Hackler (ron@htius.com) is Director of Development at Hamilton Technologies, Inc. (HTI) based in Cambridge, MA. As part of his responsibilities, he is the lead engineer for the development of both current and future versions of the 001 tool suite using 001 to define and generate itself. In addition Hackler has been responsible for many areas of the DBTF technology.

Hackler has been responsible for many other 001 designed and developed systems including the development of a simulator for the University of California Los Alamos National Laboratory; a missile tracking simulation for a large aerospace company (HTI was nominated for SBA Subcontractor of the Year as a result of this effort); several asynchronous real-time distributed applications for SDI; a factory model for an aerospace manufacturing plant; and several Internet related applications including an accident record system for state highway departments.

Prior to HTI, Hackler was Director of Advanced Concepts at Higher Order Software, Inc. where he spent many years defining and developing technologies based on research using the foundations of the HOS methodology. Here he was responsible for many applications applying this methodology and its automation, USE.IT (many components of which he was responsible for designing and developing). These applications included the development of systems in the areas of battle management and aerospace manufacturing,

Prior to this he studied composition with composer Martin Brown in Charles Ives lineage of music and applied music theory to the objects of mathematics.

[001, 001 Tool Suite, Function Map, Type Map, Object Map, Execution Map, Road Map, FMap, TMap, Escher, EMap, RMap, VSphere, RAT, Xecutor, OMap Editor, 001 Analyzer, SOO, System Oriented Object, Resource Allocation Tool, AntiRAT, Object Editor, Primitive Control Structures, Development Before the Fact, DBTF, RT(x), 001 AXES, AIOS, Agent 001DB are all trademarks of Hamilton Technologies, Inc.]

# Resource Librarian Remote Query System for the Education Resource Centre for Continuing Care of Alberta

**Steve Dolha**
**Dave Chiste**

## Introduction

Cadeon Strategic Technologies Inc. has developed an Internet based system (WWW.ERC.CALGARY.AB.CA) which provides ad-hoc query and request of library resources such as books and videos. The Resource Librarian Remote Query system allows Internet (and Intranet) users to query an online resource catalog and subsequently make requests for these resources via email to employees of the ERC. This case study describes our experience designing and developing this system using the 001 software engineering product [1].

Internet based systems are fast becoming the way to disseminate information across a wide geographic region at a very low cost. Early in 1996, Cadeon Strategic Technologies Inc. was approached to provide a remote query capability for the Education Resource Centre for Continuing Care of Alberta. The ERC is a resource library that provides materials such as books and videos to health care professionals across Western Canada. An existing system had been used to provide online public access to the ERC catalog of resources but was proving to be costly to operate because of it's dependency on a public X25 network. In addition, the software had to be manually loaded on each client machine, a process which had continued to be an administrative headache. What was needed was a solution which provided all the power of a distributed client-server system without the associated overhead of the existing system. The pervasive client-server technologies and low cost structure associated with the

Internet proved to be the perfect solution for development of an Internet based system that would better position the ERC to meet its key business objectives.

With years of experience building client-server systems, we realized that the distributed nature of Internet based systems required careful thought as to the architecture and implementation choices that were to be made. In addition, as we examined the state of software development for distributed Internet systems, we realized how much the development of dynamic Internet systems is in its infancy.

As a result, our concerns ranged from (1) ensuring the system could evolve as Internet technologies rapidly matured, and as business objectives changed, to (2) providing for the ability to scale the system as the volume of data and demand for the system's use increased. We were struck by the tendency of the software industry to dramatically oversimplify the effort to design, build and maintain Internet based systems. While technologies such as HTML, Java and ActiveX certainly provide powerful capabilities to rapidly implement Internet software, it became clear to us that much more was needed to develop what are really complex distributed client-server based systems. These systems are more complex than traditional systems for a couple of reasons:

1. The distributed nature of components of these systems means that managing them is much more difficult than a traditional "connected" straight-line application. This is due in large part to the lack of completely defined connectivity between all parts of the system (everything from requirements models right through to the actual system components). Such connectivity is necessary to ensure that all interfaces within a system are consistent and that change to parts of the system can be made without introducing errors (in other words, easy impact analysis).

2. These systems have a higher number of interfaces between distributed components which provide more places for such a system to break.

So despite the relative strengths of Internet technologies to implement distributed client-server systems, many long term challenges remain. This includes being able to:

1. Model a system independent of WEB technologies or any other existing or yet to exist technologies,
2. Provide a fully connected model of all the distributed components of the system,
3. Ensure that all interfaces between distributed components are correct and reliable,
4. Provide high levels of reuse, and reliability
5. Evolve systems easily as either technology or business requirements change.

This is where the use of a sophisticated system engineering environment called 001 fits. 001 provides the means to seamlessly model the pieces of a distributed system in a highly connected manner. It essentially provides the modeling infrastructure "glue" that binds all these distributed pieces together. 001 excels in providing the full end-to-end integration lacking in most systems designed and built without 001.

## The Development Strategy

**Figure 24-1.** The "boom and bust" approach to software development.

This project was defined by first developing a clear set of design and strategic objectives to guide the development of the software solution to meet the ERC's immediate needs as well as give the ERC with well-defined strategic position for the evolution of the solution into the future. These objectives were addressed in a way that we believe defines the best way to design, build and deploy Internet or Intranet systems for any business — large or small.

To provide you with a clear view of our development strategy we're going to present first our strategic development objectives, followed by a description of the actual development process. The design objectives for the ERC project are described following this review of the development approach.

The development approach used on this project has been designed to support the following strategic development objectives:

*Be able to incorporate and take advantage of the best of what others have created.*

This is accomplished with well-defined interfaces to existing products and components. These interfaces have a place in the system architecture that minimizes the impact of change to the interfaces on the rest of the system. Be able to build on the successes of the past and continually reduce the impact and cost of business and technology change.

For all of our projects, we have a process and the basic architectures which provide a solid basis for building evolutionary systems. Our key objective is to avoid the "boom and bust" approach to software development (figure 24-1).

Evolutionary software development must be done on a reliable and secure foundation.

*Strive toward error-free systems.*

It goes without saying that we all would like to achieve error-free systems. Our experience is that this is only going to be possible through the adoption of a "Development Before the Fact" philosophy and by continually striving toward the improvement of processes which allow errors to be introduced into a system. This includes the automation of complex processes which are error-prone when performed manually. 001 has taken a large step towards this with its analyzer capability which examines a 001 specification and reports on errors early in initial development which typically are not discovered until well into implementation of a system using traditional system development methods (whether object oriented or structured systems analysis).

*Continue to drive down the cost and complexity of building systems.*

Strategically it is important to focus on driving down the cost and complexity of systems in an iterative manner. The use of system architectures and well-defined, reliable and reusable software components provides the way to make systems development less expensive and difficult.

*Ensure an accurate design based on user objectives and requirements.*

Although it often goes without saying that one must build appropriate software solutions, without a clear understanding of user objectives and requirements this is an impossible task. We prescribe the use of a contextual inquiry and design approach which ensures that information is collected to be able to provide a software solution that is both appropriate and accurate.

## The Development Approach

The software development process used to develop the ERC Remote Query System is designed to balance the immediate needs of a system with the long-term objective of providing for reuse and the evolution of a system. This balance is managed on every project by applying appropriate levels of effort to both the specific requirements for the project and the supporting system architecture.

It is important to recognize the higher initial cost associated with building a reusable system architecture at the same time as one is producing a specific system. Within any project, hard decisions must be made to keep projects costs in line without sacrificing long-term needs. However, it is equally important to make this decision based on the total lifetime cost of a system. It is our experience that the lifetime cost of a system will be substantially lower by using an evolutionary development and maintenance approach to software. Without an evolutionary approach, one reaches a point much sooner where a software solution must be redeveloped entirely from scratch — at that point an extremely costly proposition. This is in sharp contrast to the evolutionary approach of performing less costly and "safer" incremental improvements of software solutions designed from the start to be durable. With this approach we are clearly targeting a significant reduction in the cost of the activity after the initial development which traditionally consumes 70% of the lifetime cost of a system — maintenance and update of a software solution. "Creating durable, reusable software is more expensive initially, but less costly over the long haul" [2].

It is critical that the development process embody an evolutionary approach from the start. Evolution is only reasonable when a system is structured to allow for it to happen easily. The methodology that 001 implements (called Development Before the Fact or DBTF) provides strong support for the evolution of systems because:

1. The graphical representation of 001 models dramatically improves the visualization changes to the FMaps and TMaps that comprise these models.

2. The entire 001 system model is fully connected. Thus change can be better managed because the impact of any change (especially interface changes) can be immediately traced through the 001 system model. Since every 001 module requires clearly defined inputs and outputs, changes become obvious and are reported to the developer immediately for EVERY component of the system that will be affected. This prevents any part of the system from being overlooked or forgotten by the developer making the change. This greatly increases the reliability of the system being delivered.

3. 001 provides an object model which, through encapsulation, allows functional implementation to be hidden behind well defined interfaces. This significantly reduces the impact of changes in this implementation on the rest of the system.

4. The 001 analyzer catches interface errors (75% of the errors fixed after the fact in traditional systems) are before parts of a system are deployed.

The following is a description of the primary phases of the development process to build the ERC Remote Query System:

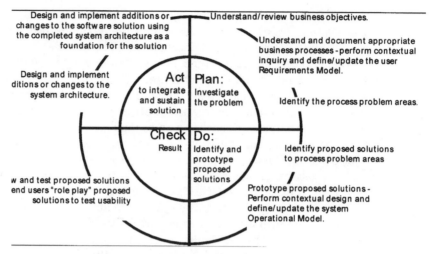

**Figure 24-2.** An iterative evolutionary development process.

1. Determine user requirements along with system and business objectives (requirements model). We prescribe a customer centered design methodology called "Contextual Inquiry and Design" [3]. This method discovers and captures detailed information about how people work in *context* while they work at real tasks in their workplace. It guides the development of a system design and provides the means to prototype and test designs with customers before any system development occurs. It is only by involving the users in the design process and, *"participate in the users' world, we want it shown to us so well that we know it — we want our feet to be sore when their shoes pinch"* [3] can we be assured that we have captured the correct design.

2. The requirements and design captured in step 1 are formalized in FMaps and TMaps.

3. Design additions or changes to the system architecture to provide the foundation to meet key long term system and business objectives. This includes making strategic implementation choices to support systems of this type. The supporting system architecture is reviewed as part of every project to determine the scope of changes to support requirements for this particular project, as well as for other similar projects.

Additions or changes to the system architecture are prioritized based on the likelihood and impact of future change in the applications supported by this part of the system architecture. Those parts of a system which have a high likelihood of change and where such change will have a dramatic impact on the system are supported within the architecture using a design that provides both powerful and intuitive customization capabilities. In the ERC system, the template mechanism where dynamic data is merged with a static defined HTML template is an example of such a component.

4. Build/revise the system architecture based on the design(s) from step 2.

5. Build the project specific components using the completed system architecture.

This process is applied in an iterative manner using a spiral development cycle. This spiral approach acknowledges that development is most successful when applied in an iterative evolutionary fashion until a level of stability is reached that meets the existing objectives. This is the initiation of a lifelong evolutionary process that supports the software solution through its entire lifetime, not just it's initial creation.

This iterative evolutionary development process is summarized in figure 24-2 as it relates to the continuous improvement process of Plan, Do, Check and Act (3.)

Having put the "cart before the horse" in terms of explaining the development process before the objectives that it supports, we now turn our attention to describing objectives for this project and showing how this development process supports successful achievement of the objectives.

## Remote Query Design Objectives

In addition to the development approach supporting the already described strategic objectives, each project has particular design objectives which are required to meet the client's particular needs. Each of ERC's objectives is listed below with a description of the supporting part of the development strategy used to address the objective:

*The system must be easy to learn and use. The key objective is the ability for ERC clients to easily locate and request appropriate ERC resources.*

The use of Contextual Inquiry and Design  helps ensure a clear understanding of the underlying process and a review of the usability of the resulting design.

*The system can be supported by non-technical administrators.*

The use of technologies that are easy to set up and provide powerful yet intuitive management facilities are key to meet this objective. We feel it is important to design automation that allows non-technical administrators to make changes, such as those changes required in the user interface using the HTML view template process. The key here is to create innovative and intuitive designs that support system operational tasks. The system must have low operational costs.

The use of the browser based client along with automation of the various regular operational activities contributes to keeping these costs low or virtually nonexistent.

*The system must have low development costs.*

The power of 001 and its large library of software components allows the development costs to remain low. In total, the entire system was developed with a total of 8 months of development activity. Our expectation is that future similar systems will require 10 to 20% of this effort because of the number of "reuseful" (see note 1) and reusable components produced within this project.

*The system must be available worldwide on a 24 hours a day, 7 days a week basis.*

By its very definition, the Internet is a 24 hour a day, 7 day a week operation. The operational environment relies on the stability of the various supporting hardware, software and network pieces of the system. Thus far, the system has run for 6 months with only one power related outage.

*The system must provide timely availability of new or updated resource catalog data and integrate seamlessly with the existing operational system.*

This objective requires a clear definition of the data shared between the existing and new system and the appropriate times to perform the updates to keep the parallel systems synchronized as required by the supported business processes. With the ERC system, it was deemed sufficient that an automated batch update process would provide updates to the system in a timely enough manner to meet the end-user requirements. This batch update is currently done weekly, although the design accommodates more frequent updates if desired.

The existing system from which the resource catalog data is drawn has been interfaced to the new Remote Query system by combining an export utility with an automated load process. This batch load process automatically updates the query database and requires no scheduled downtime of the Remote Query system. The automated load process watches a specific export file and when it's modified date and time is changed, a load is triggered for some future configurable time-frame. This allows the initial export to be done anytime and act as the trigger to start the load, but ensures that the load is automatically scheduled outside of the prime time for query activity. When a load is successful, the load process then informs the administrator who can then switch the active query database to the newly loaded query database.

## The System Architecture

Any system can be defined using components defined in layers that build upon each other to provide larger and more complex systems. It is critical that each layer and its components be well defined to support reliable interaction between them. Equally important is the need to define each layer and its components to ensure that a layer can be evolved with a minimal impact on the rest of the system.

Software makes up a significant part of the architecture needed to make computers effective and powerful tools. As such, and considering the ever

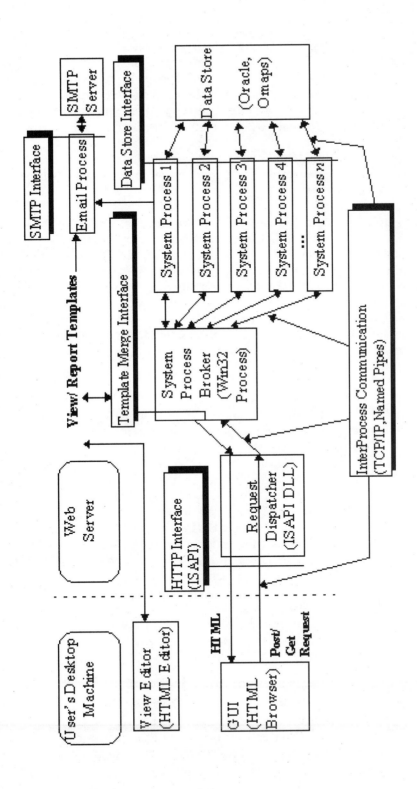

**Figure 24-3.** WEB System Architecture.

increasing complexity of computer systems, it is, more than ever, important to first architect, then build, then evolve systems.

As part of this project, we defined a system architecture (shown in figure 24-3) to support the development of the ERC system and all similar WEB based systems. In fact, the architecture shown here can be used to support many dynamic and scaleable WEB or distributed client/server based systems.

The following describes the various components of this architecture including the particular implementations chosen to support the various parts of the architecture.

Graphical User Interface (HTML Browser):
This component fulfills the role of client side interaction. Any HTML browser can provide simple user interface capabilities using standard HTML forms. Further complex user interaction is available with certain browsers (such as Netscape or MS Internet Explorer) using Java or ActiveX based components and browser scripting with VBScript or JavaScript. The 001 resource allocation tool (RAT) could be configured to generate from Function Maps to any of these languages — this was not done in this project since no scripting was required to satisfy the user interaction requirements of the ERC Remote Query system.

HTTP Interface:
The typical WEB based system will use either the CGI interface or one of a number of propriety interfaces such as Microsoft's ISAPI interface for processing POST or GET requests from the HTML Browser. A key conceptual view of this interaction is that the traditional workstation event loop has been replaced with a workstation <=> HTTP server loop. This is sufficient for the simplest user-GUI interaction (for example, actions associated with push buttons). It has the disadvantage of increased network interaction and thus may not be appropriate for certain types of GUI interaction (typically micro-level interactions such as field level edits or "drag and drop" support). The ISAPI interface was chosen for the ERC Remote Query system to coincide with the choice of Windows NT/IIS as the supporting Web server platform.

View Editor (HTML Editor):
Flexibility of the user interface and report output process is provided by a series of View Templates. The editing or modification of these templates is accomplished using an HTML editor.

Request Dispatcher and System Process Broker:
The Request Dispatcher will take the input provided by the user and pass it on to the "System Process Broker." The System Process Broker will either attach to the appropriate process that is already running, or it will spawn a new system process to handle the user's request. The ability to dynamically create and

then attach to new processes which can run as services on any number of hosts is important to allow the system to automatically scale up as demand on the system increases.

System Processes:
A system process is either already running on the server or is created by the System Process Broker. Each process will handle a user's request and pass the results of the request back. Each system process will be for a unique action on a set of data passed in from the user. After a process has been "idle" for a while it will terminate. It is up to the System Process Broker to decide if it can attach to an idle process or if it needs to create a new one.

Template Merge Interface:
The objective of the template/view processing component is to provide a means of defining dynamic HTML pages that integrate data from data stores (such as Oracle) based on user supplied data and actions — in other words, define the GUI. This part of a system is the primary control of both the look and feel of a system from the end-user perspective. As a result, it is one of the components of the architecture to be highly impacted by change in user needs or ERC business requirements. Rather than developing dynamic HTML pages using a program driven, hardwired approach — an approach which complicates change to the pages — a simple template language was developed which is embedded within the HTML describing each page of the system. This language is simple to use, yet does not in any way limit the capability to support complex user interaction within the Web Browser environment (including the use of VBScript or JavaScript). This approach is similar to the concept of server-side includes or Microsoft's "Active Server" technology.

The template language developed in phase I provided for the following:

1. Substitute data values passed from a previous POST or GET request into the page.
2. Create, alter or transform data merged in the output by calling predefined 001 generated functions. Predefined functions include one which supports the specification of a SQL based query.
3. Allow formatting of multiple row query results in an iterative manner by specifying a single "row section" around specific HTML tags.
4. Define the flow of the pages using "next template" commands which include conditional logic processing to decide which page to display next.

In the second phase of the ERC project, some work was done on the template language to align it closer to the concept of a 001 TMap. This resulted in a template language which is able to automatically apply the concepts inherent in the 001 types (such as an OSetOf implying iteration over all of it's elements).

These pages can be easily constructed using any HTML editor. We designed and built a utility program which parses, performs error checks and loads a new or updated template. The templates are stored in a 001 OMap format consistent with the definition of the TMap of a template.

As data or other results are passed back to the user, it is combined or "merged" with a particular template so that the data can be presented in many different customizable ways. Typically these templates will consist of HTML for the browser to interpret and display. Note that this is an implementation similar to the Smalltalk Model/Controller/View (MVC) architecture. The advantage of this architecture is that views can be customized without impacting the core functionality of the system.

The following figures illustrate the results of some of the pages dynamically generated using this template component in the Resource Librarian Remote query system:

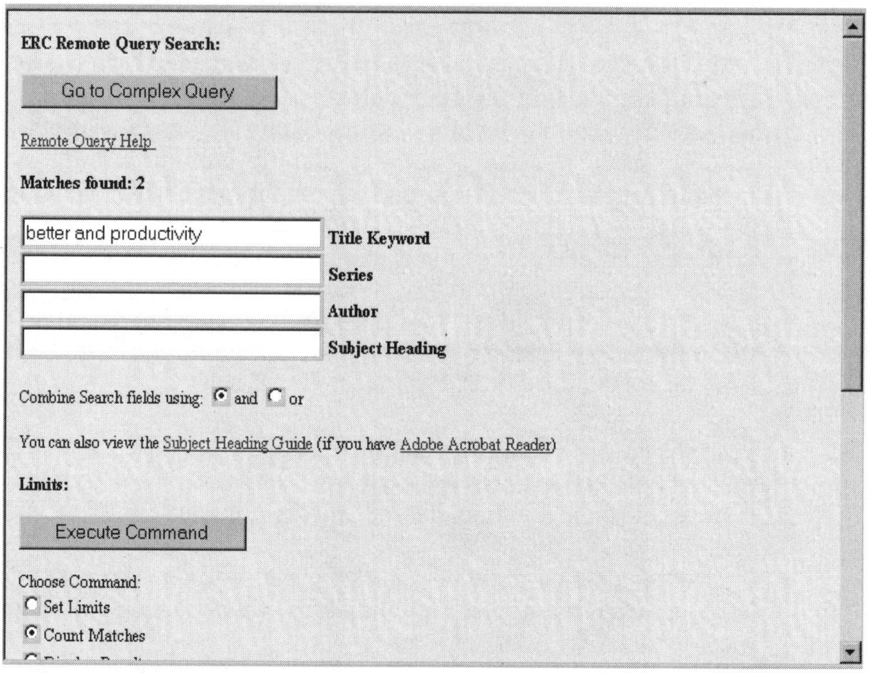

**Figure 24-4.** Simple query.

Figure 24-4 is the simple query page which is used to initiate queries. The user can enter Boolean syntax into any of the four fields (Title keyword, Series, Author or Subject Heading) and request a count or display matches found.

Figure 24-5 shows the dynamically formatted table output of query results. It includes a checkbox to allow the user to select desired resources for inclusion in the following request page.

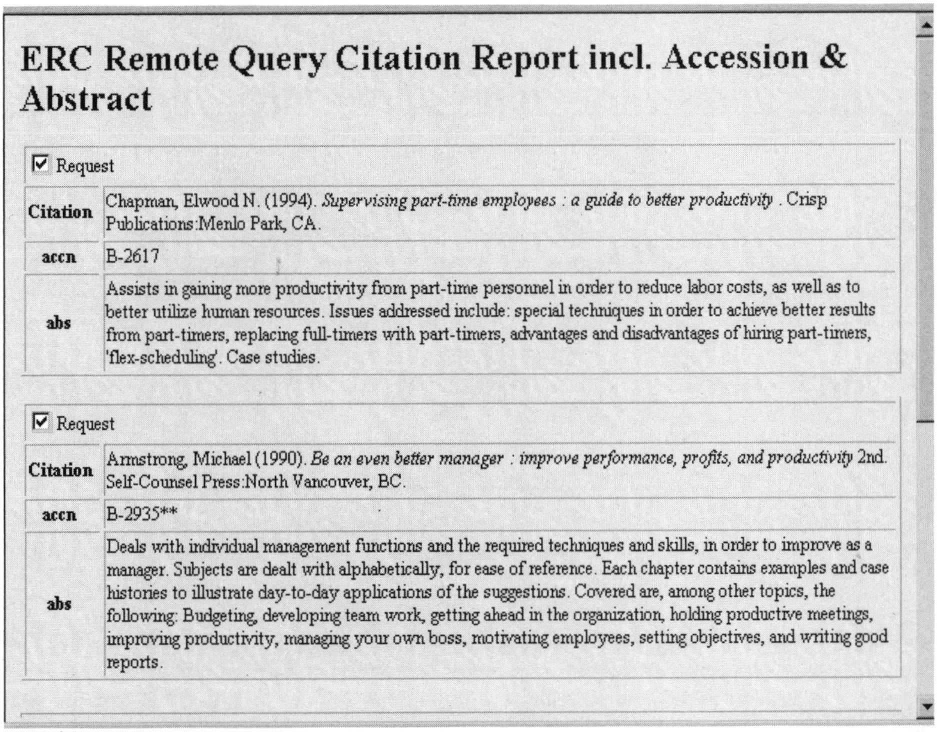

# ERC Remote Query Citation Report incl. Accession & Abstract

☑ Request

| | |
|---|---|
| **Citation** | Chapman, Elwood N. (1994). *Supervising part-time employees : a guide to better productivity* . Crisp Publications:Menlo Park, CA. |
| **accn** | B-2617 |
| **abs** | Assists in gaining more productivity from part-time personnel in order to reduce labor costs, as well as to better utilize human resources. Issues addressed include: special techniques in order to achieve better results from part-timers, replacing full-timers with part-timers, advantages and disadvantages of hiring part-timers, 'flex-scheduling'. Case studies. |

☑ Request

| | |
|---|---|
| **Citation** | Armstrong, Michael (1990). *Be an even better manager : improve performance, profits, and productivity* 2nd. Self-Counsel Press:North Vancouver, BC. |
| **accn** | B-2935** |
| **abs** | Deals with individual management functions and the required techniques and skills, in order to improve as a manager. Subjects are dealt with alphabetically, for ease of reference. Each chapter contains examples and case histories to illustrate day-to-day applications of the suggestions. Covered are, among other topics, the following: Budgeting, developing team work, getting ahead in the organization, holding productive meetings, improving productivity, managing your own boss, motivating employees, setting objectives, and writing good reports. |

**Figure 24-5.** Abstract page.

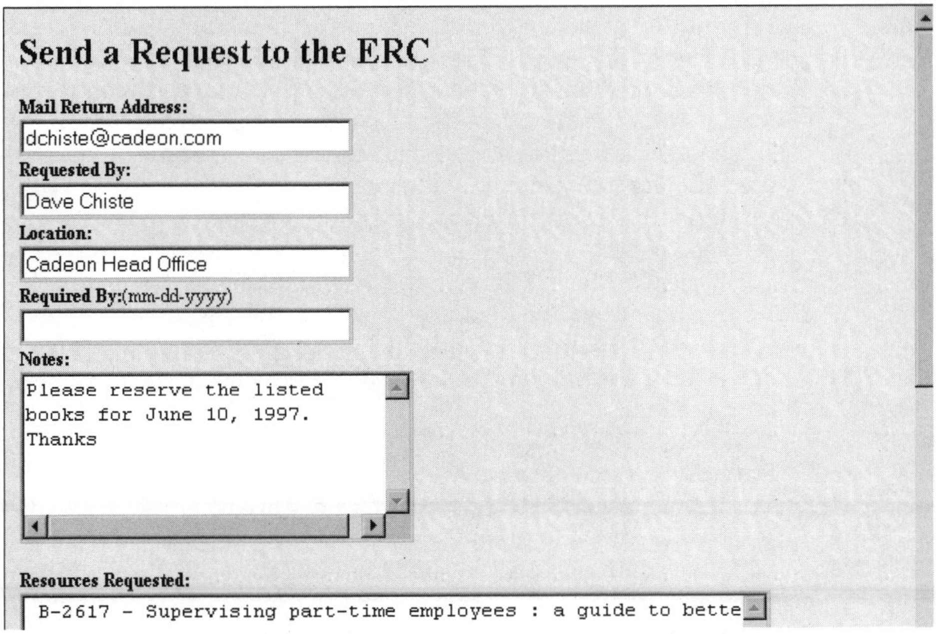

# Send a Request to the ERC

**Mail Return Address:**

dchiste@cadeon.com

**Requested By:**

Dave Chiste

**Location:**

Cadeon Head Office

**Required By:**(mm-dd-yyyy)

**Notes:**

Please reserve the listed
books for June 10, 1997.
Thanks

**Resources Requested:**

B-2617 - Supervising part-time employees : a guide to bette

**Figure 24-6.** Sending a request.

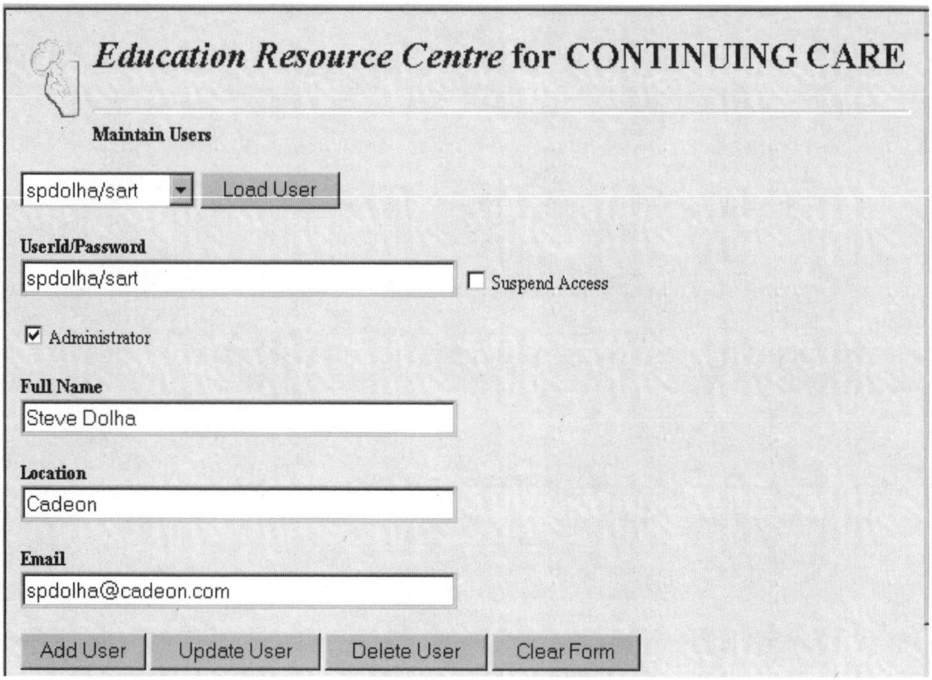

**Figure 24-7.** Maintain users.

When submitted (as shown in figure 24-6), the data from this request page is formatted using the template facility to generate an email format of the message sent to ERC staff. This is possible because the template mechanism is not tightly coupled to HTML as a formatting language. Thus it can also be used to format data into simple text messages appropriate for email.

The user administration page (figure 24-7) is an example using the newer (and simpler) template language which is more aligned with the concept of traversing 001 OMaps than the original template language used to generate the previous pages:

Our goal for future versions of this template mechanism are to allow default views to be automatically generated from 001 TMap definitions. Automation of such tasks will ultimately allow systems to be created extremely quickly without loosing the customization abilities needed to meet a particular system's requirements.

Data Store (Oracle, OMaps):
The first phase of the ERC Remote Query project used the 001-Oracle interface to query data stored in an Oracle database. The queries were defined using an SQL like syntax defined in the template language. It allows queries to be customized based on input provided by the user. In the second phase of this development project it was realized that by taking advantage of the power of the 001 environment, we could replace the implementation of the database component

of the architecture with our own custom built database engine — at an extremely low incremental cost (in fact, the cost was the same as the licensing fees charged by Oracle to provide unlimited database access on the WEB). This approach provided several advantages:

1. A significantly reduced cost to deploy the system by eliminating Oracle licensing costs.
 2. A set of high speed search algorithms that are easily tailored to the type of data in this system and are reusable in future systems.
 3. Complete control over the design and implementation of the data store and retrieval components of the architecture (keep in mind that software developed using 001 exhibits ultra-high reliability).

The decision to build a custom data storage and query mechanism was possible only because of the inherent power and reliability of 001 defined systems. With 001 it is possible to consider the option of building custom complex systems in a fraction of the time — placing them on equal footing with the option of using product based implementations (such as Oracle). It is this ability of 001 which expands the viable choices to implement systems. The result is an increased competitive edge over those who do not use 001.

Inter-Process Communication (Named Pipes, TCP/IP):
Inter-Process Communication is that infrastructure component of the architecture which supports the interaction between the various "services" (or system processes) defined in the system. Named pipes were chosen for this system implementation. It should be noted that 001 supports standard IPC mechanisms based on Berkley sockets on Unix and WinSock on Windows NT platforms.

## Innovations and Challenges

To put the scope and level of sophistication of the final Resource Librarian Remote Query system into perspective, here is a list of the key innovations/challenges that were encountered during the project:

1. Designed and developed a template language, parser and runtime engine.
2. Developed using 001 on UNIX and deployed the system under Windows NT. The 001 produced "C" code was simply copied to the Windows NT machine and compiled without any changes.
3. Developed an 001 interface to the Microsoft ISAPI and named pipe WIN32 functions.
4. Used 001's interface to Oracle's "Oracle Call Interface" (OCI) API. This demonstrated to us the ease of incorporating vendor product interfaces as primitive layers in 001.
5. Developed generic bitmap, hash table and binary tree indexing capabilities

for 001 OMaps. This allowed us to provide fast and easy to define database structures using 001 OMaps instead of an Oracle database — a choice which we feel was more appropriate for this particular system.

6. Designed a Boolean search language and implemented a parser for the language that uses the indexing capabilities described above to search OMaps. This is similar to the parsing and execution of a dynamic SQL statement as provided by Oracle.

All of this was performed by a team of two people with a total manpower effort of 8 months. We believe that it is significant that with a relatively small effort a substantial base of powerful and reusable capability has been produced for building Internet and Intranet systems. It is our belief that without 001, this effort would have been 6 to 10 times this effort and would not even come close to the level of architectural sophistication and reliability present in the Remote Query system.

## Summary

This case study illustrates an approach used by Cadeon to architect and build robust, reliable and scaleable systems based on Internet technologies. The Resource Librarian Remote Query Project demonstrates how 001 can be used to develop such systems while also accommodating the important strategic objectives of systems development — software evolution and reuse.

With 001, one is modeling systems in the pure Function Map (FMap) and Type Map (TMap) form, then choosing to implement those systems with the distributed client-server technologies used to drive the Internet (and Intranets). None of these technologies alone is radically new (except of course 001 itself) — it is the pervasive and open use of Web technologies across many different hardware and networking platforms that is significant. Web technology is the closest that the IT industry has come so far to a set of standard client-sever protocols that are supported consistently across many different desktop, server and network hardware platforms — HTML to drive the client GUI, CGI to define the server request interface, TCP/IP to provide a reliable packet transport mechanism, HTTP to serve hypertext document requests. This pervasive nature makes Web technologies the best choice yet for a highly stable implementation.

Still the major challenge remains to be able to model a system independent of this or any implementation and provide a "connected" model of all the distributed components of a system. This is where 001 fits. It is the glue that defines, as well as binds together, all the pieces of a distributed system. 001 provides a level of integration and reliability missing in systems designed and built without 001. Regardless, whether a system is implemented using traditional mainframe technologies or the latest and greatest Web technologies mixed with traditional client-server technologies such as SQL databases, 001 is a constant and stable foundation that allows one to build, maintain and evolve complex systems in an unprecedented manner.

## Author Bios

With its software strategic planning and development services, Cadeon delivers on the promise of software solutions for business that are appropriate, well designed, reliable, and adaptable.

Steve Dolha (spdolha@cadeon.com) is president of Cadeon Strategic Technologies Inc. (528 11 avenue NE, Calgary, AB, Canada, T2E 0Z5). Steve has a B.Sc. in Computing Science from the University of Alberta. Prior to founding Cadeon in 1994, Steve had accumulated five years of corporate IS experience and had founded and for seven years run a successful software consulting firm. With a total of 16 years in the information systems industry, Steve is the driving force behind Cadeon's ability to strategically position its clients with software technology.

Dave Chiste (dchiste@cadeon.com) is a senior systems analyst with Cadeon Strategic Technologies Inc. Dave has a Technical Diploma in Computer Technology from the Southern Alberta Institute of Technology in Calgary, Canada. Since 1991 Dave has applied his strong technical skills to the design and development of client server based systems at many Canadian and U.S. Fortune 1000 companies such as Citibank, Syntex, and General Electric.

## Bibliography and Notes

1. 001 Reference Manual, Hamilton Technologies Inc.
2. Arthur, Lowell Jay, "Improving Software Quality: An Insider's Guide to TQM" John Wiley & Sons Inc. 1993.
3. Holtzblatt Karen & Beyer, Hugh, "Making Customer Centered Design Work for Teams" Communications of the ACM. October 1993 p. 93.

Note 1:
"Reuseful" is a term which recognizes that it may not be possible to initially create designs or software components as fully reusable because of the constraints of cost or time for a specific project, but acknowledges that future work is justified to evolve the designs or software components towards a stronger "reusable" condition.

[001, 001 Tool Suite, Function Map, Type Map, Object Map, Execution Map, Road Map, FMap, TMap, Escher, EMap, RMap, VSphere, RAT, Xecutor, OMap Editor, 001 Analyzer, SOO, System Oriented Object, Resource Allocation Tool, AntiRAT, Object Editor, Primitive Control Structures, Development Before the Fact, DBTF, RT(x), 001 AXES, AIOS, Agent 001DB are all trademarks of Hamilton Technologies, Inc.]

Chapter

# 25

# System Oriented Solutions: The Enterprise Management Architecture Approach

**Marc and Norman Beaulieu**

## Introduction

A significant paradigm shift is under way. One in which traditional rules used to build and integrate enterprise systems will give way to more consistent and logically complete modeling approaches. Organizations will increasingly demand a more common or universal method of building and integrating systems to avoid problems of interpreting semantics and the syntax of varied languages. Automation will become commonplace — essential to improve quality and reduce manual intervention, manual coding errors and overall costs. Organizations will need an IT approach that rapidly develops totally reusable application-specific solutions to more productively assemble enterprise-wide IT solutions. This will be a critical success factor because the speed at which an organization must adapt and evolve to simply remain competitive is staggering. And no one wants to be left behind.

This technological revolution and transformation became very evident a few Internet light years ago — about 3 calendar years — as our company began integrating its first database with the Internet. It was a systems integration project related to our vision of better using technology to more productively impact the operations of non-profit organizations — including educational institutions, hospitals, charitable and government organizations. We quickly encountered the fact that integration issues between the rapidly expanding Internet and existing and/or legacy database systems presented some interesting challenges. For instance, being able to reliably collect data from multiple, simultaneous on-line users while concurrently disseminating data securely from various incompatible internal databases captured our full attention. The challenge seemed obvious: reliably integrate the Internet with both on-line and internal databases in an easy, cost efficient manner.

To meet this challenge, our company began carefully examining the traditional ways of building and integrating systems. Not surprisingly we soon concluded that commonly used existing methods, products and tools did not offer a complete solution. A major problem we found, which still is rampant today, is that products and systems are built to solve a particular problem, and therefore are not adaptable when hardware, software or the business processes change. For instance, upgrading an existing system generally has integration errors that could propagate throughout an entire system. In addition, IS departments had no universal method to build or integrate systems, so when staff changes occur, the new programmers are left to figure out the semantics of the language used.

Given these issues, the rapid pace of technological change, and increased competitive pressures spurred by a more global business community, it was glaringly apparent that a more productive and cost efficient approach to building and integrating enterprise-wide solutions was more than overdue. The future, it seemed, would belong to those organizations that could best harness technological advancements to their advantage in the most time effective and cost efficient manner.

## Approach

NetBenefit® realized that in order to build a complete solution to the problems we had identified, we had to use a radical new approach. Fortunately we were introduced to the formal Development Before the Fact (DBTF) theory upon which we could base, and use to create, our solution. What first attracted us to this approach was that DBTF concentrates on doing things right the first time, and solving problems before they happen through a formal method of specification, a preventative rather than curative technique, unlike with the other approaches we examined.

DBTF, developed by Hamilton Technologies, Inc. (HTI), had exactly what we needed including its graphical scripting language along with a process and an automation that supports it. This, together with its advanced software engineering tool called the 001 Tool Suite™ used for building software with "built-in quality assurance and built-in productivity assurance," offered the beginnings of a dynamic solutions approach.

Among other things that appealed to us, all aspects of a 001 system are expressed in the same graphical language, a language that uses reliable mechanisms to create reliable building blocks. These building blocks are automatically integrated to create systems that are inherently reusable, parallelizable, portable and understandable.

The major components of 001 with which we developed the product aspect of our solution are used to define, analyze, generate and execute System Oriented

Objects (SOO). A SOO is a system that is both object oriented and function oriented. Its function oriented definitions are inherently integrated with its object oriented definitions through a formal method of specification. This formal method is based upon its own unique mathematics of control unlike other formal or informal theories.

•Define: A system is defined in two ways: by object oriented type components called TMaps™ and functional behavior components called FMaps™. Each are trees of information that describe the objects and functions that combine to form an integrated definition of the system.

•Analyze: The 001 Analyzer™ uses a proven set of mathematical rules that guarantee the consistency and logical completeness of the system. The Analyzer automatically searches for and locates all interface errors — traditionally the hardest to find and most costly to correct.

•Generate: 001 automatically transforms the analyzed FMaps and TMaps into fully executable production quality source code (i.e., in C). Concurrently, the entire system is automatically described in English by the 001 Documentor™.

•Execute: The 001 OMap Editor™ simplifies final testing by checking for semantic errors at runtime.

NetBenefit is using 001 to create Enterprise Management Architecture(EMA)™ — the product it believes offers the foundation to a complete systems oriented solution to the aforementioned challenges of system integration and development.

## Enterprise Management Architecture™

The very foundations of Enterprise Management Architectures (EMA™) are constructed with modules that include powerful 001 components. EMA delivers an adaptable systems integration framework designed to more productively build and integrate enterprise-wide applications for the entire lifetime of a total system. Framework refers to the EMA architecture — a real time distributed SOO approach that enables the integration of various applications, databases and the Internet through open distribution between clients and servers. It has the ability to be able to integrate with any hardware, software and database available today, and it is designed to integrate with the products of the future.

EMA has three main components that comprise its framework: Integrator™, Active Object Manager™ and Internet Cooperator™. EMA Integrator is a server-based component responsible for managing the integration of client/server, database(s), legacy systems and the Internet. Integrator will be able to manage

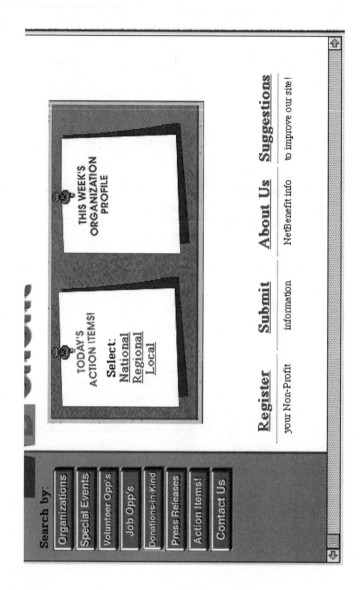

**Figure 25-1.** Enterprise Management Architecture.

all various desktop applications to be integrated or "plugged in" to the system. It coordinates application logic between the client or server and has the capability to handle changes both during development and in full operation. This functionality is to facilitate interoperability of applications and systems so end users and IT managers have seamless access to information and resources located on multiple databases, clients/servers and mainframe legacy systems. In addition, Integrator will manage the integration of data security products for encrypted communication via the Internet.

Active Object Manager (AOM) is also a server-based component that coordinates information control and access to users. Active Object Manager is the Company's version of an object request broker (ORB). AOM directs the requests of various multiple users to different resources throughout the enterprise through the use of a complex hierarchical order. This hierarchy is comprised of active agents, each with specific functions to perform and each with the ability to delegate to another agent for it to perform its designated function.- All system users log into the system via a graphical user interface that is tied to the Active Object Manager. AOM allows for n-tier levels of access and control of data through the use of different password-secure access levels. AOM manages and records all system users and the respective passwords and determines who has access to which information and resources.

Internet Cooperator is an HTML template generator that merges database information with screen descriptions to provide input and output of data to the Web browser. Users can specify where to get certain information throughout the enterprise, to which access is granted, and display it on-line for both Internet and Intranet use. Internet Cooperator greatly facilitates remote access and remote change control of information within internal databases and allows for full Web site development and management. Internet Cooperator can work directly with HTML and CGI scripting languages or it can interface with packaged Web site development and management kits like Netscape Navigator Gold or Microsoft Frontpage.

Combined, these components make up a solution set of applications and engines that do the real work, behind the scenes, for one part or for the entire enterprise system. EMA is as open, portable, extensible and scaleable as is possible. It empowers the IS manager with varying levels of control — as little as is wanted and up to complete control over the enterprise system. Unlike the traditional way of buying a product and force-fitting it to meet current needs, an organization can have a user-defined system that truly addresses current needs and can be re-defined as needs change.

As illustrated in figure 25-1, EMA acts like a metasystem offering the foundation from which design engineers can model and execute user defined specifications for an entire system or a single application. For example, design engineers interview the system users to carefully specify how to tailor an Internet database solution to best model end user functions. From these detailed specifications, design engineers are able to create a complete system that best meets user workflow. The result is a user-defined system that most accurately and most productively meets existing needs and is fully engineered to be adaptable to evolving needs. This is critical given the rapidity with which the Internet moves and the speed at which data must be managed for a business to stay ahead of the competition.

As a more specific example, the Internet Cooperator can have multiple outside users, simultaneously accessing and performing transactions to Web based databases and/or internal — new or legacy — databases. EMA Integrator is expected to be used to more productively convert existing data to a new database, integrate the new database with the Internet and any other part of the system. Legacy database(s) can be fully or partially used to provide on-line data access to users and customers.

The Active Object Manager coordinates access and change control to various information in the new system. For instance, one department of an organization can manage their part of the Web site and all data needed for it while another department has no access to that information, but can similarly manage their own part of the Web site. At a different level, management may pull reports for all departments or only certain types of reports at certain departments for n-tier  levels of control.

In addition, as system needs change, new specifications can be defined eliminating the need to change products, do more training and waste more money. For example, if an organization changed from a relational database to an object oriented database, design engineers would simply match the new primitives to the other database(s) primitives using EMA. Data migration would not be as massive an obstacle because with EMA design engineers will be able to more productively integrate the new database with the Internet and the rest of the enterprise. Consequently, by using EMA a major database project that historically has significant integration and migration issues is drastically simplified and made more reliable, more time efficient and more cost effective than traditional methods.

## Alumni Development Internet Application

A prime example of a real world application using EMA is connecting a university's alumni development database system to the Internet. Colleges and universities have alumni all around the world and there is always the problem of keeping track of where everybody is and, of course, asking them for an annual contribution.

By using EMA, a university has the ability to integrate its existing database(s) to the Web, which affords it some distinct advantages. For starters, volunteers soliciting alumni for donations can input information changes, pledge amounts and even credit card information on-line from their desktop computer via password access. This saves time and money for the alumni office because manually inputting names, pledged amounts and credit card information is no longer necessary. It also distributes a bulk of the solicitation workload to the volunteers in the "field" from the staff in the "home office" — again reducing staff costs and office expenses.

It is also more accurate. Alumni can input their own personal information changes on-line and this can be added to the Web server database and to the internal alumni development database. In addition, this information can be available to any number of various university departments that have access to alumni personal information — or it can be automatically updated to each pertinent department throughout the enterprise. Again, no manual intervention, saving significant time and money.

Certain 001 features help make this possible. Unlike traditional systems, 001 can automatically generate 100% complete production ready code for an entire system — which means an alumni development application can be created and maintained more quickly and reliably without error-prone manual intervention. The 001 graphical language enables both changes and entirely new specifications to be modeled and analyzed for errors before implementation, greatly reducing the propagation of errors after the specifications have been integrated.

## NetBenefit® Web Site

As another real world example, EMA was used to develop the NetBenefit Web site as shown in figure 25-2. This Web-based service was created to provide on-line users with information and opportunities to support the non-profit community. The NetBenefit Web site has been designed as a user-generated information center for content and commerce all relating to the non-profit community.

A non-profit can post news and information — such as special events, volunteer and job opportunities, requests for donations-in-kind, financial information, and general information for individuals to learn more about their organization. The information is automatically compiled in several non-profit-generated databases and organized in a user-friendly format for individuals to search.

Remotely, non-profits sign-in and do their own changes to the information listed from their computer — an easy, fast way to keep fresh information about their organization in front of the on-line community. Similarly, users sign-in and can remotely add items to donate to benefit a charity of their choice. Multiple non-profits and users can access and submit information simultaneously to either register or to edit existing data. All inputted information is stored on numerous Web server databases that are integrated with internal databases from which custom reports and queries can easily be generated. Every aspect of the system can be easily re-specified and regenerated to meet new requirements.

By using EMA to manage the NetBenefit Web site, we have more choices at the outset and throughout the life of the evolving system. The same is true for IS managers at other organizations. A system can be built for them, with them or they can learn how to do it themselves. There is no more total reliance on vendors for costly vendor-specific solutions that quickly become outdated. Instead, an end product that truly satisfies user needs can be built more quick-

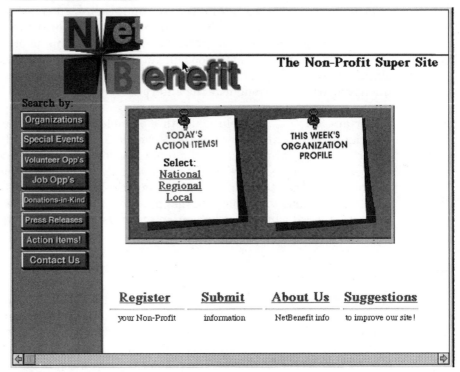

**Figure 25-2.** The NetBenefit Web site.

ly and significantly less expensively than what alternative solutions offer.

The NetBenefit Web site offers a good example of how multiple, varied organizations and multiple varied individual users can interact and conduct transactions reliably and cost effectively in a way that can flexibly respond to its participants evolving needs.

## Unique Features and Benefits

Any organization can use EMA to not only manage Internet database connectivity, but to better integrate and develop entire enterprise systems. EMA is comprised of a concentrated collection of inherently reusable SOO's purposefully composed of the most commonly needed components necessary to build, integrate and manage enterprise solutions. Combined, these are some features that make EMA unique:

Integrates the Internet, database(s) and client/server:
EMA significantly advances and makes more expeditious the integration process. A formal method of specification seamlessly integrates any and all parts of an entire system. This method inherently links objects and their functions between the Internet, database(s), and C/S for one part or for the entire enterprise system.

Integrating complete systems, like client/server, database(s) and the Internet, is a complex task for traditional systems in part because of different languages and various interfaces. Traditionally the integrated code is done manually by one or more programmers and if that same group is not available on an ongoing basis, new people must be hired to interpret the code. 001 has a consistent method of integration, so any new technician can pick up where the other left off with no concern of language misinterpretation. The EMA solution improves quality, is less time consuming and less costly.

Empowers the user; it is configurable to meet specific needs and to adapt as needs evolve:
A system or application is designed with 001's inherently configurable graphical language that defines types and functions of real world objects. User-defined specifications can thus be easily re-defined — without changing the code — to meet new requirements. This is critical since objects and their relationships change as an organization evolves. In addition, changes are made without manually tampering with code — a procedure that can propagate errors.
Once an EMA application is created, it is fully reusable and fully configurable. Another organization can use and customize the application to its preferences and integrate it with its hardware, software and databases — which may be completely different. Similarly, any non-001 created application can be more reliably integrated with EMA.

Reduces complexity and offers total control:
With EMA, IS departments significantly reduce the complexity of integrating the Internet, databases and client/server systems because the real work to accomplish integration is already done. Therefore, by using EMA organizations have a single, core framework from which new applications can be built or plugged in, and existing or legacy systems can be fully utilized and integrated. One of the benefits of simplification is more control — one architecture with one tool from which applications can be developed or fully integrated.

This powerful core of unique features and benefits establish the foundation from which radical changes can occur to replace the traditional ways of building and integrating enterprise systems.

## Conclusion

Technologically speaking it has been a long time since our initial quest began for a more reliable way to build and integrate applications with the Internet and databases. Since that time, one thing is for sure: the Internet has spurred a sweeping technological revolution. Major changes are evidenced not only with businesses embracing the Internet and the surge of database technology, but corporate culture is being jarred as well. More and more CEOs and

Executive Directors view technology as mission critical and are themselves becoming technologically competent and savvy, thus putting pressure on IT managers to locate solutions that are more reliable and cost effective.

This trend is of major significance. As organization leaders take an active, participatory role in information technology, we should witness a far less forgiving temperament with products and integration services that do not make the grade. Today's market driven technology behemoths have been providing products and services catered to a conservative mainstream marketplace which have not always been "best of breed." Interestingly enough, it appears as though this very market — with many CEO's leading the charge — may be realizing that waiting too long or compromising in any way on technological solutions can no longer be tolerable.

Coinciding with this new cultural trend are the initially described technological challenges which are critical success factors in the increasingly competitive global marketplace. A solution to meet these technological challenges must reliably interconnect various databases with n-tier levels of access and control in multiple locations via the Internet. The solution must also be cost effective to build and maintain and most certainly must adapt to any changes in hardware, software, databases or even in the business process itself. In addition, there needs to be a common or universal method of building and integrating systems to avoid problems of interpreting semantics and syntax of the languages used when there is staff turnover.

Without question, the 001 Tool Suite, together with the EMA framework, offer the originally sought total solution. The 001 Tool Suite is a "universal tool" that appeals to IS managers tired of learning new languages, manually integrating disparate applications and who feel the increased pressure from upper management to perform and cut costs. EMA provides one complete architecture that more productively enables the creation of new applications and the integration of applications with the Internet, databases, client/server and legacy systems while having n-tier levels of access and control. The combination of these products addresses our initial challenge and offers a truly revolutionary solution that satisfies CEO and IS manager alike.

Gone are the days of force-fitting products and costly, time consuming manual intervention to keep these products and their error-prone integration working. Today, leadership is demanding reliability and expectations for it will be commensurate. Fortunately, solutions are available because the new reality is that technology is fast becoming the fulcrum — the focus for solutions to remain competitive in an increasingly global economy.

## Author Bios

Marc and Norman Beaulieu are co-founders and managing principals of NetBenefit, a Boston-based systems integration and consulting firm providing solutions to both commercial and non-profit sectors. They can be reached at rep@netbenefit.com and by snailmail at 66 Charles Street #371 Boston, MA

02114.

Marc Beaulieu is Co-Founder and Managing Principal of NetBenefit. A 001 design engineer, Marc is a principal architect for EMA and chief technologist in research and development for new EMA and 001 applications. Marc has been involved with Web-based consulting and building database and Internet-related applications for over three years. Prior to co-founding the company, Marc worked with expansive financial services database applications and customer service database systems at Fidelity Investments and Liberty Financial. Marc received a BS from Cornell University in Ithaca, NY, in 1991.

Norman Beaulieu is Co-Founder and Managing Principal of NetBenefit, a systems integration and consulting services firm based in Boston, MA. Norman is chief marketing and development officer who has served on panel discussions and spoken on technology related issues. Norman has been involved with Web-based consulting and building database and Internet-related applications for over three years. Prior to co-founding the company, Norman piloted and managed creative marketing programs through new mediums with American Express through database and administration software systems and applications. Norman received a BA, cum laude, from Wesleyan University in Middletown, CT, in 1989.

[001, 001 Tool Suite, Function Map, Type Map, Object Map, Execution Map, Road Map, FMap, TMap, Escher, EMap, RMap, VSphere, RAT, Xecutor, OMap Editor, 001 Analyzer, SOO, System Oriented Object, Resource Allocation Tool, AntiRAT, Object Editor, Primitive Control Structures, Development Before the Fact, DBTF, RT(x), 001 AXES, AIOS, Agent 001DB are all trademarks of Hamilton Technologies, Inc.]

# Index

## ABOUT THE AUTHOR

**Jessica Keyes** is president of New Art Inc., a high-technology consultancy. Keyes has given seminars for such prestigious universities as Carnegie Mellon, Boston University, University of Illinois, James Madison University and San Francisco State University. She is a frequent keynote speaker on the topics of competitive strategy using information technology and marketing on the information superhighway. She is an advisor for DataPro, McGraw-Hill's computer research arm as well as a member of the Sprint Business Council. Keyes is also a founding Board of Director member of the New York Software Industry Association. She has recently been appointed to a two-year term to the Mayor of New York City's Small Business Advisory Council.

Prior to founding New Art, Keyes was Managing Director of R&D for the New York Stock Exchange and has been an officer with Swiss Bank Co. and Banker's Trust, both in New York City. She holds a Masters degree from New York University where she did her research in the area of artificial intelligence.

A noted columnist and correspondent with over 150 articles published, Keyes is also the author of ten books:

*The New Intelligence: AI in Financial Services*, HarperBusiness, 1990
*The Handbook of Expert Systems in Manufacturing*, McGraw-Hill, 1991
*Infotrends: The Competitive Use of Information*, McGraw-Hill, 1992
*The Software Engineering Productivity Handbook*, McGraw-Hill, 1993
*The Handbook of Multimedia*, McGraw-Hill, 1994
*The Productivity Paradox*, McGraw-Hill, 1994
*Technology Trendlines*, Van Nostrand Reinhold, 1995
*The Ultimate Multimedia Handbook*, McGraw-Hill, 1997
*How to be a Successful Internet Consultant*, McGraw-Hill, 1996
*Datacasting*, McGraw-Hill, 1997

*Infotrends* was selected as one of the best business books of 1992 by the Library Journal. *The Software Engineering Productivity Handbook* was the main selection for the Newbridge book club for computer professionals. The *Handbook of Multimedia* is now in its second reprint and has been translated into Chinese and Japanese.